# THE GERMAN PEOPLE
# AND THE REFORMATION

# The German People and the Reformation

EDITED BY

R. PO-CHIA HSIA

*Cornell University Press*

ITHACA AND LONDON

First published 1988 by Cornell University Press.
First printing, Cornell Paperbacks, 1988.

International Standard Book Number (cloth) 0-8014-2064-4
International Standard Book Number (paper) 0-8014-9485-0
Library of Congress Catalog Card Number 87-47863
Printed in the United States of America
*Librarians: Library of Congress cataloging information*
*appears on the last page of the book.*

⊗ The paper in this book meets the minimum requirements of the American National Standard for Information Sciences—Permanence of Paper for Printed Library Materials, ANSI Z39.48-1984.

Paperback printing  10 9 8 7 6 5

# Contents

[v]

  9. The Reformation and Its Public in an Age of Orthodoxy, *by
     Gerald Strauss*                                                     194
 10. The Laity's Religion: Lutheranism in Sixteenth-Century
     Strasbourg, *by Lorna Jane Abray*                                  216
 11. Johann Weyer and the Transformation of the Insanity Defense,
     *by H. C. Erik Midelfort*                                          234
 12. Between the Territorial State and Urban Liberty: Lutheranism
     and Calvinism in the County of Lippe, *by Heinz Schilling*         263


     Bibliographical Essay                                              285
     Index                                                              295

# Acknowledgments

To the many friends and colleagues who have supported the idea of this collection of essays, even when they were unable to contribute themselves, I express my warm appreciation. To the readers and to John Ackerman, my editor at Cornell University Press, I am grateful for many incisive criticisms that have helped to make this a better volume.

R.H.

*Ithaca, New York*

MAP OF GERMANY IN 1547 (following page)
Reproduced with the permission of the publisher from *The History of Modern Germany: The Reformation* (Vol. 1) by Hajo Holborn (New York: Alfred A. Knopf, Inc., 1959), copyright © 1959 by Hajo Holborn.

[vii]

# GERMANY IN 1547

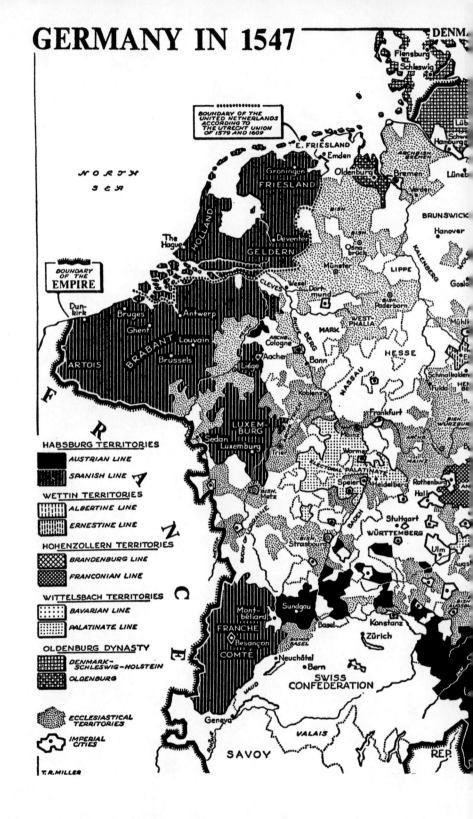

DENM.

Flensburg
Schleswig

BOUNDARY OF THE
UNITED NETHERLANDS
ACCORDING TO
THE UTRECHT UNION
OF 1579 AND 1609

E. FRIESLAND · Emden

*NORTH SEA*

Groningen
FRIESLAND

Oldenburg

Bremen

Lüneb

ARCHBISH
BREMEN

BISH

Hamburg

Lüneb

BRUNSWICK
Hanover

KALENBERG

HOLLAND

The
Hague

Deventer

GELDERN

Münster

BISH

Osna-
brück

LIPPE

Goslar

BOUNDARY
OF THE
EMPIRE

Dun-
kirk

Bruges
Ghent

Antwerp

CLEVES
Wesel

Dort-
mund

Cologne
Aachen

Bonn

ARCHBP
COLOGNE

BERG

MARK

WEST-
PHALIA

Paderborn

BISH

HESSE

Mühlh

Schmalkalden
Fulda

HEN

ARTOIS

BRABANT

Louvain
Brussels

Liège

NASSAU

Frankfurt

BISH.
WÜRZBUR

F
R
A
N
C
E

LUXEM-
BURG

Sedan
Luxemburg

Trier

BISH.
METZ

Worms

PALATINATE
Speier
Heidelberg

MAINZ

Rothenburg

Hall

AN

## HABSBURG TERRITORIES
- **AUSTRIAN LINE**
- **SPANISH LINE**

## WETTIN TERRITORIES
- **ALBERTINE LINE**
- **ERNESTINE LINE**

## HOHENZOLLERN TERRITORIES
- **BRANDENBURG LINE**
- **FRANCONIAN LINE**

## WITTELSBACH TERRITORIES
- **BAVARIAN LINE**
- **PALATINATE LINE**

## OLDENBURG DYNASTY
- **DENMARK-SCHLESWIG-HOLSTEIN**
- **OLDENBURG**

- **ECCLESIASTICAL TERRITORIES**
- **IMPERIAL CITIES**

DUCHY OF LORRAINE

MEUSE

Strasbourg

BISH.
STRASBOURG

BADEN

Stuttgart
WÜRTTEMBERG

Ulm

Augs

BISH.
AUGSBUR

Mont-
béliard

FRANCHE
COMTÉ
Besançon

Sundgau

Basel

BISHOP.
BASEL

VAUD

Neuchâtel

Bern

Konstanz

Zürich

SWISS
CONFEDERATION

INN

Geneva

VALAIS

SAVOY

REP.

T. R. MILLER

THE GERMAN PEOPLE
AND THE REFORMATION

# Introduction

Until about twenty years ago, the study of the German Reformation was represented by two major directions of research, one focusing on political history, practiced by scholars in history faculties, the other concentrating on theology and church history, the domain of theological faculties and seminaries. The political approach harks back to the nineteenth century, when Leopold von Ranke narrated the heroic actions of the Reformation as fateful events in the development of the Holy Roman Empire.[1] He set an agenda of research for future generations of German historians who would set out to explore the confessionally divided fate of the German nation by focusing on the themes of imperial and religious politics. In German historiography one can trace the genealogy of this scholarship from Ranke through Bezold, Joachimsen, M. Ritter, and G. Ritter to Skalweit;[2] in English writings, the works of Hajo Holborn and Geoffrey Elton represent this approach.[3] The achievements of these histo-

---

[1]Leopold von Ranke, *Deutsche Geschichte im Zeitalter der Reformation* (Munich, 1926). This work was written between 1839 and 1847.

[2]See Friedrich Bezold, *Geschichte der deutschen Reformation* (Berlin, 1890); Paul Joachimsen, *Die Reformation als Epoche der deutschen Geschichte,* ed. Otto Schottenloher (Munich, 1951); Moritz Ritter, *Deutsche Geschichte im Zeitalter der Gegenreformation und des Dreissigjährigen Krieges,* 3 vols. (Stuttgart, 1898–1908); Gerhard Ritter, *Die Neugestaltung Europas im 16. Jahrhundert: Die kirchlichen und staatlichen Wandlungen im Zeitalter der Reformation und der Glaubenskämpfe* (Berlin, 1950); Stephan Skalweit, *Reich und Reformation* (Berlin, 1967). In the most recent work of synthesis, Heinrich Lutz's *Das Ringen um deutsche Einheit und kirchliche Erneuerung von Maximilian I bis zum Westfälischen Frieden, 1490 bis 1648* (Berlin, 1983), there is more emphasis on history from below and on socioeconomic and cultural structures.

[3]See Hajo Holborn, *The History of Modern Germany,* vol. 1: *The Reformation* (New York, 1959); Geoffrey R. Elton, *Reformation Europe, 1517–1559* (New York, 1966).

[1]

rians culminated in the detailed analyses of both the interplay between imperial and territorial politics and the part played by confessional conflicts in shaping the constitutional character of the Holy Roman Empire in the sixteenth and seventeenth centuries. The other approach, with its emphasis on theology and ecclesiastical history, is dominated by the towering figure of Luther, whose writings have been made accessible through decades of critical scholarship, the study of whom has provided the model for examining the life and thought of other, lesser reformers. The recent splash of publications in celebration of the quincentennial of his birth attests to the enduring interest in the Wittenberg reformer.[4]

Since the early 1960s, a new approach has emerged in Reformation studies. Identified by its practitioners and critics as "social history," this new direction represents a truly international scholarship and encompasses studies published in East and West Germany, North America, Britain, and France. Animated by a common spirit, these works investigate the reform movements as they affected the lives of the elite and the common people. The studies use neglected historical sources that supplement, and often contradict, the documents generated by the "makers" of the Reformation. The fundamental premise of the social history of the Reformation is the belief that the religious messages of Protestants and Catholics were interpreted and appropriated by different social groups in the context and limitations of their daily existence. Only by focusing on this creative and active appropriation by various social groups can we understand the ideas of reformers, theological controversies, and political struggles in the larger cultural and historical context of the rise of confessional society.

The history of the Reformation is thus no longer a chapter in the history of Western Christianity, which in the past was usually written by scholars who had a sense of religious commitment or continuity. Religion is a matter not only of faith and doctrine but also the stuff of daily practice, encompassing the cultural and material universe of the peoples of early modern Europe. Above all, religion and church are not synonymous; and the recent scholarship on the German Reformation has demonstrated that rituals and doctrines represented precisely the symbols in which different social interests were articulated and different meanings defined and contested by the ruling elites, the clerical professionals, and a multitude of popular groups. New methods of research have been applied to neglected sources: prosopographical studies have mined tax records, notarial documents, and family chronicles to reconstruct the nexus between power and

---

[4]For a brief survey of Luther studies in America, see Lewis W. Spitz, "Luther in America: Reformation History since Philip Schaff," in Bernd Moeller, ed., *Luther in der Neuzeit* (Gütersloh, 1983), pp. 160–77.

piety; wills, records of marriage courts, and inventories of printers (and other serialized documents) have been analyzed to demonstrate the long-term structural changes in culture and ideas; pamphlets, woodcuts, broadsheets, folk songs, and visitation and hospital records have all become important for historians striving to understand the impact of religious changes on the lives of common men and women.

Three factors contributed to the emergence of the social history of the German Reformation: the stimulus of social anthropology and folklore studies, the dialogue with Marxist historiography, and the exploration of new sources. Before discussing the influence of social anthropology in the field of Reformation research, we need to review this intellectual tradition briefly as it is represented in Germany by the discipline of folklore studies (*Volkskunde*).

Oddly enough, the study of early modern popular religion has been undertaken primarily by historians from France, Britain, and North America, although Germany has a strong tradition of folklore studies and cultural history. From the last decades of the nineteenth century to the 1930s, German scholarship dominated the field of folklore studies. One of the leading figures was Johannes Bolte, founder and editor of the *Zeitschrift des Vereins für Volkskunde*, who studied many sixteenth-century chapbooks and coauthored a major annotation of the children's tales collected by the Grimm brothers.[5] Another major achievement of the German folklorists was the multivolume, encyclopedic *Handwörterbuch des deutschen Aberglaubens,* edited by Hanns Bächtold-Stäubli of Basel but with contributions by many German-speaking folklorists on all aspects of folk customs and beliefs.[6] The discipline of folklore studies suffered as a result of the ideological prominence given to it under the National Socialist regime but succeeded in producing a number of important studies of early modern popular culture after 1945.[7]

As folklore studies developed, cultural history (*Kulturgeschichte*) emerged as a distinctive discipline. The institutional focus was provided

---

[5]See Johannes Bolte and G. Polívka, *Anmerkungen zu den Kinder- und Hausmärchen der Brüder Grimm,* 5 vols. (Leipzig, 1913–31). On Bolte's role in folklore studies, see Stith Thompson, *The Folktale* (Berkeley, Calif., 1977), pp. 395ff.

[6]Published in Berlin and Leipzig, 1927–37.

[7]For an examination of the status of folklore as an independent discipline in Germany, see I. Weber-Kellermann, *Deutsche Volkskunde zwischen Germanistik und Sozialwissenschaft* (Stuttgart, 1969). For important contributions in the field of popular culture, see L. A. Veit and L. Lenhart, *Kirche und Volksfrömmigkeit im Zeitalter des Barock* (Freiburg, 1956); K. S. Kramer, *Volksleben in Hochstift Bamberg (1500–1800)* (Würzburg, 1957); Kramer, *Volksleben im Fürstentum Ansbach und seinen Nachbargebieten (1500–1800)* (Würzburg, 1961); Wolfgang Brückner, ed., *Volkserzählung und Reformation* (Berlin, 1974). See also the journal *Jahrbuch für Volkskunde,* edited by Wolfgang Brückner at Würzburg.

by the establishment of the Germanisches Museum in Nuremberg and the founding of the journal *Zeitschrift für deutsche Kulturgeschichte* in 1856.[8] As Johannes Falke, one of the founding editors, explains, Kulturgeschichte was essentially the history of the German people; *Volksgeschichte,* the history of a people, represented the antithesis of *Staatsgeschichte,* or the history of the state, because the aspirations of the people and the state are not always in agreement.[9] From the beginning, then, cultural history as a discipline symbolized an alternative vision of German history that challenged the hegemony of political history, especially in the Prussian universities. Georg Steinhausen defined cultural history in 1894 as *Lebensgeschichte,* or the history of daily life, which includes the history of law, art, literature, and morals *(Sitten).* Steinhausen criticized the exclusion of the field from university teaching.[10] The guidelines of German cultural history have always been interdisciplinary, and their early supporters included historians who were excluded from the inner sanctuaries of German academic history.[11] Although Kulturgeschichte occupies the crossroads between *Germanistik,* philology, history, and sociology and inspires original research in the field of the social history of the Reformation, its influence in German historiography is limited, compared with the role played by social anthropology in Western Europe and North America.

The theoretical inspiration for the social history of religion in Western Europe has often come from the writings of French- and English-speaking sociologists and social anthropologists. This is not the place to discuss at length the influence of scholars such as Durkheim, Mauss, Lévi-Strauss, van Gennep, Evans-Pritchard, and Eliade, but the major contribution of French religious sociology and British-American social anthropology is to provide the conceptual framework for the symbolic interpretation of precisely those religious beliefs and practices that were suppressed by the clerical professionals of the Reformation and Counter-Reformation. Whereas the German tradition of Volkskunde is particularly strong in the collection of data from popular literature and in the reconstruction of the material life of the past, it has until recently exerted only a limited influ-

[8]The founding editors were Johannes Müller and Johannes Falke of the Germanisches Museum in Nuremberg. The *Zeitschrift für deutsche Kulturgeschichte* was superseded by the *Zeitschrift für Kulturgeschichte* in 1894, under the editorship of Georg Steinhausen; the journal became the *Archiv für Kulturgeschichte* in 1903, and it continues to appear today.

[9]See Johannes Falke, "Die deutsche Kulturgeschichte," *Zeitschrift für deutsche Kulturgeschichte* 1 (1856):5–30, here, p. 23.

[10]See Georg Steinhausen's introduction to the first issue of the *Zeitschrift für Kulturgeschichte* (1894):1–4.

[11]For example, the German Jewish historian Ludwig Geiger was one of the contributors to the journal.

ence on the way in which professional historians in West Germany write the history of the Reformation. For one thing, interdisciplinary dialogue is rare among historians in German universities; for another, social history in West Germany is oriented toward institutional history and the analysis of political power.[12] But as historians turn their attention from emperors, princes, and bishops to the lower echelons of the social hierarchy, and as scholars raise questions of the practice of religion in daily life, folklore studies and cultural history will provide fresh insights and will prompt stimulating questions.

The second challenge to the traditional directions of Reformation research came from historians in the German Democratic Republic. Their endeavor represents an ongoing attempt to reclaim the sixteenth and seventeenth centuries for an alternative German nation of the common people, a vision first articulated by Engels and Kautsky in the nineteenth century.[13] Although some of the writings of the 1950s and early 1960s may seem dogmatic and schematic in spelling out a rigid periodization of German history, many important studies of the German Reformation have now appeared in the GDR, enriching our understanding of the social conflicts of the sixteenth century.[14] Apart from stressing the class character of social conflict and the class specificity of theological differences, as we might expect, the Marxist approach to the German Reformation argues for its importance as an "early bourgeois revolution" (*frühbürgerliche Revolution*), the forerunner of the Netherlands and English revolutions of the seventeenth century and the American and French revolutions of the eighteenth century. The major challenge of Marxist historiography is that, even among Western historians who disagree with the methodologies and concepts of Marxist historiography, the social character and the differences within the Reformation movement can no longer be ig-

---

[12]James A. Vann, "New Directions for Study of the Old *Reich*," *Politics and Society in the Holy Roman Empire, 1500–1806* (=*Journal of Modern History*, vol. 58, Supplement, December 1986), pp. 3–22.

[13]See Friedrich Engels, *The Peasant War in Germany*, first published in 1850 in the *Neue Rheinische Zeitung*; and Karl Kautsky, *Communism in Central Europe in the Time of the Reformation*, trans. J. L. and E. G. Mulliken (New York, 1959).

[14]An early programmatic article outlining the concept of an "early bourgeois revolution" is Max Steinmetz's "Theses on the Early Bourgeois Revolution in Germany, 1476–1535," in B. Scribner and G. Benecke, eds., *The German Peasants' War, 1525: New Viewpoints* (London, 1979), pp. 9–18. For assessments of the Marxist contribution to Reformation research, see the sympathetic dialogue by Robert W. Scribner, "Is There a Social History of the Reformation?" *Social History* 2 (1977):483–505. For a negative evaluation, see Abraham Friesen, *Reformation and Utopia: The Marxist Interpretation of the Reformation and Its Antecedents* (Wiesbaden, 1974). For a work of synthesis with profuse illustrations from the German Democratic Republic, see Adolf Laube and Günther Vogler, *Illustrierte Geschichte der deutschen frühbürgerlichen Revolution* (Berlin, 1974).

nored. Marxist historians have helped to place the study of the Peasants' War of 1525 squarely in the center of research on the early Reformation movement and have shown that the Evangelical movement was supported not only by disgruntled clerical intellectuals and city people but also by masses of peasants, miners, and laborers in the countryside and towns of the empire. As outstanding examples of the East German contribution, one may point to the following studies: Ingrid Mittenzwei's book on the uprising in the Joachimstal, Adolf Laube's meticulous examination of silver mining in the Ore Mountains, Manfred Bensing's careful analysis of the Peasants' War in Thuringia under the inspiration of the radical reformer Thomas Müntzer, and Siegfried Hoyer's lucid account of the military organization of the peasant armies.[15] In 1975, in commemoration of the 450th anniversary of the Peasants' War, there appeared a flood of publications in German and English that debated the various approaches to the study of rural society and the early Reformation movement. As a result, the literature on the German Peasants' War of 1525 has been quite well absorbed and is now represented in English-language works.[16]

Perhaps the most important reason for the emergence of the social history of the Reformation, however, is the exploration of new sources, many of which have become accessible only in the past ten years. The traditional political and theological approaches to the German Reformation concentrated on writings by the reformers, the correspondence of princes and councillors, the decisions of the Imperial Diets, and the city chronicles. Publications aimed at shaping public opinion in the early Reformation years, often in the form of cheap broadsheets and pamphlets, received relatively little attention.[17] In the past ten years, however, with the systematic collection of early Reformation pamphlets under the direction of Hans-Joachim Köhler at Tübingen University, five thousand pamphlets have become available on microfiche to scholars of the Reformation.[18] In addition, the pictorial images of the Reformation—woodcuts, engravings, and etchings—have begun to be studied for their social con-

[15]See Ingrid Mittenzwei, *Der Joachimstaler Aufstand 1525* (Berlin, 1968); Adolf Laube, *Studien über den erzgebirgischen Silberbergbau von 1470 bis 1546* (Berlin, 1974); Adolf Laube and Gerhard Brendler, eds., *Der Deutsche Bauernkrieg, 1524–25: Geschichte, Traditionen, Lehren* (Berlin, 1977); Manfred Bensing, *Thomas Müntzer und der Thüringer Aufstand, 1525* (Berlin, 1966); Siegfried Hoyer, *Das Militärwesen im deutschen Bauernkrieg, 1524–26* (Berlin, 1975); Siegfried Hoyer and Manfred Bensing, *Der deutsche Bauernkrieg, 1524–26,* 2d ed. (Berlin, 1970).

[16]See Bibliographical Essay, "Religion and Rural Society."

[17]The major exception is the series *Flugschriften aus der Reformationszeit,* 20 vols., published between 1877 and 1953 as part of the larger series *Neudrucke deutscher Literaturwerke des XVI. und XVII. Jahrhunderts.*

[18]The microfiche collection *Flugschriften des frühen 16. Jahrhunderts* was begun in 1978,

tent.[19] Still another category of newly explored sources, autobiographies and personal letters, provides historians with insights into the private lives of the men and women of the sixteenth century.[20] To reconstruct the texture of daily lives, historians are now exploring local city and church archives, poring over council minutes, notarial documents, wills, records of church courts, consistories, and ecclesiastical visitations, asking themselves questions that eluded generations of local historians and antiquarians. Using techniques developed in other disciplines and fields of history, they have written many monographs, which have had the cumulative effect of correcting and modifying the older broad sweeps of interpretation.

The history of the German Reformation is now moving chronologically into the seventeenth century, thereby raising a new agenda for research that transcends the traditional schema of periodization. Thematically, it compares the Protestant Reformation with the Catholic Counter-Reformation, finding the two less opposing ecclesio-theological movements than intertwined forces of a single historical era. The two movements manifest many parallels in the way that established religions became instruments for exerting tighter social controls.

The study of religion as social control has highlighted the self-assertion of the new Catholic and Protestant clerical professionals and their relationship to the common folk, especially the rural populace. It is easy to overlook the fact that the Reformation was initially a "revolt" within the

---

with planned completion for 1988. The time span is the years 1501 to 1530; both German and Latin writings are included. Inter Documentation Company AG in Zug, Switzerland, is the supplier of the microfiche series. Another important collection, less comprehensive in scope but including topically arranged pamphlets from the seventeenth and eighteenth centuries, is the Gustav Freytag Sammlung in the University Library of Frankfurt. This collection is now also available on microfiche. Another new publication project is being undertaken in the German Democratic Republic; see *Flugschriften der frühen Reformationsbewegung (1518–1524)*, vol. 1, ed. Adolf Laube et al. (Vaduz, 1983).

[19]For printed collections of sixteenth-century German woodcuts, see Walter L. Strauss, ed., *The German Single-leaf Woodcut, 1500–1550* (New York, 1974); and *The German Single-leaf Woodcut, 1550–1600: A Pictorial Catalogue* (New York, 1975); for a pioneering work on interpreting the social and religious message of visual images, see Robert W. Scribner, *For the Sake of Simple Folk: Popular Propaganda for the German Reformation* (Cambridge, 1981).

[20]For published excerpts of autobiographies, see Horst Wenzel, ed., *Die Autobiographie des späten Mittelalters und der frühen Neuzeit*, 2 vols. (Munich, 1980). Kaspar von Greyerz and Steven E. Ozment have both used autobiographies and private letters in their work; see K. von Greyerz, "Religion in the Life of German and Swiss Autobiographers (Sixteenth and Early Seventeenth Centuries)," in K. von Greyerz, ed., *Religion and Society in Early Modern Europe, 1500–1800* (London, 1984), pp. 223–41. For Ozment, see *Magdelena and Balthasar: An Intimate Portrait of Life in Sixteenth-Century Europe Revealed in the Letters of a Nuremberg Husband and Wife* (New York, 1986).

clerical hierarchy that began when zealous monks and priests detected abuses in doctrines and practices within the church. The Reformation had as one of its chief goals the creation of a new, god-fearing and learned clergy, and ministers of the new Protestant churches were recruited heavily from the middling ranks of urban society, which had provided the strongest support for the early Evangelical movement. There are only a few studies of the social origins and intellectual milieu of Protestant pastors, and among the Counter-Reformation clergy, the classic study of German Jesuits by Bernhard Duhr remains unmatched by similar efforts for other religious orders or for the secular clergy. Another lacuna is the paucity of works on the rural Reformation, although historians have begun examining visitation and court records that may shed light on the ideas and behavior of rural folk. In the countryside, magic and a materialist conception of religion seem to have persisted well into the eighteenth century, as is evident from millenarian beliefs and the appearance of rural prophets whom the urban Protestant churches found distasteful.[21]

The social history of the German Reformation, as I have suggested, does not really conflict with the more traditional approaches of Reformation research. It does not call into question the importance of biographies of reformers, churchmen, and political elites, nor does it underestimate the work of intellectual historians who labor patiently with texts and difficult theological concepts. Rather, it asserts that the religious changes of the sixteenth century were fundamentally important in shaping the history of Europe and the wider world up to the modern age, and it defines as territory for exploration that area in which religious ideas and rituals impinged upon the structures of everyday life, a realm in which the peoples of Europe resisted, obeyed, or cooperated with the clerical elites in defining the meanings and material conditions of their mundane existence and the visions of a celestial afterlife.

The twelve essays in this collection seek to provide a representative, though by no means comprehensive, picture of the recent historiographical development in the social history of the German Reformation. The contributions include seven essays from the United States, two from West Germany, and one each from Britain, Canada, and East Germany. Some of these essays represent syntheses of recently published monographs, incorporating in one case the author's reflections and response to critics; others are based on previous publications but have

[21]For rural religion in early modern Germany, see the excellent collection of essays by David W. Sabean, *Power in the Blood: Popular Culture and Village Discourse in Early Modern Germany* (Cambridge, 1985). See also the Bibliographic Essay, "Religion and Rural Society."

included new material in a broader discussion; still others may be characterized as summaries of current research and previews of forthcoming
books. Together these essays provide an introduction to the social history
of the German Reformation and offer materials not previously available in
English. In selecting the essays, I have sought to supplement, not to
duplicate, the existing readings in English; students who wish to sample
the variety of scholarship on the Peasants' War, for example, should
consult the collection of essays by Scribner and Benecke.[22]

The twelve articles in the collection fall under four thematic headings.
Brady, Vogler, and Hsia offer different interpretations and case studies of
the urban reformation in South Germany, Nuremberg, and Münster; they
argue for understanding the different religious visions of the urban populace in the context of the varying social experiences of the urban groups.
In the next group of articles, Chrisman, Scribner, and Rublack examine
the media that conveyed the message of the Reformation to the laity and
the different ways in which interpretations of religious reform reflected
social and structural norms of communication. Under the rubric "Wom-
en, Family, and Religion," Wiesner surveys women's responses to the
Reformation, which were varied and often contrasted with men's religious
experiences, and Safley analyzes the Protestant reform of marriage and
morality as it influenced the family life of early modern Germany. The
fourth and last section focuses on the impact of the Reformation: Strauss
and Abray discuss the tensions between lay and clerical visions of the new
religion and society; Midelfort argues for a transformation in the legal and
medical discourse as seen through the writings of Johann Weyer; and
Schilling offers us a case study of confessional and political conflict on the
eve of the Thirty Years' War.

[22]See Scribner and Benecke, *German Peasants' War*.

# PART ONE

# CITIES AND THE
# REFORMATION

*The publication of Bernd Moeller's essay on imperial cities and the Reformation in 1962 signaled a turning point in the social history of the Reformation. Moeller draws attention to the different social visions in the reformed messages of Martin Luther, the Saxon monk who lived in a territorial state ruled by a prince, and Martin Bucer and Huldrych Zwingli, the reformers of Strasbourg and Zurich whose theological ideas were shaped by the corporate ideology of the autonomous civic communes of South Germany and Switzerland. For the past twenty-five years the Reformation in the cities has inspired some of the most original work in the field. One line of inquiry has focused on the ways in which the urban experience—the late medieval city as a center of trade, manufacturing, printing, and culture—helped to increase and articulate discontent with the late medieval church. The townsfolk and their magistrates wanted a religion that satisfied the spiritual needs of common men and women, a clergy that was responsive to the demands of the laity, and a theology and a set of rituals that could be grasped by people whose moral concerns had been deeply shaped by their experiences of communal living and civic autonomy. With the concentration of ecclesiastical wealth in the cities, with the legal exemption of clerics from civic jurisdiction, and with the growth of a lower clergy recruited heavily from the ranks of literate townsfolk, the groundwork was laid for a fundamental crisis of conscience and a challenge to traditional ecclesiastical authority in the cities of the Holy Roman Empire. The merchants and humanists of the cities were some of Luther's earliest supporters. Through the printing press, through sermons, and by word of mouth, the Evangelical message spread rapidly from town to town. The following essay by Thomas A. Brady attempts to describe and analyze the relationship between city life and the Reformation by placing the events of the early Evangelical movement in a larger context. By transforming the theology, rituals, and institutions of the Catholic church into ideas and practices that the urban populace could understand and exploit, the magistrates and other urban social classes attempted to "domesticate" religion and turn their communal societies into "godly republics."*

*If the ideology of communalism and the attempt to make German towns into godly republics represent one side of the dialectic of the German urban Reformation, the struggles between different social classes within the cities represent the other side. The Marxist interpretation of the urban Reformation is predicated upon class differences and the conceptual opposition of a reformation from above to a spontaneous popular movement from below. This viewpoint is represented by Günther Vogler's detailed analysis of the imperial city of Nuremberg in 1524 and 1525. In Nuremberg, as in many other cities, the ruling elites and other social groups had very different visions of religious renewal: whereas the magistrates wanted to restrict reforms to the wresting of control over religion from the hands of the clergy, radical reformers and social revolutionaries often called for political, social, and economic remedies as well. Having inherited the wealth of the Catholic church, the city magistrates found themselves committed, like that institution, to defending the rights of property and the social order. When religious and social discontents merged, when artisans, workers, and peasants came together to discuss common grievances, as they did in the city and territory of Nuremberg, the ruling elite suppressed all signs of dissent. For members of that elite, religion and social criticism must not mix, and the goal of the new religion was to inculcate social discipline and deference to authority.*

*When religious renewal and social revolution fused, the result was a powerful vision of a new society. In Münster the Evangelical movement paved the way for a unique social experiment when the Anabaptists proclaimed the city "the New Jerusalem." Awaiting the end of the world, which they regarded as imminent, the saints who accepted rebaptism to mark themselves off from the ungodly turned their city into a godly republic. Later, under the leadership of Jan of Leiden, a millenarian kingdom was proclaimed: private property was abolished and polygamy was introduced during its fifteen-month-long existence. R. Po-chia Hsia's article traces the ideas and practices of the Münster Anabaptists back to the social ideology of the guilds, from whose ranks many leaders and supporters of the Anabaptist movement were recruited.*

*In Germany the Reformation began in the cities; ideas of religious renewal and the sociopolitical ideologies of civic communes merged to form a powerful current of change. The problem facing magistrates was how to harness these forces of change and bring about church reforms without simultaneously tearing apart the fabric of society. The domestication of religion in the German cities is the central theme of the work of Thomas A. Brady, Jr., professor of history at the University of Oregon in Eugene. Brady has discussed the problem in two works:* Ruling Class, Regime, and Reformation at Strasbourg, 1520–1555 *(1978), and* Turning Swiss: Cities and Empire, 1450–1550 *(1985). In the first book, Brady analyzes the composition of the Strasbourg ruling class and examines its efforts at maintaining power amid the tensions and conflicts generated by the Reformation. In the second book, he expands his perspective to the Holy Roman Empire and traces the history of the abortive alliance between the centralizing Hapsburg dynasty and the ruling oligarchs of the South German imperial cities, an alliance that fell apart when the oligarchs succumbed to internal civic political pressures during the Reformation. The following article draws upon both works and represents a reflective synthesis of Brady's thinking on this theme.*

[13]

# [1]

## In Search of the Godly City: The Domestication of Religion in the German Urban Reformation

THOMAS A. BRADY, JR.

A people's religious life, it has long been recognized, centers on the rituals that connect the people to extrahuman or suprahuman forces that can, and do, influence its collective fate.[1] A defect in ritual can lead to a people's doom, as Achilles reminded the Achaeans in the face of Apollo's wrath.[2] Explanations of such forces—myth, belief, and doctrine—arise from efforts to understand, interpret, and justify the community's situation vis-à-vis its gods and, by derivation, vis-à-vis the distribution of wealth, prestige, and power that a correct relationship demands. In complex societies, where tensions arise from the distribution of the social product, the shared symbols may be seen somewhat differently by different social groups, which in extreme cases may lead to a disruption of the ritual community and therefore to social revolt—an outcome that the ruling part of the society must naturally try to prevent. As Peter Munz has noted, there arises as a result "the normal pressure in all societies . . . to use religion as a means to promote social cohesion."[3] From this point of

---

Parts of the following essay are based on my recent book *Turning Swiss: Cities and Empire, 1450–1550,* Cambridge Studies in Early Modern History (Cambridge, 1985). I cite only quoted texts here, and I refer the interested reader to that work for additional source material.

[1]An understanding of this principle animates Bob [Robert W.] Scribner, "Cosmic Order and Daily Life: Sacred and Secular in Pre-Industrial German Society," in Kaspar von Greyerz, ed., *Religion and Society in Early Modern Europe, 1500–1800* (London, 1984), pp. 17–32.

[2]Homer, *Iliad,* Bk.I,ll. 59–67.

[3]Peter Munz, "From Max Weber to Joachim of Floris: The Philosophy of Religious History," *Journal of Religious History* 11 (1980):167–200, here at p. 182. He calls the response to this pressure mundanization, by which he means approximately what I mean by "domestication."

[14]

view, every disruption of the sacral order of ritual and myth must threaten social harmony.

Complex religious cultures, including those that offer forgiveness of sins and eternal life, do not neglect the "normal pressure" to promote social cohesion. The fourteenth-century Muslim philosopher Ibn Khaldūn (1332–1406) expressed this point perfectly. "Only by God's help in establishing His religion," he wrote, "do individual desires come together in agreement to press their claims, and hearts become united."[4] Many Latin Christian writers agreed, at least in principle. Johann Hug, for example, a priest at St. Stephen's in Strasbourg in about 1500, wrote that "government is preserved by religion, more . . . than by offices or physical labors."[5]

In medieval Latin Christendom the preservation of government through religion was complicated by the bifurcation of authority into *sacerdotium* and *imperium*, corresponding to a division of its elites into lay rulers and clergy, which gave rise to a bewildering variety of—mostly unstable— situations of governance. Right down to the Reformation era, many writers nonetheless accepted and in principle approved this bifurcation of authority as a normal and necessary situation. One such writer was a Basel law professor, Peter von Andlau (1415/25–1480), who in about 1470 wrote, "The world is chiefly ruled by two forces, that is, the papal authority and the royal power, and they are the two chief powers through which God regulates and moves the world."[6] Well and good, but many other men strove to unite religious and temporal authority as rulers of men sought to become masters of souls and as rulers of souls sought to become masters of men. Symbolically it was a struggle between two Romes. On one side, Emperor Charles V's grandchancellor, Mecurino Arborio di Gattinara (d. 1530), announced in 1519 that the work begun by Charles the Great would be completed by Charles the Greatest, giving the world "one pastor and one flock."[7] At the papal court, however, Giles of

---

[4]Ibn Khaldūn (='Abd-ar-Rahmān Abū Zayd ibn Muhammad ibn Muhammad ibn Khaldūn), *The Muqaddimah: An Introduction to History,* trans. Franz Rosenthal, abridged ed. by N. J. Dawood (Princeton, 1957), p. 125.

[5]"Conseruatur autem imperium per religionem. Vnde dicit imperator rem publicam magis religionibus quisquam officijs et laboribus corporis contineri" (Johannes Hug, *Quadrivium ecclesie Quatuor prelatorum officium Quibus omnis status tum Secularis tum vero Ecclesiasticus subiicitur* [Strasbourg, 1504], fol. 49r). See also fol. 49v: "Non solum autem conseruatur imperium per religionem sed etiam per pacem." On Hug, see Charles Schmidt, *Histoire littéraire d'Alsace à la fin du XVe et au commencement du XVIe siècle,* 2 vols. (Paris, 1879; reprinted, Nieuwkoop, 1966), 2:51–53.

[6]Josef Hürbin, *Peter von Andlau, der Verfasser des ersten deutschen Reichstaatsrechts* (Strasbourg, 1897), pp. 130–31, from his *Libellus de caesarea monarchia.*

[7]John M. Headley, "The Habsburg World Empire and the Revival of Ghibellinism," *Medieval and Renaissance Studies* 7 (1978):93–127, here at pp. 97–102.

Viterbo (1469–1532) contrasted Julius Caesar, who had merely believed he ruled the world, with Pope Julius II, who in fact did so.[8]

Latin Christendom's failure to resolve its peculiar structural bifurcation into either autocracy or theocracy had at least two extremely important consequences. First, it doomed every dream of uniting, under Roman imperial symbols, both military power and Christian religious authority into an empire of a classic type.[9] Second, it created the moral space in which much smaller units could become practically sovereign without the need for extreme religious and cultural localism. This process occurred most richly in Italy, where no great power emerged to usurp the weakened or shattered imperium, but another great zone of urban communal formation arose in South Germany, the lands that stretched from the foot of the High Alps northward to Germany's Central Highlands. Here the massive disturbances that accompanied the early Reformation movement during the 1520s forced the urban magistrates to trim civic religion more closely to their duty to preserve law and order under the symbol of the common good (in German the *gemeiner Nutz,* in Latin the *bonum commune*). They commonly did so by bringing religious personnel and practice more closely under their own control, pursuing what may be called a "domestication" of urban religion.

I

In the great debate over the Protestant Reformation and the origins of modernity that erupted in the middle decades of the nineteenth century, some identified in the Reformation, especially in the cities, the break-through to "religious freedom" or, in Engels's words, the "revolution No. 1 of the bourgeoisie." Others—notably the jurist Otto von Gierke—saw in the urban reformation the achievement by the medieval urban corporation of political, legal, and moral autonomy. Recent writing on the South German urban reform movement has highlighted its traditional, corporate thrust. Bernd Moeller, for example, wrote in 1962 that Martin Luther's southern urban colleagues—chiefly Zurich's Huldrych Zwingli (1484–1531) and Strasbourg's Martin Bucer (1490–1551)—through their emphasis on the collectivity rather than on the individual, corrected

---

[8]John W. O'Malley, "Giles of Viterbo: A Reformer's Thought on Renaissance Rome," *Renaissance Quarterly* 20 (1967):1–11, here at p. 10 (reprinted in John W. O'Malley, *Rome and the Renaissance: Studies in Culture and Religion* [London, 1981]).

[9]I mean "empire" in approximately the sense discussed by Immanuel Wallerstein in *The Modern World-System,* vol. 1: *Capitalist Agriculture and the Origins of the European World-Economy in the Sixteenth Century* (New York, 1974), p. 15.

In Search of the Godly City

Luther and deepened his concepts of church and state. Heiko Oberman agrees with this estimate: "The south German Reformation expanded [Luther's] limited purpose to include a reordering of the community; seeking to realize the horizontal implications of the gospel within the framework of the *bonum commune*." Peter Blickle, in an even more pointed judgment, ascribes to the urban reform "the tendency toward an exclusive civic jurisdiction, toward communalization of the church, and toward the rationalization of religion and piety."[10]


## II

The decades before the beginning of the German Reformation heightened the perceived need for social integration in the self-governing cities. "There was a time," wrote the Strasbourg lawyer Sebastian Brant (1457–1521) in 1504,

when we could rightly claim of our empire that it was lord and master over the world. Now, however, our society has become a haven for every kind of folly and vice. . . . Do you doubt that our end will be the same as the end of all the kingdoms and empires that went before us and all those that are still to come: dust, ashes, a scattering of rubble, a mere name? Nothing lasts in human affairs except the immortal soul.[11]

The brilliant half century between 1470 and Luther's initial blast, indeed, brought trouble to magistrates' hearts in every South German city hall. New threats to traditional civic order loomed both within and beyond the walls.

Within the walls, the very wealth accumulated through the economic recovery further polarized society as the rich got richer and the poor poorer. Poverty's claws were, indeed, very much longer and far sharper than the cities' tax registers indicate. Europe's cities held no fixed class of "the poor," for the condition of potential poverty gripped a large part of the population and threatened a still larger part, depending on the variable

---

[10]Bernd Moeller, *Imperial Cities and the Reformation: Three Essays*, trans. H. C. Erik Midelfort and Mark U. Edwards (Philadelphia, 1975), pp. 89–90 (slightly revised); Heiko A. Oberman, *Masters of the Reformation: The Emergence of a New Intellectual Climate in Europe*, trans. Denis Martin (Cambridge, 1981), p. 294; Peter Blickle, *Die Reformation im Reich*, Uni-Taschenbücher, 1181 (Stuttgart, 1982), p. 92.

[11]Sebastian Brant to Conrad Peutinger, July 1504, in *Konrad Peutingers Briefwechsel*, ed. Erich König (Munich, 1923), pp. 32–36, here at p. 34, trans. Gerald Strauss, in Gerald Strauss, ed., *Manifestations of Discontent in Germany on the Eve of the Reformation* (Bloomington, Ind., 1971), p. 225.

economic conditions, such as harvests, prices, wages, and unemployment. As a result, in a broad sense the term "the poor" was frequently and correctly used to designate the majority of the working population,[12] for the ranks of the potential poor extended far into the fat bulge on the onion-shaped representations with which social historians describe social stratification in the premodern city.[13] The fat bulge formed a political cushion for the oligarchies that was more apparent than real both because the ranks of the potential poor were so very much larger than those of the obviously destitute and because large sectors of the work force had no regular, legitimate channels of communication with the oligarchies. The ranks of the apprentices and wage workers, a fertile ground for discontent, composed between a quarter and a third of those gainfully occupied in the larger cities.[14] In German cities the polarization lent new substance to grievances against monopolists and usurers, which struck directly at the urban oligarchs and the sources of their wealth.[15]

Outside the walls lurked the great predators, the princes who had smashed the last South German urban league in the period 1449–1453 and who now strove to bring the free cities' assets—money and credit, guns, and men—under their direct control. Against such dangerous lords the urban oligarchs' natural refuge was the imperial monarchy—hence the urban humanists' strident monarchism—but the Habsburgs could not guarantee law and order. Emperor Maximilian I (r. 1493–1519), a veritable "royal locust,"[16] papered his progresses with bad debts and poured the cities' money into his Italian projects. Aided by the cities, he did humble the chief South German dynasties, but he could not provide what the oligarchies most wanted—good government.

[12]On growing impoverishment in the sixteenth century, see Catharina Lis and Hugo Soly, *Poverty and Capitalism in Pre-Industrial Europe*, trans. James Coonan (New York, 1979), pp. 71–82. For German cities in particular, see Thomas Fischer, *Städtische Armut und Armenfürsorge im 15. und 16. Jahrhundert*, Göttinger Beiträge zur Wirtschafts- und Sozialgeschichte, 4 (Göttingen, 1976), pp. 17–139; Robert Jütte, *Obrigkeitliche Armenfürsorge in deutschen Reichsstädten der frühen Neuzeit: Städtische Armenfürsorge in Frankfurt am Main und Köln*, Kölner historische Abhandlungen, 31 (Cologne and Vienna, 1984), pp. 8–19.

[13]See Erdmann Weyrauch, "Über sociale Schichtung," in Ingrid Batori, ed., *Städtische Gesellschaft und Reformation*, Spätmittelalter und Frühe Neuzeit, Tübinger Beiträge zur Geschichtsforschung, 12 (Stuttgart, 1980), pp. 5–57.

[14]Knut Schulz, *Handwerksgesellen und Lohnarbeiter: Untersuchungen zur oberrheinischen und oberdeutschen Stadtgeschichte des 14. bis 17. Jahrhunderts* (Sigmaringen, 1985), pp. 37–46.

[15]See Erich Maschke, "Deutsche Städte am Ausgang des Mittelalters," here from the reprint in his *Städte und Menschen: Beiträge zur Geschichte der Stadt, der Wirtschaft und Gesellschaft, 1959–1977*, Beiheft 68 der Vierteljahrschrift für Sozial- und Wirtschaftsgeschichte (Wiesbaden, 1980), pp. 56–99, here at p. 71.

[16]Gerhard Benecke, *Emperor Maximilian I, 1459–1519: An Analytical Biography* (London, 1982), p. 128.

The need for guarantees of law and order grew all the more desperate with the dream of the common man as far north as Franconia of "turning Swiss"—that is, of joining or imitating the Swiss and living without lords. As the Augsburg politician Ulrich Arzt (1460–1527) wrote in 1519, "I fear that we will be pushed from behind toward the Swiss. Then the old proverb will come true: when a cow stands and moos on the bridge at Ulm, she'll be heard in the middle of Switzerland."[17] Strange prophecies circulated through South Germany, among them that the Archangel Michael "proposes to set out to reestablish a firm Christian faith on earth, so that the words of our Savior may be fulfilled: 'There shall be one flock, one shepherd [John 10:16].' "[18]

Religion, which ought to have promoted peace, justice, and unity in the service of God's honor and the common good, sometimes did just the opposite.[19] Clerical rights, privileges, and practices, however much they had been honored by earlier generations, were making laymen and laywomen in about 1500 angry and confused, providing endless provocations to disputes, quarrels, and ill will. Clerical exemptions from market laws and civic duties, clerical collection of tithes and usury, clerical quarrels between monk and priest and monk and monk, and seemingly irremediable abuses in clerical life—all these breached the commune's sense of moral security and reduced the sustenance that religion was obliged to lend to good government. No matter that the magistrates themselves helped to block episcopal efforts to improve clerical discipline nor that the clergy themselves paraded the problems before the literate laity. Episcopal reform efforts amounted to little, not least because—here the contrast with Italy is illuminating—South German bishops were not civic patriarchs but great feudal magnates and often the cities' former lords. What mattered most was not whether clerical discipline had in fact worsened or improved since earlier times[20] but that lay tolerance of clerical privileges and life-styles was declining. The seemingly natural solution—

[17]Ulrich Arzt to Conrad Peutinger, Augsburg, 9 February 1519, quoted in Heinrich Lutz, *Conrad Peutinger: Beiträge zu einer politischen Biographie*, Abhandlungen zur Geschichte der Stadt Augsburg, 9 (Augsburg, [1955]), p. 147.

[18]Annelore Franke and Gerhard Zschäbitz, eds., *Das Buch der hundert Kapitel und der vierzig Statuten des sogenannten oberrheinischen Revolutionärs*, Leipziger Übersetzungen und Abhandlungen zum Mittelalter, A 4 (Berlin, 1967), p. 181, quoted here from Strauss, *Manifestations*, p. 235.

[19]The one adequate study of a pre-Reformation diocese reveals with great clarity how the structural deadlock between lay and ecclesiastical authority blocked all paths to reform from above. See Francis Rapp, *Réformes et Réformation à Strasbourg: Eglise et société dans le diocèse de Strasbourg (1450–1525)*, Collection de l'Institut des Hautes Etudes Alsaciennes, 23 (Paris, 1975).

[20]See Lawrence G. Duggan, "The Unresponsiveness of the Late Medieval Church: A Reconsideration," *Sixteenth Century Journal* 9 (1978):3–26.

full civic control over the church and the commune's religious life—could not be attained within the bounds of the law.

The communalization of the church during the South German urban reform therefore aimed to transform the civic religious establishment from an agent of disruption into one of order. How very desperate the situation had become is evident in the plaintive cry of Strasbourg's great cathedral preacher, Johann Geiler von Kaysersberg (1445–1510), a man of impeccable life and unshakable will: "You laymen hate us priests, and it is an old hatred that separates us. Whence comes your hatred against us? I believe that it comes from our insane way of life, that we live so evilly and create such scandal."[21]

### III

To this increasingly desperate situation the early Protestant reformers brought a welcome message: the identity of church and people. "The Kingdom of Christ is also external," Zwingli wrote against the Lutherans, and "a Christian city is nothing more than a Christian commune."[22] Erasmus had said much the same thing in 1518 when he asked a friend, "What else is the city but a great monastery?"[23]

The urban reformation's guiding principle was, in Heiko Oberman's words, "the slippery but irreplaceable concept of biblicism,"[24] the idea that the Bible contains binding norms of Christian social conduct. "That realm is best and most secure," wrote Zwingli, "which rules according to God alone; and that is worst and least secure which rules according to its own lights."[25] At Strasbourg the cathedral preacher Caspar Hedio (1494–1552) reminded the magistrates that they, together with the preachers and schoolmasters, were the pillars of civic welfare, who should find in the Bible "a vital, certain unerring guide against false doctrine, divisions and sects, and how one can survive dangerous times."[26] It is difficult to

[21]Johann Geiler von Kaysersberg, *Die Emeis: Dis ist das buch von der Omeissen, und auch Herr der könnig ich diente gern* (Strasbourg, 1516), fol. 28v (my thanks to R. Emmet McLaughlin for sending me this text).

[22]*Huldrych Zwinglis sämtliche Werke*, ed. Emil Egli et al., 14 vols. to date (Berlin, Leipzig, and Zurich, 1905–), 14:424, ll. 19–22.

[23]Desiderius Erasmus to Paul Volz, Basel, 14 August 1518, in P. S. Allen and H. S. Allen, eds., *Opus epistolarum Des. Erasmi Roterodami*, 12 vols. (Oxford, 1906–58), 3:361–77; quoted here from *Christian Humanism and the Reformation: Selected Writings of Erasmus*, trans. John C. Olin (New York, 1965), pp. 107–33, here at p. 130.

[24]Oberman, *Masters*, p. 277.

[25]*Zwinglis sämtliche Werke*, 2:346, lines 15–18.

[26]Manfred Krebs and Hans Georg Rott, eds., *Quellen zur Geschichte der Taüfer*, vols. 7–8,

imagine a closer coupling of the gospel to the common good than these urban reformers preached.

The urban regimes gradually responded to the preachers' and their own citizens' urgings with a new civic religious praxis. They drafted dozens of new laws and passed them around to one another: preaching ordinances, liturgical ordinances, laws on marriage courts, laws against sectarianism, laws governing parish life, and new articles of doctrine. This praxis moved beyond mere usurpation of the episcopal functions to reshape civic religious life in an autonomous and Evangelical sense. The process briefly reawakened a sense of solidarity among the Swiss, Swabian, and Upper Rhenish cities—what a Strasbourg politician called "the good old neighborliness."[27] This exchange of ideas and institutions, far more than any distinctive doctrine, formed the practical heart of South German Zwinglianism, which radiated from the three linked centers of Zurich, Constance, and Strasbourg.

Four aspects of this civic religious praxis contained especially great integrative potential. First, the urban clergy were fully domesticated through marriage, compulsory citizenship and guild membership, and reduction in numbers, and many formerly clerical functions and resources were transferred to the communal regime. Second, the regime's assumption of episcopal authority, especially in marriage law, touched every constituent household of the commune and made possible the full coordination of patriarchal authority with governmental.[28] Third, the full domestication of worship, made possible by the total uncoupling of salvation from social life, gave birth to liturgies that were frankly designed to indoctrinate. The Catholic formula, "The norm of prayer is the norm of faith" (lex orandi, lex credendi) gave way to an Evangelical "the norm of doctrine is the norm of prayer" (lex docendi, lex orandi).[29] Fourth and finally, the formation of an autonomous civic church subordinated parish life and its pastor to the government, and all subsequent efforts to restore the integrity of the parish, chiefly through the right of excommunica-

---

*Elsass, Stadt Strassburg, 1522–1535*, Quellen und Forschungen zur Reformationsgeschichte, 26–27 (Gütersloh, 1959–60), 2:262, ll. 19–21, no. 492. Oberman in *Masters* writes of the "political theology" that "declared the Gospel to be no more and no less than a function of the *bonum commune*" (p. 280).

[27]Klaus Kniebis to Bernhard Meyer, Strasbourg, 30 August 1542, in Staatsarchiv Basel, Kirchen-Akten A 8, fol. 15v.

[28]See Thomas Max Safley, *Let No Man Put Asunder: The Control of Marriage in the German Southwest, 1560–1600*, Sixteenth Century Texts and Studies, 2 (Kirksville, Mo., 1984), pp. 121–65.

[29]Thus it is elegantly put by René Bornert in *La réforme protestante du culte à Strasbourg au XVIe siècle (1523–1598)*, Studies in Medieval and Reformation Thought, 28 (Leiden, 1981), p. 596.

tion, shattered in the face of governmental intransigence. In time, the Zwinglian ideal of a partnership between regime and clergy produced a thoroughgoing official control of the urban church.

The first decade of the urban reformation thus fashioned a clean, comprehensive solution to the problem of religion and civic order. The governments, emboldened by the preachers' offer of biblicist legitimacy and pressed forward by their own citizens' agitation, took control of parishes and clergy, convents and schools, and poor relief and the custody of Christian marriage. To all appearances, the Protestant free city of South Germany became the first of those godly peoples of Reformation Europe who placed themselves under the gospel understood as the *lex Christi*, or the law of Christ.

## IV

Much is known about how the reformers' message was preached and far less about how it was received. Most arguments for a uniform reception rest on samplings of the vast flood of pamphlets aimed at the literate 10–30 percent of the urban population, though it is not yet possible to say how representative the findings are.[30] A study of the illustrations intended for the illiterate majority suggests little real doctrinal content beyond biblicism and anticlericalism. As for specific urban groups, even the ruling elites, the best documented of all the urban classes, have been studied in only a few cities.

Despite these limitations, Bernd Moeller has confidently argued that urban folk received Luther's message as he preached it and that the ruling elites displayed "a general antipathy to the Reformation" that stood in opposition to the enthusiasm of "the people." Moeller's argument rests on polls of guildsmen and guild officials (*Schöffen* and so on), which "almost always resulted in an overpowering victory for the Protestant party."[31] In contrast, the current state of knowledge about the urban reform suggests, in Günther Vogler's words, that "the movement em-

---

[30]This statement is true of Bernd Moeller's programmatic "Stadt und Buch: Bemerkungen zur Struktur der reformatorischen Bewegung in Deutschland," in Wolfgang J. Mommsen, ed., *The Urban Classes, the Nobility, and the Reformation: Studies on the Social History of the Reformation in Germany and England*, Publications of the German Historical Institute, London, 5 (Stuttgart, 1979), pp. 25–39; and of most of the contributions to Hans-Joachim Köhler, ed., *Flugschriften als Massenmedium der Reformationszeit*, Spätmittelalter und Frühe Neuzeit, Tübinger Beiträge zur Geschichtsforschung, 13 (Tübingen, 1981). On illustrations, see Robert W. Scribner, *For the Sake of Simple Folk: Popular Propaganda for the German Reformation*, Cambridge Studies in Oral and Literate Culture, 2 (Cambridge, 1981).
[31]Moeller, *Imperial Cities*, pp. 62, 64.

braced various forces and interests. They included oligarchs and humanists, artisans and journeymen, clergymen and artists, peasants and ple-
beians, who differed from one another in their views on both the
theoretical and practical aspects of the Reformation, and who reacted
variously to different situations."[32] United for a time against one target,
the clergy—liberation from whose authority was seen as self-liberation
with regard to both salvation and the common good—the various classes
and interests soon began to split apart. Still, the fruit of their brief cooperation, the communalization of religion, was achieved without a social
revolution, which suggests that the urban elites favored not the old religion but the new.

A close analysis of some of the polls of guildsmen and guild officials
yields not a clear but a murky picture of the allegiances of the urban elites.
Nearly a dozen such polls are known from the years 1525 to 1531 in which
entire citizenries or guild officials alone were polled on some reformation-
related policy. Four polls were taken at Constance, two of them constitu-
tionally mandated and two at the regime's choice. Each produced a hefty
majority for the government's policy, though none was taken on the acts
directly related to the change in religion, most notably the abolition of the
Mass.[33] Elsewhere such polls also produced strong to overwhelming support for official policy. At Strasbourg in early 1529, for example, 184 of
the 300 Schöffen voted to abolish the Mass, 94 to delay its abolition until
the end of the Imperial Diet, and only 1 to retain it under all circumstances. Ninety-three percent of the Schöffen thus approved the government's proposal to abolish their ancestors' central act of worship.[34]

In most cases the polls did not directly measure the strengths of Catholic and Evangelical parties. One reason is that much depended on the way
in which an issue was presented. At Ulm in November 1530, minorities in
the two richest guilds voted quite differently—in the *Kramerzunft* (shopkeepers' guild) for the Diet's recess and in the *Kaufleutezunft* (merchants'
guild) to reject it if no General Council met within a year—though probably both minorities supported the position that opposed outright rejection
of the Diet of Augsburg's recess.[35] In this poll—and in most of the others

[32]Günther Vogler, *Nürnberg 1524–25: Studien zur Geschichte der reformatorischen Bewegung in der Reichsstadt* (Berlin, 1982), p. 323.

[33]Moeller, *Imperial Cities*, p. 64 n. 48. On the polls at Constance, see Hans-Christoph
Rublack, *Die Einführung der Reformation in Konstanz bis zum Abschluss 1531*, Quellen und
Forschungen zur Reformationsgeschichte, 40 (Gütersloh, 1971), pp. 114, 123.

[34]Miriam U. Chrisman, *Strasbourg and the Reform: A Study in the Process of Change* (New
Haven, 1967), p. 172.

[35]Hans Eugen Specker, "Zwischen Gewissen und Gehorsam: Zur Reformationsabstimmung
der Ulmer Bürgerschaft vor 450 Jahren," in *Die Einführung der Reformation in Ulm: Geschichte
eines Bürgerentscheids*, ed. Hans Eugen Specker and Gebhard Weig, Forschungen zur Gesch-

as well—a vote on one side is probably evidence of Evangelical convictions or sympathies, but a vote on the other side is not reliable evidence of Catholic ones. There was never a single line of policy, particularly foreign policy, associated with the new religion.[36] At Augsburg (a large, wealthy, and well-connected city), since about 1525 the government's inner circle had consisted of Evangelicals—mostly Zwinglians—but they did not change the civic religion and foreign policy until 1533.[37] The political cohesion and financial interests of the oligarchies, plus the binding power of traditional ties to the emperor, varied considerably from city to city,[38] and the coming of the Reformation did not obliterate their influence on civic policy.

Although the polls do not show, as Moeller maintains, that "the opposition votes came mostly from the patricians," they do reveal that urban nobles and wealthier guilds commonly backed conservative policies.[39] Only seven of the eleven officials (*Eilfer*), for example, of Memmingen's patrician *Grosszunft* appeared for a vote on 9 December 1528, and they refused to vote, because, they said, "we fear that Memmingen will not get away with this. The Mass has not yet been abolished in quite a few of the larger and smaller free cities."[40] This is the voice of prudence, not the fire of Catholic conviction. In the Memmingen poll of 1530, the wealthy Grosszunft furnished about a quarter of the fifty-one votes against rejecting the Diet of Augsburg's recess; at Ulm the heaviest opposition came from the patricians and the two wealthiest guilds, those of the Kramer and Kaufleute.[41] The rich clearly favored more cautious policies, but their

---

ichte der Stadt Ulm, "Dokumentation" series, 2 (Ulm, 1981), pp. 39–46, with the voting lists reprinted on pp. 343–85. Though Specker reiterates the notion that the vote was a decision for one religion or the other (p. 39), his account of the vote of Matthäus Laupin the Elder (p. 45) makes my point perfectly.

[36]See the tortuous policy of Nördlingen as portrayed by Hans-Christoph Rublack, *Eine bürgerliche Reformation: Nördlingen*, Quellen und Forschungen zur Reformationsgeschichte, 51 (Gütersloh, 1982), p. 257, and see pp. 147–50.

[37]I am grateful to James E. Mininger for this information. The findings of Wolfgang Reinhard's team will demonstrate the dominance of Zwinglians at Augsburg. For now, see Olaf Mörke and Katarina Sieh, "Gesellschaftliche Führungsgruppen," in Gunther Gottlieb et al., eds., *Geschichte der Stadt Augsburg: 2000 Jahre von der Römerzeit bis zur Gegenwart* (Stuttgart, 1985), pp. 301–11, here at pp. 306–307.

[38]This point, which was made fifty years ago by Hans Baron in "Religion and Politics in the German Imperial Cities during the Reformation," *English Historical Review* 52 (1937):405–27, 614–33, seems to require frequent repetition.

[39]Moeller, *Imperial Cities*, p. 64 n. 48.

[40]Friedrich Dobel, *Memmingen im Reformationszeitalter*, 5 vols. (Augsburg, 1877–78), 2:70.

[41]Ibid., 4:22; Specker, "Zwischen Gewissen und Gehorsam," p. 45 and the lists on pp. 369–74.

ranks were not necessarily filled with Catholic recusants. This essentially social interpretation of the polls is supported by a poll of 1547 in which the Strasbourg patricians and Schöffen of the merchant guilds voted overwhelmingly for "peace with honor."[42]

The reasons why the urban nobles, big merchants, bankers, and rentiers tended to favor relatively conservative policies are not far to seek. First, they had close sentimental and symbolic ties to the sacred buildings of the old faith, which had become, through their altars, glass windows, and heraldic devices, virtual showcases of aristocratic family prestige. Anyone who has strolled through Nuremberg's churches of St. Lorenz and St. Sebald can imagine how the cathedrals of Ulm, Constance, and Strasbourg once looked. Second, because of their education, books, travels, and business and diplomatic activities, the urban rich knew much about the world outside their cities' walls. Wealthy citizens were far better informed about external political forces than their social inferiors and were far more likely as well to appreciate the need for caution in the framing of policy. Unlike some modern historians, they were not likely to believe that their cities were, in fact, autonomous organisms. Third, these classes had great material interests outside their cities, such as estates, fiefs, loans to all classes of people, patronage rights, and goods in transit. Fourth, the religious schism within families probably affected the rich, whose familial ties tended to be strong and deep, more profoundly than other classes, whose families were less protected by property, politics, and genealogical memory.[43] For all of these reasons, the urban elites kept a political eye watching over their cities' walls.

The oligarchies did include recalcitrant Catholics, of course, who in a few towns, such as Rottweil and Schwäbisch-Gmünd, defended both the old faith and patrician power against popular challenges. Occasionally, for example at Basel, a resolute oligarchy could split the alliance between Evangelical religion and demands for the devolution of power.[44]

In general, therefore, it may be said that no solidly Catholic upper class in the South German free cities resisted the changes in religion. On the contrary, as Oberman notes, "members of the patriciate and the upper *bourgeoisie* of the south German cities, in the wake of long-standing

---

[42]Thomas A. Brady, Jr., *Ruling Class, Regime, and Reformation at Strasbourg, 1520–1555* (Leiden, 1978), pp. 259–75, esp. pp. 265–68.

[43]Here I am following Erich Maschke, "Die Familie ist so gross, wie sie vom Familienbewusstsein erfasst wird"; *Die Familie in der deutschen Stadt des späten Mittelalters*, Sitzungsberichte der Heidelberger Akademie der Wissenschaften, philosophisch-historische Klasse, Jahrgang 1980, no. 4 (Heidelberg, 1980), p. 14.

[44]Hans R. Guggisberg, *Basel in the Sixteenth Century: Aspects of the City Republic before, during, and after the Reformation* (St. Louis, 1982), pp. 27–31.

efforts at communalization, tended to reject the medieval privileged church that confronted them on every hand."[45]

The urban reform enjoyed the patronage of powerful upper-class figures from the very start. The club at Nuremberg that gathered reform-minded individuals under the influence of Johann von Staupitz, for example, included such important men as Anton Tucher, Hieronymus Ebner, Kaspar Nützel, Hieronymus Holzschuher, and Sigmund and Christoph Fürer—the cream of the city's political elite. At Augsburg three of the four mayors were early Evangelicals—Georg Vetter, Ulrich Rehlinger, and Hieronymus Imhof—as was the influential Conrad Herwart. Early Evangelicals at Strasbourg included the *Ammeisters* Claus Kniebis and Daniel Mieg, the future Ammeister Mathis Pfarrer, the banker Conrad Joham, and Egenolf Röder von Diersburg, a noble with important connections in Baden. Many of Constance's patrician politicians became early converts, among them Bartholomäus and Thomas Blarer, Hans Schulthaiss, and Konrad Zwick, whereas at Zurich some very important people, such as the millionaire Hans Edlibach, backed Zwingli from an early point. At Frankfurt am Main, finally, two of the leading patrician figures, Hamman von Holzhausen and Philipp Fürstenberger, protected Evangelical clergymen. It is difficult to imagine what might have become of the urban reform if its agents and their ideas had not enjoyed such protection from the very first.

Applied to these cities, the commonly identified antithesis—the "official" or "magisterial" Reformation, or the "popular" Reformation—is badly conceived. The South German urban reformation was both "official" and "popular": without initial protection and support from urban aristocrats, the movement would never have survived long enough to move into the churches and the streets; without broad support from the common man, the pressure for religious change would not have developed as rapidly or as radically as it did; without the preachers' theological and personal leadership, the movement could not have been sustained; and without the oligarchies' actions, the movement could not have been turned to a domestication of urban religion. The urban reformation thus became viable when individual oligarchs supported and protected it and it became secure when the oligarchy collectively established it. In between, the movement awakened sympathy among large numbers of artisans, shopkeepers, petty officials, employees, apprentices, and servants. This class of common man, a German *popolo minuto* (Ital: "little people"), comprised those who would not normally take an active part in government

[45]Oberman, *Masters,* p. 293.

but who were in touch with those who did, some of whom could expect to be consulted, personally or through their officials, in times of great crisis.

The free cities' governments protested long and loudly during the 1520s that such common folk had forced the governments to make changes in religion and would not tolerate a restoration of the old ways. This apology gains credence from the very broadness of the typical body politic. At Strasbourg, for example, a city of at most 20,000 inhabitants, some 3,500 persons were enrolled in the guilds; the comparable figure for Ulm, a somewhat smaller city, was 2,270 in 1530. If an oligarchy was backed by a large majority of a body politic of this size, it was invulnerable to internal foes, but it could not coerce or punish through ordinary means a large body of guildsmen who decided to break the law in the name of a higher law. Although Augsburg's rulers appeared at city hall in full armor during the Schilling riots in 1524, displays of force were relatively rare in the urban reformation—at least at this stage—because governments could not coerce large groups of respectable citizens who acted together in, for example, iconoclastic riots. Organized violence on behalf of Catholicism was even rarer, and most significant Catholic resistance involved religious communities, usually of women.[46] In the guilds, however, there were people who possessed the political skills to organize a movement and to orchestrate agitation and pressure on the regime, and it is almost certainly correct—though it cannot yet be demonstrated—to discern in the broad middling group of respectable citizens the social motor of the urban reformation. The decisive point came when very considerable numbers of them (there is as yet no reason to conclude that they were a majority) supported the Evangelical preachers' freedom to preach and attacked the Catholic clergy and ceremonies with militancy and perseverance. No comparable parties formed to defend the old religion with sufficient militancy or in sufficient numbers. After 1525 or so the major struggles in the larger cities occurred *between* Evangelicals,[47] persons committed in some sense to the supremacy of the unadulterated Word of God.

The structure of the South German urban reformation can now be described. A magisterial or official reform, the only kind possible short of revolution, occurred during the mid-1520s and was prolonged in some

[46]This subject badly needs comprehensive study. For two well-known cases, see Greta Krabbe, *Caritas Pirckheimer: Ein Lebensbild aus der Zeit der Reformation*, Katholisches Leben und Kirchenreform in Zeitalter der Glaubensspaltung, 7, 5th ed. (Münster/Westfalen, 1982); Francis Rapp, "La vie religieuse du couvent de St. Nicolas-aux-ondes à Strasbourg de 1525 à 1592," *Histoire et sociologie religieuses,* Cahiers de l'Association interuniversitaires de l'Est (1962):15–30; and Lorna Jane Abray, *The People's Reformation: Magistrates, Clergy, and Commons in Strasbourg, 1500–1598* (Ithaca, 1985), p. 118.

[47]It is well to heed Oberman's words, in *Masters*, p. 198, about the term "Evangelical."

places until the early 1530s. It was carried out under the oligarchies' custody of fundamental civic values and through their exclusive police power; it was legitimized by the Reformation movement's biblicism and by the oligarchies' undeniable peacekeeping authority (*jus pacificandi*). The pace of reform reflected both the jolting pressures from below, created by respectable folk who insisted on religious change, and the cautioning influence of external forces and events. In an age of uncertainty, the urban Reformation promised to convert civic religion from an unsettling, disruptive force into a supportive, legitimizing force for oligarchical rule and basic civic values. The urban elites willy-nilly seized this promise, because, although the Reformation movement brought a solution to the problem of the clergy within the oligarchies' grasp, it created a fearsome new situation by dividing the city in both belief and ritual. The rise of the sects during the late 1520s gave the crucial impetus to the formation of urban state-churches. At Strasbourg, the best-studied case, the magistrates' actions reveal the slenderness of the connection between the proclamation of an official system of belief—a confession of faith—and the achievement of the most rudimentary ritual unity. Unwilling to institute either a positive policy of belief or compulsory worship, in the end the magistrates settled for a negative ritual unity: citizens were forbidden to withhold their children from the baptismal font.[48] The Catholic church's official ceremonies had never, even before the Reformation, completely captured people's full ritual life,[49] and any existing communal ritual had been grievously damaged by the Reformation movement. The long, slow path to confessionalism began with unity not of worship but of doctrine— "lex docendi, lex orandi."

The whole task of fashioning the people—enthusiastic, indifferent, recalcitrant—into civic state-churches lay ahead. The enforcement of a clerically fashioned discipline moved slowly and against much resistance.[50] The urban laity had its own ideas as to what was and was not compatible with the Christian faith.[51] Half a century after the glory days of the urban reform, a Strasbourg Jesuit named Jacob Rabus surveyed its fruits in his native city: "In poor Strasbourg you now have five or six

[48]Abray, *People's Reformation*, pp. 104–16, with full references.

[49]This fundamental point is made by Scribner in "Cosmic Order and Daily Life."

[50]Gerald Strauss, *Luther's House of Learning: Indoctrination of the Young in the German Reformation* (Baltimore, 1978). James M. Kittelson's study of visitation records from Strasbourg's territory has caused him to dissent from Strauss's findings; see "Success and Failure in the German Reformation: The Report from Strasbourg," *Archiv für Reformationsgeschichte* 73 (1982):153–75. His conclusions, however, at most slightly modify Strauss's work, which receives additional support from Abray's *People's Reformation*.

[51]Miriam U. Chrisman, *Lay Culture, Learned Culture: Books and Social Change in Strasbourg, 1480–1599* (New Haven, 1982).

sects among the common people. One fellow is an out-and-out Lutheran, the second a half-Lutheran, the third a Zwinglian, the fourth a Calvinist, the fifth a Schwenckfelder, the sixth an Anabaptist, and the seventh lot is purely epicurean.''[52] An eighth, he might have added, was of his own faith. So much for the successful domestication of religion; so much for the identity of church and people, of gospel and common good.

V

Why did the urban reform of the 1520s fail to transform the South German towns into godly cities? The historian of religion might answer, as Peter Munz did, that very often ''the momentum of religious experience has made it very difficult to contain religion within the social parameter.''[53] Instead, historians of the Reformation point to the elevation of the gospel as a critical principle above the community and the common good, noting that the ''properly interpreted gospel'' became attached not only to the city as an oligarchically ruled commune but, more important, to what Oberman calls ''the consensus of the community of true believers.''[54] Although this statement precisely describes the preachers' standpoint, it is nonetheless true that the oligarchies resisted every attempt to make the Gospel a binding norm of belief for the citizens (although they did use it as a weapon to crush the sects) or to organize true believers as ''ecclesiolae in ecclesia,'' that is, conventicles inside the church. Only in a very limited sense did the urban laity want their hometowns to become ''godly cities.''[55]

One powerful reason why the oligarchies did not favor too close an identification of the Gospel with the common good was that they lacked full hegemony over these concepts, just as—a point demonstrated by the wave of urban revolts[56]—they lacked full political control over their own citizens. A different conception of gospel and common good, embodied in the idea of the ''godly law,'' had burst onto the political stage in 1525.[57] The *Twelve Articles'* rejection of serfdom, for example, on the ground that

[52]Jacob Rabus, *Christliche bescheidne und wolgegründts ablähnung/der vermeindten Bischoffs Predigt . . . im Münster zu Strassburg* (Cologne, 1570), fol. 30r. I am grateful to Lorna Jane Abray for this text.

[53]Munz, ''From Max Weber to Joachim of Floris,'' p. 182.

[54]Oberman, *Masters*, pp. 294–95. Moeller's view is similar; see *Imperial Cities*, p. 90.

[55]Compare Bruce Lenman, ''The Limits of Godly Discipline in the Early Modern Period with Particular Reference to England and Scotland,'' in Greyerz, *Religion and Society*, pp. 124–45.

[56]Maschke, ''Deutsche Städte,'' p. 95 n. 206.

[57]Peter Blickle, *The Revolution of 1525: The German Peasants' War from a New Perspective*, trans. Thomas A. Brady, Jr., and H. C. Erik Midelfort (Baltimore, 1981), p. 91.

Christ had died for all men, was no less inherently "Evangelical" than was Luther's hammering on St. Paul's admonition to obedience (Romans 13). The gospel and the common good could be, and were, seen as commands to justice as well as order, both in the countryside and on the land. This view was expressed perfectly in 1524 by an Augsburg rope-maker named Ott, who was overheard to condemn the "dishonorable priests and the rich . . . , who pile up goods and money and keep the truth from us" and who were to blame for the fact that men treat one another as devils rather than as brothers. "We have always been Evangelicals," Ott concluded, "and we still are today. But truly, we have been fed many lies. If we were to follow truly the Gospel, we would all have to be like brothers."[58] A few years later another Augsburger was reported to have said that "there is only one lord, and He is in heaven, so there are none here below. If he had the money, he would be a lord, too. . . . There is no lord but God, the only true Lord."[59] This is the religious sense of wanting to "turn Swiss," to live without human lords. Ott and his kind needed "no lord but God," nor did they need the preacher's gospel, for they had "always been Evangelicals."

There was never only one way to couple the Gospel to the common good. If the establishment coupled it to the image of patriarchal authority in the family and hierarchy in the commune, why could the opposition not link it to the fraternal principle of cooperation? The reason was that this understanding of what it meant to be Evangelical could bring revolution to the home, the shop, the guild, the marketplace, and the city hall; no civic regime could tolerate the godly law of justice and equality. Conversely, no free city could have satisfied this understanding within the economic and social conditions then obtaining. The thirst for Christian community, which the sacramental system of the medieval church and the entire monastic tradition had sought to accommodate "without damage to the society in which it flourishes,"[60] was reinvigorated by the urban reformation, which gave it, however, no permanent home in the city. Rather, the city expelled its seekers after community to wander about until the day when a great Christian commune, built according to South German specifications, would arise at Münster on the rain-swept Westphalian plain.[61]

The urban rich and the middling folk liked this outcome well enough.

---

58Stadtarchiv Augsburg, Urgichten 1524, Produkt 3, at 27 September 1524. I am grateful to Hans-Christoph Rublack for this reference and for the following one.

59Ibid., Urgichten 1525–26, at 30 December 1526.

60Munz, "From Max Weber to Joachim of Floris," p. 182.

61On the role of communal ideas and sentiments in Münster and the continuity between the Anabaptist and post-Anabaptist eras, see R. Po-chia Hsia, *Society and Religion in Münster, 1535–1618* (New Haven, 1984).

They fought and rejected—as a "new papacy"—every clerical attempt to build stricter religious discipline, because an established church that demanded a fixed minimum of compliance, preached the godly nature of patriarchal and magisterial authority, and provided a religious life unburdened through the uncoupling of salvation from social life suited them perfectly.

In the end, South Germany saw no godly cities; the ruling classes' interests and ambitions had become incommensurable with the political worlds of their own hometowns.[62] Outside these classes had their business operations and investments, their fiefs and country estates; outside, too, their children sought education and often careers as well; and from outside came books and travelers, new ideas and curious tales, new inventions, and rumors and threats of war. Small and economically dependent, the South German city no longer formed a realm of power and imagination,[63] at least not one adequate to the talents, wealth, and ambitions of its elites' offspring. The rising world of absolutist states, whose chief business was war, had uses and rewards for urban talent and urban capital but little place for proud, self-governing little cities. The German princely states, in themselves mostly petty things, formed through confessional alliances larger systems of opportunity into which the townsmen streamed. They hardly shared, as far as we can tell, the sentiment of Machiavelli, who wrote: "I love my native city more than my own soul."[64]

[62]An extreme example of this incommensurability is presented in Olaf Mörke, "Die Fugger im 16. Jahrhundert: Städtische Elite oder Sonderstruktur?—Ein Diskussionsbeitrag," *Archiv für Reformationsgeschichte* 74 (1983):141–61.

[63]That is, society and culture, for which I borrow this phrase from Lauro Martines, *Power and Imagination: City-States in Renaissance Italy* (New York, 1979), preface.

[64]Niccolò Machiavelli to Francesco Vettori, Forlì, 16 April 1527, in *The Letters of Machiavelli: A Selection of His Letters,* trans. Allan Gilbert (New York, 1961), p. 249 (no. 225 in Alvisi's edition [Florence, 1883]). This letter was written nine weeks before Machiavelli's death.

*For historians in the German Democratic Republic, the Reformation occupies a key role in the interpretation of the transition from feudal to capitalist society. Central to the Marxist historiography of the Reformation is the concept of "early bourgeois revolution," by which is meant that a popular, antifeudal Evangelical movement, represented by the Peasants' War and the social unrests in the cities, challenged the princes, magistrates, and theologians in the struggle for social and religious transformation. Focusing on Nuremberg, the largest imperial city in the sixteenth century, and concentrating on the years 1524 and 1525, the revolutionary years of the Peasants' War, Günther Vogler, professor of history at the Alexander von Humboldt University of Berlin, examines both archival sources and published pamphlets to reconstruct the popular antifeudal socioreligious movement, a force that was quickly suppressed by the magistrates. In the following article, which is based on his book-length study, Vogler offers an alternative model to explain the urban Reformation in the German cities, one that focuses on the cultural and religious differences between different urban classes. Vogler is also the coauthor (with Adolf Laube and Max Steinmetz) of an illustrated history of the German early bourgeois revolution (1974) and the author of several articles on the Münster Anabaptist kingdom.*

[32]

# [2]

# Imperial City Nuremberg, 1524–1525:
# The Reform Movement in Transition

GÜNTHER VOGLER

Translated by R. Po-chia Hsia

Between 3 and 14 March 1525, a religious colloquy took place in the great hall of the city council of Nuremberg. Some five hundred persons, including members of the Large Council, attended, and a large crowd gathered in front of the city hall, awaiting the long overdue decision of religious reform. Although the delegated magistrates did not produce binding decisions, the city council felt that it had the mandate to further the reform movement, which had already been developing in Nuremberg under its toleration. After the religious colloquy, the city council took the lead in promulgating new religious ordinances.

The result of the religious colloquy might give us the impression that in its success the Reformation was free of conflict, that it represented the culmination of the Lutheran movement that had begun in Nuremberg some years back, and that, logically, the commune would become a Lutheran city. Such assumptions, however, would alter if we examined the problems besetting the reform movement both within the city walls and in the countryside prior to its ultimate triumph.[1]

When we turn to the phase of reform in Nuremberg that preceded the religious colloquy, certain characteristics common to the urban Reformation as a whole become noticeable. One question in particular should attract more attention in research. Recent studies on the phases of the urban Reformation have introduced a three-phase model: preparation,

---

[1] Cf. Günther Vogler, *Nürnberg 1524–25: Studien zur Geschichte der reformatorischen und sozialen Bewegung in der Reichsstadt* (Berlin-East, 1982). This article summarizes the arguments in my book and formulates some conclusions with greater precision. I cite here only works that I quote and other works that I did not use in my book.

[33]

crisis, and organization[2] or, inception, transition, and consolidation.[3] We are concerned here with the phase of crisis or transition because such a phase seems to have characterized the imperial city of Nuremberg as well in that alternative visions signaled a crisis and demanded resolutions. The task therefore is to document this development in actual events.

In 1526 the preacher Dominik Schleupner described the reform movement in the city thus: "Nuremberg is not a small or forsaken peasant mart with goings-on about which nobody cares; rather, it is a respected imperial and trading city, and if the clear, revealed truth is abandoned, or if there is faltering in any course of action, a lot of people will be hurt."[4] Not only did Schleupner emphasize the role of the city as a political and economic center, he also showed an interest in ascertaining the results of the Reformation. Still, what had happened before 1526?

I

The public appearance of Martin Luther was the decisive event for the articulation of a reform movement in Nuremberg.[5] The first supporters of the Wittenberg reformer were found among the prominent civic families. The reception of his teachings in humanist circles and the intellectual exchange in a sodality were typical forms of communication in Nuremberg as well as in other communes. But things soon went beyond the confines of the sodality. With the publication and spread of Lutheran writings, and with the appointment of Evangelical preachers, conditions were created for the popular dissemination of reform teachings, so that the struggle for the realization of the Reformation increasingly provided the occasion for public conflict.

Lutheran teachings were propagated by the preachers Andreas Osiander at St. Lorenz's, Dominik Schleupner at St. Sebald's, Thomas Venatorius

[2]Cf. Jean Rott, "La réforme à Nuremberg et à Strasbourg: Contacts et contrasts," *Hommage à Dürer* (Strasbourg, 1972), p. 92.

[3]Cf. Joseph Seubert, *Untersuchungen zur Geschichte der Reformation in der ehemaligen freien Reichsstadt Dinkelsbühl* (Lübeck/Hamburg, 1971), p. 60.

[4]Gottfried Seebass, "Dominikus Schleupners Gutachten zum Stand der Reformation in Nürnberg, 1526," *Zeitschrift für bayerische Kirchengeschichte* 47 (1978):37.

[5]Cf. Gottfried Seebass, "Stadt und Kirche in Nürnberg im Zeitalter der Reformation," in Bernd Moeller, ed., *Stadt und Kirche im 16. Jahrhundert*, (Gütersloh, 1978), pp. 66–86; Friedrich-Wilhelm Kantzenbach, "Gottes Ehre und der Gemeine Nutzen: Die Einführung der Reformation in Nürnberg," in *Zeitschrift für bayerischen Kirchengeschichte* 47 (1978):1–26; Peter Blickle, *Die Reformation im Reich* (Stuttgart, 1982), pp. 73–92; Heinrich R. Schmidt, *Reichsstädte, Reich, und Reformation: Korporative Religionspolitik, 1521–1529/30* (Stuttgart, 1986), pp. 30–33, 45–48, 51–57; *Reformation in Nürnberg: Umbruch und Bewahrung, 1490–1580*, vol. I: *Catalogue* (Nuremberg, 1979); Adolf Laube, Max Steinmetz, Günther Vogler, *Illustrierte Geschichte der deutschen frühbürgerlichen Revolution*, 2d ed. (Berlin-East, 1982).

in the Hospital of the Holy Ghost, Martin Glaser in the Augustinian cloister, and Jakob Dolmann at St. Jakob's. As early as the end of 1522, someone observed, "Everywhere there are preachers who are closely aligned with Luther, as is commonly reported."[6] The preachers made "the common man" aware of the conflict. Naturally, local differences were to be expected because the preachers differed among themselves with respect to style and directness, and the Evangelical message was spread not only by appointed preachers but also by the laity. In any case, the appointment of Evangelical preachers was the first step in the direction of the Reformation.[7]

These early years were a probation period for the Evangelical movement because after 1521 the imperial regime was located in Nuremberg, and between 1522 and 1524 three Imperial Diets met in the city; thus, the council and the citizenry were acting under the noses of the imperial estates. The city council was forced to carry out tactical maneuvers. Whenever it was admonished to enforce the 1521 Edict of Worms, it repeatedly referred to the common man, who could be provoked to an uprising if measures were undertaken against the reform-minded preachers or laymen. Its attitude must also be seen against the background of pre-Reformation church politics. Since the fifteenth century, the imperial city had followed a policy of extending the city council's ecclesiastical sovereignty at the expense of the Catholic church, which resulted in a "tendency to incorporate the Church within the civic commune."[8] The background for this development was the "pronounced sense of lordship [*Herrschaft*] of the Nuremberg patrician-dominated city council, which strove to exercise unrestrained authority over the Church and would no longer tolerate islands of corporative, ecclesiastical autonomy."[9]

Although a pronounced late medieval piety can be discerned in Nuremberg,[10] the first years of the Reformation prompted massive outbursts of

---

[6]*Deutsche Reichstagsakten unter Kaiser Karl V*, vol. 3, ed. Adolf Wrede (Gotha, 1901), p. 871.

[7]Cf. Gottfried Seebass, "Apologia Reformationis: Eine bisher unbekannte Verteidigungsschrift Nürnbergs aus dem Jahre 1528," *Zeitschrift für bayerische Kirchengeschichte* 39 (1970):34.

[8]Gottfried Seebass, "Zur Geschichte der reformatorischen und sozialen Bewegung in der Reichsstadt Nürnberg, 1524–25," *Mitteilungen des Vereins für Geschichte der Stadt Nürnberg* 71 (1984):269; and his *Stadt und Kirche*, p. 70.

[9]Anton Schindling, "Die Reformation in den Reichsstädten und die Kirchengüter: Strassburg, Nürnberg, und Frankfurt im Vergleich," in Jürgen Sydow, ed., *Bürgerschaft und Kirche* (Sigmaringen, 1980), p. 78.

[10]Cf. Karl Schlemmer, *Gottesdienst und Frömmigkeit in der Reichsstadt Nürnberg am Vorabend der Reformation* (Würzburg, 1980); *Caritas Pirckheimer, 1467–1532 (Ausstellungskatalog)* (Munich, 1982); Rainer Wohlfeil and Trudl Wohlfeil, "Nürnberger Bildepitaphien: Versuch einer Fallstudie zur historischen Bildkunde," *Zeitschrift für historische Forschung* 12 (1985):129–80.

anticlerical sentiments. Such a development was prompted by the numerous pamphlets and tracts, that spoke to and articulated the wishes and
hopes of the common man. Anticlericalism covered a broad spectrum, as
was evident in Nuremberg from the writings of the influential city secretary Lazarus Spengler, the painter Hans Greiffenberger, and the shoemaker Hans Sachs and also from the picture sheets of Sebald Beham and
other artists. These individuals publicized reform teachings in various
media intended for the common man.

With their anticlerical attitude artisans and journeymen clamored for
actions against the pope and the clergy and gave the movement a popular
character. Protests ensued: there were public criticisms of traditional
preachers and monks during mass and during processions and other occasions, giving rise to verbal battles, to physical provocation, and to various
kinds of confrontation. Anonymous slander sheets, secretly posted in
churches and in hidden corners, prompted searches by the magistrates,
who feared unrest. Protests were manifest in the singing of songs of
ridicule, and in mock processions and other events directed against the
pope, the cardinals, and the clergy. In addition, monks who had left their
cloisters spoke of their experiences and inspired aversion to the cloistered
life.[11]

The anticlerical protests turned against the teachings and behavior of
the old believers in the city. The protesters denounced priests and monks
as falsifiers of the Gospel and false leaders of the faithful, but their
criticism did not go further. The patrician city council was adamant that
such restraint must be shown, and as long as it was, magisterial reactions
were limited to admonitions and warnings. As early as December 1522,
however, the imperial Statthalter, Archduke Ferdinand, who was attend-
ing the Diet in Nuremberg, appeared before the city council and demanded that measures be taken against the Evangelical preachers and that
Lutheran tracts be suppressed. In January 1523, during another Diet ses-
sion, the papal nuncio, Francesco Chieregati, reiterated the demand.

When the laity demanded communion of both kinds in early 1523,
developments took a new turn. Although the city council denied the
request, it did abolish some religious ceremonies and customs that had
been attacked as ungrounded in theology and as mere "external pomp."
Although some of the obstacles to reform had been removed, the expectations of the supporters of the Reformation remained to be fulfilled.

On 1 June 1524, the provosts of Ss. Lorenz's and Sebald's took a

---

[11]The former monk Gallus Korn wrote of his experiences in the work "Eyn handlung, wie es
eynem Prediger Munch czu Nurmberg mit seynen Ordens brudern von wegen der Euangelischen
warheyt gangen ist" (1522).

further step and introduced a decisive reform of the liturgy of the mass. Although these innovations did not go unopposed by the council—because these changes "had not been instituted by any other places outside of Wittenberg,"[12] and the Bishop of Bamberg had also been provoked to intervene—the reforms were not rescinded. "The sign of a civic uprising proved to be the most convincing argument against the demand to restore the status quo by force."[13]

The *unity* of the reform movement manifested itself in the anticlerical opposition, in the critique of clerical institutions, traditional preachers, monks, and nuns. The movement's heterogeneity began to be more clearly discernible when it was recognized that adherents intended to apply the reform teachings to secular life and the social realm. The background for this development was increasing external pressure: the city council was bound to obey the decisions of the Imperial Diets (which had spoken against the Reformation) but was still hoping that a future national church council would resolve the issue.[14] When the social classes that had hitherto acted in relative unison under the banner of anticlericalism began to exhibit conspicuously different interests and expectations, the movement entered a perceptibly new phase of crisis or transition.

## II

Our interest thus turns to the period from early 1524 to March 1525, when the social character of the reform in Nuremberg emerged prominently. Although we may only infer the contents of reform sermons in the imperial city, Evangelical preaching must have benefited from an existing social vision. Albrecht Dürer and Hans Sachs represented two good examples that attested to the existence of a social vision before this phase of crisis. Dürer's position on the Reformation was tied to Luther's programmatic writings, with a further emphasis on the needs of the common man, who was often portrayed in his pictures. Dürer not only received reform

[12]*Quellen zur Nürnberger Reformationsgeschichte: Von der Duldung liturgischer Änderungen bis zur Ausübung des Kirchenregiments durch den Rat (Juni 1524–Juni 1525)*, ed. Gerhard Pfeiffer (Nuremberg, 1968), p. 5.

[13]Kantzenbach, "Gottes Ehre," p. 11.

[14]Cf. Martin Brecht, "Die gemeinsame Politik der Reichsstädte und die Reformation," *Zeitschrift für Rechtsgeschichte* 94 (1977):186–202; Georg Schmidt, "Die Haltung des Städtecorpus zur Reformation und die Nürnberger Bündnispolitik," *Archiv für Reformationsgeschichte* 75 (1984):194–232, and his *Der Städtetag in der Reichsverfassung: Eine Untersuchung zur korporativen Politik der Freien und Reichsstädte in der ersten Hälfte des 16. Jahrhunderts* (Stuttgart, 1984), pp. 478–86; Heinrich R. Schmidt, *Reichsstädte, Reich, und Reformation*, pp. 86–112, 130–52.

ideas but he also problematized them through a personal effort to understand the message of Christ. He saw his actions and artistic output as
serving "the honor of God and . . . the common good." Dürer's position
reflected an intense religious earnestness, and he attacked "the laws of
men" and advocated social responsibility for the common man.[15]

The involvement with the Reformation of the shoemaker poet Hans
Sachs was first reflected in a poem of animal allegory, "The Nightingale
of Wittenberg," which was published in 1523. It was an effective com-
pilation of the current complaints and grievances against the papal church
and the clergy and a defense of Luther's teachings against the tradi-
tionalists. The literary critique of clerical abuses reflected the anticlericalism of the reform movement. By stressing the greed of the Catholic clergy, Sachs emphasized the social dimension of the Reformation. He
could very well have been thinking of the situation in his hometown.

On 23 March 1524, Balthasar Wolf wrote an anxious letter to the
Elector of Saxony: "The preacher of St. Lorenz is doing remarkable
things: Be careful, he might do too much, because he might stir things up
against the secular authorities."[16] His opinion was off the mark, but it
suggested a potential consequence of Evangelical sermons. Sachs had
denounced the clergy for "badly abusing the people with the tithe in the
countryside."[17] He was actually drawing attention to a problem that was
real enough for the village communities in the large rural territory under
the jurisdiction of the city. Since mid-May 1524, there had been gatherings of peasants and refusals to pay the tithe. There were peasant assemblies on 29 May in Grundlach, on 1 June in Poppenreuth, and on 5 June in
Reichelsdorf. In each case, representatives of many villages met to discuss matters of common concern. More than sixty villages probably participated in these peasant assemblies. Artisans from the city also attended
the meetings and pledged their support.

The movement in the countryside was directed above all against the
payment of tithes to clerics and to ecclesiastical institutions, possibly also
against many feudal obligations that grew out of manorial relations of
dependence. At the same time that the gatherings occurred, there were
refusals to pay the tithe by the majority of peasants and even by whole
village communities. Although not all villages in the Nuremberg territory
participated, a greater number did; the actions of protest drew the attention
of the city council, which tried to contain them.

[15]Albrecht Dürer, *Schriften und Briefe*, ed. Ernst Ullmann (Leipzig, 1971), p. 240.

[16]Wilhelm Möller, *Andreas Osiander: Leben und ausgewählte Schriften* (Elberfeld, 1870), p.
16.

[17]*Flugschriften der frühen Reformationsbewegung (1518–1524)*, ed. Adolf Laube, Annerose
Schneider, and Sigrid Looss, vol. 1 (Berlin-East, 1983), p. 596.

Attacked by reform sermons, the tithe became an anachronism. The following argument was central for the protesting peasants: Established in Mosaic Law, the tithe was now invalid because it could not be shown to be an obligation in the New Testament. Economic anticlericalism thus received a theological foundation. In a mandate dated 20 May, the Nuremberg city council criticized its rural subjects for trying to "defend their unseemly conduct with the Gospels."[18] In the public magisterial pronouncement of 9 June, the peasants were again denounced for attempting to justify tax evasion by the Gospels.

The refusal to pay the tithe became the focus of a social confrontation in the countryside; the Reformation had sown its seeds here. "The Freedom of a Christian," as espoused by Luther, was also understood to represent liberation from social oppression. The council undertook preventive measures: peasant assemblies were spied on; those who refused to pay the tithe were arrested; and precautionary steps were undertaken to prevent citizens from supporting the rural movement.

Above all the Nuremberg magistrates intended to keep the rural movement out of the city, within whose walls the contours of a civic opposition movement could be discerned, a movement directed specifically against the excise, a consumer tax on food. The impetus for this movement was the social condition of the lower classes and their predicament in the face of rising food prices and inflation. Although the refusal to pay the excise was based on the argument that it was a heavy economic burden, reform sermons may very well have prepared the ground. Where Christian neighborly love was preached, the unequal distribution of burden on different segments of the populace contradicted the principle of Christian brotherhood.

The first stirring and the public demand to abolish the excise occurred on 2 June 1524, when eleven deputies from the villages met at the Peasant Inn in St. Jakob's district (inhabited mostly by the poor and artisans) to discuss common grievances and possible action. When they were arrested and interrogated by the city council, a crowd gathered before city hall and vehemently demanded the abolition of the excise. On this occasion the civic tax (*Losung*) seems also to have been criticized; threats were made against the magistrates, and there were demands that guilds be organized. Articles of grievances were not drawn up, as they had been in other cities, however, and citizen committees were not formed. As a result it is impossible for us to know this urban opposition movement in greater detail.

The Nuremberg city secretary, Spengler, wrote later "that it was not

---

[18]*Quellen zur Nürnberger Reformationsgeschichte*, p. 259. For the events, see also Heinrich R. Schmidt, *Reichsstädte, Reich, und Reformation*, pp. 154–68.

right, nor was it in the interest of civic peace and harmony, when those who contribute nothing for the common good, be it taxes, council, or help, should live on the blood and sweat of the common man—on those who toil day and night for the benefit of others, who nourished themselves by the sweat of their faces and win their bread with much effort, in the face of danger on the open roads, risking their bodies and lives and bearing the burdens and heat of the day—that they should be free and idle about; they should enjoy no pity in a Christian community."[19] Although the invective was directed against the clergy, this attitude quite possibly also determined the relationship between the people and the secular authorities, given the social antagonism in the city and in the countryside.

Given the threat of an uprising, the city council undertook measures to contain the opposition movement. On 4 June 1524, it decreed an ordinance for the maintenance of security in the city; on 7 June several craft masters were questioned concerning suspects. A public decree was issued on 9 June from city hall warning against uprisings. In this connection, some concessions were also made to alleviate the conditions of the lower classes. The council concentrated its effort on punishing peasants who had refused to pay the tithe and on searching for artisans who had promised the peasants support and had incited the opposition to the excise. The investigation ended with the execution of an innkeeper and a clothier's apprentice as well as the exile of a third man.

The extraordinary steps undertaken by the council underscored its perception of the situation as very dangerous. There is so far no agreement as to whether the ecclesiastical reforms introduced by the provosts had anything to do with these developments—whether the provosts themselves exploited the situation while the council was preoccupied with other problems or whether the city council tried to prevent the reform movement from being extended into the social realms. Perhaps the council wanted to show that the demands of reform could be met without their having to pay a heavy price in fulfilling the social expectations of the people.[20]

We must also bear in mind that it was possible to politicize this movement. The incidents in front of city hall on 2 June and many activities in St. Jakob's quarter clearly demonstrate this point. The demand for the creation of guilds (which did not exist in Nuremberg) revealed hostility toward the authorities but also showed that an important organizational prerequisite for the formation of a bourgeois opposition was lacking in the imperial city.

[19]Seebass, "Apologia Reformationis," pp. 63–64.
[20]Seebass, "Zur Geschichte," p. 271. The questions raised here cannot be answered definitively at this time.

Although the council accused the peasants of wanting to refuse payments of annuities, interests, and ground rents, we cannot confirm this point from peasant sources. We cannot rule out the possibility either, however, because the refusal to pay the tithe could very well have grown into a broader social movement that challenged feudal land obligations. There were occasional references to fishing and the right to use the woods as well as to conflicts over poaching. Generally speaking, the problems that would play a role in the making of the Twelve Articles of the Swabian Peasants (1525) were already apparent. It was not unthinkable that these early actions in the countryside around Nuremberg could have developed into an uprising and that the uprising would have become part of the Peasants' War, but the security measures and the concessions of the city council prevented such an outcome. Perhaps the existing social contradictions in the countryside were also not sharp enough to stimulate a radicalization of the movement.

### III

When we state that the social movement was stimulated by reform sermons, preached from the pulpits of the city, we must add that lay preachers also appeared occasionally and exerted an influence whose extent cannot be precisely determined. In the records of the council of 30 December 1523, the former priest Diepold Peringer, who called himself a layman, appeared for the first time. Two pamphlets ascribed to him showed that he held Lutheran ideas.[21] The ideas were already part of the general heritage of the reform movement. Called "the Peasant of Wöhrd" in Nuremberg, Peringer attracted many to his open air sermons; he belonged to a type of popular preacher who lacked intellectual originality. It is noteworthy that the Nuremberg council forbade him to appear publicly in early May 1524, when the antitithe movement began in the rural areas.

From the seven tracts composed by the painter Hans Greiffenberger between 1523 and 1524, we can see how a layman understood the ideas of the Reformation.[22] These tracts reflected numerous current themes: Anti-

---

[21]The two pamphlets are: *Eyn Sermon, geprediget vom Pawren zu Werdt bey Nürmberg am Sonntag vor Fassnacht von dem Freyen willen des Menschen* (1524); *Ein Sermon von der Abgötterey, durch den Pawren der weder schreyben noch lesen kan gepredigt zyu Kitzing im Franckenland auff unsers Herren Fronleychnamstag* (1524).

[22]These are: *Die Welt sagt, sy sehe kain besserung von den, die sy Lutherisch nennet* (1523); *Diss biechlin zaygt an, was uns lernen und gelernet haben vnsere maister der geschrifft* (1523); *Ein kurtzer begrif von gutten werckenn, dye gott behagen vnd der welt ain spot seynd* (1524); *Ein Christenliche Antwordt denen, die da sprechen, das Evangelion hab sein krafft von der kirchen*

christ and idolatry, the veneration of saints and the cloistered life, justification by good works and scriptural authority. Greiffenberger defended
the right of the laity to know and read the Bible and demanded emphat-
ically that it be possible to propagate the Gospels without hindrance.
Besides repeatedly stressing the opposition between faith and the devil's
work, he showed concern for the common man, who was threatened by
the Antichrist and who must be shown the right way to faith. Greiffenberger had no aim to inspire social change. In his condemnation of monetary offerings, requiem masses, and other customs, he touched on social
themes but never drew any logical conclusions. His polemic against the
world, nature, and reason, however, as well as his use of the terms
"Spirit," "Cross," *Gelassenheit,* and "suffering," made possible a radical development in the movement that he himself had not intended.

New problems that arose after the reform of church service and the birth
of an opposition movement in the city and countryside were reflected in
four prose dialogues of Hans Sachs, with which he engaged in literary
polemics in the second half of 1524.[23] They deal with a broad spectrum of
questions, including social problems. The lay critique of clerics reached
its climax in the demand that they should turn to useful labor. In propagat-
ing the idea of labor and in demanding that clerics take up civic burdens
and duties, Sachs disclosed the core message of the Reformation in the
social realm. He focused on the interests of the common man in his
dialogues. He was concerned with the respect of Evangelical norms but
did not give them a social revolutionary interpretation. In the fourth
dialogue, however, he asks poignantly: "What use is our freedom to us,
when you are not allowed to use it?"[24] One obstacle was the behavior of
those who called themselves Lutheran without living as such. Thus his
criticisms were directed not only against the old believers but also against
many "new Evangelicals."

Peringer, Greiffenberger, and Sachs offered each in his own way a

---

(1524); *Ein warnung vor dem Teuffel, der sich wider übt mit seinem dendelmarckt* (1524); *Ein trostliche ermanung, den angefochten im gewissen, von wegen gethaner sündt* (1524); *Disz biechlin zaigt an die Falschen Propheten, vor denen vnss gewarnet hat Christus, Paulus, und Petrus* (1524).

[23]The titles of the dialogues are: "Disputation zwischen einem Chorherren vnd Schuhmacher, darinn das wort gottes vnnd ein recht Christlich wesen verfochten würdt" (1524); "Ein gesprech von den Scheinwercken der Gaystlichen vnd jren gelübten, damit sy zu verlesterung des bluts Christi vermaynen selig zu werden" (1524); "Ein Dialogue, des inhalt ein argument der Römischen wider das Christlich heuflein, den Geytz, auch ander offenlich laster etc. betreffend" (1524); "Ain gesprech eines Ewangelischen christen mit einem Lutherischen. Darinn der ergerlich wandel etzlicher, die sich Lutherisch nennen, angezaigt vnd bruderlich gestrafft wirdt" (1524).

[24]*Die Prosadialoge von Hans Sachs,* ed. Ingeborg Spriewald (Leipzig, 1970), p. 154.

Lutheran vision and expressed different perspectives. Peringer and Greiffenberger merely exhorted their hearers to neighborly love without examining whether it could eradicate evil. Conversely, Hans Sachs argued directly and poignantly against clerical exploitation. Every religious ceremony asked for money: "Thus they plucked our wool."[25]

Sachs repeatedly cited the spiritual and material burdens introduced by the Roman horde and also mentioned in conclusion the equally harmful practices of "the new Evangelicals." For Sachs, the abolition of material burdens is an essential part of the necessary Reformation.

The pamphlets and literary polemics—the three named authors are exemplary—reflected the demand that one make one's life conform to the norms of the Gospels. Because the first new reform ordinances obviously did not achieve this result (if indeed such a goal was attainable), criticisms of old believers were joined by polemics against those who called themselves Lutherans but did not live accordingly or who behaved badly toward their fellow men. Behind this critique stood "a circle that was disappointed with the absence of true Christianity in the reform movement."[26] We can understand this situation as a crisis in which the reform movement found itself and in which alternative ideas were advanced.

## IV

When Sachs complained that Christian freedom could not be put to use, his interpretation was not to be understood as merely subjective. Given the sharpening of social conflicts and the frustration of expectations associated with the Reformation, such ideas expressed publicly a more pervasive mood. In this situation it also happened that more radical reform influences infiltrated from the outside and exerted some impact. When Luther and the Saxon court suppressed the influence of Thomas Müntzer and Andreas Karlstadt in the Thuringian-Saxon territory, exiling them and some of their followers, Müntzer, Heinrich Pfeiffer, and Martin Reinhart sought contacts in Nuremberg.

With Heinrich Pfeiffer there appeared for the first time a follower of Müntzer in Nuremberg. When the council noticed Pfeiffer's activities on 26 October 1524, it ordered his exile, claiming that he had tried to attract followers and together with Müntzer had caused an uprising in September in the city of Mühlhausen, Thuringia. Pfeiffer wanted to publish two manuscripts in Nuremberg, whose contents can only be reconstructed

[25]*Flugschriften der frühen Reformationsbewegung*, 1:596.
[26]Seebass, "Zur Geschichte," p. 273.

from Osiander's verdict. They concerned the September uprising in Mühlhausen and Mosaic Law. The council intervened immediately, not only forbidding the printing of the two works but also exiling the author in order to suppress possible radical influences.

Many traces indicate that Thomas Müntzer also stayed incognito in Nuremberg for a few days in November or early December 1524. It was important for him to publish his tracts here—*Expressed Unmasking of the False Beliefs of the Untruthful World* and *A Most Necessary Defense and Answer against the Spiritless, Soft Living Flesh in Wittenberg*—because it was no longer possible to publish them in Saxony. The first work was delivered by Hans Hut, an accountant known to Müntzer, to the printer Hans Hergot before Müntzer's sojourn, whereas the second was passed on by an unknown "foreign traveler" to Hieronymus Höltzel after Müntzer's stay. The council confiscated the press runs and destroyed most of the copies. During his stay, Müntzer probably came into contact with the schoolmaster of St. Sebald, Hans Denck. If he had ever entertained the plan to create another center of the popular reformation after his exile from Mühlhausen, he must have been convinced in a short time that such a plan was unfeasible in Nuremberg.

The spread of Karlstadt's teachings in Nuremberg was connected with the work of Martin Reinhart, the exiled preacher from Jena, who stayed in Nuremberg for a short time before his expulsion on December 17, 1524. He was expelled principally because he was suspected of being Müntzer's follower. Thus the Nuremberg council followed Luther's arguments in ascribing the same intentions to Müntzer and Karlstadt. One can assume that, during his brief stay, Reinhart worked to arouse interest in Karlstadt's teachings. He too, however, was unsuccessful in gaining a foothold.

By expelling "the foreigners" from the imperial city and by forbidding the spread of their ideas and writings, the council succeeded in keeping away radical influences but did not quite manage to suppress them completely. This point became clear in the trials of Hans Denck and the painters Sebald Beham, Barthel Beham, and Georg Pencz in January 1525.

On 10 January 1525, the three painters were first interrogated in a normal court proceeding. The charge was blasphemy, sectarianism, and disrespect of secular authority. The question of their relationship to secular power moved the trial from the sphere of religious errors into the realm of secular rule and the attitude of the citizens toward the civic regime.

Denck was likewise involved in the trial. His "confession" shows that his doubts culminated in the question of whether he had already achieved the right faith. It was no coincidence that Denck's transformation took place precisely at the moment when Karlstadt's influence was discernible in the city. The schoolmaster had already conversed with Hans Hut and probably also with Müntzer. The investigations of Denck ended on 21 January 1525 with his expulsion. Crucial for this extreme punishment was not Denck's personal doubt but the possible influence that he might have exerted on others.

In the case of the three painters, what mattered in deciding the punishment was not only the suspicion of blasphemy but also their influence in a volatile situation. Therefore the council decided on 26 January 1525 on expulsion. The painters knew the writings of Müntzer and Karlstadt. They had contacts with Pfeiffer or Reinhart as well. The most important influence on them, however, came from Denck; there is no key evidence to document any intellectual agreement between Müntzer and the painters.[27]

Through their denial of the Eucharist and baptism, the three painters belonged to the group that was bitterly attacked by Luther. During the trial their hostility toward authority showed itself in the assertion that they recognized God alone as their lord. Nevertheless they did not try to undermine secular authority. The fact that they did not do so distinguished them from Müntzer and the revolutionary popular movement. Their critical attitude toward the church and secular authority manifested itself in doubt but did not transcend the phase of negation.

In its argument against them, the council reasoned mainly from the separation of religion and politics; it pleaded for "sermons of unanimity." This decisive argument, which had already arisen in the context of the peasant movements, was used in the disputes with the monks as well as against the more radical influences; it was also decisive for the religious colloquy.[28]

V

When one follows the process of the Reformation in Nuremberg in the phase from early 1524 to March 1525, one finds a broad spectrum of

[27]Cf. Frank Ganseurer, "Hans Hergot und der 'linke Flügel der Reformation' in Nürnberg," *Mitteilungen des Vereins für Geschichte der Stadt Nürnberg* 71 (1984):149–66. His conclusions cannot be documented by sources (p. 165).

[28]Cf. Gottfried Seebass, "Der Nürnberger Rat und das Religionsgespräch vom März 1525 mit den Akten Christoph Scheurls und anderen unbekannten Dokumenten," *Jahrbuch für fränkische Landesforschung* 34–35 (1974–75):467–99; Bernd Moeller, "Zwinglis Disputationen: Studien zu den Anfängen der Kirchenbildung und des Synodalwesens im Protestantismus," pt. 2, *Zeitschrift für Rechtsgeschichte* 91 (1974):255–65; Günther Zimmermann, "Das Nürnberger Religionsgespräch von 1525," *Mitteilungen des Vereins für Geschichte der Stadt Nürnberg* 71 (1984):129–48.

expectations and attitudes. Luther's teachings were accepted by a majority in the city, and in general they characterized the Reformation there. Reform preachers, pamphleteers, even the three painters all belonged to the early Lutheran reform movement. Many of them, however, found themselves subsequently facing specific conditions that contradicted the position represented by the original point of departure, so that there were different understandings of the Reformation.

Many views tended toward the vision of a People's Reformation (*Volksreformation*). Examples include Albrecht Dürer (his diary of the journey to the Netherlands and his artistic creations), Hans Sachs (the "Wittenberg Nightingale" and prose dialogues), and Sebald Beham (his graphic works and his trial). It is thus justifiable to see points of departure for a popular reform movement in Nuremberg. Some forces in the city spoke out for using the Reformation for the good of the common man. In this sphere, the influences of Müntzer, Pfeiffer, and Reinhart were also at work for a while.

Alternative visions that showed their beginnings could not be realized because their development was blocked by the counteractions of the Lutherans and magistrates. An influential party on the city council identified itself with the Lutheran Reformation. It succeeded in pursuing a policy of toleration of reform long before the official recognition of the Reformation. The council, however, observed and controlled all steps. It tolerated, encouraged, protected, or hindered all activities. The result was a mixture of cooperation and opposition in the relationship between the council and the reform movement. The council channeled the movement particularly through moderate reform measures.

The politics of the city council reflected the idea that salvation was not only a personal matter but came under magisterial competence as well. The common good that the council saw itself obligated to promote was linked to the question of religious allegiance. Later Spengler wrote: "It is without doubt clear to everyone that the duty and highest office of every Christian authority is to have the greatest concern, not only for those things which are useful for the general civic order, universal peace, and ordinary bodily nourishment, but even more so for the things which are useful for the spiritual salvation of the subjects under its command, for their righteous, godly lives and fraternal, friendly harmony, because the Almighty will demand the blood of subjects from their rulers, as the godly script demonstrates."[29] In the eyes of the council, the securing of "unanimous sermons" and the preservation of "civic peace" were related.

[29]Seebass, "Apologia Reformationis," p. 51.

The division in the city, repeatedly deplored by the city council, was rooted, as the magistrates saw it, in the polemics preached from the pulpits and in the coexistence of Catholic and Evangelical services. "Out of the opposing, polemicizing sermons of evangelical and Catholic theologians one expected a deep uncertainty and confusion on the part of the individual; out of the civic factions—primarily the evangelical 'Common Man'—one feared violent excesses."[30] Thus the city council made known its standpoint in the introduction to the religious colloquy: for a long time "many divisive teachings and discordant sermons have arisen, and yet both sides claim that theirs is the truth and grounded in Holy Scripture. From this not only has great extremity, disobedience, and agitation come about in behavior and civic conduct, but also great burdens, entanglements and irredeemable vexation in the conscience of men, for whom danger grows daily regarding the sanctity of their souls, as one experiences this."[31] The council adds further "that these offensive and extreme sermons not only contribute to unrests, extremities and the ensnarement of human conscience, but also undermine the morals of the subjects, which in time give no little cause to uprisings, disobedience, adversity, and also the destruction of civic peace."[32]

The situation criticized by the council was not caused by Catholics alone. One must also take into account the polemics of the Evangelical preachers and the mood of the people.[33] The council had reacted with efforts to repress the social movement and the more radical reform influences. Now it set out to eliminate the influence of the Catholics as well. It sought, in the first place, to dissolve cloisters, forcing clerics to become citizens and establishing Evangelical sermons and communion.

In reply to a query of the city of Goslar in 1528, the Nuremberg magistrates sent a "list of reformed abuses and ceremonies": Christian preachers had been appointed to the parish churches, to the nunneries that were not closed, and to the towns and villages in the territory; the abuse of pecuniary mass was eliminated; processions, saints days, feasts days, and requiem mass, auricular confessions, baptism, and marriage had been reformed; a community chest had been set up; cloisters had been dissolved, and clerics had become citizens; and a Christian school had been established.[34] By making the clergy and the church no longer exempt, the council wanted to remove causes for unrest; it also eliminated simul-

---

[30]Seebass, "Der Nürnberger Rat," p. 475.
[31]Ibid., p. 488.
[32]Ibid., p. 490.
[33]Kantzenbach, "Gottes Ehre," p. 14.
[34]*Quellen zur Nürnberger Reformationsgeschichte,* pp. 440–47.

taneously the feudal vestiges in civic communalism, using the Reformation as the basis for a process of communalization. The result was the strengthening of magisterial power through the incorporation of ecclesiastical sovereignty, but it was in the final reckoning a revolutionary step, part of the phenomenon of the German early bourgeois revolution.


## VI

We can at last draw certain conclusions. For the process of reform in the imperial city of Nuremberg, the phase from early 1524 to March 1525 was an interesting and important period. The emergence of differences and early radicalization culminated on the one hand in a stronger emphasis on social expectations and on the other in a broad acceptance of Evangelical norms. Thus after the inception of the Reformation, which began in patrician and humanist circles, and after its growth into a broad reform movement, the varied expectations gained new prominence in this phase.

The Reformation hence reached a turning point because the council was forced into open action, both by pressure of the growing opposition movement in the city and the countryside and by the more radical ideas from outside. The moment of decision was at hand. Its consequence was the religious colloquy of March 1525, initiated by the council, which ended the fluid situation and led to the institutionalization of the Reformation.

Karl Marx has concluded that, for the revolution of a people and the emancipation of a particular class of bourgeois society to coincide, "a particular state of affairs must be the state of general offense, the incorporation of universal barriers; moreover, a particular social sphere must stand for the notorious crimes of the entire society, so that the liberation from this sphere would appear as a universal self-emancipation."[35] During the Reformation, this general obstacle was represented by the clergy and the church, as the intellectual, social and political representation of the feudal order. The actions in Nuremberg were directed against this clergy, and in part also against feudal landownership and a patrician civic regime. Although these class conflicts had not yet become an attack on the feudal order, given the existing social tensions and oppositions in the summer of 1524, the danger of a violent conflict was real.

The fact that in this situation a more comprehensive social or political movement did not develop is to be explained by the existence of a firm, experienced, and cautious city council, which reacted decisively and ef-

[35]Karl Marx, *Zur Kritik der Hegelschen Rechtsphilosophie*, in *Karl Marx/Friedrich Engels, Werke*, vol. 1 (Berlin-East, 1981), p. 388.

fectively. This council was flexible enough to turn danger away from itself in conflicts, both by its firmness and by some concessions.

The council succeeded in mastering the crisis, in cutting short the transition phase, and in leading it to an organization of a new order, thanks both to the freedom of action and the abilities of the council and to the absence of an organizational base for the opposition. The city was not free from future tensions, but these came from external factors and no longer from internal dangers. In the research on city and Reformation,[36] the process described above offers a remarkable example of how alternative visions arose in a critical phase, before the definitive legitimation of the Lutheran Reformation.

[36]Cf. Kaspar von Greyerz, "Stadt und Reformation: Stand und Aufgaben der Forschung," *Archiv für Reformationsgeschichte* 76 (1985):6–63.

*The interest of historians has often focused on the dramatic events of the early Reformation: Luther, the Peasants' War, the Anabaptist movement, and the Religious Peace of Augsburg. From there, one jumps eagerly to the denouement of the Thirty Years' War. The intervening years, between 1555 and 1618, however, were a crucial period during which the confessional identities of the German territories, the origins of the later conflict, and the character of early modern German society were formed. In his book* Society and Religion in Münster, 1535–1618 *(1984) R. Po-chia Hsia, an associate professor of history at the University of Massachusetts, Amherst, analyzes in detail the interplay between the social, political, and religious forces in the Westphalian metropole between the demise of the Anabaptist kingdom and the beginning of the Thirty Years' War. The following article is an examination of an earlier period in Münster's history. The story of the Anabaptist kingdom is well known, but the article represents an attempt to understand the millenarian revolution within the context of guild ideology, civic conflict, and family history. Hsia is also the author of* The Myth of Ritual Murder: Jews and Magic in Reformation Germany *(1988).*

# [3]

## Münster and the Anabaptists

R. Po-chia Hsia

The sixteen-month-long Anabaptist kingdom of Münster, with its millenarian fervor, polygamy, and communalism, was certainly the most dramatic event in the Reformation, and its siege and destruction probably the bloodiest. Although the story itself is well known and the historical literature is immense, the Anabaptist revolution resulted in the systematic destruction of city records, and so the story of the rise and fall of the "New Jerusalem" has been narrated only by its enemies. Historical reconstructions of the movement have also had to rely mostly on hostile sources.[1] The remarkable course of the Reformation in the Westphalian

[1] There is an immense literature on the Münster Anabaptist kingdom. For a Marxist interpretation, see Gerhard Brendler, *Das Täuferreich zu Münster, 1534–35* (Berlin, 1966); for a meticulous archival reconstruction of the social composition of the Anabaptist community, see Karl-Heinz Kirchhoff, *Die Täufer in Münster, 1534–35: Untersuchungen zum Umfang und zur Sozialstruktur der Bewegung* (Münster, 1973). Heinz Schilling sees the revolution as an urban conflict between the traditional patriciate and a new group of civic leaders; see his "Aufstandsbewegungen in der Stadtbürgerlichen Gesellschaft des Alten Reiches: Die Vorgeschichte des Münsteraner Täuferreichs, 1525–1534," *Geschichte und Gesellschaft, Bauernkrieg-Beiheft* (1975):193–238. For the impact of Münster on Germany, see Robert Stupperich, "Das Münsterische Täufertum im Blickfeld des Reichs," *Westfalen: Hefte für Geschichte, Kunst, und Volkskunde* 58 (1980):109–16; Günther Vogler, "Das Täuferreich zu Münster im Spiegel der Flugschriften," in Hans-Joachim Köhler, ed., *Flugschriften als Massenmedium der Reformationszeit* (Stuttgart, 1981), pp. 31–48, and "Das Täuferreich zu Münster als Problem der Politik im Reich: Beobachtungen anhand reichsständischer Korrespondenzen der Jahre 1534–35," in *Mennonitische Geschichtsblätter* 42 (1985):7–24. For a short English overview of the major events and an analysis of the millenarianism of the Anabaptists based essentially on the tracts of Bernhard Rothmann, see James M. Stayer, *Anabaptists and the Sword* (Lawrence, Kan., 1972). For the impact of Münster on the Anabaptist movements in central and south Germany, see Claus-Peter Clasen, *Anabaptism: A Social History, 1525–1618* (Ithaca, 1972). There are two major contemporary sources on the Anabaptist kingdom: an account written by the shoemaker

metropole has been variously interpreted as a revolution of the common man, an antipatrician urban insurrection, a sectarian revolution,[2] a reign of terror,[3] a millenarian psychodrama,[4] and an episode in collective religious fanaticism.[5] Even after 450 years of polemics and scholarship, however, we still do not fully comprehend the social complexity and the multiplicity of meaning of the Anabaptist kingdom, nor, as it seems, have historians uncovered all the sources that relate to the revolution.[6] In this essay I offer tentative interpretations on three themes that have not received sufficient attention in the analysis of the Münster Anabaptist movement: women and the Anabaptist movement, kinship and religious revolution, and guild ideology and millenarian communalism. First, however, I will briefly summarize the sequence of events.

In the wake of the Peasants' War of 1525, unrest spread to the north German cities, fusing the late medieval social and constitutional struggles in the cities with the new anticlerical movement. Urban insurrections spread from Frankfurt northward to Cologne, Münster, and Osnabrück but were suppressed after the defeat of the common man in the spring and summer of 1525. Voices raised in Münster against the economic privileges of the clergy were silenced in 1525, but the Evangelical movement found its leader six years later in the person of a fiery young priest, Bernhard Rothmann.

---

Heinrich Gresbeck, who betrayed the city to the besieging troops, and the historical work of the Münster schoolmaster Hermann von Kerssenbroch. For Gresbeck's personal account, see *Berichte der Augenzeugen über das Münsterische Wiedertäuferreich* (Münster, 1853), pp. 3–214. For Kerssenbroch, see Hermann von Kerssenbroch, *Anabaptistici Furoris Monasterium inclitam Westphaliae Metropolim evertentis historica narratio*, ed. Heinrich Detmer, 2 vols. (Münster, 1899–1900). The most recent survey of the historiographical debate over the Münster Anabaptists is James M. Stayer, "Was Dr. Kuehler's Conception of Early Dutch Anabaptism Historically Sound? The Historical Discussion of Anabaptist Münster 450 Years Later," *Mennonite Quarterly Review* 60 (1986):261–88.

[2]See Otthein Rammstedt, *Sekte und soziale Bewegung: Soziologische Analyse der Täufer in Münster (1534–35)* (Cologne, 1966). This study applies Max Weber's concepts of "church/sect" distinction and "routinization of charisma" rather mechanically to the archival analysis of Kirchhoff.

[3]Eike Wolgast, "Herrschaftsorganisation und Herrschaftskrisen im Täuferreich von Münster, 1534–35," *Archiv für Reformationsgeschichte* 67 (1976):179–201.

[4]Hedda J. Herwig, "Das Münsterische Täufertum: Prototypische Charakteristika und Ursachen einer politischen Erlösungsbewegung, dargestellt am historischen Beispiel," *Zeitschrift für Religions- und Geistesgeschichte* 31 (1979):173–84.

[5]Robert Stupperich, "Das Königreich Zion in Münster (1534–35): Fragen zur Täuferherrschaft in einer belagerten Stadt," in Wilhelm Bitter, ed., *Massenwahn in Geschichte und Gegenwart* (Stuttgart, 1965).

[6]Robert Stupperich has recently discovered two autographs by Bernd Knipperdolling, second in command to Jan of Leiden in the Anabaptist kingdom, in the Staatsarchiv Marburg. See Robert Stupperich, "Zwei bisher unveröffentlichte eigenhändige Briefe Berndt Knypperdollyncks," *Jahrbuch für Westfälische Kirchengeschichte* 77 (1984):41–58.

Appointed to a vicarship in 1531, Rothmann won rapid fame and widespread civic support by his biting sermons against clerical abuses. In its structure the Evangelical movement in Münster resembled that in many other German cities: a popular preacher echoed Luther's message and called for reform, attacking monasticism and clerical abuses; citizens rallied to his cause, adding their resentment of the church's economic competition to the call for moral regeneration; spontaneous sacramental and liturgical innovations were tolerated by the magistrates, who disagreed regarding their responses; the reform movement became part of the struggle between burghers and magistrates, which often took the form of opposition between the guilds and the city council, and a final, usually bloodless constitutional reform incorporated many of the demands of the Evangelicals while averting a social revolution; cloisters were closed, clerics took civic oaths, ecclesiastical properties were secularized, and reforms institutionalized in a new Evangelical church ordinance; finally, the magistrates came out with more authority, a few ruling families lost power, but the social order was preserved.[7]

The events in Münster from 1531 to the spring of 1533 followed roughly this model of urban reformation. Rothmann appealed to the city council to take up the cause of religious reform, and the Evangelical movement turned into a popular political movement when the guilds pressured the city council to protect Rothmann against the prince-bishop. A public debate in the summer of 1532 pitted Rothmann against the Franciscans; the momentum of reform culminated in the mustering of the civic militia, which captured the Catholic patrician magistrates and cathedral canons in a surprise attack on nearby Telgte, one of the sites of the *Landtag*, on Christmas Day 1532. Elections in February 1533 returned a solidly Evangelical city council, with the guild elite replacing the Catholic patriciate, who had evacuated the city, and an Evangelical ordinance was promulgated in April to consolidate the gains of the Reformation.

In the summer of 1533 the alliance of reformers and magistrates fell apart. Persuaded by the teachings of wandering preachers who believed in a symbolic understanding of the Eucharist, Rothmann, now superintendent of the new church, parted company with the Lutheran magistrates. The city council, under the leadership of its syndic, Dr. Johann van de Wyck, saw developments in Münster as part of the larger picture of religion and politics in the empire: as one of the Evangelical cities,

---

[7]See, for example, Thomas A. Brady, *Ruling Class, Regime, and Reformation at Strasbourg, 1520–1555* (Leiden, 1978); Hans-Christoph Rublack, *Eine bürgerliche Reformation: Nördlingen* (Gütersloh, 1982), and *Die Einführung der Reformation in Konstanz von den Anfängen bis zum Abschluss 1531* (Gütersloh, 1971); and Günther Vogler, *Nürnberg, 1524–25: Studien zur Geschichte der reformatorischen Bewegung in der Reichsstadt* (Berlin, 1982).

Münster needed to protect its newly won full autonomy from the prince-bishop and to ally itself with the other Protestant princes and cities in the Schmalkaldic League. After the promulgation of the Evangelical church ordinance, the reformation movement was over, and the duty of the new ministers was to inculcate the new religious teachings and obedience of magisterial authority and to preach civic morality and harmony. Roth-mann's sacramentarian ideas smacked of Zwinglianism; there was too much of the common man, too much "turning Swiss" for the magistrates to stomach. For many authorities after the Peasants' War of 1525, "turn-ing Swiss" meant assuming the antifeudal and antinoble aspirations of the common people of the Alpine Highlands. It symbolized disobedience and rebellion, and Zwinglianism was, at least in the eyes of many magistrates and princes, the religiopolitical ideology of commoners.[8] The split be-came public in August 1533 when Rothmann and the "radical" preachers confronted the Evangelical ministers and the council in a disputation. Political divisions followed the pattern of the theological split. The "com-mon men," represented most visibly by the craftsmen organized in the *Gesamtgilde*,[9] faithfully supported Rothmann and forced a confrontation with the council when the magistrates attempted to exile the popular preacher and church superintendent. In the autumn and winter of 1533–1534, the influx of Anabaptists, primarily from the Netherlands, to the godly city more than compensated for the voluntary exile of alarmed Catholic ruling families. In the elections of February 1534, the radical party won handily, with most of the Evangelical magistrates of 1533 reelected and the few who continued to oppose the turn of events voted out of office.

The elections took place in an atmosphere of imminent civil war. The prince-bishop, Franz von Waldeck, had actually called up his feudal levies to attempt to crush rebellion and heresy. Thus one of the very first acts of the new regime was the enforcement of rebaptism on all inhabitants and the exile of dissidents. In the New Jerusalem under siege, the regime was an unstable mixture of traditional civic government and informal prophetic leadership. The former comprised artisans of the Gesamtgilde, who had supported Rothmann and the Evangelical movement from the beginning, substantial burghers, and native Münsteraners; the latter were

---

[8]See Thomas A. Brady, *Turning Swiss: Cities and Empire, 1450–1550* (Cambridge, 1985).

[9]The Gesamtgilde was the union of seventeen independent craft guilds. It represented the corporate political strength of the artisans and defended their interests versus the city council. Officers of the Gesamtgilde were chosen by the masters of the member guilds; together, the *Olderlude* and *Mesterlude* formed a sort of shadow city council and were guaranteed certain positions in the city government. See Robert Krumbholtz, *Die Gewerbe der Stadt Münster bis zum Jahre 1661*, (Leipzig, 1898), Section 1, chap. 4.

immigrant Netherlanders, the prophet Jan Matthys and his disciple Jan Bockelszoon of Leiden. Alongside the traditional city council, headed by the patrician Bürgermeister Hermann Tilbeck and the shopkeeper Bürgermeister Bernd Knipperdolling, the Dutch prophets exercised their personal charismatic and extrainstitutional power over the believers. Their influence rested partly on the massive migration of Anabaptists from many parts of northwest Germany and from the Netherlands to Münster, people for whom the political traditions of the Westphalian metropole meant little in comparison with their vision of a heavenly city, but the remaking of Münster into the New Jerusalem also depended on cooperation between the old civic elite and the new religious leadership.

The turning point came after the death of Matthys during the first days of the siege. His disciple, Jan of Leiden, assumed the prophetic mantle and organized a successful repulsion of the first major attempt by the episcopal troops to storm the city. The first step toward the dissolution of the dual civic-religious power structure was the institution of a community of goods. Acting according to the historical example of the earliest Christian communities recorded in the Acts of the Apostles and responding to the real need to house, clothe, and feed the many immigrants, the leadership abolished private property in the city of the saints; outlawed the use of money inside Münster; confiscated ecclesiastical properties and the possessions of burghers who had fled the city; and appointed twelve elders who were to supervise the stockpiling of surplus food, clothing, and wealth in communal stores and to oversee their distribution to the needy. Native Münsteraners took on many of the new positions of power, all modeled after the institutions of the ancient Israelites. The authority of the city council was effectively bypassed when Bürgermeister Knipperdolling became the swordbearer of the new prophet Jan of Leiden.

Since the community of goods was rooted in a deep civic sense of communal solidarity and represented, moreover, a siege economy, it was accepted without perceptible opposition. The next policy of the Anabaptist regime, however, brought to the fore the tensions within the community. It provoked a bloody uprising and effectively eliminated all vestiges of traditional civic society in Münster.

The introduction of polygamy must be understood in terms both of the ambitions of one man and of the larger demographic picture. When Jan of Leiden first arrived in Münster, he married a daughter of Bürgermeister Knipperdolling. After the death of Matthys, Leiden wanted to marry the prophet's beautiful young widow in order to bolster his own claim to prophetic leadership. Eventually he found biblical justification in the Old Testament and succeeded in persuading Knipperdolling and the civic elite to take more than one wife. For the Anabaptist leadership, polygamy also served as a means by which the many single women in the city could be subjugated to male authority. The decree that all women must find husbands to protect and rule over them, however, met with fierce opposition from many native Münsteraners. Led by the blacksmith Heinrich Mollenhecke, they denounced the tyranny and false prophecy of the Dutchmen, clamored for the restoration of traditional civic ways, and devised a plan to turn the city over to the bishop. The Anabaptist elite, however, stood firm, and the uprising was crushed mercilessly; two hundred men were killed in battle or were subsequently executed. Opposition from the women to polygamy was also fiercely repressed; the former beguinage of Rosenthal became a prison for women who defied spousal authority.

With the successful implementation of polygamy and the defeat of internal dissent, Jan of Leiden acquired sufficient power to proclaim himself king, justifying his royal pretensions by claiming divine revelation. His kingship was to be a restoration of the holy kingship of David; his mission was to eradicate the godless, to establish the kingdom of God on earth, and to pave the way for the return of Christ. Having set up his court, Leiden had lavish costumes cut and gold coins struck; the pomp and circumstance of the eschatological king were to reflect the glory of Christ.

While this theater of power and vanity was being played out in Münster, the military situation was becoming desperate. In the winter of 1534, the imperial estates of Westphalia and the Lower Rhine joined hands to fight the Anabaptists. Catholic as well as Lutheran princes closed ranks against this grandiose rebellion of the common man: the archbishop of Cologne, the duke of Cleve, and the landgrave of Hesse all pledged financial assistance, and Bishop Franz was able to raise enough troops to blockade Münster, effectively cutting off provisions.

Leiden sent out apostles to seek help from Anabaptist communities in northwest Germany and the Netherlands. Many of them were caught and killed by the besiegers, but others made their way through the lines. During the winter months of 1534–1535, the Anabaptists in Wesel, Amsterdam, Friesland, and other towns and territories made preparations to send munitions, food, and reinforcements to their brethren in Münster. The promised deliverance never came, however, because the bishop of Münster quickly and ruthlessly suppressed these preparations within Westphalia, and Habsburg authorities quickly crushed concurrent Anabaptist uprisings in the Netherlands.[10] In Münster itself, famine took a

---

[10]For the Anabaptist movement in the Netherlands, which had close theological and personal ties with the Münster kingdom, see Albert F. Mellink, *De wederdopers in de noordelijke nederlanden, 1531–1544* (Leeuwarden, 1981), and *Amsterdam en de wederdopers in de zestiende eeuw* (Nijmegen, 1978). For published archival sources on the suppression of the Dutch Anabaptist uprisings, see *Documenta Anabaptistica Neerlandica, I: Friesland en Groningen (1530–1550)*, ed. Albert F. Mellink (Leiden, 1975).

heavy toll among the women and children; by the spring of 1535, some had begun to desert the city. In spite of the hardship, the faith of the majority remained firm, and the writings of Rothmann consoled the Anabaptists with the vision of a final reckoning, when the wrath of God would wreak vengeance upon the godless. In the end, Münster's fall was due not to hunger or cowardice but to betrayal by a mercenary who opened the city gates to the besieging troops. In the night of 24 June 1535, the city was taken after intense street fighting and great slaughter. Leiden and his lieutenant, Knipperdolling, were captured, tortured, and executed. After eighteen months of siege warfare and great loss of life, the Münster kingdom was finally destroyed, but the spectacle of the Anabaptists was to become a moral and political example for the succeeding centuries.

I

Estimates of the Anabaptist population differ, but they range between eight and ten thousand; some fifteen hundred to two thousand were able-bodied men, and most of the rest were women.[11] What accounts for the preponderance of women in the godly city? Some historians argue that Anabaptism, and the Radical Reformation in general, found more sympathy among women because of the greater independence that some of the sects allowed for female religious leadership.[12] Other historians have argued that the Reformation in general was welcomed by women and that it resulted in the creation of improved gender roles for the oppressed sex.[13] There is, in fact, some evidence that women in Münster took an active part in the Evangelical movement. The chronicle of Überwasser Convent recorded in 1533 that many of the sisters had been seduced by evil teachings and agitated for permission to leave the cloister; others defied authority and returned to their families or got married.[14] The Anabaptists who paraded about the streets of Münster crying for repentance included many women.[15] We have the names of a few women whose zeal

[11]See Gresbeck, *Berichte der Augenzeugen,* p. 107.

[12]George H. Williams, *The Radical Reformation* (Philadelphia, 1962), pp. 505–17; the position of women in the Münster Anabaptist kingdom has received almost no attention, the only exception being one article: A. J. Jelsma, "De koening en de Vrouwen, Münster 1534–1535," *Gereformeerd Theologisch Tijdschrift* 75 (1975):82–107.

[13]See Steven E. Ozment, *When Fathers Ruled: Family Life in Reformation Europe* (Cambridge, Mass., 1983). Along a different line, Thomas Max Safley has demonstrated that women had the right to divorce in reformed territories; see his *Let No Man Put Asunder: The Control of Marriage in the German Southwest: A Comparative Study, 1550–1600* (Kirksville, Mo., 1984).

[14]See "Klosterchronik Überwasser während der Wirren, 1531–33," ed. Rudolf Schulze, in *Quellen und Forschungen zur Geschichte der Stadt Münster,* vol. 2 (Münster, 1924–26), pp. 149–65.

[15]Jelsma, "De koening," p. 103.

in supporting the religious convictions of their husbands was prominent enough to merit notation by hostile Catholic writers.[16] Still other women apparently chose the new faith over the objection of their spouses and remained in the city when their husbands fled. The most dramatic example was Hilla Feicken, who imitated the example of Judith in the Old Testament and attempted to assassinate Bishop Franz in the camp of the besieging army.[17] At least in the early stages of the Anabaptist movement in Münster, women enjoyed greater freedom: they could divorce their unbelieving husbands and enter into new marriages.

To focus our attention only on the relationship between women and the Anabaptist movement, however, is to ignore the entire spectrum of the very different experiences of men and women during the Reformation. In the case of Münster, there is scattered evidence that many women were violently opposed to the reform. Not only did an older generation of nuns resist first the reform and later the Anabaptist takeover, but also laywomen, probably members of parish confraternities, clung to their religion with vehemence. The Franciscans of St. Catherine had many female supporters who defended their beloved cult with violence, as a later Franciscan chronicle notes in praise, and according to the same source many women accepted rebaptism under duress but secretly remained steadfast to their faith.[18] It seems reasonable to assume that the common people, women and men alike, were for the most part too preoccupied with the toils of daily life to be able to devote very much time and energy to the religious movements. Many women and men were overtaken by the onrush of events; they did not bequeath records of their thoughts and reactions. Active female supporters and opponents of the Anabaptist movement probably constituted a minority of all women in Münster. The preponderance of women among Anabaptists in Münster can be explained by the conjunction of two factors. First, fearing for their safety, many men left Münster, leaving their wives behind to look after the family property. Women generally were not targets of political repression, and many Münsteraners thought that the Anabaptist episode was but a short interlude during which the men could ride out the storm in the haven of the neighboring towns while their womenfolk remained behind,

[16]A 1532 "list of Lutherans" compiled by their opponents in Münster named eighty individuals, including three women. See Kirchhoff, *Die Täufer*, pp. 17–18.

[17]Kerssenbroch, *Narratio*, pp. 605–6. For her confession after capture, see Josef Niesert, ed., *Münsterische Urkundensammlung, I: Urkunden zur Geschichte der münsterischen Wiedertäufer* (Coesfeld, 1826), p. 40.

[18]Stadtarchiv Münster Mss. 4, "Chronik des Minoritenklosters zu Münster," p. 19. The chronicle was compiled in the mid-eighteenth century by the cloister archivist, brother August Westmark, and was based on documents that are no longer extant.

safeguarding the family possessions. A second factor was the demographic structure of Münster, which resembled all premodern cities in that women usually outnumbered men because of higher death rates among males. Moreover, single working women—spinsters, widows, and young servant girls—constituted a distinctive segment of the urban population, one which formed the lowest stratum of urban society. They were often recipients of public charity, dwellers in sheds, and paid the least taxes. They were the ones who could not flee Münster even if they had wanted to and became, by default, Anabaptists when rebaptism was declared obligatory for all inhabitants in February 1534.

Seen in this context, the introduction of polygamy in July 1534 takes on a new significance. The ostensible reason given by Jan of Leiden and the Anabaptist elite was the emulation of the patriarchal age of the Old Testament; theologically, the saints must heed the call "to be fruitful and multiply" and to fill the earth with the eschatological number of 144,000.[19] The practical concern was, however, to ensure political control over the majority of the population, whose religiopolitical loyalties were manifest only in a minority of cases. For the women of Münster, the initial promise of the Anabaptist movement quickly turned into the reality of subjugation. Religious ecstasy and prophecy could challenge the hierarchy of Anabaptist rule, and women visionaries were forbidden to communicate their messages. Furthermore, Anabaptist women were denied direct access to salvation and sanctity. They were to their husbands as their husbands were to Christ; the salvific path for women was a tortuous one through a double intermediacy of men and Christ.[20] It is not surprising that the introduction of polygamy provoked the active resistance of some women, who were either incarcerated in the women's prison or, in a few outstanding cases of female defiance of male authority, executed, as was the fate of one of Jan of Leiden's many wives.[21]

The women of Münster enjoyed a relatively high degree of rights and freedom before the Anabaptist regime: although they were excluded from political office and from some of the guilds, wills and other notarial papers testified to their right to own real property, retain their dowry, practice many handicrafts, act as business partners with husbands, make their own wills, represent themselves in court, keep their patrilineal names in legal documents, and by and large choose their own mates and lovers. In the Catholicism of the Rhineland, Westphalia, and the Low Countries,

---

[19]See Bernhard Rothmann's treatise "Restitution rechter christlicher Lehre," chaps. 14–16, in Robert Stupperich, ed., *Die Schriften Bernhard Rothmanns* (Münster, 1970), pp. 258–69.
[20]Ibid., p. 269.
[21]Kerssenbroch, *Narratio,* pp. 688–89.

beguinages assumed a crucial role in providing an institutional outlet for the pietistic expression of laywomen who did not have either the wealth or the inclination to enter into a religious life in a noble cloister. In pre-Reformation Münster there were four beguinages, and the sisters enjoyed a high degree of civic esteem as being economically and spiritually independent.[22] In spite of the initial excitement and promises of the Evangelical and Anabaptist movements, the Reformation in Münster represented an attempt to subjugate women by restricting their social and religious roles, by transforming them, ultimately, into obedient (and protected) wives and daughters of a polygamous, patriarchal, and sacred tribe.

## II

Enemies of the Anabaptist kingdom ascribed the worst motives to the introduction of polygamy; it was supposedly an excuse to satisfy the lust of the seditious heretics.[23] What they failed to grasp was the meaning of polygamy in creating a fictive tribe, a chosen people, the "New Israel," a holy nation for a sacred city. It was the means by which the new social order was literally to be created, a theocratic ideology endowing a fictive ethnicity with the power of blood and sanctity. Unlike the family, the godly people as a tribe was comprehensive, not exclusive; communal, not private; sacred, not profane; eternal, not ephemeral; harmonious, not divisive; spiritual, not material. In the months before the Anabaptist regime, Münsteraners noticed how the Anabaptists would greet one another only as brother and sister, exchanging the kiss of peace and ignoring the other citizens on the streets. The fictive sacred kinship of the saints was comprehensive in the strictest endogenous sense because intercourse with the "impure" members of society was prohibited. When the Anabaptists transformed Münster into the New Jerusalem, they extended this idea of a sacred endogeny to the understanding of urban space. Boundaries between parishes and districts no longer existed, nor were distinctions between sacred and secular and between public space and private recognized. Food, clothing, wealth, and living space were to be shared by all; the Anabaptist elite ordered all doors to be kept open to signify the abolition of private, familial, and exclusive space.[24] The city, the houses, and the

---

[22]For the beguines in pre-Anabaptist Münster, see Karl Zuhorn, "Die Beginnen in Münster," *Westfälische Zeitschrift* 91 (1935):1–149; for the beguines after 1535, see R. Po-chia Hsia, *Society and Religion in Münster, 1535–1618* (New Haven, 1984), pp. 36–37, 40–41.

[23]Kerssenbroch, *Narratio*, p. 619.

[24]See Gresbeck, *Berichte der Augenzeugen*, p. 47.

community were all sacred bodies within which corpuscular distinctions were abolished, whereas the exogenous boundaries were reinforced to protect the pure from contamination. This sense of a sacred kinship as well as the contingencies of siege warfare prompted the Anabaptist leaders to prohibit all trade and contact between the saints and the outside world.[25]

In stark contrast, the structure of family life in pre-Anabaptist Münster showed that the boundaries between public and private spheres, urban and family space, and sacred and secular interests overlapped in a complex and intricate matrix, as is evident from an examination of the family structure of the ruling elite before the Reformation.[26] It has been astutely observed that the family was the basis of social power in medieval German cities.[27] The more relatives and friends (in premodern German usage, the term often denoted kinship) one had, the more physical and social security one enjoyed, and the family of the urban upper classes in late medieval and early modern Germany resembled a network of power alliances that linked the patrician and mercantile elites of many cities. In Münster the families of the patriciate (called *Erbmänner*), the rentier, and the mercantile and guild elites were institutions that inherited, accumulated, and bequeathed wealth, cemented marriage alliances with others like themselves, and exercised political power by providing civic and corporate offices with successive generations of males. In addition to being a kinship group organized around sizable property holding, the upper-class families impressed the city with their private space by building the most sumptuous townhouses, by purchasing family pews and burial lots in parish churches, by endowing chantry mass for the salvation of the lineage, and by memorializing themselves in the many artistic works commissioned for pious donations. The socioeconomic space of upper-class families was not confined to the city but extended into the countryside, where patricians and the leading burgher families held feudal fiefs, owned allodial estates, and imagined themselves lords of their manors. There, too, the guild and mercantile elites invested their family wealth in farmlands and pastures.

In the complexity of upper-class family structure we find reflected the multifarious social and spiritual character of pre-Reformation Catholicism: kinship and salvation were linked in a curious mixture of sublimity and crass self-interest, piety and greed, equality and hierarchy. Precisely

[25]Kerssenbroch, *Narratio*, p. 561.

[26]See Hsia, *Society and Religion*, pp. 16–23, for an analysis of the family structure of the restored Catholic ruling elite after 1535.

[27]See Erich Maschke, *Die Familie in der deutschen Stadt des späten Mittelalters* (Heidelberg, 1980).

because upper-class families were often marriage alliances of power, the status of women was better protected. The spouses often acted as partners who had the luxury to grow in love and mutual respect in the common management of family wealth, the direction of domestic servants, and the rearing of children. On the other hand, upper-class family life of course also provided numerous causes for disputes engendered by disagreements over inheritance, which pitted siblings against one another, patrilineal relatives against matrilineal relatives, and children against mothers and stepmothers. The crucial point nonetheless remains clear: the upper-class urban family was a powerful institution of kinship and wealth with the strength to resist change. Except for one patrician family, none of the families that constituted the ruling class in Münster, dominating the city council and the leadership of the Gesamtgilde, went over to Anabaptism. The Catholic church gave these families the means to unite kinship solidarity and salvation. To Borchard Heerde, a wealthy merchant who belonged to the ruling elite, the lessons of heresy taught that steadfastness to the true religion (Catholicism) and family prosperity went hand in hand.[28] For these families, corporate unity was the real blood tie that connected specific people to wealth and the bond between past, present, and future generations that created the corporate perpetuity of the ruling class.

As the above discussion of models of kinship and salvation makes apparent, family structures in Münster had a class specificity that expressed itself in terms of its ability to respond to changes and its predilection for certain forms of religiosity. We have seen how the upper classes were successful in resisting the Evangelical and Anabaptist challenges by maintaining family solidarity. Who were the Münsteraners who found the Anabaptist idea of a fictive sacred kinship compatible with their own understanding of society? In reconstructing the Anabaptist community from records of confiscated Anabaptist houses, Karl-Heinz Kirchhoff has shown conclusively that the saints were recruited heavily from the ranks of the handicraft guilds. They were house owners, taxpayers, solid burghers, and heads of families. Since Kirchhoff's sources are records of the confiscation of the real properties of burghers implicated in the Anabaptist regime, two other groups are automatically excluded: the poor and the immigrants.

From extant documents it is impossible to reconstruct the extent of participation by the unpropertied lower classes in the Anabaptist movement. In the lists of known Anabaptists, however, men employed in a low-status occupation—construction work, gravedigging, milling, weaving, street cleaning—hardly ever appear. Single women who belonged to

28Hsia, *Society and Religion*, p. 16.

the lower strata of urban society, as I have argued above, probably represented the poor in the Anabaptist kingdom. In any event, whereas the middle strata of urban society were overrepresented in the millenarian movement and provided the overwhelming majority of the regime's leadership, there is no evidence to indicate any active lower-class support of the Anabaptist revolution.[29]

There are only scraps of information about the immigrant Anabaptists. Those who came from the Westphalian towns and villages seem to have arrived in family groups. Catholics charged that entire communities in the Münsterland turned Anabaptist.[30] Sources on the Dutch Anabaptists who wanted to move to the heavenly city are much more abundant. Entire communities were affected by the preachings of the Anabaptist prophets and apostles; the Hapsburg authorities in Holland found hundreds of men, women, and children—whole families—waiting for transportation to take them to the promised sanctuary.[31] Underlying the self-concept of the Anabaptists as a holy people were the collective emotions of communal solidarity. The common theme that ran through the Evangelical and Anabaptist movements was the assertion of Christian communalism, or literally, the "common weal" (*Gemeinnutz*) over selfishness (*Eigennutz*). By communalism, sixteenth-century Christians meant concern for the welfare of some larger social corporation above the family, whether the confraternity, the neighborhood, the village, the parish, the guild, the city, or all of Christendom. Selfishness meant not only the greed of an individual but also that of a family, a craft, or a corporation that pursued its interest to the detriment of the good of the whole. Thus a grain merchant who inflated prices in times of famine was just as selfish as a guild that practiced its craft to the disadvantage of a civic community or a group of powerful families that exchanged private wealth and kinship solidarity for salvific credit. The domination of the Catholic church by the feudal nobility, the preponderance of patricians and rentiers on the city council, and the control of the Gesamtgilde by a small group of guild families could all be interpreted as manifestations of Eigennutz; for the urban ruling classes, the family bred power, confusing the boundaries between private and public in the marriage of kinship and salvation. The Anabaptist revolution attempted to restore the sense of a Christian community and, by imposing the ideology of a fictive sacred kinship, hoped to do away with the inherent tensions between private and public, family and civic society. The ideology of a sacred tribe aimed to compensate for the absence of real

[29]Kirchhoff, *Die Täufer*, pp. 78–88.
[30]Kerssenbroch, *Narratio*, pp. 508–11.
[31]Mellink, *Amsterdam en de wederdopers*, pp. 30ff.

blood ties in the fictive kinship community and to create an ideal nation from diverse social elements, just as the Israelites created their sacred nation out of many peoples. Although the Old Testament furnished the Anabaptists with the historical precedent, the theological arguments, and the social images for their creation of a Christian community—the language, one may say—the social and political ideology of the guild community in Münster formed the underlying grammar for the text of the millenarian drama.

### III

In binding individuals and families that practiced the same craft, the urban mercantile and handicraft guilds harked back to Germanic, pre-Christian forms of fictive kinship associations. Guilds arose after the eleventh century with the rapid spread of urbanization in the Holy Roman Empire, when first merchants and then artisans banded together in sworn associations for common defense and the promotion of mutual interests. Guild rules, rituals, communal feastings, common religious practices, and intermarriage solidified the bonds of occupational interests, and members of a particular guild would often inhabit a specific street or neighborhood in the medieval city.[32]

In many ways the guilds in Münster resembled other forms of associations in early sixteenth-century Westphalia: the parish confraternities that banded laymen and laywomen in a collective struggle for salvation and the many neighborhood associations (*Nachbarschaften*) found in the small towns and villages of the Münsterland. The other associations that promoted social solidarity, however, lacked the elaborate corporate ideology and political power that the guilds had developed by the later Middle Ages. The history of cities in late medieval Germany abounds with examples of guild revolts as merchants and artisans demanded a share of the power held by the patrician regimes. Guildsmen formed civic militias, overthrew old regimes, battled feudal armies, and shaped the face of urban society between the late fourteenth and early sixteenth centuries.[33] The Münster guilds played a pivotal role in the war of the Münster bishopric (1450–57), which gave the Gesamtgilde a share of power on the city council for the first time. The Evangelical and Anabaptist movements were supported primarily by the artisans; after the Catholic restoration in

---

[32]See Hans Planitz, *Die deutsche Stadt im Mittelalter: Von der Römerzeit bis zu den Zunftkämpfen* (Graz-Cologne, 1954), pp. 205ff.

[33]Ibid., pp. 325ff.

June 1535, the prince-bishop abolished all guilds, condemning the Gesamtgilde as the instigator of heresy and rebellion. Only with the full restoration of civic liberties in 1554 were the individual guilds and the Gesamtgilde allowed to reconstitute themselves. In his *History of the Anabaptist Fury,* Kerssenbroch boldly asserted that the guildsmen were to be blamed for the debacle of 1534–1535; a libel suit followed immediately, and the hapless schoolmaster of the Gymnasium saw his manuscript confiscated by the city council and its publication prohibited.

How did guild ideology and practices engender widespread artisanal support for the religious movements? First, the Catholic church represented a powerful economic competitor: the cloisters manufactured their own products, the clergy were exempted from guard duty and taxation, and the domination of the church by arrogant feudal noble families was all too apparent. Beyond economic anticlericalism and implicit class antagonism, however, the guilds had developed a socioreligious ideology of their own, which posited an ideal of Christian communalism against the corruption of the Catholic church by selfish familial interests. This ideology of Christian communalism can be described as a sacred corporatism, and it was enshrined in the statutes of the Gesamtgilde and in the practices of the guilds.

In Article 43 of the Redbook, which contained the statutes of the Gesamtgilde, compiled between the mid-fifteenth and early sixteenth centuries, the guilds were defined as Christian organizations whose economic and social practices conformed with pious religion.[34] This identification of a particular socioeconomic practice with religiosity was characterized by an obsession with defining boundaries. The officials of the Gesamtgilde arbitrated disputes between guildsmen and other citizens and between member guilds over the delineation of economic activities; the individual guilds themselves defined the rules of apprenticeship, work, the quality and prices of products, admission criteria, marriage, feasting, and burial customs. The object was to define a boundary between guild and city, between a qualified, incorporated craft and a common one, between artisan and citizen, and between quality and vulgarity. Underlying the various demarcations was the fundamental idea of maintaining corporate purity: substandard merchandise was to be destroyed; the socially undesirable were to be kept out. Thus the statutes of the Gesamtgilde barred from entry Jews, heretics, bastards, parsons' sons, and people from "tainted" occupations—executioners, millers, gravediggers, and others. All of these groups carried with them elements of impurity, whether false re-

---

[34]Krumbholtz, *Die Gewerbe,* pp. 15–16.

ligion, illegitimate birth, or the results of pollution by sex and death.[35] The stigma attached to bastardy was an important means by which the guild community distinguished itself from both its social superiors and its inferiors. Bastardy was not only common among the lower classes—servants and maids who did not have the permission or means to marry—but was also a distinctive feature of the amorous life of the nobility and the urban aristocracy. Men from patrician and ruling families often mentioned "natural children" in their wills and provided for their upbringing. Illegitimacy was an important fact of demographic history, and it did not close the doors of social advancement for those with important family connections.

For the guilds, however, the preservation of corporate purity depended on a strict endogamy, which was enforced de facto if not de jure: artisans almost always married daughters or widows who were, if not from the same craft, then from other guilds. The statutes of most of the crafts within the Gesamtgilde gave preferential treatment to accepting sons of masters as members, usually by setting a much lower entry fee; foreign journeymen had to prove their purity of blood by showing a birth certificate of legitimate burgher heritage.[36] Purity of blood and piety seem to have formed the twin pillars of guild corporate status upon which rested the entire body of practices and ideas of the urban guild economy.

It is thus not surprising that the Evangelical movement in the 1520s conjured up many voices attacking usury, monopolies, and unbridled commercial greed, in addition to criticizing the burdens of the old religion. Besides being the fusion of the sacred and the economic, Christian communalism, as it was manifested in guild ideology, also expressed itself in articulating a corporate view of human society.[37] Like the guild community in Florence, the ideology of the Münster Gesamtgilde was also characterized by a tension between a corporatist and a consensus model.[38] The tension was implicit in the metaphorical use of the body in political language: a body may be unified in its functions, but the status of the various organs and members differs. Thus the head and eyes, or the rational faculty, must rule and direct the movements of the limbs and control the appetite. The consensus model argued or implied the rule of

[35]Cf. Werner Danckert, *Unehrliche Leute: Die verfemten Berufe* (Bern, 1963), and Redbook, statutes 39–41, in Krumbholtz, *Die Gewerbe*, pp. 13ff.

[36]See Helmut Lahrkamp, ed., *Die Geburtsbriefe der Stadt Münster, 1548–1809* (Münster, 1968).

[37]For a synthetic study of guild ideology, see Anthony Black, *Guilds and Civil Society in European Political Thought from the Twelfth Century to the Present* (Ithaca, 1984).

[38]See John M. Najemy, *Corporatism and Consensus in Florentine Electoral Politics, 1280–1400* (Chapel Hill, 1982).

the body by its "better parts," whereas the corporatist model defended the equality of all the constituent members. In the statutes of the Gesamtgilde, each of the seventeen member guilds was guaranteed an equal vote in electing officials to the umbrella guild, as "no one should put himself before others." Likewise, within each guild, all master artisans ideally stood on the same footing, sharing responsibilities and exercising equivalent power. The reality of guild politics, however, was that some guilds dominated the Gesamtgilde by virtue of their wealth, whereas the wealthier artisans controlled affairs within each guild. In Münster the most powerful of the seventeen guilds was that of the clothiers, who supplied most of the Olderlude to the Gesamtgilde. The reality of hierarchical gradations was perpetuated by an electoral system within member guilds and the Gesamtgilde, whereby presiding guild masters and Gesamtgilde officials nominated the electors, who inevitably elected the outgoing officials for another term. Although the facade of equality and democracy was preserved, the reality, at least by the beginning of the sixteenth century, was the consolidation of a guild oligarchy that formally exercised power through guild institutions of professed egalitarianism but that in reality based its influence on family wealth and status, much as the families of the ruling elite maintained their hold on the city council. In fact, some of the families of the ruling elite belonged to the clothiers' guild in the mid-fifteenth century but severed their ties to the corporate world of the guilds when family wealth alone could sustain their standing in the political class.

Although we do not have direct evidence of tensions within the Gesamtgilde prior to 1533 (the protocols of the Gesamtgilde are extant only from 1569), three conclusions can be drawn from the fragmentary lists of officeholders within the Gesamtgilde and the individual guilds and from the guild statutes. First, there was evidently a "guild aristocracy," which collectively controlled the politics of the member guilds and the Gesamtgilde; in some guilds, sons succeeded fathers as guild officials, and in almost all guilds, outsiders had to pay hefty entry fees to become masters. Second, during the Evangelical movement from 1531 to 1533, the guildsmen were solidly behind Rothmann, and the officials of the Gesamtgilde signed petitions to the city council on his behalf. Third, a crucial split seems to have occurred within the Gesamtgilde during the transition from the Evangelical movement to the Anabaptist movement: the elections to the city council of 1533 (the Evangelical council) and 1534 (the Anabaptist council) returned artisans and merchants of the Gesamtgilde who had at most held minor civic offices before, and none had served on the city council before 1533. More significant is the fact that, although individuals of the guild aristocracy served on the 1533 council as Evangelicals, they were not returned to office in the 1534 elections.[39] New men, more committed to radical religious ideas and to a more thorough transformation of society, took their places in city hall. These new men, also drawn from the guilds, were committed to the restoration of Christian communalism, a vision that informed the egalitarian ethos of the guilds. For them, the Anabaptist movement was the fusion of a religious renewal and a sociopolitical restoration, a return to an ideal age of moral purity and corporatist communal politics.

To the men who supported the Evangelical movement throughout its Anabaptist metamorphosis and on to the bitter end of the millenarian kingdom, the underlying vision was the consensus of a Christian republic. Their preacher Rothmann expressed it best when he expounded on the symbolic nature of the eucharist, before his conversion to Anabaptism. A sacrament, Rothmann reminded his flock, was simply an oath, something sacred not by virtue of the object of remembrance, be it bread or wine, but by the act of consensus that constituted the community. The eucharistic feast thus became a symbolic rite to commemorate and celebrate the existence of the community of believers.[40] The structural parallel with guild practice and ideology is exact. Guilds and communes arose as sworn associations, conjurations, constituted by the mutual consent of equals. Not surprisingly, communal feasting played a ritualistic role in articulating the sense of fellowship and reaffirming the social boundaries of the guild community. Eating was quintessentially a social act and food a social object. The repeated criticisms of gluttony and drunkenness in the sermons and moral tales of the early Reformation years amounted to a critique of antisocial selfish eating habits. Similarly, the disagreements between the reformers on the correct understanding of the Last Supper touched on the different social meanings of food. For the Catholics and the Lutherans, the sanctification of bread and wine implied the reification of a hierarchical, coercive social relationship: only a clerical elite could "prepare" the sacred food, the consumption of which by the laity depended on the censure of their behavior and attitudes by the very same clergy.[41] Alternatively, in the case of a prominent Catholic in Münster, food was a display of wealth and piety when he endowed a fund in his will to feed the poor after his death for the salvation of his soul. In these cases, food was not so much eaten as it was fed—forcibly, as in the requirement

---

[39]Kirchhoff, *Die Täufer*, pp. 65–69.

[40]Rothmann, "Bekenntnis von beiden Sacramenten," in Stupperich, ed., *Die Schriften Bernhard Rothmanns*, p. 141.

[41]For communion as coercion in Lutheran Württemberg, see David W. Sabean, *Power in the Blood: Popular Culture and Village Discourse in Early Modern Germany* (Cambridge, 1984), pp. 37–60.

to take communion in Catholicism and in the new Evangelical ordinances, or voluntarily, when the strong, wealthy, and pious fed the poor and the weak in body and spirit. In Rothmann's exposition of the eucharistic sacrament and in the communal feasting of the Anabaptist kingdom, the act of communal eating, sharing, and equal exchange was restored: food was to the saints merely a symbol of the voluntary community constituted by equals.[42]

In line with the social meaning behind Rothmann's interpretation of the eucharist, his advocacy of believers' baptism also stressed the need for consensus in defining the community of the faithful. Rothmann's sermons must have encouraged the artisans in the Gesamtgilde in their struggle to restore corporatist politics against the elitist domination of a few families; in civic life, the restitution was the renewed quest for communal equality of all citizens versus the selfish regime of the self-styled *Obrigkeit*.

The Christian republic, however, granted equality only to males. The creation of a fictive, patriarchal sacred kinship received its inspiration partly from the Old Testament and partly from the social practices of the guilds. Outside the Catholic clergy, the guild community was the social locus in which exclusive male association was most clearly defined. The youthful members of the guild community, the unmarried apprentices and journeymen, formed their own associations, with the permission of the masters, and played a prominent role in the traditional celebration of carnival. Women were excluded from officeholding in the member guilds and Gesamtgilde, even though widows were occasionally permitted to continue practicing the craft before they turned over the shop to a new husband or a grown son. Unlike the upper classes, with their powerful families, and the lower classes, with their precarious existence as married or single individuals, the artisans of the guild community lived in a social world in which an extrafamilial male corporation, with its ideology of a fictive kinship, a fraternity, reinforced their own positions as heads of households, as fathers and husbands, within the nuclear family. For the guildsmen of Münster, there was a fundamental continuity between patriarchal domination in family and corporate life, on the one hand, and patriarchal rule in a polygamous sacred "tribe," on the other.

---

[42]Jan of Leiden and his wives fed the entire Anabaptist community every Sunday in a communal feast on the cathedral square. See Gresbeck, *Berichte der Augenzeugen,* p. 103.

PART TWO

# TRANSMITTING
# THE REFORMATION

*One of the most fascinating problems in Reformation research is the question of how the Evangelical message was so swiftly communicated. The printing press was an obvious agent: thousands of copies of Luther's writings were published in his own time, and hundreds are still extant in libraries all over Germany and Europe. Unlike incunabula, most of these were pamphlets—short, in other words—and written in German; many had woodcut illustrations, often with captions, to convey the same message, albeit in a cruder form, to the illiterate. Many other reformers also got into print, as did lay preachers and social critics. The numerous pamphlets give us a vivid picture of the vibrant debates and diverse opinions of the early Reformation years. Although scholars have long been aware of the importance of printing, and of pamphlet literature in particular, no one has undertaken the task of examining the role of the printing press in the long-term cultural and religious development of sixteenth-century Germany. The situation has changed, however, with the publication of Miriam Usher Chrisman's two-volume study of printing in Strasbourg between 1480 and 1599. One of the major findings of her research is the documentation, based on the analysis of more than five thousand Strasbourg imprints, of the independence and vitality of a lay culture that hungered after all types of knowledge—scientific, religious, historical, and magical. Her study paints a fascinating picture of the cultural universe of one of the most important cities in the empire and certainly one of its chief intellectual centers in the sixteenth century.*

*Communication of the ideas of the Reformation depended on much more than books and pamphlets: the shaping of "public opinion" resulted from sermons, gossip, rumors, discussions in public and private places, woodcuts, and popular festivals as well. The context of this process of communication in the imperial city of Nördlingen is evoked in all its details by Hans-Christoph Rublack. In addition to various forms of printed, visual, and oral communication, music, or more precisely a ballad in this case, also played a crucial role. By examining the composition, singing, and text of the "Song of Contz Anahans," Rublack suggests a method by which the vast repertoire of folk songs of the sixteenth century could be tapped for social analysis. His study shows how a particular popular cultural medium was used to transmit political and religious messages during the Peasants' War of 1525 and the way in which music could stir up "seditious" passions that the magistrates could not afford to ignore.*

*Still another method of reconstructing the meaning of religious practices for the common people is the examination of ritual behavior and its symbolism. The vast array of rituals associated with the Catholic church functioned as a language by which the clergy conveyed theological ideas and acted as mediators between the laity and God. By rejecting, mocking, and mimicking Catholic rituals, the supporters of the Evangelical movement were in fact engaged in a rite of desacralization, the aim of which was to purify Christianity of its accrued corruptions. Robert Scribner's subtle analysis of popular rites suggests a way to "read" ritual behavior as the practices of reformed religious ideas. The power of the Evangelical message lay not only in the Word as it was read or heard but also in the way it enabled the laity to turn Catholic rituals inside out to create their own religion.*

*Historians have often written intellectual and cultural history on the basis of a few major texts. Miriam Usher Chrisman, professor of history at the University of Massachusetts at Amherst, has followed upon her previous publication on Strasbourg,* Strasbourg and the Reform *(1967), to study the intellectual and cultural history of the great Alsatian imperial city. Unlike traditional intellectual historians, Chrisman has amassed a huge data base consisting of the title, the date, and a content analysis of all books published in Strasbourg between 1480 and 1599. Using computer analysis to help identify intellectual trends, generations, and styles, she demonstrates the vitality and diversity of a lay vernacular culture in sixteenth-century Strasbourg. The result of her study is the most comprehensive cultural history of any sixteenth-century city. She discusses, among other things, the techniques of book production and the work of individual printers. Her research results are presented in* Lay Culture, Learned Culture: Books and Social Change in Strasbourg, 1480–1599 *(1982), upon which the following article is based. A companion volume,* Bibliography of Strasbourg Imprints, 1480–1599 *(1982), lists the 5,677 imprints according to themes and subjects.*

# [4]

# Printing and the Evolution of Lay Culture in Strasbourg 1480–1599

MIRIAM U. CHRISMAN

Recent scholarly interest in the sixteenth century has focused on popular culture and is reflected in studies of religious pamphlets, religious propaganda, and popular education.[1] Is it possible at this point to develop a view of popular culture in its entirety? The analysis of surviving books published in one sixteenth-century city, Strasbourg, provides at least a starting point.[2] The published books reveal a lay culture that, although dependent on the clergy and the intellectuals in some areas, pursued its own goals in terms of knowledge and had its own distinctive values.

This article is based on the evidence from printed materials that include not only books but also pamphlets, broadsheets, maps, songs, and calendars—any type of printed paper that came off the presses. Together, these documents make it possible to reconstruct the intellectual milieu of ordinary men and woman. Written in the vernacular language, the books cover a broad range: popular medical treatises, technical handbooks, religious pamphlets, books on how to bring up children, biblical plays,

[1]The most important contribution to this study is the massive bibliography now under way at Tübingen and edited by Hans Joachim Köhler, *Flugschriften des frühen 16. Jahrhunderts,* Microfiche Serie, 1978, Zug, 1978. Also see Steven Ozment, "Pamphlet Literature of the German Reformation," in Steven Ozment, ed., *Reformation Europe: A Guide to Research* (St. Louis, Mo.: Center for Reformation Research, 1982), pp. 85–106; and R. W. Scribner, *For the Sake of Simple Folk: Popular Propaganda for the German Reformation,* Cambridge Studies in Oral and Literate Culture, ed. Peter Burke and Ruth Finnegan (Cambridge, 1981).

[2]Miriam Usher Chrisman, *Bibliography of Strasbourg Imprints* (New Haven, 1982). I cite this book below as Chrisman Bibliography with book numbers. Because the complete reference in each case appears in Chrisman, I provide only author, short title, printer, and date in my notes. Place of publication is omitted because all of these works are Strasbourg imprints. I refer to series of books only by number, including the date of publication of the works.

propaganda songs, drinking songs, riddles and jokes, and music for the lute and other stringed instruments. Many of these, according to their title pages, were explicitly written for a popular audience.

Five major elements characterized what I will call lay culture. First, there was a fascination with the world of nature. In sharp contrast to the assumption that the sixteenth-century world was governed by superstition and the pursuit of magical formulas, books published in the vernacular reveal a consistent and informed curiosity about the physical world. This inquisitiveness was reflected in anatomy books, botanicals, herbals, geographical treatises, and books on astronomy and in journalism that reported on comets, voyages of exploration, and meteorological phenomena. Second, this interest in the natural world was strengthened by a desire for technical skills. Whether these were seen as a means of harnessing the natural forces is a matter for conjecture. In any case, the quest was reflected in a variety of technical manuals and treatises, ranging from texts on surveying and applied mathematics to books on mining and scientific agriculture. Ordinary men and women also bought popular medical handbooks that would help them to meet the health needs of their families. A third element in lay culture was a passion for self-instruction, already witnessed in the technical manuals. In addition there were all sorts of how-to books: how to conduct a case in court (without a lawyer); how to write letters to officials; how to make wine; how to make beer; how to build a sundial in your own backyard; how to teach yourself Latin. People were obviously eager to increase their knowledge and their skills. A fourth element was a search for religious meaning that, in this period, found expression in acceptance of the teaching of the reformers. Finally, there was a moral quest that reflected a desire for an ethic relevant to everyday life as lived within the community and the family. This search was expressed in novels, songs, poems, and, above all, plays that the townspeople put on themselves. Popular culture expressed little cynicism; it was affirmative and optimistic and displayed pragmatism and empiricism rather than superstition and credulity.

The development of this lay culture resulted from no one group of writers but from several different groups. Established intellectuals—men of advanced education connected with the church, the schools, or the law courts—wrote in the vernacular for a popular audience. Equally important were the printers who chose to devote a significant part of their repertory to vernacular books. These were not *winkel drucker,* marginal job printers grinding out materials for the masses. Johann Grüninger, one of the earliest of the Strasbourg printers to publish a considerable number of vernacular books, was a major humanist printer, and he also did a great deal of work for the Catholic church. Later in the century, the Rihel press was the established press for the Strasbourg Gymnasium and Academy, but it also published vernacular works. The tastes and interests of the printer could play a significant role in opening up new areas of vernacular publication. The repertories of Christian Egenolff and Jacob Cammerlander both reflected an interest in technical books and popular scientific texts, and their output made these books available in Strasbourg and in the markets it served.

Finally, laymen and laywomen themselves contributed to the development of the vernacular culture. I define laymen as men and woman without a university education who were not involved in the intellectual establishment, such as the church, the schools, and the law courts. Some of these men were civil servants in the lower echelons of the urban or town bureaucracy. Others were military men, patricians, artists, designers, engineers, apothecaries, accountants, veterinary surgeons, and housewives. Even before the Reformation, ordinary people wrote down their ideas,

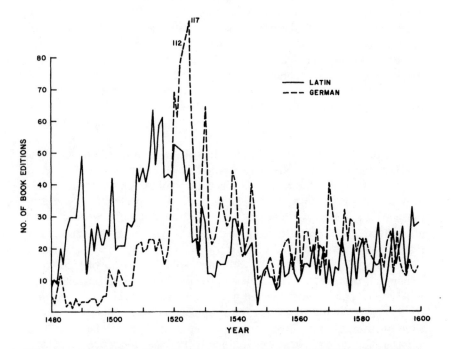

*Figure 4.1.* The Linguistic Division of Latin and German Books Published in Strasbourg, 1480–1599. From Miriam U. Chrisman, *Lay Culture, Learned Culture: Books and Social Change in Strasbourg, 1480–1599* (New Haven: Yale University Press, 1982), figure 1. Reprinted by permission.

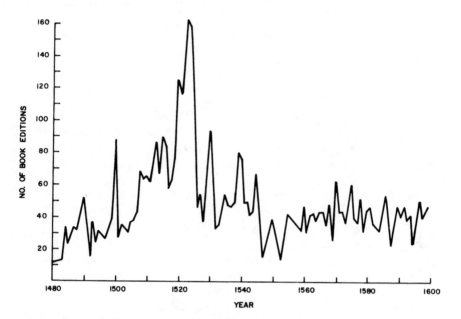

*Figure 4.2.* Total Production of Book Editions by All Printers by Year. From Miriam U. Chrisman, *Lay Culture, Learned Culture: Books and Social Change in Strasbourg, 1480–1599* (New Haven: Yale University Press, 1982), figure 2. Reprinted by permission.

summarized their expertise, and published these works. Together with the printed works of the intellectuals, these books created a flourishing lay culture that developed alongside, but often quite independently of, the learned culture.

The importance of vernacular books is reflected in the statistics. A total of 5,677 surviving books formed the base of the current study. Of these, 2,812 (49.5 percent) were in Latin, and 2,608 (45.9 percent) were in German (figures 4.1 and 4.2).[3] The evolutionary development of the lay culture falls into five periods, whose dates should not be considered to be rigidly fixed because there was always some overlap from one period to another except in the case of the abrupt ending of Catholic publication with the Reform. The five periods of the development of lay culture are: a nascent period from 1480 to 1499; a period from 1500 to 1519, when the lay culture drew on traditional sources and on the literary elite; the period

---

[3]Miriam Usher Chrisman, *Lay Culture, Learned Culture: Books and Social Change in Strasbourg, 1480–1599* (New Haven, 1982). Other vernacular languages included French, English, and Spanish. Together they constituted only 1 percent of the total production. The only other important language of publication was classical Greek.

of the Reform, from 1520 to 1528; a period of relative independence from 1530 to 1570; and finally a period of synthesis with the learned culture from 1571 to 1599.

### The Printers Create a Lay Market, 1480–1499

In the earliest decades, 1480 to 1499, the overwhelming proportion of books were printed for the church. The printers served a clerical market and printed volumes of sermons, books on doctrine, and liturgical books, especially missals and breviaries.[4] A few printers, however, in particular Heinrich Knoblochtzer, began to experiment with books with a broad popular appeal. In 1477 he borrowed woodcuts from the editions of an Augsburg printer to publish a version of the story of Belial. It went through two later editions, and Knoblochtzer followed this success with the story of Herzog Ernst and a version of the Lucretia story. Johann Prüss and Martin Schott were attracted by the experiment and began to produce popular books on their presses; indeed, Prüss used some of Knoblochtzer's woodcuts.[5] Johann Grüninger, with the largest volume of any Strasbourg printer, used illustrations in a variety of books and developed new techniques. At first he borrowed woodcuts from other printers, but by 1500 he had begun to commission new woodblocks, calling on major artists—Hans Baldung, Johann Schaufelin, and Johann Wechtelin.[6] These illustrated books were designed for laymen, whether they could read or not.[7] Sebastian Brant, in a foreword to an illustrated version of the *Narrenschiff* printed by Grüninger in 1494, states that people who could not read could nevertheless see their foolishness in the woodcuts.[8] Illustrated books played a vital role in making the world of print accessible. In these early decades, by printing picture books the printers made books attractive to ordinary men and women and helped to teach them to read. After 1520 the use of illustrations diminished noticeably.[9] Furthermore,

---

[4]Chrisman Bibliography; see the section on Catholic literature, pp. 3–38, especially subsections C3.1, C6.1, and C6.2.

[5]VI.1.2a–b, Jacobus de Theramo, *Buch Belial* (H. Knoblochtzer, 1481, 1483); VI.1.1, Johannes Hildesheimiensis, *Buch der Heiligen drei könige* (J. Prüss I, circa 1480); V2.1.1a–b, *Dass oventurlich buch beweiset . . . von einer frouwen genant Melusina* (H. Knoblochtzer, n.d.; J. Prüss I, circa 1480); V2.1.2b–c, Egenolf von Staufenberg, *Geschichte von Peter Diemeringer* (J. Prüss I, 1483; M. Schott, 1490); V2.1.7, Andreas Capellanus, *De amore et de amoris remediis*, Latin title, German text, J. Hartlieb, trans. (M. Schott, 1481); François Ritter, *Histoire de l'imprimerie alsacienne aux XVᵉ et XVIᵉ siècles* (Strasbourg-Paris, 1955), p. 69.

[6]Ritter, *L'imprimerie alsacienne*, p. 86.

[7]Rolf Engelsing, *Analphabetentum und Lektüre* (Stuttgart, 1973), p. 23.

[8]Chrisman, *Lay Culture, Learned Culture*, p. 106.

[9]Ibid., table 11, p. 106.

the pictures were used differently. In the early period the pictures were carefully tied to the story line, and there might be only one line of text. Later the text was far more important, and the illustrations were used to ornament rather than to explain the text.

Significantly, even at this very early stage, autodidactic works began to appear. There were books on rhetoric and letter books that provided models for letters to one's superiors, such as counts, barons, or city magistrates.[10] The printers used the presses to increase the literacy skills of ordinary people, and they also provided practical manuals, one for making wine, another for distilling alcohol from wine, and a standard astrological handbook that was used as a medical guide because the taking of baths or medication was strictly regulated by astrological signs.[11] Missing from the printers' repertoire of popular books were religious materials. From 1480 to 1499 no sermons were printed in the vernacular, nor were any prayer books or devotionals, psalters, or hymnbooks. Grüninger did bring out a complete German Bible in 1485, which would have been accessible to the literate laity but may have been designed for church use. The most popular religious books were lives of the saints, but the major collections were published in Latin and were only for the use of the clergy. Vernacular versions were restricted to brief accounts of the lives of individual saints.[12]

In the next two decades, from 1500 to 1519, vernacular books came to play an increasingly important role in the repertoire of the Strasbourg printers. Johann Grüninger's new workshop created handsome woodcuts for his books, and these were quickly copied and imitated by others. Mathias Hupfuff began to specialize in popular publications. From 1508 to 1519, popular vernacular books constituted approximately 12 percent of the total volume of books produced in the city.

The basic stock in trade for these popular works continued to be chivalric tales, tales based on Greek and Roman legends, and lives of the

[10]V4.1.1a–b, [Heinrich Gessler], *Formulare und Tutsch Rhetorica* (J. Prüss I, 1483, 1486); V4.1.2, Stephanus Fliscus de Sontino, *Formulare Loquendi,* in German and Latin (J. Prüss I, 1487); V4.1.3, *Biechlin . . . wie man einem jeglichen Tütschen Fürsten und Herren schreiben soll . . .* (M. Hupfuff, 1499).

[11]S2.1.1a, Michael Schrick, *Von den ausgebrenten und Distillierten Wassern* (M. Scott, 1481; n.p., 1483); S2.1.2a–b, Arnoldus de Villa Nova, *Tractat von der bereytung der Wein* (H. Knoblochtzer, 1483; M. Schott, 1484); S4.1.1a–c, *Ain lieblichs Biechlin zu lesen von dem hochgelerten Meister Lucidarius . . .* (n.p., n.d.; H. Knoblochtzer, circa 1482; M. Hupfuff, 1499).

[12]C4.2.1, Jacobus de Voragine, *Legenda Aurea* (G. Husner, 1479, 1480, 1483, 1485, 1486, 1489, 1492, 1496, 1498; H. Eggestein, 1480; n.p., 1482, 1487, 1496; J. Grüninger, 1496, 1497); V3.1.7, *Lesen von sant Brandon was wunders er uff dem mer erfaren hat* (M. Hupfuff, 1494, 1499); V3.1.8, *Von Sant Ursulen schifflin* (B. Kistler, 1497); V3.1.9, *Leben, das ist sant Pauls Leben* (B. Kistler, 1498).

saints. The chivalric tales and the Greek and Roman legends had nothing to do with the realities of the everyday lives of their readers; they were meant to entertain. The heroes and heroines were knights and ladies, kings and queens, and French princesses. The authors did, nevertheless, attempt to make knightly life a model for burgher behavior, as the subtitle of one book ran: "The Knight of Turn . . . a pretty and valuable story for instructing your children."[13]

Printers continued to bring out self-teaching manuals, and their scope was now broadened to include legal handbooks, books on agronomy, and books of pseudoscience. Letter-writing books were still important to the repertoire. One of these explained its goals with great precision in the title: "How one should write to German princes and lords, also knights and servants, cities and villages, men of clerical and civil status, for every letter the proper beginning and end."[14] Clearly, ordinary folk had to write about their grievances, legal matters, and business affairs. This need was further evidenced in the success of popular legal handbooks, Ulrich Tengler's *Layenspiegel*, which went through seven editions in eight years, and a similar manual by Sebastian Brant, which went through two editions in this period. Tengler's book attempted to provide the ordinary citizen with the material a person needed to appear in court without a lawyer. The reader was instructed in preparing a defense, in drawing up a complaint, and in presenting a case. In this way, Tengler concluded, justice could be achieved.[15] The book became a permanent best-seller; it had gone through fourteen editions by the middle of the century.

The printers not only gave ordinary citizens the legal tools they needed but also discovered a market for popular medical books. They began with rather specific treatises—in particular, health rules to be followed in case of plague.[16] In 1507 Martin Flach published the first edition of Eucharius Rösslin's gynecological book, designed for the instruction of midwives and the improvement of obstetrical care. The manual was popular all over Germany and went through one hundred editions in the course of the century.[17] Similarly, a popular herbal provided remedies that could be

[13]V2.1.25, Geoffroy de La Tour de Landry, *Der Ritter vom Turn* (J. Knobloch, 1519; J. Cammerlander, 1538), title page.
[14]V4.1.3, *Biechlin . . . wie man einem jeglichen Tütschen Fürsten und Herren schriben sol . . .* (M. Hupfuff, 1499), title page.
[15]L1.3.4, Ulrich Tengler, *Layenspiegel: Von rechtmässigen ordungen in Burgerlichen und peinlichen regimenten . . .* (M. Hupfuff, 1510, 1511, 1514; n.p., 1513, 1515, 1516; J. Knobloch, 1518, 1527), title page of 1527 edition.
[16]S1.4.3, *Ein Tractat contra pestem, preservative und regiment* (B. Kistler, 1500). S1.4.4, *Hie in disem büchlin vindest du ein gut regiment für die Pestilenz* (M. Hupfuff, 1502); Johann Wydman, *Regimen . . . Wie man sich in pestilentzischem lufft halten soll* (M. Schürer, 1511, 1519; J. Knobloch, 1519).
[17]S1.2.2, Eucharius Rösslin, *Der Schwangeren Frauen Rosengarten* (M. Flach II, 1507, 1513, 1522; B. Beck, 1529).

made at home for ordinary illnesses.[18] The interest in improved agricultural techniques was reflected in a German translation of the medieval agronomist Petrus de Crescentius.[19]

Still, the interest in the world of nature was not solely practical. People were interested in the larger world that was being revealed by the voyages of discovery. Reports of these voyages, translated into German, appeared relatively quickly after the event. An account of the voyages made to the Far East in 1498–1499 under the patronage of the king of Portugal was published in 1506. Amerigo Vespucci's account of his voyage to the New World, first published in Italian in 1505, was available in German from the Strasbourg presses by 1509. The Portuguese conquest of Malacca in 1511 was described in a treatise published in 1513. Ludovico di Varthema's travels through the Far East, printed first in Italy in 1510, had been translated into German by 1515.[20] There was an intense interest in these voyages, and in travel accounts generally, and the printers made them available as quickly as possible. In Strasbourg several of the humanists served as translators. The books make plain the cooperation between the scholars and the printers.

## Humanists, Clergy, and the Lay Readers, 1500–1520

The vernacular culture in the decades from 1500 to 1520 was shaped by scholars, particularly by the group of Alsatian humanists centered in Strasbourg. Johann Geiler von Keysersberg, Sebastian Brant, Jacob Wimpheling, and Thomas Murner wrote in the vernacular for a popular audience. Brant's *Narrenschiff*, first printed in 1494, created a type of popular satire that was enjoyed by everyone—clergy, merchants, artisans, and townspeople—the very people parodied in the poem. Thomas Murner, a Franciscan frair, modeled his *Narrenbeschwörung* on Brant's poem and continued with a series of satirical poem-stories. These por-

---

[18]S3.1.4, *In disem Buch ist der Herbary; oder, Kruterbuch genannt der Gart der gesuntheit* (J. Prüss I, 1507, 1509; R. Beck, 1515, 1521; B. Beck, 1528, 1530; J. Grüninger, 1529).

[19]S8.1.3, Petrus de Crescentius, *Von dem nutz der ding die in äckern gebuwet werden* (n.p., 1512; J. Knobloch, 1518; J. Schott, 1518; J. Knobloch II, 1531).

[20]S6.2.3, (M. Ringmann), *Von den nüwen Insulen und landen so yetz kürtzlich erfunden synt durch den Künig von Portugall* (M. Hupfuff, 1506); S6.2.4, Amerigo Vespucci, *Diss Büchlin saget wie die zwen . . . Herren Fernandus Künig zu Castilien und Herr Emanuel: Künig zu Portugal haben das weyte mör ersüchet unnd funden vil Insulen unnd eine Nüwe Welt . . .* (J. Grüninger, 1509); S6.2.6, Emanuel, King of Portugal, *Abdruck eines Lateinischen Sendtbrieves an Bapstliche Heiligkeit von der Eroberten Stat Malacha* (M. Hupfuff, 1513); S6.1.4, *Die ritterlich und lobwürdig reiss des . . . erfanen Ritters . . . Herren Ludovico Vartomans von Bolonia* (J. Knobloch, 1515, 1516).

trayed men and women at their worst, as dishonest, grasping, ambitious, and driven by pride and vanity to achieve a higher position in the social hierarchy. The result was a chaotic, disordered world that would change only if men and women rejected false values and dedicated themselves to an ascetic way of life.[21] Murner's satires denigrated burgher values, ridiculing rather than praising family life, friendship, and loyalty to the community. The poems were popular because they were entertaining, not because the burghers were attracted to the ideal of ascetic withdrawal from the world.

The most important departure in the decades before the Reform was in the publication of religious materials for the laity. Having neglected these in the earlier period, the printers discovered that there was a market for popular religious literature and turned to the work of the popular preacher Geiler von Keysersberg. Geiler died in 1510, but his sermons and devotionals were a major feature of the popular repertoire from 1508 to 1520. In his lifetime Geiler had packed the cathedral week after week with his sermons, which called on people to repent and to give themselves up to a more moral and religious way of life. It was not a new message, but Geiler preached in a marvelously direct way, using the idiom of his listeners and drawing them to him by his genuine human empathy. The sermons had a clear moral point that could be applied to everyday life. One set of sermons took the ant as an example. Humans, Geiler said, should learn from the ants to store up during the summer what would be needed in the winter. He contrasted the industry of the ants with the laziness and idleness of humans. He praised the division of labor among the ants because it developed a sense of common purpose. The moral was clear: men should not compete against one another but should work together for the common good. Life on earth, Geiler pointed out, was short. The human should prepare for the winter.[22]

The printers also worked with Geiler and Brant to develop other types of religious books for the laity. In 1502 Brant edited a collection of saints' lives based on a fifteenth-century German text. Divided into a summer section and a winter section, it was lavishly illustrated with a woodcut on nearly every page.[23] Brant's volume was quickly followed by other German collections of the lives of the saints published first by Mathias Hup-

---

[21]V6.2.4, Thomas Murner, *Narrenbeschwerung* (M. Hupfuff, 1511, 1512; J. Knobloch, 1518, 1522; G. Messerschmidt, 1556, 1558); V6.2.5, Thomas Murner, *Der Schelmen zunft* (M. Hupfuff, 1512; J. Knobloch, 1516; J. Cammerlander, ca. 1540; n.p., 1568, 1574); V6.2.8, Thomas Murner, *Die Mülle von Swyndelsheim* . . . (M. Hupfuff, 1515).

[22]C3.3.13, Johannes Geiler von Keysersberg, *Die Emeis* . . . (J. Grüninger, 1516, 1517), fols. vii–xxv.

[23]V3.1.14, Sebastian Brant, *Der heiligen Leben nüw mit viel me Heiligen* (J. Grüninger, 1502, 1508, 1510, 1514).

fuff and later by Johann Knobloch. The timing of these volumes, which were issued in quick succession, reflects a ready market.[24]

In 1506 Johann Knobloch created a new kind of popular religious book, an illustrated version of the Passion of Christ with the text from the four Gospels. He commissioned Urs Graf to prepare handsome illustrations facing each page of the texts. This book was a significant departure. The scripture was presented as straight text, without any commentary or explanation. The sources, chapter and verse, were carefully cited in the margin. All four Gospel accounts were given so that the reader could absorb the different emphases of the apostles. The illustrations sharpened the impact of the texts and conveyed their own message. Jesus was depicted as calm, unmoved, and accepting, almost withdrawn. The crowd, the Roman soldiers, and the Jews were shown as hostile, aggressive, and menacing. The message of the illustrations was the patient endurance of suffering in a hostile world, as seen in the burdens and sorrows of Christ. At the end of the 1506 edition, Knobloch included an admonition: "The book had been printed so that every thoughtful reader could seek out the story more frequently and thus experience the bitterness, the compassion, the sorrows which the Savior had suffered. While it might not affect moralistic sinners deeply, those who were God's companions (*Gott gesellen*) would be truly moved."[25]

The success of the book was immediate. Knobloch reprinted it the following year and again in 1509. By 1509, Johan Grüninger had published an edition of the same work, and Mathias Hupfuff brought out his version in 1513. It is significant that these editions appeared before the first Strasbourg publication of Erasmus's biblical texts; his Latin New Testament would appear in 1521.[26] Luther's German New Testament would also come out in 1521.[27] Biblical texts were not, in this case, opened to the laity by the scholars, the humanists, or the clergy. It was the printers acting independently and on their own initiative who first put the German text of the Bible into the hands of ordinary men and women.

### Laity, Clergy, and Religious Propaganda, 1520–1528

By 1520, before the Reformation had had its impact, publications for the lay audience had already come to manifest certain characteristics. The

---

[24]V3.1.16, *Der heiligen leben neüw getruckt* . . . (M. Hupfuff, 1513; J. Knobloch, 1517; M. Flach II, 1521).

[25]VI.1.6, *Der Text des passions oder lidens christi, usz dem vier evangelisten* . . . (J. Knobloch, 1506), end page.

[26]B5.1.3, Erasmus Roterodamus, *Testamentum Novum Latinum* (U. Morhard, 1521, 1522; J. Knobloch, 1522, 1523, September 1523; J. Herwagen, 1523).

[27]B5.1.5, Jhesus, *Das Neuw Testament Deutsch*, trans. Martin Luther (J. Schott, 1522; J. Knobloch, 1524, 1525, 1528; J. Grüninger, 1527, 1529).

printing presses were used for self-education and to gain knowledge of the physical world. The public had a desire for entertainment and diversion and delighted in satire. At the same time people exhibited a moral seriousness and were engaged in a search for ethical values and in a spiritual quest. In the years from 1520 to 1528, the spiritual quest took precedence over the other interests. Religious literature commandeered the presses, reducing scientific and popular vernacular books to a mere trickle. The figures are clear. There were 43 scientific, autodidactic, or literary books published in German in this period, but there were 383 religious books: books of Protestant and Catholic doctrine, Luther's sermons, polemics from both sides, biblical texts, and devotional works. The 1520s were characterized by a total immersion in religion. The overwhelming presence was, of course, Luther, but the Strasbourg reformers, the printers, and laymen and laywomen also played a part in diffusing the new religious ideas.

It is important to recognize that the new faith was not communicated to the laity in logical, carefully argued sermons or books of doctrine. It was communicated in polemic pamphlets that vigorously attacked Catholic doctrine, the pope, the bishops, and the central ceremony of the Catholic church, the mass. The printing presses made these pamphlets available, creating one of the first modern propaganda campaigns. The polemical works were followed by doctrinal treatises, also written and published in German, which introduced the new teachings with regard to justification by faith, penance, and the Eucharist. Doctrinal treatises also addressed the role of Christians in society, their subordination to the secular authorities, and their responsibility in the marketplace. Separate treatises discussed issues of family life, the relationship of married partners to each other, and the duty of parents to provide education for their children.[28] Thus the ethical search of the earlier decades was at least partially satisfied by the reformers.

It is not necessary to describe these publications in detail. The important point is their impact on the development of the vernacular culture. Their linguistic significance can hardly be overstated. The fact that these polemical and doctrinal treatises were written in German, together with the publication of Luther's German New Testament, gave the vernacular language an importance it had never had before. For the first time in the history of Christianity, a vernacular language had achieved equality with Latin. This phenomenon was short-lived. By 1524, even before the Peasants' War, Luther and the Strasbourg reformers had begun to cut back on doctrinal publication in the vernacular. The number of Lutheran treatises

---

[28]Chrisman Bibliography, see secs. PI.1, PI.6, PI.7, PI.8.

published in German in Strasbourg dropped from forty-three in 1523 to eighteen in 1524.[29] The liturgy for the new services, however—the new hymns and prayers—had been and continued to be written in German. The new liturgy was first printed in 1524, and numerous editions of the psalms were set to music, as were hymnals and prayer books. The vernacular language was thus an integral element of the new faith, and this role strengthened the language as a cultural force.

Still, how did the outburst of religious propaganda and doctrine influence laypeople? The answer to this question can be found in the polemical pamphlets that they themselves wrote. In the five years from 1520 to 1524, some forty-eight such pamphlets were published in Strasbourg, the work of ordinary men and women. The peak came in 1523. In theme the pamphlets were not very different from those written by the reformers, and their influence is clear. The laity attacked the old church, particularly the clergy. There was a vociferous rejection of monasticism. The lay authors attempted to draw up rules for the Christian life. What they said was not as important as how they said it. The pamphlets demonstrate that these men and women, few of whom had any formal higher education, could organize their ideas clearly and present them persuasively, drawing on Scripture to prove their point. The primacy of the Bible was the all-pervasive theme of the lay tracts; indeed, their major criticism of the Roman clergy was that the latter had withheld the Scriptures from the laity and falsified it in accordance with their own opinions.[30] The lay writers provided copious biblical citations, either in the text or in the margins. These reflect an impressive familiarity with the Scriptures. The lay writers did not just pick one Gospel or Epistle and work through that single source. They organized their own thoughts and then found support in appropriate texts. In a single paragraph Clement Ziegler, a Strasbourg gardener, referred to Deuteronomy, Acts, Isaiah, Baruch, and Corinthians.[31] A major impact of the Reform was that ordinary men and women, gardeners, artists, and military men felt free to address themselves to religious questions and to interpret Scripture according to their own understanding. Not one of these lay religious treatises refers to or defers to a reformed cleric. Neither Luther nor any of the Strasbourg reformers are quoted to support an argument. As early as 1522, laymen and laywomen

[29]Chrisman, *Lay Culture, Learned Culture*, p. 157.

[30]Lux Gemmiger, *Ob einer wissen wolt wie der heiss . . . Das hat gethon ein freyer student/auss ursach das man Luther seine bücher verbrant* (n.p., n.d.) fol. aiv; P4.1.14, Clement Zyegler, *Von der waren nyessung beyd leibs und bluts Christi . . .* (J. Schott, 1524), fol. biiii; Hanns Greyffenberger, *Dies biechlin zaygt an was uns lernen und gelernet haben unsere maister der geschrifft* (n.p., 1523), fol. Dii.

[31]B8.3.1, Clement Ziegler, *Ain Kurt Register und ausszug der Bibel* (n.p., 1524), fol. Aiiv–Aiii.

were confident that they could read the Scriptures properly and find the truth. Luther's doctrine of the priesthood of all believers helped to legitimize the lay culture, but the laity took the initiative in expressing their own opinions.

The religious changes also gave the laity a new self-confidence. In the early decades no lay writer would have dreamed of publicly criticizing the clergy or those in authority. Luther's attacks on the clergy and the monks emboldened the laity, and both men and women wrote to their own sisters, brothers, or sisters-in-law, urging them to leave their convents and to resume a secular life that, they asserted, would be more Christian than life behind the cloister walls. Mathis Wurm von Geydertheym, for example, a member of a Strasbourg patrician family, wrote a hundred-page treatise marshaling the reasons why families should take their children and relatives out of convents and should prevent young people from entering them. The vow of celibacy, he wrote, ignored God's decree to work.[32] In another treatise a married woman wrote to her sister, who was a nun. The latter, together with her mother superior, was fearful that her sister and brother-in-law had become Lutherans. The problem, answered the sister, was not whether one was Lutheran. The problem was how best to lead a Christian life. Christ taught, "I am the door through which you must go to the Father." The monastic orders, however, instead of following that simple path, had created a special life that demanded tonsures, special clothing, and all sorts of food rules. They had set up their own rules, forgetting the spirit of unity and the bond of peace that Christ had taught.[33] The lay sister not only believed that life in the world was closer to the Christian ideal; she was willing to defend her ideas before her sister, the mother superior, and the other sisters in the convent.[34] Furthermore, she went so far as to publish these ideas. One result of the Reformation was to make laymen and laywomen more self-assertive, more independent. As a consequence lay culture was stimulated.

### The Apogee of Lay Books, 1530–1570

The development of lay culture after the Reform was the result not only of this new independence but also of economics, in particular the economics of printing. Until the Reformation the major market for books was the Roman church. Until 1520, Catholic books composed 35 percent of

[32]Mathis Wurm von Geydertheym, *Trost Clostergefangner* (n.p., 1523), fol. biiv–biiiv.
[33]P3.3.22, *Ayn Bezwungene antwort uber eynen Sendtbrieff eyner Closter nonnen an ir schwester im Eeliche standt zugeschickt* (n.p., 1524), fols. aiiiiv; Biv; Bii.
[34]Ibid., fol. aiiv.

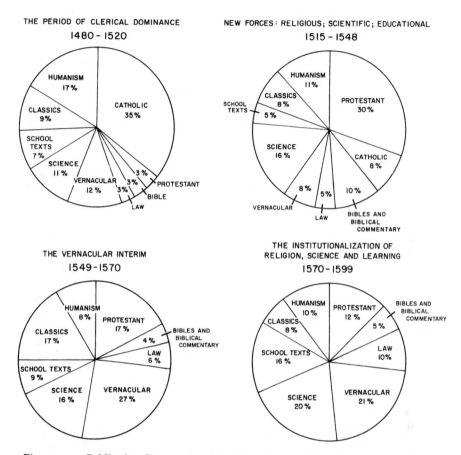

THE PERIOD OF CLERICAL DOMINANCE
1480 - 1520

HUMANISM 17%
CLASSICS 9%
SCHOOL TEXTS 7%
SCIENCE 11%
VERNACULAR 12%
CATHOLIC 35%
3%
PROTESTANT
3%
BIBLE
3%
LAW

NEW FORCES: RELIGIOUS; SCIENTIFIC; EDUCATIONAL
1515 - 1548

HUMANISM 11%
CLASSICS 8%
SCHOOL TEXTS 5%
SCIENCE 16%
PROTESTANT 30%
CATHOLIC 8%
VERNACULAR 8%
LAW 5%
BIBLES AND BIBLICAL COMMENTARY 10%

THE VERNACULAR INTERIM
1549-1570

HUMANISM 8%
CLASSICS 17%
SCHOOL TEXTS 9%
SCIENCE 16%
PROTESTANT 17%
BIBLES AND BIBLICAL COMMENTARY 4%
LAW 6%
VERNACULAR 27%

THE INSTITUTIONALIZATION OF
RELIGION, SCIENCE AND LEARNING
1570-1599

HUMANISM 10%
CLASSICS 8%
SCHOOL TEXTS 16%
SCIENCE 20%
PROTESTANT 12%
BIBLES AND BIBLICAL COMMENTARY 5%
LAW 10%
VERNACULAR 21%

*Figure 4.3.* Publication Patterns by Class and Time Periods. From Miriam U. Chrisman, *Lay Culture, Learned Culture: Books and Social Change in Strasbourg, 1480–1599* (New Haven: Yale University Press, 1982), figure 22. Reprinted by permission.

the output of all Strasbourg's printers (see figure 4.3).[35] An analysis of the production of several of the major Protestant printers provides an insight into the problem of markets.[36] Johann Schott was early drawn to the Reform and dedicated his press to the publication of Luther and Ulrich von Hutten as early as 1520. Between 1521 and 1523, 90 percent of his press runs were devoted to Protestant polemic. In 1524 and 1525 he

[35]Chrisman, *Lay Culture, Learned Culture*, p. 298.
[36]Ibid., pp. 32–33.

printed nothing but polemic. Then in 1526 the Protestant tracts disappeared completely from his repertoire. The major works that came off his press in this year were a reedition of Hans Gersdorff's surgical text, which he had first published in 1517, and an almanac prepared by Otto Brunfels. Schott filled out this list with an edition of Luther's Twenty-seven Sermons and a biblical commentary by Johann Brenz. He was fortunate in his close friendship with Otto Brunfels because the latter had completed a compendium of the Old and New Testaments and two volumes of popular biographies of biblical figures in the vernacular. These latter works were the mainstay of Schott's printing shop until 1529. Between 1526 and 1529, however, he began to add medical works to his repertoire, editions of Dioscorides, Lanfrancus, and the Italian physician Manardo. By 1530 he had managed to shift the emphasis of his press and had become a printer of medical and technical books.[37]

The Beck press made a similar adjustment. Reinhardt Beck had taken over the shop of Johann Prüss I at the time of his marriage to Prüss's daughter, Margarethe Prüss. Prüss I had specialized in printing missals. He worked, among others, for the bishops of the far-flung dioceses of eastern Germany. Beck deserted this Catholic repertoire to print humanist works. In 1521 he had begun to print Lutheran tracts. His death in the following year meant that this Reformation printing could go no further. In 1525 Margarethe married again. Her second husband was also named Beck, Balthasar in this case. Balthasar carried the press through the difficult years after 1525 by reprinting the traditional herbal, the *Garten der Gesundheit,* which had been part of the Prüss repertoire since 1501. By 1529 he had begun to print the works of Anabaptists and Spiritualists, and Anabaptists came from all over Germany to bring him their books. He balanced these controversial tracts and treatises with popular medical texts, many of them prepared and edited by Walter Ryff, and he was able to keep the press at a prosperous level.[38] These examples, and that of Jacob Cammerlander, who combined vitriolic anti-Catholic polemical treatises with medical and scientific manuals, indicate that the mixture of medical with religious publication was an effective solution for the printers. No printer in Strasbourg could depend on a repertoire of Protestant books alone; the market was not big enough.

These economic requirements were complemented by intellectual factors. Sixteenth-century men were fascinated by the world of nature. Curious about the structure and functions of the human body, they wanted medical information for themselves and their families. Plants and animals,

[37]See Chrisman Bibliography for listing in index under Johann Schott, pp. 415–16.
[38]Chrisman, *Lay Culture, Learned Culture,* pp. 22–23, 179.

agronomy and veterinary medicine—all were of interest to them. They were eager to extend their computing skills and their knowledge of the techniques of measurement and simple mechanics. The scientific publications of the period indicate that concern for life in the world to come was balanced by a strong interest in the here and now. In part because of market conditions for books, in part because of interest in the natural world, there was a surge of vernacular medical, scientific, and technical publication from 1530 to 1555.

The scientific and technological publications were more professional in style and content than the work of the earlier decades. The outstanding example was Otto Brunfels's *Kreüterbuch*. The earlier botanies were traditional compilations that described the plant, provided a rather generalized woodcut in some cases, and listed the various medical uses. Brunfels's work was on a different scale from the very beginning. He had started to work on the Greek botanical sources as early as 1525 and had been encouraged by Johann Schott, the printer, to continue his reading and translations. Schott drew together a working team that included Brunfels, Michael Herr, and Nikolaus Prügner—all learned men with scientific training—as well as several apothecaries and herb gatherers, and, most important, the artist Johann Weyditz. Herr, a doctor, worked as the medical consultant, translator, and editor. Prügner gathered botanical samples. The herb gatherers drew on their long experience in the fields. Weyditz drew the plants from life, where they grew.[39] The book was published first in 1530, a folio edition in Latin. Michael Herr's German translation was available two years later. The text for the German edition was simplified, so that the book became essentially a field guide rather than a scientific text, but Weyditz's illustrations were all included. These were the first botanical drawings from life. The root system of each plant was shown, and even more significant, the plant was shown in all stages of development, from blossom to seed pod. Thus the observer could identify the plant at any time in the season. The German edition also included information on when the plant should be gathered and its various medical uses.[40] Brunfels also published a German treatise on the special pharmaceutical needs of women and children and the first pharmaceutical text written in German.[41] In this way the most advanced scientific knowledge of the time was made available to ordinary people.

[39]Kenneth Thibodeau, "Science and the Reformation: The Case of Strasbourg," *Sixteenth Century Journal* 7 (1976):42.

[40]Oth. Brunnfelsz, *Contrafayt Kreüterbuch Nach rechter vollkommer art, und Beschreibung der alten, besstberumpten ärtzt* . . . (vol. 1, J. Schott, 1532, 1534; *Ander Teyl*, J. Schott, 1537).

[41]S1.2.5, Otto Brunfels, *Weiber und Kinder Apotheck* (J. Cammerlander, 1534); S1.9.14, Otto Brunfels, *Reformation der Apothecken* (W. Rihel, 1536).

Popular anatomical treatises also reflected the printers' growing profes-
sionalism and accuracy. Heinrich Vogtherr, who was an engraver and
printer as well as an optometrist, published two so-called anatomical
charts, one of a man, the other of a woman, in 1537 and 1538. These were
in fact crude and highly generalized diagrams of particular organs. The
drawing of the heart, for example, strongly resembled the heart symbolized in a modern valentine. Four years later, however, Walter Ryff
compiled an anatomical treatise, in German, which presented the human
body over the life span of an individual. Beginning with diagrams of the
fetus in the womb, which Ryff took from Rösslin's gynecology, he proceeded to illustrations of the human body, male and female, based on
Vesalius's *Tabulae Sex.*[42] The skeleton, the vascular system, and the
organs were shown for both the male and the female. In this case the
organs were well drawn, obviously on the basis of a dissection. The point
is that the information was made available to the common reader and that
it represented the highest state of knowledge at the time. Ryff was a
notorious plagiarist, but he knew from whom to plagiarize. The drawings
were probably the work of Hans Baldung.

Technical manuals were an increasingly important part of Strasbourg
book production in these decades, in part because of the particular efforts
of Christian Egenolff, Jacob Cammerlander, and Heinrich Vogtherr, all of
whom were interested in this type of publication and were active in the
city from 1530 to 1555. The quantitative significance of the technical
manuals can best be seen comparatively. Over the time span 1500–1599,
a total of ninety-five Catholic and Protestant devotional books were published in German. In the same period, eighty-five technical manuals were
printed, 30 percent of them between 1528 and 1550.[43]

The technical manuals were not innovative; indeed, several of them had
circulated in manuscript form in the fifteenth century. What was different
was that the printers were disseminating technical information at the artisanal level. The books on metallurgy, the books on how to temper iron
and steel, the books on the dyeing of cloth, and the mining books were all
clearly aimed at people in these trades. The style of the manuals suggests
their intended audience. It was direct: "Take gilded silver, as much as
you wish, and grains of powder . . ."[44] Most writers used the second
person singular. From these manuals men could acquire trade information

---

[42]S1.10.8, Walter Ryff, *Das aller . . . höchsten unnd adelichsten geschöppfs . . . von
Gott . . . Das ist der menschen . . . warhafftige beschreibung oder Anatomi . . .* (B. Beck,
1541).

[43]Chrisman, *Lay Culture, Learned Culture*, p. 182.

[44]S11.4.1, *Probier Büchlin, Auff Goldt, Silber, Alle Ertz und Metall . . .* (C. Egenolff,
1530), fol. 28v.

without being a member of a guild, or as guild members they could add to their knowledge. Technical manuals printed between 1530 and 1570 provided information for a broad spectrum of trades: mining, assaying, the making of steel and iron, dyeing, cabinetmaking, and architecture. There were also books for domestic use—cookbooks, books on how to make wine, and the favorite: how to make a sundial.

Books on applied mathematics were a new departure in the decade of the 1530s. Education for business careers was taken seriously in Strasbourg. Private schools that taught the basic skills to boys and girls and to men and women were fairly common. There were special schools for instruction in French, a useful skill for the businessman.[45] At a higher level, the *Rechenmeister* taught arithmetic, algebra, and techniques of bookkeeping and systems of business accounting. Their work was reflected in a series of applied mathematical texts that began to appear in 1525. Six were printed between 1530 and 1546. Although the academic mathematicians limited themselves strictly to arithmetic and geometry, the Rechenmeister taught algebra as well. Their books used algebraic equations to solve everyday problems of exchange and profit and loss.[46] Ulrich Kern's treatise on measurement described the systems of measurement used by different cities, the basic rules of measurement, and the way to compute the volume of fluids and solids. The section on fluid measurement addressed itself particularly to the problems of the vintner—how much wine did a vat hold? The book included a section on surveying with a rod and a sight.[47]

These medical and technical books were descriptive rather than theoretical in nature. They did not propose a new world system, nor did they suggest innovative methods or experiments. The world of nature was opened to people at all levels of society, with the quality of the descriptions improving greatly in the decades from 1530 to 1570. Furthermore, the technical books and mathematical treatises gave their readers the opportunity to master a given skill.

Although scientific and technical publication was a dominant element in the lay culture of the middle of the century, popular vernacular literature was developing a new independence. In the earlier decades, chivalric tales and stories drawn from Greek and Roman legends formed the

---

[45]François J. Fuchs, "Quelques aspects de la vie économique à Strasbourg" (paper presented at the Colloque Internationale, Strasbourg, May 1975).

[46]S5.4.6, Georg Waelckl, *Die Wälsch Practica, gezogen ausz der kunst der Proportion* (M. Apiarius, 1536); S5.4.7, Christophorus Stiltz, *Eyn new Rechenbuch . . . Wie mann eyn ordenliche Raittung oder Rechnung . . . auch uber eyn gantze Amptsverwaltung . . .* (J. Cammerlander, 1542).

[47]S5.4.5. Ulrich Kern, *Eyn new Kunstlichs wolgegrundet Visierbuch . . .* (P. Schaeffer, 1531).

basis of the vernacular repertoire. Sebastian Brant and Thomas Murner had added their satirical poems to these traditional tales. After the Reformation the printing of chivalric tales dropped way back; only nine were printed in the forty years from 1530 to 1570, and most of these were reprints. Greek and Roman stories also dropped off, and the lives of the saints, as might be expected in a Protestant city, disappeared altogether. In their place, new works appeared. These were written not by humanists or learned men but by laypersons, often men who held minor civil service or administrative posts in the towns surrounding Strasbourg. Several of the writers were burgomasters of their towns. The important point is that burgher society had now produced its own writers, people who could articulate the values and aspirations of their fellow burghers. Drawn from the middle ranks of urban society, not from the educated elite, they wrote unaffectedly on the dignity of burgher life, the felicity of the married estate, and the virtue of family life. Tied to neither the church nor the schools, they expressed the moral and ethical concerns of ordinary men and women.

The starting point seems to have come in civic theaters. Miracle plays, plays for special church festivals, were a familiar part of medieval and late medieval life. The Reformation brought an end to the traditional farces, and new plays had to be written for Mardi Gras and Christmas. By 1530 these plays had begun to be published by Strasbourg printers, and thirty were published between 1530 and 1570. Biblical plays were a favorite, with the Old Testament serving as a major source. Joseph was the most popular hero; three different playwrights addressed themselves to the Joseph story. Old Testament women were particularly important, with plays on Susanna, Judith, Jephtha's daughter, Esther, and Rebecca. The favorite New Testament text was the parable of the prodigal son. These biblical stories were used to illustrate familial and domestic virtue and to point the way to the good, moral life. Jephtha's daughter served as a model of filial obedience and total devotion to her father, and Rebecca provided another example of obedience and the obligations owed by the young to their parents. The stories of Esther and Judith honored their patriotism, furthering the cause of national pride and dedication to one's city.[48] Plays based on Roman legends developed similar themes.[49] The theater clearly played an active part in the development of lay culture.

It is important to recognize that these plays bore little resemblance to traditional miracle plays. They were often modeled on classical sources,

---

[48]Chrisman Bibliography; see section V8.1 for list of thirty-four plays in German printed between 1533 and 1599.
[49]V8.2.7, *Ein schön Spil von . . . Lucretia . . .* (J. Frolich, 1550); V8.2.11, Martin Montanus, *Von zweien Römern, Tito Quinto Fulvio und Gisippo . . .* (P. Messerschmidt, 1560).

with a prologue, an epilogue, and the correct division into scenes and acts. They were performed by the burghers themselves, with the published version often listing the cast by name. The performances were important occasions, sometimes requiring two days from the opening prologue through to the closing epilogue, with perhaps a cast of nearly a hundred citizens.[50]

By 1539 Georg Wickram, the illegitimate son of a wealthy burgher of Colmar, had begun to write novels. His first novel was simply a longer version of a traditional chivalric tale about a knight who defended a countess suspected and accused of adultery; the knight challenged the lady's slanderer to combat and exonerated the innocent noblewoman.[51] Gradually, however, Wickram broke away from these traditional subjects. By 1555 he was writing on themes of family and burgher life. In the *Jungen Knaben Spiegel,* the hero is a peasant's son who is adopted by a childless count and countess. They then have a child of their own, and the point of the story is the comparison between the adopted child, of poor and humble origin, who behaves responsibly and manifests love and devotion toward his parents, and his foster brother, of noble lineage, who brawls, drinks, gambles, and finally runs away from home. In the end the peasant finds his noble foster brother ruined and drinking in a tavern and brings him back to the bosom of the family, where all is forgiven. This is a reversal of the usual tale: the nonnoble behaves nobly, whereas the noble lives a life of debauchery.[52] Wickram continued to write novels that asserted the superiority of burgher life. In a later novel the heroes are two businessmen. As merchants they experience the adventures formerly reserved for noble knights. They travel far on business, but are shipwrecked and captured by Turkish pirates. They are saved by their faithful servant, who happens to speak Arabic. Meanwhile, at home their wives help and support each other.[53] The moral of the book is that strength comes from cooperation and mutual aid, a far cry from the stress on the individual derring-do of knightly valor.

Wickram's novels marked a new attitude toward burgher life. He depicted merchants and tradesmen as having their own ways, which no longer had to be considered inferior to aristocratic life. Urban men and women did not have to look to the nobility for heroes; they could create their own. Family relationships—a deep, reciprocal love between hus-

[50]Chrisman, *Lay Culture, Learned Culture,* pp. 218–219.

[51]V6.3.3, Georg Wickram, *Der Ritter Galmy* (J. Frölich, 1539, 1540, 1548, 1550, 1554; n.p., 1588).

[52]V6.3.7, Georg Wickram, *Der Jungen Knaben Spiegel* (J. Frölich, 1554; n.p., 1555).

[53]V6.3.11, Georg Wickram, *Von Guten und Bösen Nachbaurn* (G. Messerschmidt, 1556).

band and wife and responsibility toward children—took the place of the romantic love of the chivalric tale.

The plays and novels of midcentury reflect the continuing desire of the burghers for a code of ethics and standards of behavior related to the reality of their daily lives. Once the reformed clergy had married, the virtues of marriage and the dangers of celibacy disappeared as themes from their sermons and treatises. Laymen picked up these themes and, through popular literary forms, shaped them into a new ethic. The education of children, courtship and engagement, and marriage—all became subjects for popular literature. Loyalty to the family, obedience to parents, and the responsibility of each member of the family to the others emerged as cardinal virtues. The family was given new status as the foundation of society.

Although scientific, technical, and popular literature increased in the years from 1530 to 1570, religious publication was dramatically curtailed. Polemical tracts were reduced to about two a year. Jacob Cammerlander printed violent attacks against the pope, and the call to the Council of Trent gave rise to some five tracts, but the period of confrontation was over. Significant religious publication for the laity centered on the Bible. Luther's Bible was completed in 1527, but it was not printed in its entirety by a Strasbourg printer until 1535. There were five more editions between 1537 and 1547 and then no more.[54] There were also eight editions of the German New Testament between 1532 and 1549, then no more until 1576.[55] These biblical editions meant that it was increasingly possible for a layperson to own the Bible or part of it. It was, however, still an extremely expensive book, and probably more people owned the New Testament or the psalms than the whole Bible. The popularity of the psalms is reflected in the twelve editions of these decades in which the psalms are set to music.[56] Significantly, the Protestant clergy wrote few books directly for the laity—only a handful of devotionals and prayer books.[57] The clergy were diverted by the external political problems of

---

[54]B1.1.5a–g, Martin Luther, *Biblia, Das ist: Die gantz Heylige Schrift Deütsch* (W. Köpfel, 1535, 1537, 1544, 1547; W. Rihel, 1535, ca. 1540, ca. 1542).

[55]B5.1.5g–i, Jhesus, *Das Neuw Testament Deutsch*, trans. Martin Luther (J. Grüninger, 1532; G. Ulricher, 1533; W. Köpfel, 1538); B5.1.7, *Das Neüwe Testament* (W. Köpfel, 1537); B5.1.8a, *Das Newe Testament Mart. Luth.* (W. Rihel, 1542); B5.1.9, *Das Newe Testament mit schonen Figuren* (W. Rihel, 1549).

[56]B4.1.3b; B4.1.4a–f; B4.1.7; B4.1.10; B4.1.11a–b; B4.1.5.

[57]P5.1.16, Otto Brunnfels, *Biblisch Bettbüchlin Der Altvätter, und herrlichen Weibern, beyd Alts und Newes Testament . . . wie man recht betten sol* (J. Schott, 1531); P5.1.17, Jacob Otther, *Ein Kurtzer bericht, wie man sich bey den krancken und sterbenden halten soll* (M. Apiarius, 1534); P5.1.23, *Der Psalter in gebett gestellt . . .* (W. Rihel, 1550); P5.1.24, Jacobus Ratz, *Vomm Fastenn: Welches das Recht, Christlich, unnd notwendig, auch das falsch und onchristlich Fasten sey . . .* (J. Frölich, 1554).

the new church and the problems within it. The Protestant church was shaken by the war, the collapse of the Protestant League, and the settlement that permitted the resumption of Catholic services in the city parishes. In the aftermath of the defeat, the Magistrat took positive diplomatic steps to preserve the autonomy of the city and to forestall further Catholic influence. From 1549 to 1570 there was little doubt in Strasbourg that the leadership was firmly in the hands of the secular authorities. The church was also weakened by internal strife as Johann Marbach and Johann Pappus struggled to assure that orthodox Lutheranism prevailed in the Strasbourg churches. The Gymnasium was drawn into the struggle because Marbach understood the need to control the faculty. The conflicts preoccupied the clergy and the faculty, so that lay culture flourished without competition from the learned.

### The Learned Resume Control, 1570–1599

In the last three decades of the sixteenth century, the basic elements of lay culture continued in much the same pattern, producing technical books, books on natural science, popular literature, religious devotionals, and catechisms. Books printed for the laity, however, became more serious and professional. In a sense, there was a return to the period of 1500 to 1515, when the Strasbourg humanists had written the important new vernacular books. After 1570 the academic scientists turned their attention to preparing treatises for the vernacular market rather than leaving this area to the popularizers. Solid historical books and careful scholarly accounts of recent events became increasingly important. The histories appeared as early as the 1550s and began to be important in the 1560s. In the 1570s Comines's history of the Burgundian war and Jean Sleidan's history of the reign of Charles V were important elements of the vernacular repertoire. The interest in history reflected a new preoccupation with politics, a desire to know about the war against the Turks and the religious wars of the period. This concern was further evident in popular journalism, which, again, began to develop in the 1550s, became more important in the 1560s, and flourished in the 1570s. Religious publication also became more important in these decades as Pappus began to achieve the stability that Marbach had envisioned. In the field of vernacular literature, there was a significant shift. The popular plays were now written by schoolteachers rather than burghers. Scientific works and histories were the work of academicians, men with formal, university training. Thus a sort of synthesis occurred. The importance of vernacular publications was recognized, and the learned became more involved in creating these materials.

The most important vernacular scientific publication in these last decades was an edition of the work of Paracelsus undertaken by Michael Toxites. Paracelsus was hardly an accepted academician. He had practiced in Strasbourg for a few brief months in 1526 and 1527 and had then left for Basel, where he was expelled from the city and the university. Very early in his career he rejected the use of Latin in medical practice, believing that it restricted men's thoughts. He was also convinced that his work would be scorned by trained university physicians but would be understood by artisans and common people. Forced to wander from one German or Austrian city to another, he died in 1541. In 1564 Michael Toxites, who taught in Jean Sturm's Gymnasium until he was fired for drunkenness, began a complete edition of Paracelsus's work. By this time there was a definite split within the medical community between those to whom Paracelsus was anathema and those who accepted his teaching, particularly his pharmacopia, which was based on the use of chemical substances instead of the traditional herbal mixtures. Paracelsus related these changes in medical treatment to a new worldview and a new view of the nature of man. Toxites, after leaving the Gymnasium, apprenticed as a physician. As an enthusiastic disciple of Paracelsus, he wanted to make the latter's work available not only to doctors but also to ordinary men and women. In Strasbourg Guinther von Andernach, a prestigious figure in the medical world, adopted some Paracelsan methods, but greater support came from two non-university-trained men, Lucas Bathodius, a doctor-astronomer-astrologer, and Valentinus Kosslitius, a disciple of Toxites.[58] Paracelsus also had a following among the lower classes, who hoped to understand the secrets of nature through a combination of empirical observation, technical skill, and numerical codes based on occultism and alchemy.[59] The impact of Paracelsus is further reflected in a spate of alchemical books published at this point, both his own and those of Bernardus Trevisanus.[60] Alchemy had not played an important role in Strasbourg scientific publication before except in several editions of Phillipus Ulstadus and the standard Geber text in the late 1520s. Seven edi-

---

[58]Theophrastus Hohenheim Paracelsus, *Sämtliche Werke*, ed. Karl Sudhoff, 3 vols. (Munich and Berlin, 1929–30), 3:xxxviii.

[59]Manfred Fleisher, "The Institutionalization of Humanism in Protestant Silesia," *Archive for Reformation History* 66 (1975):258.

[60]S16.1.9, Theophrastus Hohenheim Paracelsus, *Archidoxa: Von Heymlichkeyten der Natur* (T. Rihel, 1570; Chr. Mylius II, 1574); S16.1.10, Theophrastus Hohenheim Paracelsus, *De lapide philosophorum drey tractat* (N. Wyriot, 1572); S16.1.11, Bernardus Trevisanus, *Von der hermetischen Philosophia . . .* (Chr. Mylius II, 1574; Chr. Mylius Erben, 1582; A. Bertram, 1586); S16.1.12, Theophrastus Hohenheim Paracelsus, *De Secretis Creationis: Von Heimligkeiten der Schöpfung aller dingen* (Chr. Mylius II, 1575).

tions of alchemical books were published in the six years from 1570 to 1575.

The other important scientific publications, again reflecting a more serious and more professional approach, were the botanical books of Hieronymus Bock and Bartholomaeus Carrichter, which were based on Brunfels's work;[61] Jean Liebault's agronomy text, several veterinary texts; and hunting books.[62] In all cases these were more instructive and represented a higher standard than the earlier popular manuals. More information was included, and it was presented in a more logical way. The naïveté of the earlier how-to books was gone; among other things, the reader was no longer called by the familiar pronoun "du." Significantly, the veterinary texts were written by laymen who were specialists in their field.

The interest in history was a response to the times. Buffeted by war and the threat of war, ordinary men and women turned to historical accounts of their own time. Jean Sleidan's history of the reign of Charles V, with its brilliant account of the formation of the Schmalkaldic League and the Schmalkaldic War, saw nine editions in German between 1568 and 1598.[63] There were chronicles of Saxony and Alsace and a general history of the Empire.[64] Even more important were the journalistic accounts of the war against the Turks, the Dutch Revolt, and the French Wars of Religion.[65] In part these were religious propaganda. Many of the accounts of the Dutch and French wars were written by Johann Fischart, a zealous Protestant who worked for his brother-in-law, the printer Bernard Jobin. These two together made Strasbourg the center for a new outburst of

---

[61]S3.1.1oh–l, Hieronymus Bock, *New Kreuter Buch* . . . (J. Rihel, 1572, 1577, 1580, 1587, 1595). S3.1.17a–g, Bartholomaeus Carrichter (Martinus Pegius), *Kreutterbuch,* ed. Michael Toxites (Chr. Mylius II, 1575, 1576, 1577; A. Bertram, 1589, 1595, 1597; L. Zetzner, 1596).

[62]S8.1.7a–d, Johannes Libaltus (Jean Liebault), *Siben Bücher von dem Feldbau* . . . (B. Jobin, 1579, 1580, 1592, 1598); S9.1.5, Caspar Reuschel, *Hippiatra: Gründlichter un eigentlicher Bericht . . . von Art und Eygenschafft der Pferde . . . Kranckheiten . . . Artzneyung* (B. Jobin, 1593, 1599); S9.1.6, *Ross Artzney Buch* . . . (L. Zetzner, 1599); S10.1.6, Johann von Clamorgan (Jean de Clamorgan), *Wolffsjagt* . . . (B. Jobin, 1590).

[63]V9.3.7e–m, Johannes Sleidanus, *Beschreibung . . . Geistlichen und Weltlichen sachen so sich under der regierung des Groszmechtigsten Keysers Caroli disz namen des V. verlauffen,* trans. Marc Stamler (J. Rihel, 1568; T. Rihel, 1568, 1570, 1574, 1575, 1579, 1588, 1593, 1598).

[64]V9.3.10, Carolus Sigonius, *Deutschen Römischen Reichs Hoch Achtung und dessen von Teutschen Keysern* . . . (B. Jobin, 1584); V9.3.12, Cyriacus Spangenberg, *Sächsische Chronik* (n.p., 1585); V9.3.13, Christophorus Reusner. *Contrafacturbuch: Ware und lebendige Bildnussen etlicher weitberhümbten und Hochgelehrten Männer in Teütschand* (B. Jobin, 1592); V9.3.14, Bernhard Hertzog, *Chronicon Alsatiae* . . . (B. Jobin, 1592); V9.3.15, Cyriacus Spangenberg, *Hennebergische Chronica* (B. Jobin Erben, 1599).

[65]Chrisman Bibliography, see secs. VII.2, VII.3, VII.4.

polemic far more bitter than the earlier polemic written by the reformers. Fischart was an educated man, but he had no interest in a career as a scholar or a preacher. Instead, he devoted himself to a campaign against the papacy, the Guise, and the Spanish Hapsburgs. Jobin had earlier assembled a team of translators who worked tirelessly, converting Hugenot tracts, treatises, and accounts of the Wars of Religion into German.[66] However biased, these accounts were complete. Ordinary men and women were well informed with regard to the introduction of the Inquisition in the Netherlands, the reign of the duke of Alva, and the Saint Bartholomew's Day massacre. Thus, vernacular publication continued to inform and instruct the laity.

The propaganda-journalism was written to strengthen the Protestant cause, to make clear the difference between the true faith and the idolatry of the Roman church. It helped to create a climate of emotion. Suspicion and doubt were inculcated; the other side was not to be trusted. All loyal Protestants must band together, or terrible consequences would result. Part of the religious search at the end of the century was a search for a common identity with other Protestants, a goal that might be achieved if Roman Catholicism were made the common enemy.

At the same time, the inner religious needs of the laity were met by a concentrated attempt on the part of the Strasbourg ministry to make available basic instructional materials. Luther's *Kleyne Catechismi* and the Strasbourg catechism went through three editions.[67] These were reinforced by vernacular explications of the doctrine of the Eucharist.[68] Most important were the prayer books and hymnbooks. Clearly, for most Protestants sharing in the worship service was central, and by active participation in the singing of hymns and psalms they could express their devotion.[69] Prayer books were also written for family prayers and for private intercessions.[70] The major aim of the Protestant clergy in these last decades was to achieve religious orthodoxy. From this, they believed, an ordered community would evolve. The inner religious needs of the laity were not, however, forgotten. Through congregational worship and an

---

[66]Pierre Besson, *Etude sur Jean Fischart* (Paris, 1899), p. 290.

[67]P1.6.16b, Martin Luther, *Der Kleyne Catechismi für die Gemeyne Pfarrher und Prediger* (S. Emmel, 1570); P1.6.15d–f, *Catechismus: Christliche Underrichtung . . . zu Straszburg* (B. Jobin, 1578; A. Bertram, 1585; B. Jobin, 1591).

[68]Nicolaus Florus, *Kürtze . . . erinnerung . . . das H. Abendmal . . .* (T. Berger, 1579).

[69]P1.1.8–P1.1.13.

[70]P5.1.30a–d, Martin Luther, *Beteglöcklin Doctoris Martini Lutheri . . .* (B. Jobin, 1571, 1579, 1580, 1591); P5.1.32, Johannes Habermann, *Wöchentlich Christliche Gebeten . . . verdeutscht* (B. Jobin, 1575); P5.1.33a–d, Samuel Neuheuser, *Ein Christliches Trostbüchlein in zwolfe . . . Capitel abgetheylet* (B. Jobin, 1575, 1580, 1585, 1593; B. Jobin Erben, 1595).

active life of prayer, ordinary men and women could develop spiritual depth and understanding and a sense of communion with God.

The analysis of vernacular books helps us to move on beyond the question of whether lay culture derived from learned culture or was independent. It was both. For some elements it drew on the learned—the lawyers, the university-trained physicians, and the theologians. For others it drew on practitioners—applied mathematicians, businessmen, apothecaries, civil servants, and ordinary men and women. The difference between the two cultures stemmed not only from the difference in sources. Their purposes were dissimilar. Learned culture was meant to preserve the whole Greco-Roman-Christian heritage and hand it down from one generation to the next. The aims of the lay culture were more immediate, more pragmatic. It was meant to provide useful information for problem solving, to pass along skills and knowledge, to provide precise guidelines for conduct and behavior.

In certain areas, particularly in religion, the goals were similar. During the early period of the Reform, the two cultures could thus draw closely together, almost becoming intertwined. The split in the scientific disciplines, on the other hand, was deep and fundamental. The science of the learned was still based on Aristotle and on Euclidean geometry. This theoretical scientific study did not attract the laity. Laypeople were interested in applied mathematics, in technology, in precise descriptions of the natural world. Similarly, the laity had little interest in the classical studies that so absorbed the humanists and that were the foundation of the Gymnasium and the Academy curriculum. Ordinary men would never be called on to speak before the city council, to muster arguments for a particular policy; the rules of rhetoric and Latin grammar were irrelevant to their lives. Indeed, one of the marks of lay writing is that it lacks the grammatical control that characterizes the work of the literary elite. The only element of humanism that aroused the interest of the laity was the classical historians. The patriotism that lay at the core of Livy's republican ethic spoke directly to the sixteenth-century urban dweller.

Lay culture drew what it wanted or needed from the learned culture, particularly with respect to religious ideas. On the whole, however, lay culture was more innovative. Learned culture, by very definition, had to continue in the traditional paths of grammar, rhetoric, logic, and theology. New techniques of analysis and new teaching methods were developed, but there were few innovations in subject matter or form. Lay culture could develop new forms. The autodidactic book, the popular medical manuals, and the illustrated technical manuals were created. The novel, biblical plays, and journalism appeared. The result was a mixed creation that drew on the work of the humanists and theologians as well as on that of businessmen, apothecaries, and civil servants. No school, university, or Gymnasium, however, disseminated lay culture and assured its continuity. It depended on the printers for its development and for its diffusion. The printers, finally, played the major role in shaping the intellectual world of ordinary people.

*The research of Hans-Christoph Rublack, professor of history at Tübingen University in the Federal Republic of Germany, has focused on the problem of the city and the Reformation. The author of four previous books, Rublack has studied the introduction of the Reformation in Constance (1971); the failed Protestant movements in the southern and western German episcopal cities (1978); the city and the church in Kitzingen (in a book coauthored with Dieter Demandt, 1978); and the Reformation in Nördlingen (1982). The following article grew from his research on the imperial city of Nördlingen, in which a folk song about the Peasants' War of 1525 became the subject of an official inquest. The essay shows how communal and civic political ideas can be reflected in popular culture; it argues that music and other nonverbal forms of communication were just as effective as published pamphlets and woodcuts in mobilizing or controlling public opinion. It represents an innovative attempt to evaluate oral sources from the sixteenth century and an analysis of the relationship between politics and culture. For Rublack's reflections on city and religion, see his essay in English in* Religion, Politics, and Social Protest: Three Studies on Early Modern Germany, *ed. Kaspar von Greyerz (1984).*

# [5]

# The Song of Contz Anahans:
# Communication and Revolt
# in Nördlingen, 1525

HANS-CHRISTOPH RUBLACK

## I

The city of Nördlingen, once an imperial city but today a country town situated on the Romantic Road along the border of Swabia and Bavaria, has in its city archive seven versions of a "song." The song may be placed within the broader context of the Peasants' War and can be related more specifically to a civic revolt that took place in Nördlingen in April 1525. The council considered the texts of this song to be directed against the Swabian League, the only effective stronghold against the peasants' armies. Because of the apparent partisan nature of the piece, it remained unprinted until the end of the nineteenth century. Thus it continued to document purely oral communication.[1]

---

[1]A text of the song was edited by Ludwig Müller, "Beiträge zur Geschichte des Bauernkriegs im Ries und seinen Umlanden," *Zeitschrift des Historischen Vereins für Schwaben und Neuburg* 16 (1889):23–160; 17 (1890):1–152, 253–76. This first edition did not take the versions into account. It has been reprinted by Wolfgang Steinitz, *Deutsche Volkslieder demokratischen Charakters aus sechs Jahrhunderten*, vol. 1, Deutsche Akademie der Wissenschaft zu Berlin: Veröffentlichungen des Instituts für deutsche Volkskunde 4/I (Berlin, 1954), pp. 14–17. For a full edition with critical notes, see my "Das Lied des Nördlingers Contz Anahans, April 1525," in Hans-Martin Maurer and Franz Quarthal, eds., *Speculum Sueviae: Beiträge zu den historischen Hilfswissenschaften und zur geschichtlichen Landeskunde Südwestdeutschlands: Festschrift für Hansmartin Decker-Hauff zum 65. Geburtstag*, vol. 2 (Stuttgart, 1982), pp. 58–74. See also my *Eine bürgerliche Reformation: Nördlingen* Quellen und Forschungen zur Reformations-Geschichte 51 (Gütersloh, 1982). For songs on the German Peasants' War, see Hermann Strobach, "Die Bauern sind aufrührig worden: Lieder aus dem Bauernkrieg," in Strobach, *Der arm Man, 1525: Volkskundliche Studien* (=Akademie der Wissenschaften der DDR, Zentralinstitut für Geschichte, Veröffentlichungen zur Volkskunde und Kulturgeschichte, 59) (Berlin, 1975), pp. 237–73; Siegried Bräuer, *Die zeitgenössischen Lieder über den Thüringer Aufstand von 1525*

It is possible that the civic authorities became aware of the song only when some verses were sung by a weaver on night watch on 8 May 1525. In a drunken state, Hans Trumer banged on the doors of the houses he passed and, stopping in front of the preacher's home, he endeavored to rouse the latter to a disputation. This reveling bore a certain resemblance to activity on a night the previous month when the town had risen in revolt. Triggered by the rumor that the city gates had been left open so that the knights of the Swabian League could enter the city to suppress the common man, there was a spontaneous resort to arms and a rallying of mercenaries, who declared their leader to be Anton Forner, a coũncillor and populist head of the reform movement.

A detailed account of the events of the night of 4 April 1525 may be gained from an examination of the council's protocols of the torture to which the rebels were later subjected. Following the restoration of law and order, the council ensured loyalty and obedience not only by consent but also by executing the leaders who spearheaded the revolt. This action prompted a roper's wife to challenge the "evangelical" nature of such methods, thereby expressing her concern with religious reform. What the sources reveal is a confused narrative of irrational revolt, thwarted ambitions, and the arrogance of the civic authorities. Is it possible to interpret historically what appears to be a sequence of disorder? Is it indeed possible to give a structural meaning to events and emotions when they are related to institutions and roles and to particular types of actions? What is the meaning of conflict, revolt, and torture in a city that stressed its sense of unity and the concept of sacral corporation?

II

Today it is still possible to form an impression of the whole town of Nördlingen by either walking around the city walls or viewing the town from its church tower. Nördlingen may be considered an ideal, if romantic, city that gives the sense of being an integrated unit. At the beginning of the sixteenth century, it was even more of a "hometown." The city gates were closed at night, citizens alternated on guard duty, and the community gathered in the marketplace and assembled for religious service in the church, whose construction they had recently financed. The

(=Mühlhäuser Beiträge Sonderheft 2) (Mühlhausen, 1979). For Nördlingen, see Christopher R. Friedrichs, *Urban Society in an Age of War: Nördlingen, 1580–1720* (Princeton, 1979) for suggestions. For the English translation of the song, I warmly thank Thomas A. Brady, Jr., and Helga Robinson-Hammerstein of Trinity College, Dublin.

civic oath united the citizens, exhorting them to perform services for the common good of the community.

The unity of the citizens in political and religious life suggests that they were an ordered organic unit. The idea of a revolt against the authorities is not easy to reconcile with this impression unless we accept and thereby stress the dichotomy between godly order and ungodly disorder. It may be advantageous to analyze this city in terms of a social system.[2] Such an analysis necessitates an investigation that differentiates between individual roles within a social action and examines their interchange therein. Moreover, the focus on social interaction and the process of institutionalization emphasizes that a social system is evolving, fluid, and not static.[3] Although a concept of mere divisive antagonism of the dominated versus the dominant would be overly simplistic, it is nonetheless a truism that those who held power were in a position to effect consent. "Power" is a considerable term that implies ultimate recourse to physical force. Though force was indeed employed, as the use of torture indicates, generally power functioned in defining the meaning of situations and setting the themes of social and political discourse. Those who controlled oral communication in effect held authority. Thus the city council was exercising authority when it summoned the citizens and addressed them in carefully drafted speeches. Preaching could serve as an alternative, giving or withholding religious meaning to social action and political authority. In 1522 the Nördlingen council had assumed control of this vital function in appointing a preacher, Theobald Billican.[4] Oral communication and discourse were vital elements of civic life. Controlling them was an essential part of holding power. For this reason a song could be considered to

[2]For analytical approaches, see the articles by Bernd Moeller and Thomas A. Brady in Wolfgang J. Mommsen et al., eds., *Stadtbürgertum und Adel in der Reformation: Studien zur Sozialgeschichte der Reformation in England und Deutschland* (Stuttgart, 1979), pp. 25–39, 40–43; see also Thomas A. Brady, Jr., *Ruling Class, Regime, and Reformation at Strasbourg, 1520–1555* (Leiden, 1978). The state of research on the Reformation in the cities has been analyzed by Kaspar von Greyerz, "Stadt und Reformation: Stand und Aufgaben der Forschung," *Archiv für Reformationsgeschichte* 76 (1985):6–63. See also my "Is there a 'New History' of the Urban Reformation?" in Tom Scott and E. I. Kouri, eds., *Politics and Society in Reformation Europe: Essays for Sir Geoffrey Elton on his Sixty-Fifth Birthday* (London, 1987) pp. 121–41. For theoretical approaches, see Niklas Luhmann, "Einfache Sozialsysteme," in his *Soziologische Aufklärung*, Vol. 2 (Opladen, 1982), pp. 21–38; Erdmann Weyrauch, *Konfessionelle Krise und soziale Stabilität: Das Interim in Strassburg, 1548–1562* (Stuttgart, 1978); and David Sabean, *Power in the Blood: Popular Culture and Village Discourse in Early Modern Germany* (Cambridge, 1984).

[3]See my "Political and Social Norms in Urban Communities in the Holy Roman Empire," in Kaspar von Greyerz, ed., *Religion, Politics, and Social Protest* (London, 1984), pp. 24–60.

[4]Gerhard Simon, *Humanismus und Konfession: Theobald Billican: Leben und Werk* (Berlin and New York, 1980); Gustav Adolf Benrath, "Theobald Billican. 1554," in Kurt Baumann, ed., *Pfälzer Lebensbilder*, 3:31–63.

threaten peace and its further publication was suppressed. For this reason too the interpretation of the Scriptures was to be controlled. The Reformation, with its recourse to the biblical message, expanded discourse, widening its spectrum to include new forms of religious, political, and social meaning. Religious discourse defined the sociopolitical situation. Because salvation was of central importance, any redefinition of religious truth had an automatic bearing on socioreligious authority. As the new definition of religious thought generated sociopolitical action, control of the word was vital. We may distinguish, on an analytical basis, between the problems of salvation and those of society, but they were bound together by more than rational deduction because religion served as the general reference for social discourse. During the "Reformation" religion was invoked as the truth and the word of God. Such uniformity has as one of its consequences a restriction of choices: there was hardly any room for a plurality of religious creed within social systems, all the more so because their vulnerability admitted of no complexity that would endanger authority.[5] For this reason social systems were delimiting beliefs, distinguishing between tolerable and intolerable beliefs and excluding the latter. A large part of the spectrum of religious meaning opened up by Luther's reference to biblical scripture had to be negated or domesticated for the purpose of mere internalization. In order to protect the social system, a stricter control of the word was essential.

## III

The author of the song was a Nördlingen citizen and weaver, Contz Anahans. His song is the only one that allows us to trace its origin and development with relative accuracy as well as identifying the audience to whom it was directed.[6] The social context can be identified as an imperial city, subject only to the emperor and represented by delegates from the city council to the Imperial Diet. Thus Anton Forner represented the city in 1524 at the Diet of Nuremberg, whereas in 1526 Jakob Wiedenmann, in his function as mayor, was present at the Diet of Speyer. Forner and Wiedenmann were both respectable and wealthy members of the city's oligarchy, which was influential in the city council. The council decided matters of policy, enacted laws, and exercised a judiciary function. The councillors, including representatives of the guilds, defined the rules of behavior on both the social and economic fronts. It was within their power to decide appeals, and they determined matters to be officially negotiated

[5]Arthur E. Imhof argues this point in *Die verlorenen Welten* (Munich, 1984).
[6]Bräuer, *Die zeitgenössischen Lieder*, p. 3.

with citizens. Closer to social and economic interest were the guilds, which incorporated the artisans. The guilds aligned their own interests with the general good of the city. The citizens had the opportunity to communicate, but by no means in an uncontrolled fashion, in the streets and taverns and in their houses. Verbal communication among them constituted a network to which ecclesiastical rites and sermons imparted a religious meaning.

Nördlingen was of medium importance in the context of South German imperial cities. When matters of great importance arose, the city council consulted with legal expertise and the councils of either Nuremberg or Augsburg. Although Nördlingen employed a learned scribe, Georg Mair, the council turned to outsiders for legal expertise, such as the famous Augsburg lawyer Conrad Peutinger.

Nördlingen had not remained untouched by what we now globally term the Reformation. The prior of the Carmelite monastery, Caspar Kantz, had married in 1523 and had had to leave the town as a result, whereas Billican, the civic preacher appointed in 1522, had married in 1524 and had met with no objection. More effective was the action of the citizens who withheld offerings in support of the priests. If this rising anti-clericalism can be taken as indicating the progress of the Reformation, Nördlingen was well on the way to changing beliefs. A more cautious assessment would describe rising disloyalty to the established church. Some citizens clearly demonstrated their understanding of change in religion by rejecting the church's fasting requirements and by removing sacred images. The council endeavored to halt this activity by an ordinance of 1524. It then became clear that the magistrate was no longer able to control the enforcement of authority. The crisis of religion thus fostered a crisis of authority.

Public opinion was not confined to issues of religion, such as defying the clergy and the church, nor was it confined to citizens. Nördlingen was a market town serving a considerable region. There are references in the sources to a bookseller who caused a disturbance at a fair in 1524 and left behind "several unbound German and Latin booklets, letters of indulgence and other minor things."[7] Inventories show that the citizens tended to have rosaries, crucifixes, and paternosters as well as Marian images, but few books. The Franciscans had no library, although their convent had twenty-eight books, large and small, as recorded in 1526.[8] The convent was clearly no stronghold of the new faith. The implication is that, al-

---

[7]"Allerlaylay [*sic*] vneinbundne teutsche vnd lateinische biechlach, lass zettel vnd anders vnachtpers ding" (Nördlingen Stadtarchiv [hereinafter cited as NöStA], Inventurbücher 1524–26, fol. 335.
[8]Ibid., 1526, fol. 90v–92.

though mass communication in print may have swept the larger cities,[9] such as nearby Augsburg, it should not be overestimated here. There was no printer in Nördlingen before 1538, when the first press was installed.[10] A venture by Simprecht Froschauer, son of John Froschauer of Augsburg, had failed in 1524. Public opinion in Nördlingen was predominantly formed through oral communication and was parochial in nature, either from individual to individual or within clearly defined groups. This facilitated the spread of sermons' content and, of course, the spread of our song.

It should be stressed that the particular situation in 1525 was influenced by a gathering of peasants who had established a camp in Deiningen, a village just east of the town.[11] This event took place in March 1525 and may be said to have been instrumental, at least as far as timing is concerned, in sparking the revolt in the city in April. It only served to highlight tensions in a time of a crisis of authority. The tension was heightened by the discovery that Forner, as a member of the council, had a private interest in an inheritance dispute that was pending before the council. This conflict of interest resulted in Forner's arrest and the bringing of a suit against him, which was headed by the city scribe, Georg Mair, representing civic law and order. Although this matter had absolutely nothing to do with religion, Forner was reputed to be the most influential supporter of the Lutheran cause. More important, he commanded a web of patronage comprising not only those who controlled wealth and influence but also the weavers. The weavers, already roused by the Gospel message, found common ground with the poorer elements in the city whose friends and relatives were among the peasantry encamped outside. The eruption of hitherto latent tensions was triggered by a letter that Georg Mair had sent to Ulm, the capital of the Swabian League, which had been intercepted by the peasants.[12] The letter, which informed the League that the peasant forces at Deiningen were neither well organized nor well equipped, expressed surprise at the delay in taking action against them. The Deiningen peasants interpreted this letter as an invitation to the league to slaughter them. Then, on the night of 3 April, rumor spread within the city that the gates had been left open to enable the knights of the League to enter the city and suppress the common man.

---

[9]Hans-Joachim Köhler, ed., *Flugschriften als Massenmedium der Reformationszeit* (Stuttgart, 1981).

[10]NöStA Handwerksakten, Buchdrucker, fols. 6–7, 12r–13v, 57r.

[11]For a short narrative account, see Günther Franz, *Der Deutsche Bauernkrieg,* 10th ed. (Darmstadt, 1975), pp. 212–16.

[12]There is a copy in the Bayerisches Hauptstaatsarchiv Munich, Reichsstadt Nördlingen Akten 992, no. 18.

Some citizens awakened the town and called for a meeting. A committee formed the same night was given the task of obtaining Mair's letter. Some citizens who had assembled at Forner's house were heard to shout that the lords (the councillors) should be stabbed. Because Forner remained loyal to the established authority and another mayor had the presence of mind to show the crowds that the gates were actually closed, it was possible to calm the people.

The following day at an assembly of the citizens, the peasants' sympathizers asked the citizens to support the Gospel and the peasants. The majority of the citizens, however, proved loyal to the civic authority. The council also achieved appeasement by expanding the membership of the larger council, sending Mair to prison, and securing Forner's release. The latter seems to have been a central figure until late May by effectively playing his role in keeping peasants and citizens apart. By the beginning of May, the peasants' cause was already clearly lost, and Forner escaped on horseback before the arrival of the troops of the Swabian League. Law and order remained a paramount concern: in September the larger council was purged, and from January 1526 onward the rebel citizens were systematically arrested and subjected to council investigation or torture or both. In March, Fend, the innkeeper, was publicly executed. A satisfied Georg Mair could state in April 1526 that there had been sufficient terror to stem the unrest. In early 1526 the council ordered an investigation of the song and its author.


### IV

The following version of the song is authenticated by a note stating that Anahans himself had handed it over to the council. This is the song of Contz Anahans:

| Das Lied | The Song |
|---|---|
| (1) Ain geyr ist aüß geflogen | A vulture[13] has soared on high |
| Im hegeu am schwartz wald | Over the Hegau[14] near the Black Forest |
| er hat vil Jüngen auß Zogen | And has raised a brood of offspring |
| die baurñ allent halb | The peasants everywhere |
| sy Send auff Rierig worden | They have become rebellious |
| In teyscher nacian | In the German nation |

[13]The bird of prey symbolizes those who harm the people, especially avaricious usurers and feudal lords.

[14]The Hegau in the southwestern part of the Black Forest was one of the earliest centers of the peasants' uprising of 1524–25.

vnd hand ain psünder orden
voleycht wirtz In wol gun.

And made an organization[15] of their own
Perhaps they will succeed.

(2) Was mach Sein Ir begern
der frumen bider leytt
es scheint ain warhaft stern
es ist erst warn Zeyt
es gschick mit gotes wilen
ist vnßer sunden schuld
er kans vnd wirtz wol stilen
got geb vnß gnad vnd huld.

What is it that they want
These good and honorable folk
A true guiding star now shines
Showing that now is the time
It all happens with God's will
And because of our own sins
He can and may suppress it
God give us grace and favor.

(3) Jetz Red ich von den baurn
vnd Irem rögen ment
mencher haist Sy laüren
vnd waist noch nit das end
Es denß schinder vnd schaber
die treybñ über mutt
merckt auf Ir wůcherß knaben
es dut In leng kain gůt.

I speak now of the peasants
And of their government
Though some call them rogues
And know not how it will end
Saying, it's all renderers and butchers
Who act so arrogant
Look sharp, you usurers
You'll get it in the end.

(4) nemant důt sich mer schemen
er Sey Jung oder alt
all bößhait den Zu nemen
In mancherlay gestalt
důt durch ain nander laufen
man weng der warhait acht
Hofart geytz vnd vir kaufen
ist In der welt der bracht.

Nowadays no one feels any shame
Be he young or old
All wickedness can flourish
Of every possible kind
The folk run to and fro
And have little need of truth
While arrogance, greed, and hoarding
Become the world's own pomp.

(5) Zů trincken vnd gots schwören
hat gnamē über hand
man kan schier nimen wörñ
es ist vur war ain schand
nemand vmß ander gebñ
man Sag gleych was man wel
In aller vnZucht leben
macht ictz das vn gefel.

Now swilling and bad swearing
Have got the upper hand
There's little help against it
Which is a dirty shame
No one deals squarely
And all say what they please
This living in such disorder
Is the cause of all our woes.

(6) der bund der hat geratten
ictz her ain lange Zeyt
es wil nit wol geratten

The League[16] has been consulting
For quite a long, long time
But it will come to nothing

[15]*Orden* probably combines two meanings: a corporative meaning, as in the name "Teutonic Order," and the Latin *ordo*, a social group necessary to maintain the world order.
[16]The reference is to the Swabian League, whose army defeated the peasants.

das loch ist worden weyt
wer mach das ictz Zu flicken
das kan ich nit verstun
die Sach wil sich nit schicken
es wirt noch ÿbel gun.

For the rift has grown so large
And who can mend it now
I really don't understand it
Things will not get in order
But will get worse and worse.

(7) Herschaft die den Sy schröckñ
das Sy kam waiß wa naüß
die baurn den auf wocken
vnd nemanß nach der bauß
es Send mir Selczsam künden
Sy wagen dir Ir haut
Sy hand ain sin erfunden
wer het In das zu draut.

Their lordships are so frightened
They don't know what to do
The peasants get them well awake
And see quite well what to do
This is all strange news to me
They risk their own skins
They've got a reason on their side
Who would have thought they had.

(8) baurn Send ainig warden
vnd kriegen mit gewalt
Sy hand ain geroßn orden
vnd send auf manig gfalt
vnd dent die schlöißer ereyßen
vnd breñe klester auß
So kan man vnß nit pseyßen
was sol ain böß Rab hauß.

The peasants have united
And now make war with might
They have made a mighty army
And revolt in many ways
They tear down the castles
Burn monasteries to the ground
Thus we can't be cheated
In such a den of thieves.

(9) Ietz wil ichs laußen bleybñ
got In der ewigkait
mir dent vil müt wil treybñ
vur war es ist Im laid
das mir So übel leben
In disem Jamer dal
wer kan ietz ain frid gebñ
wen Sein gettliche wal.

Now I will commend it
To God in all eternity
We've done a lot of mischief
And done him very wrong
When we live so wickedly
In this vale of tears
Who can grant us peace
Except his godly will.

(B10)[17] Sy seind In feld geZogen
Ir kainr wolt laßñ ab
ist war vnd nit clogen
vil mancher baurn knab
Sy hand Zamen geschworen
dem adel laid Zu ton
Sy hand In fast geschoren
was mag In werden Zlon.

They have set out for war
And none wanted to stay behind
This is true, I do not lie
Many a peasant's son
They took on oath among them
To do the nobles much harm
They nearly sheared them clean
What will they get out of it.

[17]B 10 replaced in version *a* the sixth verse and in *d* the seventh verse; see my edition, cited in n. 1.

It is possible to interpret the text in various ways. One way involves focusing on the symbols in the text and placing them in their frame of reference. Clearly the song sympathizes with the rising peasants while calling them rebellious. The rebels are praised as good and honorable people. Anahans wishes them well in their fight against evildoers, who are characterized by arrogance, pomp, and usury. It is implied that, unlike their opponents, they are fighting for the common good. That the rising is of more than regional significance is acknowledged in the phrase "In the German nation," and symbolized by the contrast of a vulture and the star of truth. This symbolism embodies the age of renewal, representing the peasants' rising as being in accordance with God's will. Then there is ambivalence, however, because the author includes his community and himself among the sinners: we have done wrong, and God is now punishing us. The peasants are mentioned as a third party. Ultimately God alone can grant peace; it is not to be achieved by a rebellion. The author here indicates his distance from, as well as sympathy with, the peasants and their cause.

The distance is that of a citizen who shares the sins of the peasants' opponents, sins that stand in opposition to the common good. The moral tone of the fourth verse, as the marginal note indicates, was heightened by the case of Anton Forner. The fourth and fifth verses add traditional civic morality to the song, which is in keeping with civic regulations to promote fair trade. Here we find the religious dimension interpreted in social terms, although strangely there is no reference to Reformation gospel. The traditional tone suggests that this is an interpretation of the period of renewal in accordance with the Gospel. It may be noted that there is no specific reference to Lutheran teaching, nor are there references to justification by faith, the priesthood of all believers, or biblicism.

Another interpretation of the song might be that, according to one version, the last two lines were sung in chorus. We may infer that those who heard the text identified with it. The last two lines emphasize identification with the peasants and distance from their antagonists. This identification is reinforced in the alternative two lines of verse 8, which expresses gratitude to the laudable peasants and commends them for their bravery.


V


Although the song was clearly intended to generate sympathy for the peasants, it was not a song of revolt as such because it did not aim at a revolt in the city and included no personal slander although, as the city scribe noted, it contained verses and statements that opposed the Swabian League and certain people in Nördlingen. Thus we must trace the process of communication that manifests itself in the progress of the song. It is possible to establish the circumstances in which the song was first communicated. It was sung at Balthasar Fend's inn; Fend was one of the leaders of the revolt on the night of the uprising. Later in April 1525, Anton Forner asked Anahans to sing it in his house. We may speculate that Forner heightened the contents of verses 4 and 5. A third singing occurred yet again in an inn. The song was therefore communicated in public at the nodal points of oral communication, and it obviously remained within the urban network of communication, because there is no indication of its being spread elsewhere. By May the song was so well known that even the drunkard Hans Trumer could render it. He claimed to have heard it in Spangenberg's inn, where fifty citizens had been present, including the master of the weavers' guild, Hans Husel. Hans Trumer had been a student at Heidelberg, and he later worked in his father's shop as a weaver. In his drunken state he had roamed about the town, declaring that the common man would now be lord. He wished to involve the town's preacher, Billican, in a disputation to support his claim. When Billican did not appear, Trumer turned to his companion, Hans Mock, and said, "Methinks the preacher takes his wife and he rightly does so as King Solomon had 400 concubines and King David killed Uriah and then slept with his wife." This was a strange biblicism, apart from being incorrect. It was apparently intended to justify Billican's breach of celibacy.[18] This mixture of Reformation propaganda and artisan status can be seen in Anahans himself. He was a poor weaver and had himself been charged with failure to comply with the fasting regulations. In the process of communication, the text was expanded or contracted in accordance with the given circumstances or situation. The surviving versions show that the core had been impressed on people's minds but that certain lines or phrases had been altered. So in verse 7 instead of "This is all strange news to me," another version ran, "The peasants have been exploited and picked to the bone." In the sixth verse, the less reprehensible line "Things will not get in order" was replaced by words expressing the hope that the League would be destroyed by its unsolved problems of usury and

---

[18]I Kings 11:3: "And he [i.e., Solomon] had seven hundred wives, princesses, and three hundred concubines; and his wives turned away his heart." Another witness stated that Trumer referred to the preacher "and his Madonna." See NöStA Bauernkriegsakten V, "Zeugen Hansen Trumeris." See also Rolf Häfele, "Die Studenten der Städte Nördlingen, Kitzingen, Mindelheim, and Wunsiedel bis 1580: Studium, Berufe und soziale Herkunft" (D. Phil. diss., History Faculty, Tübingen University, 1986), p. 341: Trumer (no. 133, matriculated in Heidelberg on May 5, 1513).

moral disorder. Again, in verse 9 a more pious version that God may preserve body and soul had been replaced by the religiopolitical wish that he grant peace.

In this process of communication, the song could be made to stress opposition or could be made more acceptable by moralizing and adding a pious note. The text went through a process of "negotiation" and was not simply reproduced as an integral version. The recipients did not remain passive; the text and its variations resulted from a process of social action.

## VI

How is the song to be related to a social context and public opinion? The antagonists of the peasants are defined as those of the artisans as well. Usurers had been cited in written grievances that the Nördlingen guild of fine-cloth weavers had submitted to the city council.[19] From 1499 onward there were frequent complaints about increased competition from neighboring cities as well as about preemption of goods. In this context the grievances named members of the Nördlingen oligarchy—Nicholas Vesner, in 1525 a delegate to the Swabian League at Ulm, or Hans Husel and his brother-in-law, Sixt Sprentz. Usury threatened a basic norm providing that the work of one's hands should be sufficient to supply the individual with his basic needs. Similarly, avarice was not just an unacceptable character trait but was contrary to the concept of the commonweal. It constituted a violation of basic norms. Thus it was possible to cite lords and monks alike as thieves, as the eighth verse of the song demonstrates.

The last list of grievances had been presented by the weavers in 1524. It was a summary of specific complaints that extended into an evaluation of the state of the world. The world, it said, has become so hostile, greedy, and full of avarice that people do not hestiate to destroy their neighbors. The poor man is unreasonably burdened because of people who are not content with their own income and possessions and have no regard for the well-being of others. Anahans's song thus expressed the fears as well as the needs of the poor common folk. Here is the social root of the Nördlingen revolt, as an analysis of its participants confirms.[20] The weavers paid an average tax of one guilder per annum, and they represented 45 percent of the insurgents. Anahans himself belonged to this group, a poor weaver who nonetheless proved traditional in his religious beliefs, as seen

---

[19]NöStA Zunftakten, Geschlachtwander I, 1540.

[20]I thank Ingrid Batori for the figures; for details, see my *Eine bürgerliche Reformation*, pp. 123–24.

in his reflection that God punishes social sins by evil, hunger, disease, and death or, as in this instance, by disorder. The appropriate course is to commend oneself unto God, to improve one's life, and to expect guidance from the authorities. The Old Testament God prevails here; there is no hint of Lutheranism.

Anahans was not punished, as indeed his role in the revolt had been only a minor one. Balthasar Fend had played the most prominent part. In his inn the committee had been founded and the demand had first been raised to execute Georg Mair and to rally the citizens in support of the peasants' cause. His inn was frequented by many weavers who, after coming into contact with the peasants, reported having told them, "Dear brethren, you should be evangelic and brave and refuse clergy and monks their dues."[21] Fend, like Forner, had escaped from the city, and was arrested in January upon his return. Subjected to torture on two consecutive days, he denied the charge that he had promised to hand over the city's cannons to the peasants. Under torture he admitted having said to the peasants, "Brethren, we will soon be with you." This statement must refer to his having been sent to get Mair's letter. Fend stated that other citizens in his company had entered into treaties with the peasants, and he ultimately admitted to having been a party to such treaties. This involvement he endeavored to excuse by stating that the ultimate goal of his revolt had been to punish the clergy, expel the lords, and unite town and country to establish and protect the Gospel. Fend had thus become the spokesman of the party within the city that aimed at a coalition of peasants and citizens. Whether they aimed at ecclesiastical or secular authority or merely objected to the power of wealth cannot be determined. Yet we can see what meaning the Gospel takes on in this context, when its contents are transformed into social terms.

The council ordered Fend's execution only when the Swabian League demanded that it do so "as an example to others." Georg Husel's wife, who questioned whether the execution conformed with the content of the Gospel, was arrested, and charges were brought against her. The charges illuminate popular feeling. The accused maintained that, before the citizens took up arms against the peasants, it would be advisable to remove incompetent individuals from positions of authority within the town. Without protest, there would be no change. She was also of the opinion that her husband and she were both as entitled to control the city's defense system as any councillor. She even admitted having said that, if the men were unwilling to turn the cannons over to the peasants, then the women would do so. She added, however, that much had been said in the heat of

21NöStA Bauernkriegsakten III, IV, for this and following quotations.

the moment. Nevertheless, she reaffirmed her distrust of the council. It was essential to help good Christians (that is, to help the peasants) by providing them with the cannons. In the whole council, she said, there was not one good Christian, nor were the councillors willing to tolerate such a man in their circle, clearly a reference to Anton Forner. The popular pattern linked to the basic rights of the citizens thus disclaimed the Christian authority of the council and increased sympathy for the cause of the peasants as good Christians.

The social meaning of what Husel's wife called Christian was by no means shared by all the women living in Nördlingen. Anna Strauss had opened her shutters after the night of the revolt. "After the sun had risen, and when she realized that the gates were still closed in broad daylight she sent her maid to find out [the reason why]." When she learned that a revolt had taken place, she remarked: "If this were true as they say, one would hardly feel safe at night in one's bed." She was exiled for repeating this rumor, showing that her sense of self-protection and security were not considered to reflect obedience.

Hans Trumer tried the same excuse. If he had not been awakened by his mother, he said, he "would have slept through the whole affair." When tortured he admitted that he had indeed shouted to Mair that he might be scribe today but not tomorrow and that he had called to another councillor that he had been in the council too long and that tonight he would resign. He admitted recommending that certain individual councillors should be removed from power, but he stressed that he had not wished to undermine authority as such. Trumer's drunkenness was not accepted as a mitigating circumstance. The city scribe noted wryly: "Drunk men and fools like to tell the truth." Trumer's apprentice called people of influence by nicknames during the revolt, including Nicholas Vesner, whom he called "Batzenmann," which implied a charge of usury. Trumer admitted that this apprentice had to be reprimanded often for his impudence.

The case of another weaver, Hans Han, arrested in March 1526, reveals different aspects of civic roles. In April 1525 he had been elected to the enlarged council. Charges were brought against him for disclosing the contents of council consultations as well as conspiracy. He claimed that he had been forced to disclosure for his own security. The charges thus leveled against him were of a serious nature, involving a breach of his citizen's oath. It is clear that Han represented the political consciousness of the *menu peuple* (middling sort). The city and its autonomy, however, remained the central issue. Han was exiled from the city for life.

It is possible to reconstruct Anton Forner's role on the basis of information already presented. Most striking was his behavior following his release. Challenged by the crowd that had gathered before his house on the night of the revolt, he responded that, without permission from the mayor, he could not become involved. Because this assertion was unacceptable to the crowd, he found himself in a dilemma. His official position demanded allegiance to the authorities, but his popularity demanded that he conform to the expectations of the people. Confronted with this decision, he wept.

In analyzing attitudes and reactions during the revolt, we view individuals not only biographically but above all in their social contexts. In examining their roles, we try to establish their social identities. The process of revolt brought with it a distancing of individual roles as prescribed by authority, roles that cannot be cited as stereotypes. Roles proceeded along an axis, a continuum that comprised their positions as previously defined but developed according to situational demands and latent patterns. One pattern refers to a tradition that understood communal life as the creation of citizens. Another sees little distance between the urban and rural populations. The country folk were neighbors and were addressed as dear brethren. Brotherly love was a social relation that was sanctified by religion and that may have been reinforced by preaching. These patterns interfered with each other and constituted concepts for action.

Balthasar Fend accepted a role as the spokesman of a revolt, just as, in his accustomed position as an innkeeper, he communicated news. Trumer's state of drunkenness caused him to break the imposed silence. His description of councillors as the lords in high places reflected a belief that the common man was fundamental to the commune, not the authority. In revealing antagonisms against the authorities, the citizens were responding to a situation of potential change, which they transformed into a revolt.

Others remained within their roles in accordance with their oath of obedience. This compliance, together with the council's flexible response, facilitated the abandonment of the revolt. The council raised the level of participation and removed one source of grievance by relieving the taxes on wine and beer. In June 1525 external factors had turned from destabilizing to stabilizing elements within the civic system. In September a further step toward pacification was possible: the enlarged council was reduced to its normal size. The following spring the council proceeded to intimidate those who had been involved in the uprising.

Individual citizens became less conspicuous and assumed their accustomed roles. An analysis that proceeds in terms of social roles can break down integral concepts such as "community" and "the city as a corporate unity." These concepts acted as a framework and could function in a normative sense, but they did not produce or fully incorporate social interaction. Nor is it useful to analyze events in social systems by simply asking how ideas or economic interests were guiding motives. We must enter the complex world of the human being, its complexity reflecting the interchange of social roles, patterns of political and religious tradition, economic interests, political and social concerns, religious beliefs and devotion, and popular as well as official religion. The web of communication and interaction thus determined the urban social system.

## VII

The variety of ways in which political and religious traditions could be coupled is manifested in the addresses of the Nördlingen council to the citizens in 1525.[22] From the end of March to the beginning of May, or even as late as September 1525, appeals to the citizenry varied. In April an appeal to autonomy, unity, and tradition, together with an emphasis on the "city" that was created by the peaceful unity of all the citizens as good and honorable lovers of their fatherland, failed to restrain the revolt or stem the tide of sympathy for the peasants. A second address manifested a distinct religious strain. The council stressed that God granted peace and unity, just as every good thing was granted by him. His grace and Holy Spirit appear to be indispensable to attain that which is good and profitable. Godly values were to be ranked above temporal ones. In order to make the consent based on religion effective, the civic preacher Billican was required to deliver sermons that were to be attended by the councillors; he was instructed to stress the notion of brotherly love and peaceful concord. Here the Gospel was defined as a proclamation of civic unity, delimiting an alternative concept of brotherly love, which included the peasants as "dear brethren." In keeping with the civic tradition of autonomy, the Gospel as the pure word of God was directed toward political aims. Religion was therefore to be deprived of its ambiguity, which had fostered the revolt. This second address neglected to stress the superiority of the council and instead aimed to make the people feel that community kept the city intact, a ploy that was designed to separate the citizens from the peasants.

One month later, however, at the beginning of May, the religious keynote was replaced by a stress on the individual character of the imperial city and its privileged position, its liberty. It was the duty common to all citizens and was in line with the tradition they had received from their forefathers to foster the common good. The council referred explicitly to the emperor, but the League was meant, with the emperor as its head. Any

---

[22]For full references, see my *Eine bürgerliche Reformation*, pp. 44–51, and my "Political and Social Norms."

damage to the city was to be prevented, in accordance with the citizen's oath. Thus everyone was to abstain from collaborating with the peasants. By the end of September, when it was clear that order had been firmly reestablished, the smaller council again assumed its dominant role.

In 1526 the council invoked the League as the authority above the city's autonomy. In order to demonstrate this authority, there was recourse to exemplary punishment; Fend was decapitated, and other opponents were imprisoned. The revolt forced the lords to appeal to variable norms to integrate the community and in this way to produce consent. That appeals were varied suggests that the councillors were aware of rival patterns of political legitimacy; it also suggests the necessity of retaining control of the word in order to retain authority. In times of revolt, with authority endangered, the council almost desperately attempted to recover the power of communication. The flexibility of the communicated word responded to the complexity of the various patterns. As the lords interfered in social action, they carefully varied basic norms as they appealed to civic unity, ancestral autonomy, and brotherly love.


## VIII

In the spring of 1526, then, torture simply served again as a way of eliciting consent. Apart from extorting confessions and denunciations, it aimed to reaffirm subjection to the authority of the council. Because the notes of the city scribe during investigation and torture are most precise, it suffices here merely to quote from them:[23]

So then as he would not do otherwise (i.e., confess), he was drawn up (on ropes) and allowed to hang there some time. (He) behaved badly (i.e., he cried and lamented), asked for water and to be allowed to die. So then after a long time when the sweat had run dry he was let down and allowed to rest. Once again he was drawn up, left hanging so long that sweat and excrement poured from his body. He (said) he neither knew anything nor did confess (to anything). He said that they (i.e., the council) do injustice to him and that one should support justice. He wished to die this minute and they should rather decapitate him. When he had however been hanging for a good while the lords went away and left him hanging. Later they went down to him and told him that they would allow him to rest. (They added) that they would have to return on the next day or the day after as they knew and had information and well founded knowledge in this matter.

[23]NöStA Bauernkriegsakten IV; Michel Foucault, *Discipline and Punish: The Birth of the Prison* (New York, 1979).

Georg Husel asked the lords to refrain from tearing off his limbs, as "they had heard everything from him (which he could tell them)." "As he would not do otherwise [i.e., confess], he was drawn up again." Similarly, Hans Trumer was then drawn up on ropes. "[He said] that he rather wanted to die. He had said nothing nor shouted to the city scribe nor to Althaimer [a councillor]. Why should he have his limbs torn apart if he had done all this. [He] asked the honorable council that they should decapitate him and relieve him of this torture." Another example of this phase of torture is given by the account of Balthasar Fend, the innkeeper and glassmaker. The glazier pleaded that "for God's sake an honorable council should not make a total cripple of him. He had confessed everything he knew in fullest truth [and] he could say no more than he knew."

The next day led to subjection, as in Fend's case. "[He] asked for the sake of God and the last judgement as before that they should be satisfied with what he had said previously. [It should also] be considered that even Christ had had false witnesses brought against him. They should take this torture and imprisonment as punishment and graciously let him be released in consideration of his youth, his wife and children." Finally, he pleaded that "after all this, an honorable council, for the sake of the last judgement should be gracious and grant him pardon, for what he had done he had not fully understood, the almighty God should be his witness, and he wished to remain loyal to the honorable council until eternity." A certain Balthasar Boschge asked the council to relieve him from his torture, promising to do everything the council would ask of him for the rest of his life. Hans Trumer was even more explicit. "He not only wanted to hold the honorable council as lords but as a father and behave forever so that they would have no complaint against him. And other lamenting, submissive and pitiful words and offers [of compliance]."

Terror was an accepted method of producing subjection and restoring lawful authority. Ultimately the threat of terror was effective with every citizen who resorted to opposition. Terror was therefore used to subject citizens who dared to act according to self-defined patterns. Appeals, as well as physical force, were used to define civic roles in accordance with the particular definition of the council in power. We have therefore to admit that a concept of the city that focuses on concord and harmony demonstrated by consent and instituted by a civic oath, is of limited value as a key to unlock the problem. We must adopt a view of the sixteenth-century German city that allows for a greater degree of structural complexity. We may claim that the will to command power by established political techniques was ultimately based on the city's exposure to catastrophes, such as fire, hunger, pestilence, or external enemies, whether prince or peasant. As a result internal tensions were all the more dangerous. Powerful states had been ruined by disunity and small republics preserved by concord, as citizens and humanists observed repeatedly.[24]

It may be a well-accepted fact that the Reformation was an urban event. It remains, however, for us to determine what we really mean when we call the Reformation an urban event. As we come to realize how complex life in the cities was, we have still more to learn about the Reformation city as a city, a place where ideas moved through channels of communication and social interaction. We must consider the Reformation as a social movement.[25]

[24]See my "Political and Social Norms."

[25]See my "Reformation and Society," in Manfred Hoffmann, ed., *Martin Luther and the Modern Mind: Freedom, Conscience, Toleration, Rights* (New York, 1985), pp. 237-78.

*Why did the early Evangelical movement enjoy enormous popular support? What was on the minds of common men and women when they defied the authority and symbols of the Catholic church? In his many publications, Robert W. Scribner, lecturer in history and fellow of Clare College, Cambridge, tries to answer these questions. Drawing on the theoretical concerns of literary criticism and social anthropology, Scribner investigates the meaning of collective social and religious actions in Reformation Germany. He has studied pre-Reformation popular rituals, the use of carnival during the Reformation, and the various media that played a part in communicating the Evangelical message. In his pioneering study* For the Sake of Simple Folk: Popular Propaganda for the German Reformation *(1981), Scribner analyzes the iconography of the many woodcut illustrations of the 1520s that were crucial in stirring up support for the Reformation. The problem of historical representation and subjective meaning in the Reformation is again taken up in the following essay, which argues that the attack on the authority of the Catholic church amounted to a popular ritual of desecration. Using a number of illuminating incidents, the article suggests new ways of understanding the complexity and nuances of popular piety and protest actions. It also appears in Scribner's collection of essays,* Popular Culture and Popular Movements in Reformation Germany *(1988). Scribner's other publications include a historiographical essay,* The German Reformation *(1985), and many pioneering articles on the social history of the German Reformation.*

[121]

# [6]

## Ritual and Reformation

ROBERT W. SCRIBNER

### I

On 9 March 1560 the provost von Rottenmann reported to the archbishop of Salzburg that a great scandal had occurred on the recent *Faschingtag,* the eve of Ash Wednesday, in Liezen in the Ennstal in Styria. During Mass the local innkeeper had run into the church dressed in a fool's costume. He took up the holy water vessel, placed it on the altar, and "made his offering in it," perhaps a euphemism for urinating in it. As each person approached to take communion, as was customary that day, he struck them on the buttocks with a whip. A second villager, a peasant also dressed in a fool's costume, rode up and down the church on a hobbyhorse and shouted from the pulpit at the priest: "Pfaff, da iss!" ("Eat, priest!"). The priest scolded until he went away, but during the sermon another peasant pushed his way through the crowd behind the altar and paraded up and down with a great crucifix slung over his shoulder like a pike, as if he were going to war. At the request of the provost, all three culprits were arrested, but we have no further information about the incident—indeed, the original document is now lost.[1] We cannot, therefore, tell whether the three were Protestants, but their irreverent behavior clearly showed that they set little store by the Mass.

This seems no more than a trivial occurrence, a little local scandal of no wider significance. It is striking, however, how often such incidents oc-

[1]Leopold Kretzenbacher, "Zur Frühgeschichte der Masken in der Steiermark," *Zeitschrift des historischen Vereins für Steiermark* 46 (1955):256 and n.66.

[122]

curred during the Evangelical movements in sixteenth-century Germany. Almost four score such events can be documented during the early years of the Reformation, without resort to any systematic collection of data. Almost all of them share the common feature of involving moments of a predominantly *ritual* character. This character was expressed in roughly four ways. First, there were incidents more or less loosely framed by ritual occasions, although we might think that their connection to ritual properly understood is rather tenuous. In Weissenhorn, near Augsburg, in 1524 a number of "godless folk" sang "scurrilous songs" in the streets at Christmas and then tried to disrupt the liturgical singing of Christmas hymns by satirical parodies of them. In Magdeburg in 1524 a number of journeymen upended a reliquary with the remains of St. Florentinus, which had been set out in the cathedral prior to the formal display of the relics in a procession. In Heggbach, near Biberach, on Palm Sunday 1525, a common day for hearing pre-Easter confessions, a number of peasants ran into the church and thrust their swords into the confessional (*bichthus*), in the belief that a confessor was sitting in there.[2]

A second category of incident is close to the first, but I believe it is analytically distinct. There are numerous events involving the disturbance of Catholic cult or liturgy, often taking on the appearance of a kind of antiritual action through their apparent expression of disbelief in the efficacy or relevance of Catholic ceremonies. In Wittenberg on 6 October 1521, for example, the annual preaching round of the Antonine monks was disrupted. Just as the preacher was about to consecrate "St. Anthony's Water," one of several kinds of blessed water revered for its apotropaic qualities, the vessel was overturned and the consecration prevented. In Senden, near Neu-Ulm, on the feast of the Ascension 1527, thirteen men and a boy disrupted the reenactment of the Lord's ascension into heaven, a ceremony that involved pulling a figure of the risen Christ up through a hole in the church roof. In Pirna, in Saxony, at the beginnings of the 1520s, the elevation of the crucifix from the Holy Sepulcher on Easter night was disrupted, as was the subsequent Easter procession through the streets with the "newly risen" crucifix. This latter disruption was effected by several men hung about with sheep and cattle bells, so dishonoring the decorum of the occasion.[3]

---

[2]For Weissenhorn: Nicolaus Thomann, "Weissenhorner Historie"; Heggbach: "Heggbacher Chronik von einer heiligen Nonne geschrieben"; both in Friedrich L. Baumann, ed., *Quellen zur Geschichte des Bauernkriegs in Oberschwaben* (Tübingen, 1876), pp. 61, 290, respectively; for Magdeburg: Friedrich Hulsse, "Die Einführung der Reformation in der Stadt Magdeburg," *Geschichtsblätter für Stadt und Land Magdeburg* 18 (1883):265.

[3]For Wittenberg: Felicien Gess, *Akten und Briefe zur Kirchenpolitik Herzog Georgs von Sachsen*, vol. I (Leipzig, 1905), p. 207 n.1; Senden: Thomann, "Weissenhorner Historie," p.

Third, some of these events seem to create, or attempt to create, a counterliturgy, although it was essentially negative in intent, more a parodied liturgy. Thus there were mock processions in Senftenberg in Saxony in 1524, in Radkersberg in Styria in 1528, and in Hildesheim in 1543. There was a mock administration of the last rites to a playacting sick man in Münster in 1534 and mock mounted processions in Augsburg in 1527 and 1529. In Buchholz in Saxony there was a parody of the elevation of the relics of a saint in 1524, and the same year there was a mock eucharistic procession in Ulm. In the priory of Oberried in 1525, a peasant celebrated a parody of the Mass during which he "sang Mass," elevated the host (which had been in a monstrance that he had just smashed), and forced his companions to ring the Sanctus bells.[4]

The fourth category of event involves iconoclasm within a ritual framework. The fact that acts of iconoclasm often occurred within a ritual context imparted a quite different meaning to them from mere vandalism or thoughtless destruction. To take an obvious example, the most common form of iconoclasm, the damaging of retable altarpieces, was clearly not unrelated to the central role they played in the Mass. On a given saint's day, if Mass was not said at his or her altar, a procession would be held to this altar during the Mass, and it would be solemnly blessed with water and incense. Images were also carried in solemn processions, and in Senftenberg in Albertine Saxony we find just such an occasion provoking an act of iconoclasm in February 1523. The images (*Tafeln*) that the clergy usually carried in procession, and the carrier on which they were borne, were defiled, an indulgence bull (apparently also carried in the procession) was removed, and a skull was put in its place. Meanwhile, outside on the churchyard a mock procession was held with a straw man on a bier.[5] The significance of the defilement, presumably a smearing with filth (the German word is *verunreyniget*), emerges from the date of the report (3 February), indicating that the reported events most probably took place on 2 February, the feast of the Purification of the Virgin. That is, a feast of purification was made impure. This example shows how

143; Pirna: Rudolf Hofman, "Reformationsgeschichte der Stadt Pirna," *Beiträge zur sächsische Kirchengeschichte* 8 (1893):46.

[4]For Senftenberg: Gess, *Akten und Briefe,* 1:456; Radkersberg: Kretzenbacher, "Frühgeschichte der Masken," p. 253; Buchholz, Hildesheim, Münster, and Ulm: Bob Scribner, "Reformation, Carnival, and the World Turned Upside Down," *Social History* 3 (1978):306, 308; Augsburg: "Clemens Senders Chronik," *Chroniken der deutschen Städte,* vol. 23 (Leipzig, 1894), pp. 185, 218; Oberried: Stadtarchiv Freiburg im Breisgau, C1, Criminalia 7 (confession of Blesy Krieg, 1527)—I am grateful to Tom Scott for this reference.

[5]Gess, *Akten und Briefe,* 1:456.

complex the ritual connotations of a single act of iconoclasm could be, and I shall discuss later some of its details.

At this stage it may be thought necessary to justify the treatment of some of these events as *ritual* occasions or performances. They sometimes seem more like carnivalesque parody, a matter of play rather than of ritual. The disparity, however, is only superficial, for play (or carnival) and ritual can be seen as complementary and homologous forms of metacommunication. Both are stylized forms of behavior marking out a distinctive "set aside" time and place; both provide symbolic models of social relationships; both break away from the means-ends nexus of the mundane world to provide something valued in and for itself; both provide a form of "transcendence" of the normal world (the one in "make believe," the other in "let us believe"); and both play and ritual may serve to integrate or to subvert the social order by providing symbolic messages about the nature of social reality. When play appears as "counterritual," it stands in close dialectical tension with the ritual it seeks to mock.[6]

It is also necessary to bear in mind that the Evangelical movements in Germany took place within a "ritual culture" fully permeated with various kinds of rites and rituals through which all human life was ordered and maintained. Rituals created orderly relationships with the sacred powers on which the world and human life depended, as well as among humans and between humans and the material world. When any kind of disorder threatened this world, people were able to use various rites and rituals to overcome that disorder.[7] Such rituals included not only the usual "rites of passage" (these were not confined only to the most crucial life stages, but encompassed a variety of other transitions and transformations);[8] there was also a cycle of seasonal rituals, and what we might call "occasional rituals," rituals used ad hoc and pragmatically, the so-called Sacramentals. It is customary to see the seven Sacraments as a distillation of this ritualistic mentality, although the Sacramentals were probably used much more frequently than the Sacraments.[9] In either case, we can rightly label

[6]Don Handelman, "Play and Ritual: Complementary Frames of Meta-Communication," in Antony J. Chapman and Hugh Foot, eds., *It's a Funny Thing, Humour* (Oxford, 1977), pp. 185–92; see also on the role of celebration in ritual: Ronald Grimes, *Beginnings in Ritual Studies* (Washington, D.C., 1982), pp. 47–49.

[7]See Robert W. Scribner, "Cosmic Order and Daily Life: Sacred and Secular in Pre-industrial German Society," in Kaspar von Greyerz, ed., *Religion and Society in Early Modern Europe, 1500–1800* (London, 1984), pp. 17–31.

[8]Arnold van Gennep, *The Rites of Passage* (London, 1977), see esp. chaps. 2 and 9 for the various rites of transition and transformation.

[9]On Sacramentals, see Robert W. Scribner, "Ritual and Popular Religion in Catholic Germany at the Time of the Reformation," *Journal of Ecclesiastical History* 35 (1984):69–71 and the literature cited there.

this ritual mode of thought as "sacramental," although it could just as easily be called "magical." The essence of such rituals was that they made spiritually and physically effective that which they symbolized. Semiologically, the signifier became the signified; iconographically, representation became presence, the *effigies* became a *vero imago*.[10]

Only when we understand these basic ontological assumptions of the age can we understand phenomena such as iconoclasm and the kinds of incident under discussion here. Indeed, this point is so central to the events of the Evangelical movement that we can regard it, for all its antiritualistic elements, as itself a *ritual process*. To elucidate, I want to examine three interesting "incidents" or examples showing this ritual process at work. The first was a public event with broad public participation. The second took place in the public sphere but with a select group of protagonists. The third was more a private matter, acted out among a small group of individuals. Any form of ritual always contains numerous moments or aspects within itself, which are very complexly interwoven, and my examples focus on two such moments, the first and second on the social moment and the third on the moment of sacred power. All three, however, reveal the clash of ontological views involved in the Evangelical movements in sixteenth-century Germany.

## II

The first incident occurred in Magdeburg on Sunday, 15 August 1524, the feast of the Assumption of the Virgin. It was customary on this feast to consecrate in honor of the Virgin various flowers and herbs, which were gathered fresh in the morning dew before being blessed at the first Mass of the day. These blessed herbs had many symbolic and magical connotations, but after being blessed, they were commonly taken away and used for apotropaic purposes: in the house, in barns and stalls, in fields and meadows, as protection against illness in humans and animals, and against bad weather such as hail or storms. In Magdeburg that Sunday the Evangelical preacher preached against the custom, mentioning that the previous year in Jena some youths had taken the herbs and flowers from the church and scattered them in the street outside; if the same were to occur that day, he went on, he would certainly turn a blind eye. Some of the congregation took this as a cue to remove the herbs from the church and to

[10]Grimes, *Beginnings in Ritual Studies.* p. 45; Sally F. Moore and Barbara Myerhoff, "Secular Ritual: Forms and Meanings," in Sally F. Moore and Barbara Myerhoff, eds., *Secular Ritual* (Amsterdam, 1977), pp. 3–24, esp. p. 13; Hans Belting, *Das Bild und sein Publikum im Mittelalter* (Berlin, 1981), esp. pp. 251–63.

scatter them around outside, and the action quickly spread, as the crowd went from church to church, carrying out the herbs and flowers in each and strewing them around on the marketplace. This activity was accompanied with much gleeful dancing, as if it were Carnival. The crowd arrived at the Franciscan church in time to heckle the midday preacher, whom they pelted with stones and eggs. Some in the choir returned their fire, and this aroused the crowd to image breaking. Images were torn from the altars and carried outside. The scene of the action then moved to St. Nicolaus church, the Pauliner church, and the cathedral. In the end all religious services in Magdeburg were suspended.[11]

Attempts to implement the demands of the evangelically minded inhabitants in Magdeburg had been rather stormy well before this incident, but the tumult in the Franciscan church was a decisive leap from militant agitation and rowdiness to public disorder. From the first public appearance of Evangelical opinions at the beginning of May 1524, the conflict over religion had grown with a rising tempo until this decisive point of open public breach of social norms was reached. Each stage of the growing agitation had involved some aspect of public ritual life: baptism. marriage, the Mass, burials.[12] This was an extended struggle over the control and reordering of the town's ritual life. Victor Turner has described such incidents as "social dramas," which proceed through a sequence of conflicts to a moment of crisis, experienced ritually as a moment of catharsis.[13] Such catharsis can be seen in Magdeburg when the preacher designated the blessed herbs and flowers not as holy and healing but as dangerous; he called for their removal "so that they can do no one any more harm." This statement echoed a common Evangelical view of the old rituals, that they were positively harmful. In the removal of the herbs, the change in their ontological status was acted out through a threefold inversion. First, they were not consecrated but dishonored, trodden underfoot. Second, the desecration of the formerly holy was underlined by a profane custom, by a carnival dance, performed in profane space in the market rather than in the sacred space of the church. Third, the preacher chose not to recall a feast of the Virgin in his sermon; instead he abused the pious women who had gathered them as "the old whores, who take so much trouble with the blessed herbs."[14] Thus we see the further inversion of ritual involved: instead of uniting and sanctifying the

[11]Hulsse, *Einführung der Reformation in der Stadt Magdeburg*, p. 309; Sebastian Langhans, "Historia," *Chroniken der deutschen Stadte*, vol. 27 (Leipzig, 1899), pp. 171–72.

[12]Ibid.

[13]See Victor Turner, *Dramas, Fields, and Metaphors* (Ithaca, 1974), chap. 1, and more recently *From Ritual to Theatre: The Human Seriousness of Play* (New York, 1982), pp. 61–88.

[14]Langhans, "Historia," p. 171.

community, the events of the day had produced schism and division—disintegration, not integration.[15]

The second example is just as charged with social and ritual electricity as the first. It took place in 1533 in Augsburg, where the city's religious life had long been disputed between Lutherans, Zwinglians, and orthodox believers. The strongly orthodox Fugger family were the patrons of St. Moritz's church, whereas the churchwarden Marx Ehem, member of another patrician family, was just as fervently Evangelical. On 1 February that year Ehem and his two assistants sought to prohibit celebration of the Mass in St. Mortiz's by locking the sacristy and preventing access to Mass vestments and vessels. The Fuggers countered by supplying at their own expense new vestments, a chalice, altarcloth, candles, and candlesticks. Meanwhile, Ehem had, by having the Holy Sepulcher sealed up, made sure that one popular liturgical event, the ceremony of "laying Christ in the grave" on Good Friday (11 April), would not be performed. Here Ehem sought to disrupt some of the most beloved customs of the popular liturgy, the dramatic depiction of the sacred events known as the *functiones sacrae,* the presentation in dramatic and popular visual forms of the ritual actions occurring on Palm Sunday, Good Friday, Easter, the Ascension, Pentecost, and the Assumption.[16] Similarly, he had spirited away all the things necessary for the Ascension Day ceremony—the flags, incense, vessels, monstrance, and especially the image of Christ seated on a rainbow, accompanied by angels and the Holy Spirit, which was usually drawn up through a hole in the roof to dramatize the ascension of the Lord into heaven. Antonius Fugger, however, secretly had a new figure made, more elaborate than the first, at a cost of twenty gulden. When Ehem heard of this, he went to the church and had the hole through which the figure was usually drawn sealed up with timbers and iron fastenings.

On Ascension Day the Fuggers used a stratagem to enter the church and had the hole reopened. The ceremony took place in its traditional form before a packed church. Meanwhile, when Ehem realized that the hole had been reopened, he went hurriedly to the city mayor, Ulrich Rehlinger, who told him that he should go in haste to St. Moritz's, and if the Ascension had not taken place, he was to command that the figure of the Lord on the rainbow be left on the ground, but if it had already taken place, he was to go home, do nothing, and leave the image hanging in the

[15]It is worth noting here, however, that rituals do not always serve to integrate communities, as is assumed in many recent studies of ritual in early modern Europe; as Charles Zika has recently noted, ritual events such as processions served as frequent occasions of conflict within communities; see his forthcoming article in *Past and Present,* "Hosts, Processions, and Pilgrimages: Controlling the Sacred in Fifteenth Century Germany."

[16]On these ceremonies, see Scribner, "Ritual and Popular Religion," pp. 53–59.

church. Ehem went to the church with a crowd of supporters, to find that he was too late. He roundly abused the sexton for allowing the church to be reopened and gathered his supporters in a threatening circle in the middle of the church, on the spot where the figure had rested before the Ascension. They stood with half-drawn knives, and the Catholic chronicler Clemens Sender commented that if anyone of their opponents had drawn a knife, there would have been a bloody tumult. The congregation was singing nones, but Ehem's supporters scattered the canons and vicars from the choir and many of the congregation, including the Fuggers, fled from the church. Ehem then began to let down the figure from the roof, with the aid of his brother Jeremiah, until it was about twenty feet from the ground, when it was let slip so that it smashed to pieces ᾿ .. ᾿᾿ ᾿ floor. Jeremiah Ehem claimed that the rope had slipped.[17]

The town council regarded the incident as a provocation to disturbance but tried to take a middle course. It allowed Ehem to keep the church closed for three hours, then reopened it for public worship. Antonius Fugger was summoned before them, was lectured sternly on causing disturbance, and was sentenced to a token night in the tower. There was no decisive breach in the community such as that which occurred in Magdeburg, but the fissures that crisscrossed this "social drama" were complex. Apart from the contest between a Catholic champion and a leading Evangelical zealot, this was also a contest between proud patricians, with social face as much at issue as religious belief. There was also a conflict between church patron and elected churchwarden, summed up by Clemens Sender. Sender stated that the Fuggers had far more rights over the church than Ehem, for whereas the latter was elected for only three years, the Fuggers were founders and patrons in perpetuity.[18] For the wider circles of the Augsburgers, however, it was a case where conflict over the new religion was conducted through ritual actions, and the dangers of a wider crisis were inherent in the deep emotionality involved in the incident. Sender described how the "good old Christians" cried from joy and reverence during the Ascension ceremony, whereas the "perverted heretical Christians" cursed and cried out that hellfire should strike in the church. This was no haphazardly chosen curse, for it was a common form of the ceremony that when the Christ figure was pulled through a hole in the roof, there was a tumult up above, representing the battle in the heavens between the risen Christ and the devil, and a devil puppet was hurled from the hole onto the ground below, accompanied by strips of burning paper, to symbolize the devil's being thrust down into

[17]*Chroniken der deutschen Städte*, 23:342.
[18]Ibid., p. 341 (in variant Handschrift b).

hell.[19] These examples show not only that Reformation events were closely interwoven with ritual events but also that social conflicts could very
easily be precipitated from them. In my third example, I shall begin
examining more closely some of the ritual processes involved.


### III


On 25 January 1530 Anna Mentzen of Tomerdingen near Ulm confessed to having taken part in an iconoclastic act during the previous fast
days. With another woman, Anna Breitingerin, she had gone from Jurgen
Keller's house, where a spinning bee (*Gunkelhaus* or *Spinnstube*) was
being held, to the churchyard. There the two women had taken away the
Christ figure from the *Ölberg*, the depiction of Christ suffering in the
garden of Gethsemane that was commonly set up in churchyards, which
formed a focal point both for popular devotion and for the Passion Week
liturgy. The figure was taken to Claus Keller's house, where another
spinning bee was in progress, and it was placed on a table set before the
door. Then Ulrich Keller, Marx Nibling, and Hans Mair came up and
spoke to it. When it would not answer them, Ulrich Keller drew his sword
and cut off its hand. Then Hans Mair took the figure off to his spinning
bee, where it was again set upon a table and addressed: "If you are Paul
[*sic!*], help yourself!" It was then knocked from the table while some
song was sung, the nature of which Anna Mentzen did not recall. Someone next took the image and threw it from the window, and afterward
Anna Breitingerin and another woman returned it to its place in the
Ölberg.[20]
To appreciate the full ritualistic dimensions of this incident, we need to
recall the liturgical connections of the Ölberg. It was customary during the
Passion Week and Easter liturgy to "lay Christ in the grave" on Good
Friday, usually by laying a crucifix in a specially prepared "Holy
Sepulcher," from which it was then "resurrected" on Easter morning.
Frequently the ritual was accomplished using a figure with movable arms,
which was taken down from the cross and laid in realistic fashion in the
grave. Sometimes the consecrated Host was laid in the grave, usually in a
monstrance.[21] I have already mentioned above the disruption of this ceremony that occurred in Pirna at the beginning of the 1520s. A similar

[19]For this ceremony, see Scribner, "Ritual and Popular Religion," p. 57.
[20]Stadtarchiv Ulm, A5327.
[21]On the Ölberg, see *Lexikon der christlichen Ikonographie*, ed. Engelbert Kirschbaum, vol.
3 (Freiburg im Breisgau, 1971), cols. 342–48; for references to crucifixes with movable arms I
am grateful to Peter Jezler, Zürich, who has collected numerous examples of the usage.

incident took place in Ammern, near Mühlhausen in Thuringia on Easter night 1524: as the priest elevated the crucifix from the tomb, a peasant wrenched it violently from his hands and mishandled the celebrant. The eucharistic version of this event was disrupted in Augsburg in 1528. As the priest laid the Sacrament in the Sepulcher in St. Ulrich's church on Good Friday, a man marched up to the tomb, and with the words "Fie on you, Christ, what are you doing in that little fool's house?" bared his buttocks at it.[22]

The Ölberg also had an important role in this liturgy. It was often used as the site for the Holy Sepulcher, and formed a particular focus of devotion. That set up in Ulm in 1517 was very elaborate, with twelve life-sized figures and a tabernacle-sepulchre, and it cost seven thousand gulden. In 1534, after the introduction of the Reformation, the town council learned that a number of people were kneeling before it and lighting candles on Maundy Thursday, and they decided to move it at once, taking away all the figures and leaving only the tabernacle. The Ölberg was sometimes attacked directly during the Evangelical movements: in Augsburg cow's blood was smeared over the crucifix and the other images in the Ölberg there on 13 April 1524, whereas in Pirna in 1527 the Jesus figure was taken from the Ölberg and was "handled derisively."[23]

A further link between iconoclasm and liturgy involves the crucifix. Crucifixes were often mocked, defiled, dismembered, and destroyed during the Reformation. A man spat on the crucifix in Pirna in 1523, for example, and more drastically, a man in Ulm defecated into the mouth of a crucifix that had just been removed from Our Lady's Gate in 1534. The crucifix was derided by being carried around in Carnival processions, as occurred in Nuremberg in 1524 and in Hildesheim, where a travestied figure representing the crucifix was paraded through the streets.[24] Crucifixes were also smashed, dismembered, and decapitated, as occurred in Neuendorf in the district of Wolkenstein in Saxony in 1525, in Augsburg in 1529, in Ulm in May 1531, and in Cologne in 1536.[25] These incidents

[22]For Ammern, Gess, *Akten und Briefe,* vol. 1, p. 747 n.2; for Augsburg, "Clemens Senders Chronik," p. 197.

[23]For the Ulm Ölberg, Hans Rott, *Quellen und Forschungen zur südwestdeutschen und schweizerischen Kunstgeschichte im XV. und XVI. Jahrhundert,* vol. 2: *Alt-Schwaben und die Reichsstädte* (Stuttgart, 1934), p. 75; Stadtarchiv Ulm, Ratsprotokolle 12 (1533–35), fol. 183 (6 April 1534). For Augsburg, "Clemens Senders Chronik," p. 155; Pirna: Hofman, "Reformationsgeschichte der Stadt Pirna," p. 47.

[24]Pirna: Hofman, "Reformationsgeschichte der Stadt Pirna," p. 46; Ulm: Thomann, "Weissenhorner Historie," p. 196; Nuremberg and Hildesheim: Scribner, "Reformation, Carnival," pp. 306, 309.

[25]Wolkenstein: Walter P. Fuchs, ed., *Akten zur Geschichte des Bauernkriegs in*

may have had many overtones besides hostility to image worship. Indeed, Lutheranism largely exempted the crucifix from its desire to remove images from churches, and the crucifix came to symbolize its central doctrine, Christ as the sole mediator of salvation, providing a very striking example of the continuity between the piety of the fifteenth century and the religious reforms of the sixteenth. It has recently been argued that Luther's Christocentric perceptions owed much to the concentration of fifteenth-century piety upon the crucified Christ.[26] Luther's views on this matter were well understood at the time, as he engaged with Carlstadt's more radical views on images. In 1522, as he made a tour of various towns in Saxony, preaching against Carlstadt, he mounted the pulpit in the Thuringian town of Kahla to find strewn around it the pieces of a smashed crucifix, clearly a provocation to his views.[27]

It seems highly likely that many attacks on crucifixes were less a matter of mere rejection of images, and more an attack on the doctrine of the Real Presence, with which the crucifix was closely associated in popular belief and folklore. The crucifix played the same role as the host, for example, in the belief that archers or marksmen could achieve an infallible aim (in another version, invulnerability) by firing a shot into the holy object. This practice is attested as late as 1565 in Protestant Württemberg.[28] In the same way, stories of the bleeding host found a parallel in stories of the bleeding crucifix. The two motifs combined in the officially approved iconographic tradition of the Mass of St. Gregory. This was based on the story that, while St. Gregory the Great was celebrating Mass, a woman in the congregation doubted in her mind the Real Presence only to find that the communion host presented to her had changed into a bloody finger. The approved iconographic tradition depicted not this scene but rather a wondrous vision experienced by St. Gregory, in which the elevated host was changed into the crucified Christ himself. In some versions, the blood flows from Christ's wounds into the celebrant's chalice; in others, the Christ figure is merged along the viewer's sight line with the elevated host.[29] This idea was clearly in the minds of iconoclasts in Basel in 1529,

*Mitteldeutschland*, vol. 2 (Jena, 1942), p. 500; Augsburg and Ulm: Thomann, "Weissenhorner Historie," pp. 152, 177; Cologne, Historisches Archiv der Stadt Köln, Verf. und Verw. G205, Thurmbuch, fol. 34–35.

[26]Dieter Koepplin, "Reformation der Glaubensbilder: Das Erlösungswerk Christi auf Bildern des Spätmittelalters und der Reformationszeit," in *Martin Luther und die Reformation in Deutschland: Ausstellung zum 500. Geburtstag Martin Luthers* (Nuremberg, 1983), pp. 333, 352–78.

[27]On Luther's views, Margarete Stirm, *Die Bilderfrage in der Reformation* (Gütersloh, 1977), p. 33; on Kahla: Hermann Barge, *Andreas Bodenstein von Karlstadt*, vol. 2 (Leipzig, 1905), p. 130.

[28]Hauptstaatsarchiv Stuttgart A209, Büschel 1700.

[29]*Die Messe Gregors des Grossen: Vision, Kunst, Realität: Katalog und Führer zu einer*

when they carried the great crucifix from the cathedral to the marketplace in a satirical procession. Here the figure was addressed with the words: "If you are God, help yourself; if you are man, then bleed!"[30]

Acts of iconoclasm were therefore often deeply involved in forms of ritual action. If we return to the incident that occurred in Ulm in January 1530, we can discern a further dimension, for the actions performed on this occasion have all the features of a *rite of passage*. Rites of passage consist of three essential stages: disaggregation, transition, and reintegration. First, the person undergoing the ritual is separated from the mundane world and brought into a distinctive time and place. There he or she is subjected to various trials and tests, which can even threaten life itself. On successfully enduring these tests, the person is reintegrated into daily life, having been essentially changed by the ritual. In the case of the Ulm image, a figure of Christ from the Ölberg—that is, an object laden with ritual and sacred power—it was no rite of consecration or integration but the very reverse, a rite of desecration. The phases and the structural relationships, however, were the same.

First, the Christ image was removed from the Ölberg—that is, taken from sacred space into the profane space of daily life—not just into any ordinary profane space but rather to a Gunkelhaus or Spinnstube, a house where a spinning bee was in progress. Spinnstuben were commonly places for communal spinning in winter, but they also served as occasions for popular entertainment and youth courting rituals. They were notorious in polite society of the early modern period as occasions for immortality and license, and the houses in which they were held acquired the same bad reputation as inns or bathhouses.[31] The kind of disorderly, undisciplined and immoral behavior that was believed to take place there has been captured in a well-known woodcut by Hans Sebald Behem.[32] The removal of objects from sacred into profane space was a common occurrence in acts of iconoclasm.[33] Images were, at the very least, carried from the sacred space of the church into the street or into the marketplace, but often they were taken to more disreputable places. In 1543 an image of Christ as the Man of Sorrows was carried around to all the guild taverns in turn, and

*Ausstellung im Schnütgen-Museum der Stadt Köln,* ed. Uwe Westfeling (Cologne, 1982), pp. 23, 44, and illus. 15.

[30]Cited in Scribner, "Reformation, Carnival," p. 307, with references.

[31]On the spinning bee, see Hans Medick, "Village Spinning Bees: Sexual Culture and Free Time among Rural Youth in Early Modern Germany," in Hans Medick and David W. Sabean, eds., *Interest and Emotion: Essays on the Study of Family and Kinship* (Cambridge, 1984), pp. 317–39.

[32]Reproduced in ibid., p. 320.

[33]This idea was suggested to me some time ago by Lee Wandel, to whom I am grateful for numerous perceptive comments on the theme of iconoclasm.

in Wolkenstein in Saxony an image of St. John was taken to the bathhouse to be hung upside down.[34]

In the second phase the image was tested, subjected to trial. That occurred in various ways during acts of iconoclasm, but it was often done in imitation of the custom of the "defamatory image," the *Schandbild,* in which the honor of the person depicted was defamed and destroyed.[35] The punishment of images was nothing new in pre-Reformation Germany. Images that failed in their protective apotropaic function were subjected to derision and scorn. When it rained on St. Urban's day, weather that was taken to signify a bad harvest, the image of the patron saint of vintners was dragged through the mud.[36] What is often very striking about this testing of images, however, is that they were often addressed as though they were persons. It is an established feature of late medieval popular belief that sacred images were believed to have an inherent personality.[37] Thus when an image was addressed, it was a challenge to prove its personality. The Christ-image in Ulm was twice challenged to speak and was asked, "If you are Paul, then help yourself." The challenge issued to the Christ image in Hildesheim was somewhat different but appropriate to the occasion: in each guild tavern toasts were drunk to the image, and it was challenged to return them. At the tavern of the tailors' guild, beer was flung over it when it did not respond. This was surely a challenge that could not go unanswered by any person who valued his male honor! The challenge issued to the Ulm image, however, has overtones of the way the crucified Christ was challenged to prove his divinity, and the same challenge was put to the crucifix in Basel in 1529: "If you are God, help yourself; if you are man, then bleed!"[38] This was no less than a challenge to the twofold nature of Christ and echoes the challenge of the man in Augsburg who tested the Real Presence of Christ in the consecrated host with the words: "O Christ, what are you doing in that little fool's house?" The test was underlined here with a gesture of contempt, the baring of the buttocks.[39] By means of such tests, the images experienced a change of their being. They were no longer sacred objects, laden with sacred power,

---

[34]Hildesheim: Scribner, "Reformation, Carnival," p. 309; Wolkenstein: Fuchs, *Akten,* 2:500–501.

[35]On Schandbilder, see Robert W. Scribner, *For the Sake of Simple Folk: Popular Propaganda for the German Reformation* (Cambridge, 1981), pp. 78–81.

[36]For the St. Urban's day ceremony, see Sebastian Franck, *Weltbuch: Spiegel und Bildtnis des gantzen erdbodens* (n.p., 1534), fol. li$^v$.

[37]See Richard Trexler, "Florentine Religious Experience: The Sacred Image," *Studies in the Renaissance* 19 (1972):20; W. A. Christian, *Local Religion in Sixteenth-Century Spain* (Princeton, 1981), p. 198.

[38]Scribner, "Reformation, Carnival," p. 307.

[39]"Clemens Senders Chronik," p. 197.

but were exposed as profane objects, mere matter. In the case of the crucifixes, the images of Christ and the host, we could see this as a form of inverted transsubstantiation.

In the third stage of the rite of passage, the Ulm image was returned to its place but now as a failed, depersonalized image. In this stage, images were often burned or used for building materials, in the latter case so transformed by their rite of passage that they could safely be put to profane uses. In Mühlhausen in Thuringia in 1525, images were used for a cooking fire, to cook foodstuffs taken from the abbey in which they had stood. In Esslingen, this "domestication" of the formerly sacred was taken a symbolic step further. There the preacher married a nun at Easter 1532 and cooked all the food for the wedding feast with the images from his church, thus neatly combining two rites of passage, a rite of consecration with a rite of deconsecration. Finally, there was the case of a man in Cologne who pulled the arms off a crucifix in 1536 and then gave it to his children to use as a toy.[40]

## IV

Not all instances of iconoclasm or ritual attacks on traditional belief can so easily be interpreted as "rites of passage." Sometimes they have features of other rites such as degradation or scapegoating rituals, sometimes of judicial rituals of redress. Martin Warnke, writing about iconoclasm in Münster in 1534, noted that the mutilation inflicted on the images resembled forms of judicial punishment. Common in sixteenth-century Germany were the gouging out of eyes; cutting off of hands, fingers, or the tongue; slitting of the ears, nose, or cheeks; and dismemberment with the wheel, hanging, and decapitation.[41] These forms certainly appear in numerous cases of iconoclasm. When peasants attacked the abbey of Anhausen in Saxony in 1525, they chopped off the arms, feet and heads of images of Christ and the Virgin, while cases of decapitated images can be found in Augsburg in 1529, Kempten in 1525 (where the head was sawed off a statue of the Virgin), and Rothenburg in March 1525, where a crucifix was decapitated and had its arms torn off.[42]

[40]Thuringia: Fuchs, *Akten*, p. 62; Esslingen: Thomann, "Weissenhorner Historie," p. 85; Cologne: Historisches Archiv der Stadt Köln, Verf. und Verw. G205, Thurmbuch, fol. 34–35.

[41]Martin Warnke, "Durchbrochene Geschichte? Die Bildersturm der Wiedertäufer in Münster 1534–1535," in Martin Warnke, ed., *Bildersturm: Die Zerstörung des Kunstwerks* (Munich, 1973), pp. 65–98.

[42]Anhausen: Johannes Knebel, "Donauwörther Chronik," in Baumann, ed., *Quellen*, p. 257; Augsburg, Thomann, "Weissenhorner Historie," p. 152; Kempten: "Flachsschutzes

Some of these examples may seem like gratuitous acts of rage, especially those committed during the heat of the Peasants' War, although the sawing off of the head of the Virgin in Kempten has a certain deliberate quality. In many cases, however, the judicial parallel is unmistakable. In St. Gallen in 1526 images were placed in the stocks, as was an image of St. Francis in Königsberg in 1524, before it was decapitated. The image in Ulm discussed above was virtually "interrogated under torture," and there are several instances of images being hung. In Nebra in Saxony, an image of St. Francis was hung from the gallows on Palm Sunday 1524; in the following year, an image of St. John was hung upside down in Wolkenstein (Saxony); and in 1525 an image of St. Peter in the Abbey of Irrsee near Kaufbeuren was first hung upside down and then was disemboweled.[43] We can see this activity as merely another form of the use of *Schandbilder,* visiting on images the punishments held to be deserved by those they depicted or symbolized, but the same processes of judicial redress are involved.

Schandbilder have been interpreted primarily as an attack on the honor of the person depicted, as a form of social degradation, and we could view the forms of defilement or degradation visited upon images as ritualized acts of degradation. Sometimes the degradation was only lightly suggested, as with the case of an image of the Virgin that was hung under the pulpit in Leipheim near Ulm in 1524. We could see this as a symbolic subordination of the alleged mediatrix between God and man to the true mediator, the Word. Another interesting example is found in Memmingen in 1527, where an image of the Virgin was sold for ten gulden. This event aroused such comment that it became a common saying that the Memmingers "had sold our blessed Lady." The overtones of prostitution here perhaps echo the frequent criticism of many Reformers that the indecency of many statues made the churches reminiscent of whorehouses rather than places of worship. It is perhaps significant that at the same time that the Virgin was sold, the priests of Memmingen were told either to put away their "scandalous maids" or take them in marriage.[44]

There were several forms of satirical degradation, such as the case of the man who bared his bottom at the host in Augsburg. In 1524 an image

Chronik des Stifts Kempten," in Baumann, ed., *Quellen,* p. 383; Rothenburg: "Michael Eisenharts Rothenburger Chronik," in Baumann, ed., *Quellen,* p. 596.

[43]St. Gallen: Rott, *Quellen und Forschungen,* vol. 1, pt. 2 (Stuttgart, 1933), p. 256; Königsberg: Martin Perlbach, "Regesten der Stadt Königsberg," *Altpreussische Monatsschrift* 18 (1881):38, no. 101; Nebra: Gess, *Akten und Briefe,* 1:691; Wolkenstein: Fuchs, *Akten,* p. 501; Irrsee: P. Marcus Furter, "Historia belli rusticorum," in Baumann, ed., *Quellen,* p. 341.

[44]Thomann, "Weissenhorner Historie," pp. 137, 148–49.

of St. Francis wearing asses' ears was set up on the town fountain in Zwickau. In May 1527 the annual cross procession in Frankfurt was mocked by persons who fashioned a carnival puppet in the form of a wolf. As the procession went by, the puppet was waved out of a window and the procession mocked by cries of "A wolf! A wolf!"[45] This was probably a form of degradation by satirical inversion. It recalls the symbolism of Christ as the shepherd who protects his flock from wolves, neatly inverted in Reformation propaganda that labeled the old clergy as wolves preying on their flocks.[46] It may also, less directly, recall the designation of the Eucharist as the Lamb of God: satirizing it as a wolf would be an apt form of degradation of this holiest of objects.

The strongest form of degradation by inversion can be found in the uses of Carnival for propaganda purposes, which I have discussed elsewhere.[47] This occurred especially in the inversion of sexual roles, for example, where the clergy were hunted by women, as occurred in Zwickau (the proverbial sexual predators, the monks, were now themselves the prey), or where monks were made to pull the plow, as happened in Stralsund and in Prussia in 1522 and in Münster in 1532 and 1534 (the punishment of unmarried women applied to unmarried clergy); or where women expelled the clergy from the city, as in Hildesheim in 1543 (an inversion, perhaps, of the ritual expulsion of prostitutes and female sexual offenders).[48] Though many of these incidents lack any formal ritual or liturgical frame, they do in general fit the type of the "degradation ceremony." The persons or objects are first removed from the realm in which they enjoy their everyday character and dignity and are exposed by reference to some dialectical counterpart. This procedure establishes an ironic disparity between what the persons once appeared to be and the way in which they are now understood. Their origins are thus reexamined and redefined. A fixed distance is established between them and their denouncers, who act in the name of public order. the public realm, and the universal values to which these give allegiance. Examined and found wanting in terms of these values, they are now established as deviant.[49]

There are other redressive rituals, although they need not always involve degradation, and we also see rituals concerned with purification

[45]Zwickau: Anneliese R. Fröhlich, "Die Einführung der Reformation in die Stadt Zwickau," *Mitteilungen des Altertumsvereins für Zwickau* 12 (1919):71; Frankfurt: "Scheffers Kreinchens Chronik," in R. Jung, *Frankfurter Chroniken und annalistische Aufzeichnungen der Reformationszeit* (Frankfurt, 1888), p. 282.

[46]Scribner, *Simple Folk*, pp. 50–58.

[47]Scribner, "Reformation, Carnival," pp. 303–29.

[48]References in ibid., pp. 304–309.

[49]Harold Garfinkel, "Conditions of Successful Degradation Ceremonies," *American Journal of Sociology* 61 (1955–56):420–24.

and/or scapegoating. Purification was involved, for example, in Buchholz in 1524, where the figure of a pope was tossed into a fountain following a mock ceremony to "purify" the parodied relics of St. Benno. A more subtle note was struck in Wittenberg in Lent 1522, when students threatened the forthcoming Passion Week ceremonies with the promise that all the altars would be washed down with strong lye, a reference to the liturgical custom of washing down the altars with holy water on Maundy Thursday. This was also a veiled threat of iconoclasm, for the liturgical allusion would also have called to mind the associated practice of stripping the altars of their ornaments.[50]

Scapegoating rituals were a specific form of purification and were found frequently in sixteenth-century Germany. In Augsburg each year on St. Gallus day (16 October), there was a ritual expulsion from the city of all those held to have offended community norms, a ritual cleansing of the social body. Originally all kinds of marginal elements were the object of the expulsion, but increasingly by the end of the fifteenth century, it became an expulsion of prostitutes. Although they were supposed to be expelled for a whole year, their reentry into Augsburg was almost immediate. Parallel to this custom was an annual procession of whores held in Leipzig at Carnival time, intended to free the city from the threat of plague, in which a straw man was carried out on a bier and was thrown into the river.[51] A similar ceremony was the "Halberstadter Adam." On Ash Wednesday each year a man was chosen as "Adam," his head was covered, and he was dressed in rags. At the end of the Mass, he was hunted from the cathedral, and throughout Lent he had to go barefoot through the streets, without any rest during the day until midnight, bowing deeply whenever he passed a church. If he was invited into a house he was permitted to eat what was set before him but must utter no word. On Maundy Thursday he was absolved in church and was given the alms collected for him throughout Lent. He was then "as innocent as Adam," and it was believed that his absolution applied to the entire city and its inhabitants.[52]

The most common form of scapegoat ceremony, however, was the *Judas-jagen*, the expulsion of Judas, which occurred at various times in Passion Week, according to local custom, but most commonly on Maundy Thursday during *tenebrae*, as the candles were extinguished in church to mark the arrest of the Lord. Throughout the darkened church, rattles and

---

[50]Buchholz: Scribner, "Reformation, Carnival," p. 306; Wittenberg: Nicolaus Muller, ed., *Die Wittenberger Bewegung, 1521 und 1522* (1911), p. 158, no. 68.

[51]For the Galli custom in 1470, Istvan Bloch, *Die Prostitution*, vol. 1 (Berlin, 1912), p. 708; for Leipzig: Daniel Pfeifer, *Lipsia seu originum lipsiensium libri IV* (Leipzig, 1689), p. 312.

[52]Franck, *Weltbuch*, fol. li.

clappers were sounded as a means of "driving Judas from the church." In some areas this expulsion of Judas continued on the morning of Holy Saturday, with a dawn procession mocking the betrayer of the Savior and singing the German Judas song (*Judaslied*). Some places also had a "burning of Judas," with a straw puppet that was burned in the Holy Saturday fire.[53] The appellation of Judas was quickly applied to the pope and the clergy, and the Judaslied was adapted for antipapal polemic. "O du arm Judas, was hast du gethan" ("O wretched Judas, what have you done?") became "O du armer papst, was hast du gethan" or "O ihr monch und pfaffen, was habt ihr gethan" ("O wretched pope, O wretched monks and priests, what have you done?"). The Judaslied was sung by students who burned the books of Luther's opponents in Wittenberg in December 1520, and they had a mock pope who tossed his tiara into the flames, perhaps in analogy to the burning of Judas. The Judaslied was sung again in Basel when a Carnival procession took the great crucifix from the cathedral to the corn market, where it was burned.[54]

A second form of scapegoat ritual in use in sixteenth-century Germany was more secular in its origins than the Judasjagen. It too had strong features of a purification rite but was also linked to the notion of a rite of rejuvenation. This was the expulsion of death at mid-Lent (*Mitfasten*), which occurred either on Laetare Sunday or on the previous Wednesday (the proper mid-Lenten day). It consisted of a procession with a straw puppet, which was interred, thrown into a river, or burned, usually accompanied by the song *Nun treiben wir den Tod hinaus* ("Now let us expel Death"). This signified the expulsion of Winter, and on the way home, "Summer was fetched in." The expulsion of Death in the form of an expulsion of Winter had many similarities with the idea of "burying carnival," which can also be interpreted as an expulsion of Winter. In this ceremony, a puppet is also burned or buried or occasionally thrown into a river.[55]

This kind of ceremony was adapted for Evangelical purposes. Merchants in Radkersberg in Styria staged a mock procession on Ash Wednesday 1528, carrying a figure on a bier with a pumpkin for a head "in the shape of a dead man," the whole thing hung around with herrings. Two men walked before the bier, one carrying a book, and another dressed in woman's clothes behind it. Whenever the procession went past a priest, he was greeted mockingly. In Bautzen in 1523, on the feast of Cathedra Petri

[53]Scribner, "Ritual and Popular Religion," pp. 56–57.

[54]Scribner, *Simple Folk*, pp. 80, 100, for the Judas parallel in broadsheets; Scribner, "Reformation, Carnival," p. 118, for Wittenberg; for Basel, Wilhelm Fischer and Alfred Stern, eds., *Basler Chroniken*, vol. 1 (Leipzig, 1872), p. 447.

[55]Franck, *Weltbuch*, fol. li; *Wörterbuch der deutschen Volkskunde* (Stuttgart, 1974), p. 493.

(St. Peter's elevation as pope), two men dressed as monks carried a pope-figure made of paper on a bier in procession to the market, where it was burned.[56] There were other incidents of this kind, involving the burial or interment of the pope or papal religion: in Senftenberg on 2 February 1523 and in Münster in 1534, where there was a mock procession with crosses, flags, and tolling bells, in which a figure was carried around on a pile of faggots. In Buccholz, during the mock elevation of the relics of St. Benno at the end of June 1524, a figure of the pope was placed on a dung carrier before being tossed into the fountain. These were all in some sense mock burials akin to the burial of Carnival or expulsion of Death, and we might add to them an occasion in Goslar in which the Mass was "interred" on the marketplace.[57]

The thought content of such incidents is clear: the pope and papal religion are death, not just earthly death but the death of the soul, and must be expelled. Luther was so taken by the idea that he composed a hymn on the theme, first published in 1541 and entitled "A hymn for children, that they might expel the pope at mid-Lent."[58] Of the six events mentioned above, only one actually occurred at mid-Lent, that in Bautzen, but only one of them falls outside the paradigm of expelling Death, that in Buchholz. Three others—those in Münster, Radkersberg and Goslar—occurred at Carnival time, when a straw doll was also carried out to be buried or burned. As with the expulsion of Death, this also signified the ending of winter, the turning of the seasons and the approach of summer. Where the Carnival expulsion of winter leads to an intermediate period before the full joys of Easter, in some areas of central and eastern Germany, however, there was no inter-mediate period (spring); one simply changed abruptly from winter to summer at mid-Lent. Thus the other side of the expulsion of Death was the "fetching in of Summer."[59] Luther was well aware of this custom, for the last verse of his hymn matches the expulsion of the murderous pope with the coming of summer and the return of Christ. In the 1569 edition of the hymn, the editor replaced Luther's last verse with new verses "to sing on the way home," making quite explicit the links:[60]

[56]Radkersberg: Kretzenbacher, "Zur Frühgeschichte der Masken," p. 253; Bautzen: Karl Haupt, *Sagenbuch der Lausitz*, vol. 2 (Leipzig, 1863), p. 53.
[57]Münster, Buchholz, and Goslar: Scribner, "Reformation, Carnival," pp. 306, 308; Senftenberg: see n. 4 above.
[58]M. Luther, *Werke: Kritische Gesamtausgabe*, vol. 35 (Weimar, 1923), pp. 568–77.
[59]For *Mitfasten* or *Laetare*, see *Wörterbuch der deutschen Volkskunde*, pp. 493–94.
[60]Luther, *Werke:* "Der Bapst und Grewel ist aussgetriben, / Christus bringt uns den sommer wider, / Den sommer und auch den Meyen, / der Blümlin mancherleye" (35:570).

The papal abomination has been expelled
Christ brings us the summer again
The summer and the May-blossom
and many kinds of blooms.

Here the popular apotropaic element of the old ceremony has been "reformed," so that Christ brings in the joys of summer, new blooms, and hopes for the new year.

This is no more than implicit in my six examples: the pope is expelled, but Christ is not so explicitly fetched in to take his place. Perhaps it was unnecessary to spell out this point, or perhaps the dislike of the pope prevailed to the exclusion of all else. This seems to be the case in Bautzen, if we recall the occasion of the ceremony there, the feast of St. Peter's elevation as pope. There are, however, implicit hints of the return of summer, for example in Senftenberg, which took place on 2 February. Besides being the Feast of the Purification of the Virgin, it was also Candlemas, a feast of new light. The expulsion of the pope on this day recalls the woodcut of Hans Holbein the Younger, showing Christ as the light of the world, to whom the true Christians are drawn but from whom the papists flee into a dark pit.[61] The other side of the expulsion of the pope/death is thus implicitly the light of the Gospel and the new light of Evangelical faith. In this sense, these rituals are rituals of rejuvenation.

## V

I stated at the outset that we could perceive the Reformation as a "ritual process." Let me now summarize what is meant by that term. With all of the examples cited above we are dealing with forms of learned behavior, ritual modes of action learned in and through popular practices and popular belief, often drawing on both religious and profane rituals. In most of the cases cited, we can also discern a good deal of "Evangelical content" expressing some of the central ideas of the Reformation: rejection of papal religion as dangerous to salvation, the repudiation of various aspects of Catholic cult, and even, as I have argued in the case of attacks on crucifixes, rejection of the doctrines of Transsubstantiation and the Real Presence. These ideas are not always expressed explicitly but are attested through deeds within ritual action, even if they sometimes take the form of anti-

[61]Scribner, "Cosmic Order," pp. 18–19; Scribner, *Simple Folk,* p. 46.

rituals. Still, there can be no doubt that the process was a ritual process for the participants.

What is meant by "ritual process"? We can see ritual as teaching a "vocabulary of right action," but ritual is more than that.[62] In essence, it involved the metaphysical shaping of the world. Rituals work through symbolizing processes by which anything indicated symbolically is made metaphysically efficacious. In theological terms, they work sacramentally. People of the sixteenth century were probably not very theologically educated, but they were certainly well schooled in ritual behavior. Through various rites and rituals, they learned how the symbolic world was constructed. This involved construction both of a profane-social world and of a sacred cosmos. Through ritual activity, people were constantly building, rebuilding, and reshaping their world. This activity was reflected only partially and rather inadequately in the liturgy.[63] Ordinary people exercised their metaphysical and symbolizing activity in popular rites, in play and game, and especially in magical customs and practices. It is worth remarking, furthermore, that they did not just construct this cosmos—on occasions they also deconstructed it. Through such a ritual process, times, places, and persons, as well as the participants themselves, were sacralized and desacralized.[64]

What does this mean, however, as "reformation activity"? In all of our cases there were three possibilities. First, the participants were carried away by Evangelical conviction and sought to express their zeal in such forms, perhaps even to propagate it. Second, they attempted to implement their zeal and to reshape the world according to their new convictions—although this process was carried out in and through traditional forms and a traditional mode of ritual action. Third, the ritual process was itself a means of attaining such Evangelical convictions: incipient or half-formed views about the old church were put to the test and through a process of ritual were found wanting. We could say that the participants were putting themselves to the test, and by living through the process of ritual they acquired fully formed convictions. Interesting in this respect is the element of catharsis that is one of the major characteristics of ritual action. Victor Turner has labeled this aspect "flow," an experience of emotional distancing and

[62]For the most extensive exploration of ritual within the confines of an early modern society, see Richard C. Trexler, *Public Life in Renaissance Florence* (New York, 1980). The expression "vocabulary of right action" is Trexler's.

[63]See Grimes, *Beginnings in Ritual Studies,* esp. chap. 2; this is one of the important misemphases in John Bossy, *Christianity in the West, 1400–1700* (Oxford, 1985).

[64]For these functions of ritual, see Terence S. Turner, "Transformation, Hierarchy, and Transcendence: A Reformulation of van Gennep's Model of the Structure of Rites de Passage," in Moore and Myerhoff, *Secular Ritual,* pp. 53–70, esp. 60–64.

discharge. Flow, as Turner understands it, involves the merging of action and awareness; a centering of attention through a narrowing and intensification of consciousness of the present moment; a loss of ego, immersing the actor in the performance; control of the actions and the environment in which they are carried out, thereby overcoming any inherent sense of danger involved in the actions; a clear and unambiguous awareness of the need and demand for action that feeds back into self-evaluation of the action; and a sense of the action as something autotelic, as self-contained and needing no goals or rewards outside itself.[65]

An understanding of the role of catharsis in ritual behavior helps us to explain some rather curious features of many of our ritual incidents. Take the case of the extraordinary behavior of an Augsburg weaver in 1533. This man went into St. Ulrich's Church on the feast of the consecration of the church, marched up to St. Ulrich's altar just as compline was ending, undid his flies, held up his penis in his hand, and approached St. Ulrich's tomb as if about to urinate on it.[66] Such actions, like defecation on an altar or on the crucifix, seem wholly inappropriate for people inspired by a new religious perception. We should also include here less outrageous behaviour that would still be considered abnormal and deviant in the usual run of daily life, such as parodying the Mass or disturbing it with a fool's game. Such acts could, of course, be dismissed as the work of "the mob" or "fanatics," but this merely begs the question of the kind of experience involved and how it might be related to religious revival. Some sixteenth-century commentators spoke of such incidents as expressions of "excessive religious zeal."[67] The description of flow or catharsis set out above seems rather similar to the conversion experience, certainly as it was described by Luther. Perhaps such actions performed in a state of ritual flow or catharsis expressed the abnormal experience of conversion, and sought to replicate or even induce it.

All these elements were perhaps present in any single moment or instance of Evangelical ritual, according to the stage of encounter with Evangelical ideas. We know a good deal about how these ideas were acquired through forms such as listening to sermons, reading, discussion, reflection, or prayer. I suggest, however, that there was another major and neglected form of acquisition of such ideas, a popular cultural acquisition through

---

[65]For "flow" see Turner, *From Ritual to Theatre*, pp. 55–58; for catharsis, T. J. Scheff, *Catharsis in Ritual, Healing, and Drama* (London, 1979), pp. 12–25; and in a similar vein, Grimes, *Beginnings in Ritual Studies*, chap. 8.

[66]"Clemens Senders Chronik," p. 218.

[67]Cf. the expression "aus einem christlichen Eifer," used by the (Protestant) chronicler Enoch Widman to describe an act of iconoclasm in Hof in 1529, "Die Chronik M. Enoch Widman," *Hohenzollerische Forschungen* 2 (1893):106.

ritual action, in which Evangelical convictions were assembled and experienced in a form of bricolage, drawing on traditional modes of action. This notion presents a new field for exploration but one that may tell a good deal about popular reactions to the Reformation.

It has been said that ritual teaches us a "vocabulary of right action" and does so because it is paradigmatic, because it can inscribe a kind of cosmic order on the minds, hearts, and wills of the participants. It can also generate change by creating a new version of the social order that is meant to be believed and acted upon. It is a profoundly searching experience for the individuals concerned, showing them their innermost selves and arousing new states of consciousness. In this sense, the ritual performances described here were themselves "acts of reformation," driving the pope and papal religion out of the minds and hearts of those who took part in them. It is ironic that this should have been achieved by means of a "vocabulary of right action" learned under the papacy. The Reformation was in this sense fundamentally a ritual process. Given what we can now perceive about the nature of this process, it is clear that, when some reformers attempted to "reform popular culture," they should have experienced so much difficulty in their task. Because they believed erroneously that the only way to reform was through theology, formal piety, or doctrine, it is scarcely surprising that they should have failed. They were asking a "reformed people" to deny not only their popular roots but the very means itself of their reformation.

# PART THREE

# WOMEN, FAMILY, AND RELIGION

*The Reformation intruded very directly into the private lives of women and men of the sixteenth century, instructing them in how to mate, love, and raise children. Our knowledge of women's experiences during the Reformation is still rather sketchy, but Merry Wiesner's article provides a much needed survey of the current findings. A fact often overlooked in Reformation research is the resistance to reforms from cloistered women and laywomen. Among opponents of the Catholic Church, women appeared not infrequently as leaders and speakers in the public, a phenomenon that characterized many radical sects. During the Counter-Reformation Catholic women often showed initiative in advancing the claims of the Roman church, but they, like their sisters in the Protestant churches, were quickly put under the control of male clerics. Surveying the history of women in the sixteenth and seventeenth centuries, Wiesner reaches the conclusion that the status of women in both Protestant and Catholic regions suffered a serious setback: women were gradually excluded from the work force; stricter female gender roles were defined; the religious roles of women were limited; and a growing misogyny took its toll in the witch hunts.*

*It is crucial to see the history of women during the Reformation in relationship to the history of the family; one of the major goals of the Protestants was the reform of marriage and the establishment of a relatively more equitable status for wives as partners. The reordering of marriage was one of the most important differences between the Protestant Reformation and the Catholic Counter-Reformation: the former declared it a civic institution and allowed the injured party to petition for divorce, whereas the Council of Trent upheld its sacramental character and introduced stricter clerical supervision. This new emphasis on individualism in the Protestant marriage, however, ran contrary to another development—the concern for family solidarity. The assertion of parental authority over children's marriages, the ideal of a clear division of labor within the household, with the husband as the economic and religious head, and the intrusion of communal authority in the settling of marital disputes acted as counterweights to the individualistic tendencies of Protestant marriages. The essay by Thomas M. Safley stresses the need to understand the early modern German family as both an affective and an economic unit.*

*For a long time, European history was the record of adult males; in recent years, historians have developed a keen curiosity regarding the lives of women and children of the past. In Reformation historiography, questions are now raised as to how various religious movements, both Protestant and Catholic, might have affected men and women differently. Some scholars have suggested that the social restraints placed on women became more onerous in the sixteenth century: negative sexual stereotypes were reinforced, and gender roles became more narrowly defined. It is important to understand the witch hunts of the sixteenth and seventeenth centuries in the larger context of women's history and to balance the picture of family history with a portrait of those excluded from the institution of marriage. An important question was the degree of female participation in the work force. In her recent book, Merry E. Wiesner, associate professor of history at the University of Wisconsin at Milwaukee, examines the social, economic, and ideological changes that affected the lives of working women. The following article is based upon* Working Women in Renaissance Germany *(1986) but also includes a general discussion of all aspects of women's history in Reformation Germany.*

# [7]

# Women's Response
# to the Reformation

MERRY WIESNER

Historians of the Reformation have traditionally dealt with issues of gender in one of three ways. Most have simply ignored them, assuming that women shared their fathers' and husbands' experience and that gender made no difference. A second group has focused on the few women for which there are numerous sources, generally queens or noblewomen who supported or suppressed the Protestant Reformation.[1] Their studies make comparisons with male rulers possible but are limited to a very small group of extraordinary people. The third type of study examines male opinions about gender roles.[2] Law codes, sermons, church and school ordinances, tracts, and other prescriptive sources give many clues to male opinions about the proper roles for men and women. The "debate about women," whether women were moral or immoral, good or bad, rational or emotional, and sinful or saved, was a hot topic for humanists, theologians, and satirists during the early modern period. Both Protestant and

The research for this article was carried out in several archives in France and Germany and at the Newberry Library in Chicago. I thank the Deutsche Akademische Austauschdienst, the American Council of Learned Societies, and the Exxon Foundation for their support.

[1]Nancy Lyman Roelker, "The Appeal of Calvinism to French Noblewomen in the Sixteenth Century," *Journal of Interdisciplinary History* 2 (1971/72):391–418, and "The Role of Noblewomen in the French Reformation," *Archiv für Reformationsgeschichte* 63 (1972):168–95; Charmarie Blaisdell, "Renee de France between Reform and Counter-Reform," *Archiv für Reformationsgeschichte* 63 (1972):196–225; Gordon Griffiths, "Louise of Savoy and Reform of the Church," *Sixteenth Century Journal* 10 (1979):29–36.

[2]Ian MacLean, *The Renaissance Notion of Woman* (Cambridge, 1980); Manfred P. Fleischer, " 'Are Women Human?' The Debate of 1595 between Valens Acidalius and Simon Geddicus," *Sixteenth Century Journal* 12 (1981):107–22; Steven Ozment, *When Fathers Ruled: Family Life in Reformation Europe* (Cambridge, Mass., 1983).

Catholic reformers entered into this debate, adding their opinions about the nature of women. Male attitudes formed the legal and intellectual structures within which men and women operated, but they are only part of the story. To assess the impact of gender adequately as a significant variable in the Reformation period, women's actions and opinions must be analyzed along with those of men.

It can be very difficult to find sources on women during the Reformation. Fewer women than men in early modern German society were literate, so fewer recorded their thoughts, ideas, and reactions. The few who did write rarely published their works, as publishing required money, connections, and a sense that what one was writing merited publication. Women's unpublished works, such as letters and diaries, were rarely saved, for they were not regarded as valuable. (Many of Luther's letters to women, for instance, are still extant, but only a few of their letters to him are. None of his wife's numerous letters to him survive, though most of his to her do.) The few that have survived were generally written by upper-class women or women married to reformers, and so they are atypical.

Because of this scarcity of personal records, we must rely heavily on official sources to find information about women. These sources, such as tax lists, guild records, city council minutes, and court documents, are also those used to discover information about lower-class and illiterate men who left no personal accounts of their activities. Finding information in them about women poses special problems, however, for they are arranged by male names, occupations, and places of residence, with women recorded only sporadically and then often only when the women were widowed or single. Prescriptive sources such as laws, regulations, and ordinances also frequently mention women, but as they were drawn by male authorities, they are a better source for male attitudes toward women than for actual female experience.

In addition to source problems, historians face conceptual problems when looking at women. Because male experience has been defined as the norm throughout history, all standard categories of analysis—social and economic class, occupation, level of training, and education—are male-defined categories. Women were very likely to change occupations, places of residence and even social class on marriage, and to decline in income and wealth drastically on widowhood. They received little formal training, and yet worked at occupations for which formal training was theoretically required. The turning points in their lives—marriage, births of children, deaths of children, and widowhood—were often very different from what have been considered the turning points in male lives—finishing an apprenticeship or coming into contact with a great teacher.

The changing importance of class and gender make the picture even more complex. In medieval Europe, there were more restrictions by class than by sex, but the gap between men and women in education, political influence, and economic power grew wider in the Renaissance, at least among the upper classes.[3] Women shared a great deal with the men of their class and identified with the aims and aspirations of their fathers and husbands but could not themselves achieve the same aims. As sixteenth-century men debated women's nature, becoming more obsessed with women's sexuality and with controlling unmarried women, gender became increasingly important as a determinant of human experience.

Very recently, a few historians have begun to look beyond male attitudes, gathering material about women from the scattered archival sources to permit comparison with the more familiar story of men. They are examining the reformers' ideas about women, paying careful attention to how they were communicated to the general population. They are assessing political and institutional changes accompanying the Reformation that had a particular effect on women. Most important, they are exploring women's responses to the Reformation, responses in both words and actions. This research is far from complete, but by examining their findings, we can begin to see how gender shaped the way one responded to the Reformation message.[4]

### The Reformers' Ideas about Women

The Protestant reformers did not break sharply with tradition in their ideas about women. For both Luther and Calvin, women were created by God and could be saved through faith; spiritually women and men were equal. In every other respect, women were to be subordinate to men. Women's subjection was inherent in their very being and was present from creation—in this they agreed with Aristotle and the classical tradition. It was made more brutal and harsh, however, because of Eve's

---

[3]Joan Kelly Gadol, "Did Women Have a Renaissance?" in Renate Bridenthal and Claudia Koonz, eds., *Becoming Visible: Women in European History* (New York, 1977), pp. 137–64.

[4]Many of these discuss women in areas other than Germany. In addition to articles cited below, see Natalie Davis, "City Women and Religious Change" and "Women on Top," in her *Society and Culture in Early Modern France* (Stanford, Calif., 1975); Sherrin Marshall Wyntges, "Women in the Reformation Era," in Bridenthal and Koonz, *Becoming Visible*, pp. 165–91, and "Women and Religious Choices in the Sixteenth Century Netherlands," *Archiv für Reformationsgeschichte* 75 (1984):276–89; Joyce Irwin, *Womanhood in Radical Protestantism* (New York, 1979); Retha Warnicke, *Women of the English Renaissance and Reformation* (Westport, Conn., 1983).

responsibility for the fall—in this they agreed with patristic tradition and with their scholastic and humanist predecessors.[5]

There appears to be some novelty in their rejection of Catholic teachings on the merits of celibacy and championing of marriage as the proper state for all individuals. All Protestant reformers agreed on this point, though they disagreed on so much else; the clauses discussing marriage in the various Protestant confessions show more similarities than do any other main articles of doctrine or discipline. Even this tendency was not particularly new. Civic and Christian humanists also thought that "God had established marriage and family life as the best means for providing spiritual and moral discipline in this world," and they "emphasized marriage and the family as the basic social and economic unit which provided the paradigm for all social relations."[6]

The Protestant exhortation to marry was directed to both sexes but particularly to women, for whom marriage and motherhood were a vocation as well as a living arrangement. Marriage was a woman's highest calling, the way she could fulfill God's will; in Luther's harsh words, "Let them bear children to death; they are created for that."[7] Unmarried women were suspect, both because they were fighting their natural sex drive, which everyone in the sixteenth century felt to be much stronger than men's, and because they were upsetting the divinely imposed order that made woman subject to man. Even a woman as prominent and respected as Margaretha Blarer, the sister of Ambrosius Blarer, a reformer in Constance, was criticized for her decision to remain unmarried. Martin Bucer accused her of being "masterless," to which she answered, "Those who have Christ for a master are not masterless." Her brother defended her decision by pointing out that she was very close to his family and took care of the poor and plague victims "as a mother."[8]

The pious and obedient housewife was idealized by the Protestant reformers, but most other women were described quite negatively. Nuns and prostitutes were both encouraged to leave their houses and marry, and the level of morality in convents was compared with that in brothels.[9]

[5]Merry Wiesner, "Luther and Women: The Death of Two Marys," in Raphael Samuel, James Obelkevich, and Lyndal Roper, eds., *Disciplines of Faith: Religion, Patriarchy, and Politics* (London, 1987); John H. Bratt, "The Role and Status of Women in the Writings of John Calvin," in Peter de Klerk, ed., *Renaissance, Reformation, Resurgence* (Grand Rapids, Mich., 1976); Charmarie Jenkins Blaisdell, "Response to Bratt" in ibid.

[6]John C. Yost, "Changing Attitudes toward Married Life in Civic and Christian Humanism," *ASRR Occasional Papers 1* (December 1977):164.

[7]*D. Martin Luthers sämmtliche Werke*, vol. 20 (Erlangen and Frankfurt, 1826–57), p. 84.

[8]Maria Heinsius, *Das unüberwindliche Wort: Frauen der Reformationszeit* (Munich, 1953), p. 45.

[9]Lyndal Roper, "Discipline and Respectability: Prostitution and the Reformation in Augsburg," *History Workshop* 19 (Spring 1985), p. 10.

Female saints and martyrs, according to Luther, were lucky to have died young, as only their early deaths sent them to heaven still virgins.

The combination of women's spiritual equality, female subordination, and the idealization of marriage proved problematic for the reformers, for they were faced with the issue of women who converted although their husbands did not. What was to take precedence, the woman's religious convictions or her duty of obedience? Luther and Calvin were very clear on this point. Wives were to obey their husbands, even if they were not Christians; in Calvin's words, a woman "should not desert the partner who is hostile."[10] Marriage was a woman's "calling," her natural state, and she was to serve God through this calling. Even later Puritan writers, who had such a strong view of the liberty of conscience, were unwilling to extend this liberty to wives with unbelieving husbands.[11]

Not all reformers agreed, however. As might be expected, Catholic Counter-Reformation leaders encouraged young women to disobey their parents and enter convents to escape arranged marriages.[12] Though they did not encourage married women to leave their husbands, they followed pre-Reformation tradition in urging husbands to let their wives enter convents if they wished. More surprisingly, John Knox persuaded at least one woman, Anne Locke, to leave her husband and family in England and come to Geneva by telling her it would please God if she did so.[13]

Wives received a particularly ambiguous message from the radical reformers, ambiguity that is reflected in a sharp disagreement among historians about the impact of the Radical Reformation on the status of women.[14] Bernardo Ochino advised one noblewoman simply to hide her beliefs, for it did not hurt to participate outwardly in Catholic ceremonies. He recognized that hiding one's beliefs, termed Nicodemitism, was a particularly appropriate solution for women, although Calvin made no distinction between men and women in his harsh tract against the Nic-

---

[10]Quoted in Bratt, "Role and Status of Women," p. 9.

[11]Katherine Davies, "Continuity and Change in Literary Advice on Marriage," in R. B. Outhwaite, ed., *Marriage and Society: Studies in the Social History of Marriage* (New York, 1981), p. 70.

[12]R. Po-Chia Hsia, *Society and Religion in Münster, 1535–1618* (New Haven, 1984), p. 82.

[13]Patrick Collinson, "The Role of Women in the English Reformation Illustrated by the Life and Friendships of Anne Locke," in G. J. Cuming, ed., *Studies in Church History*, vol. 2 (London, 1975), p. 265.

[14]G. H. Williams in *The Radical Reformation* (Philadelphia, 1962) states: "The Anabaptist insistence on the covenantal principle of the freedom of conscience for all adult believers constituted a major breach in the patriarchalism and a momentous step in the Western emancipation of women" (pp. 506–507). Claus-Peter Clasen, on the other hand, comments in *Anabaptism: A Social History, 1525–1618* (Ithaca, 1972): "Revolutionary as Anabaptism was in some respects, the sect showed no inclination to grant women a greater role than they customarily held in sixteenth-century society" (p. 207).

odemites. Though the radicals stressed the equality of all believers, rejecting the need for specially educated and ordained pastors and emphasizing
revelation over reason, they still forbade women to preach or hold important church offices. Some radical groups allowed believers to leave their
unbelieving spouses, but women who did so were expected to remarry
quickly and thus to come under the control of a male believer. The most
radical Anabaptists were fascinated by Old Testament polygamy, and
accepted the statement in Revelation that the Last Judgment would only
come if there were 144,000 "saints" in the world; they actually enforced
polygamy for a short time at Münster, though the required number of
saints were never born. In practical terms, Anabaptist women were equal
only in martyrdom.

Though the Jesuits applauded young women who joined convents instead of marrying, they, and the rest of the Counter-Reformation church,
blocked all efforts by women who wanted to form active orders out in the
world.[15] Catholic women still had the approved option of celibacy, but
they were to be strictly cloistered in a convent. Catholic writers also began
to publish their own marriage manuals to counter those published by
Protestants, but the ideal wives and mothers they described were no
different from those of the Protestants; both wanted women to be "chaste,
silent, and obedient."[16]

The reformers communicated these ideas to women in a variety of
ways. Women who could read German might read Luther's two marriage
treatises or any number of Protestant marriage manuals, the first of which
was published in Augsburg in 1522. They could read tracts against celibacy by many reformers, which varied widely in their level of vituperation
and criticism of convent life. Upper-class and noble women could write
directly to Luther, Calvin, or other reformers, who were always careful to
answer women who had political power.[17] Both Protestant and Catholic
authors wrote books of commonplaces and examples, which contained
numerous references to proper and improper female conduct attributed to
classical authors, the Church fathers, and more recent commentators.

The vast majority of women could not read but received the message
orally and visually. Sermons, particularly marriage sermons but also regular Sunday sermons, stressed the benefits of marriage and the proper

---

[15]Ruth Liebowitz, "Virgins in the Service of Christ: The Dispute over an Active Apostolate
for Women during the Counter-Reformation," in Rosemary Radford Ruether, ed., *Women of
Spirit* (New York, 1979), p. 140.

[16]Suzanne Hull, *Chaste, Silent, and Obedient: English Books for Women, 1475–1640* (San
Marino, Calif., 1982).

[17]Charmarie Blaisdell, "Calvin's Letters to Women: The Courting of Ladies in High
Places," *Sixteenth Century Journal* 13 (1982):67–84.

roles of husband and wife. Women's funeral sermons stressed their piety, devotion to family, and trust in God through great trials and tribulations and set up models for other women to follow. Vernacular dramas about marriage replaced pre-Reformation plays about virgin martyrs suffering death rather than losing their virginity.[18] Woodcuts depicted pious married women (their marital status was clear because married women wore their hair covered) listening to sermons or reading the Bible. Protestant pamphlets portrayed the Pope with the whore of Babylon, which communicated a message about both the Pope and women. Catholic pamphlets showed Luther as a lustful glutton driven only by his sexual and bodily needs. Popular stories about Luther's home life and harsh attitudes toward female virginity circulated by word of mouth.

It may be somewhat misleading to focus only on works directed toward women, discussing marriage, or using female imagery, for women read, saw, and heard the more general message of the Reformation as well. Nevertheless, the majority of women probably paid most attention to works they could relate to their own experience, just as one would expect princes to listen more closely to works directed at them and magistrates likewise.

### Institutional and Political Changes

In terms of actually affecting women's lives, and demanding some sort of response, the institutional and political changes that accompanied the Reformation were more important than changes in religious ideas alone. Some of these political and institutional changes were the direct results of Protestant doctrine, and some of them were unintended, though not unforeseeable, consequences.

One of the most dramatic changes was the closing of the convents, with the nuns either ordered to leave or forbidden to take in any new novices. In some cases the nuns were given a pension, but in most cases there is no record of what happened to them. Former monks and priests could become pastors in the new Protestant churches, but former nuns had no place in the new church structure. Lay female confraternities were also forbidden, and no similar all-female groups replaced them. Women's participation in rituals such as funerals was limited, for Protestant leaders wanted neither professional mourners or relatives to take part in extravagant wailing and crying.

---

[18]Susan Karant-Nunn, "Continuity and Change: Some Effects of the Reformation on the Women of Zwickau," *Sixteenth Century Journal* 13 (1982):20.

Charitable institutions were secularized and centralized, a process that had begun before the Reformation and was hastened in the sixteenth century in both Protestant and Catholic territories. Many of the smaller charities were houses set up for elderly indigent women, who lived off the original endowment and small fees they received for mourning or preparing bodies for burial. They had often elected one of their number as head of the house but were now moved into large hospitals under the direction of a city official. The women who worked in these hospitals as cooks, nurses, maids, and cleaning women now became city employees rather than church employees. Outwardly their conditions of employment changed very little, but the Protestant deemphasis on good works may have changed their conception of the value of their work, particularly given their minimal salaries and abysmal working conditions.

Every Protestant territory passed a marriage ordinance, which stressed wifely obedience and proper Christian virtues, and set up a new court to handle marriage and morals cases that had previously been handled by church courts. They also passed sumptuary laws that regulated weddings and baptisms, trying to make these ceremonies more purely Christian by limiting the number of guests and prohibiting profane activities such as dancing and singing.[19] Though they were never completely successful, the tone of these two ceremonies, which marked the two perhaps most important events in a women's life, became much less exuberant. Religious processions, such as Corpus Christi parades, had included both men and women, with even the city's prostitutes taking part in these or other public rituals. They were prohibited, and the public processions that remained were generally those of guild masters and journeymen, with women as onlookers only.

The Protestant reformers attempted to do away with the veneration of Mary and the saints, which affected both men and women, as some of the strongest adherents of the cult of the Virgin had been men. For women, the loss of St. Anne, Mary's mother, was particularly hard, for she was the patron saint of pregnant women; now they were instructed to pray to Christ, a celibate male, rather than to a woman who had also been a mother during labor and childbirth. The Protestant martyrs replaced the saints to some degree, at least as models worthy of emulation, but they were not to be prayed to, nor did they give their names to any days of the year. The Protestant Reformation not only downplayed women's public ceremonial role, but stripped the calendar of celebrations honoring women and ended the power that female saints and their relics were felt to exert

---

[19]Lyndal Roper, "Going to Church and Street: Weddings in Reformaton Augsburg," *Past and Present* 106 (February 1985):62–101.

over people's lives. Women who remained Catholic still had female saints to whom they might pray, but the number of new female saints during the Counter-Reformation was far fewer than the number of male saints, for two important avenues to sanctity, missionary and pastoral work, were closed to women.[20]

Because of the importance placed on Bible reading in the vernacular, many of the Protestant reformers advocated opening schools for girls as well as boys. The number of such schools that actually opened was far fewer than the reformers had originally hoped, and Luther in particular also muted his call for mass education after the turmoil of the Peasants' War.[21] The girls' schools that were opened stressed morality and decorum; in the words of the Memmingen school ordinance from 1587, the best female pupil was one noted for her "great diligence and application in learning her Catechism, modesty, obedience, and excellent penmanship."[22] They taught sewing as well as reading and singing, with religious instruction often limited to memorizing the catechism.

Several female occupations were directly affected by changes in religious practices. The demand for votive candles, which were often made and sold by women, dropped dramatically, and these women were forced to find other means of support. The demand for fish declined somewhat, creating difficulties for female fishmongers, although traditional eating habits did not change immediately when fast days were no longer required. Municipal brothels were closed in the sixteenth century, a change often linked with the Protestant Reformation. The closing occurred in Catholic cities as well, however, and may be more closely linked with general concerns for public order and morality and an obsession with women's sexuality than with any specific religion.[23]

Midwives had long performed emergency baptisms if they or the parents felt the child would not live. This practice created few problems before the Reformation because Catholic doctrine taught that, if there was some question about the regularity of the baptism and the child lived, it could be rebaptized "on the condition" it had not been baptized properly the first time. The parents could thus rest assured that their child had been baptized correctly without being guilty of rebaptism, which was a crime in the Holy Roman Empire. In 1531, however, Luther rejected all baptisms

[20]Peter Burke, "How to Be a Counter-Reformation Saint," in Kaspar von Greyerz, ed., *Religion and Society in Early Modern Europe* (London, 1984), pp. 45–55.

[21]Gerald Strauss, "Lutheranism and Literacy: A Reassessment," in Greyerz, *Religion and Society*, p. 113.

[22]Merry Wiesner, *Working Women in Renaissance Germany* (New Brunswick, N.J., 1986), p. 81.

[23]Roper, "Discipline and Respectability," p. 21.

"on condition" if it was known that any baptism had already been carried out and called for a normal baptism in the case of foundlings. By 1540, most Lutheran areas were no longer baptizing "on condition," and those who still supported the practice were occasionally branded Anabaptists. It therefore became extremely important for midwives and other lay people to know how to conduct an emergency baptism correctly.

Midwives were thus examined, along with pastors, church workers, and teachers, in the visitation conducted by pastors and city leaders in many cities, and "shocking irregularities" in baptismal practice were occasionally discovered. As one perhaps apocryphal story tells it, a pastor found one midwife confident in her reply that, yes, she certainly baptized infants in the name of the Holy Trinity—Caspar, Melchior, and Balthazar! During the course of the sixteenth century, most Protestant cities included a long section on emergency baptisms in their general baptismal ordinance and even gave copies of this special section to the city's midwives. They also began to require midwives to report all illegitimate children and asked them to question any unmarried mother as to the name of the father of the child. If she refused to reveal his identity, midwives were to question her "when the pains of labor are greatest," for her resistance would probably be lowest at that point.[24]

In areas of Germany where Anabaptism flourished, Anabaptist midwives were charged with claiming that they had baptized babies when they really had not, so that a regular church baptism would not be required.[25] In other areas the opposite seems to have been the case. Baptism was an important social occasion and a chance for the flaunting of wealth and social position, and parents paid the midwife to forget that she had baptized a child so that the whole normal church ceremony could be carried out.

Along with these changes that related directly to Protestant doctrine, the Reformation brought with it an extended period of war and destruction, in which individuals and families were forced to move frequently from one place to another. Women whose husbands were exiled for religious reasons might also be forced to leave or their houses and goods might at least be confiscated. If they were allowed to stay, they often had to support a family and were still held suspect by neighbors and authorities. A woman whose husband was away fighting could go years without hearing from him and would never be allowed to marry again if there was some suspicion that he might still be alive.

[24]Merry Wiesner, "The Early Modern Midwife: A Case Study," *International Journal of Women's Studies,* vol. 6, no. 2 (1983):26–43.
[25]Clasen, *Anabaptism,* p. 149.

## Women's Responses

Women in convents were the first to confront the Protestant Reformation. In areas that were becoming Protestant, religious change meant both the actual closing of their houses and a negation of the value and worth of the life they had been living. Some convents accepted the Protestant message and willingly gave up their houses and land to city and territorial authorities. The nuns renounced their vows, and those who were able to find husbands married; the others returned to their families or found ways to support themselves on their own. Other convents did not accept the new religion but recognized the realities of political power and gave up their holdings in return for pensions; these women often continued living together after the Reformation, trying to remain as a religious community, though they often had to rely on their families for support.

Many convents, particularly those with high standards of learning and morality and with members who were noblewomen or women from wealthy patrician families, fought the religious change. A good example is the St. Clara convent in Nuremberg, whose nuns were all from wealthy Nuremberg families and whose reputation for learning had spread throughout Germany. The abbess at the time of the Reformation was Charitas Pirckheimer, a sister of the humanist Willibald Pirckheimer, herself an accomplished Latinist. In 1525, the Nuremberg city council ordered all the cloisters to close; four of the six male houses in the city dissolved themselves immediately, but both female houses refused. The council first sent official representatives to try to persuade the nuns and then began a program of intimidation. The women were forced to hear Protestant sermons four times a week and were denied confessors and Catholic communion; their servants had difficulty buying food; people threatened to burn the convent, threw stones over the walls, and sang profane songs when they heard the nuns singing. Charitas noted in her memoirs that women often led the attacks and were the most bitter opponents of the nuns. Three families physically dragged their daughters out of the convent, a scene of crying and wailing witnessed by many Nurembergers. The council questioned each nun separately to see if she had any complaints, hoping to find some who would leave voluntarily, and finally confiscated all of the convent's land. None of these measures was successful, and the council eventually left the convent alone, though it forbade the taking in of new novices; the last nun died in 1590.

Charitas's firmness and the loyalty of the nuns to her were perhaps extraordinary, but other abbesses also defended their faith publicly. Elizabeth Gottgabs, the abbess of Oberwesel convent, published a tract against the Lutherans in 1550, denigrating her own work as that of a "poor woman" but hardly holding back in her language: "The new evangelical preachers have tried to plug our ears with their abominable uproar . . . our gracious God will not tolerate their foolishness any longer." She was not the first woman to attack Luther's ideas in print. In 1528, Anna Bijns, a Dutch schoolteacher, had published an eighty-page pamphlet of poems against the "foolishness and errors of the Lutheran sect"; this was reprinted thirteen times, with the last edition appearing as recently as 1875. The letters of two sisters, Katherine and Veronica Rem, about why they would not leave their convent in Augsburg were later published without their knowledge by their brother; the volume containing them went through several editions, a sure sign that it was being read or was at least being purchased.[26]

Nuns who chose to leave convents occasionally published works explaining their actions as well. Martha Elizabeth Zitterin published her letters to her mother explaining why she had left the convent at Erfurt; these were republished five times by Protestant authorities in Jena, who never mentioned that the author herself had decided to return to the convent. Even if the former nuns did not publish their stories, they often became part of Protestant hagiography, particularly if the women had left the convent surreptitiously or had been threatened. Katherine von Bora and eight other nuns were smuggled out of their convent at night after they had secretly made contact with Luther. The fact that this occurred on Easter and that they left in a wagon of herring barrels added drama to the story, and Katherine's later marriage to Luther assured that it would be retold many times.

Nuns and other female religious responded to the Counter-Reformation as well and tried to establish groups for women that would reinvigorate Catholicism and would provide the opportunity for an active apostolate. Though none of these groups was started in Germany, several of them set up houses in Germany that attracted women searching for a life of religious service. Isabella Rosella, an associate of Ignatius Loyola in Barcelona, tried to start a female order of Jesuits in 1541. She was fiercely opposed by Loyola, and Pope Paul III would not give his approval. Her group nevertheless continued to grow, setting up houses in the Netherlands and Germany that taught the Jesuit catechism, until Pope Urban VIII published a bull against them in 1636. Francis de Sales and Jane Frances de Chantal originally founded the Visitandines to visit the sick and poor in their homes; in 1615 they were ordered to adopt strict enclosure, and during the seventeenth century Visitandine houses in Germany accepted

---

[26]"Literarische Gegnerinnen Luthers," *Historische-politische Blätter für das Katholische Deutschland* 139(1907):375–85.

the new rules. Only Vincent de Paul's Daughters of Charity succeeded in remaining a religious confraternity and avoided claustration, primarily because they placed themselves under the direction of his male congregation and so evaded control by bishops.[27] All attempts by women to set up a missionary order responsible only to the Pope were blocked, and the Jesuits remained the only nonmilitary order not to have female members or a female branch.

The Counter-Reformation church pressured beguines, Franciscan tertiaries, and other sisters who had always moved about somewhat freely or worked out in the community to adopt direct rules of cloister and to place themselves under the strict control of a bishop. The women concerned did not always submit meekly, however. The beguines in Münster, for example, refused to follow the advice of their confessors, who wanted to reform the beguinage and turn it into a cloistered house of Poor Clares. The women, most of whom were members of the city's elite families, appealed to the city council for help in defending their civil rights and traditional liberties. The council appealed to the Archbishop of Cologne, the cardinals, and eventually the Pope, and though the women were eventually cloistered, they were allowed to retain certain of their traditional practices.[28] In some ways, the women were caught in the middle of a power struggle between the archbishop and the city council, but they were still very able to use the city's pride in its traditional privileges to argue for their own liberties and privileges. Perhaps the fact that they had not been cloistered kept them aware of the realities and symbols of political power.

Most of the women in sixteenth-century Germany were not nuns or other female religious, of course, but laywomen who lived in families. Their first contact with the Reformation was often shared with the male members of their families. They heard the new teachings proclaimed from a city pulpit, read or looked at broadsides attacking the Pope, and listened to traveling preachers attacking celibacy and the monasteries.

Swept up by the enthusiasm of the first years of the Reformation, women often stepped beyond what were considered acceptable roles for them. Taking Luther's idea of a priesthood of all believers literally, women as well as uneducated men began to preach and challenge religious authorities. In 1524 in Nuremberg, the city council took action against a certain Frau Voglin, who had set herself up in the hospital church and was preaching. In a discussion after a Sunday sermon by a Lutheran-leaning prior, a woman in Augsburg spoke to a bishop's representative who had

[27]Sr. A. M. McGrath, *Women and the Church* (Garden City, 1972), pp. 96–99.
[28]Hsia, *Society and Religion*, pp. 142–47.

been sent to hear the sermon and called the bishop a brothel manager, as he had a large annual income from concubinage fees.[29] Several women in Zwickau, inspired by the preaching of Thomas Müntzer, also began to preach in 1521.[30]

All of these actions were viewed with alarm by civic authorities, who even objected to women's getting together to discuss religion. In 1529, the Zwickau city council banished several of the women who had gathered together and preached.[31] In the same year, the Memmingen city council forbade maids to discuss religion while drawing water at neighborhood wells. No German government forbade women outright to read the Bible, as Henry VIII of England did in 1543, but there were attempts to prevent them from discussing it publicly.

After 1530, women's public witnessing of faith was more likely to be prophesying than preaching. Ursula Jost and Barbara Rebstock in Strasbourg began to have visions and revelations concerning the end of the world. When Melchior Hoffman, the Spiritualist, came to Strasbourg, they convinced him that he was the prophet Elijah born again and thus one of the signs of the impending Apocalypse. He published seventy-two of Ursula's revelations, advising all Christians to read them. They were written in the style of Old Testament prophecy and became very popular in the Rhineland and Netherlands.[32] Several other female Anabaptists also had visions that were spread by word of mouth and as broadsides or small pamphlets. Though these women were illiterate, their visions were full of biblical references, which indicates that, like Lollard women in England, they had memorized much of the Bible.[33] Female prophecy was accepted in most radical sects, for they emphasized direct revelation and downplayed theological training. The fact that these sects were very small and loosely structured was also important for the continued acceptance of female revelation; in Münster, the one place where Anabaptism became the state religion, female prophecy was suppressed.

Not all female visionaries were radicals, however. Mysticism and ecstatic visions remained an acceptable path to God for Catholic women and increased in popularity in Germany after the works of St. Theresa were translated and her ideas became known. Even Lutheran women reported miracles and visions. Catherine Binder, for example, asserted that her

[29]Hans-Christoph Rublack, "Martin Luther and the Urban Social Experience," *Sixteenth Century Journal* 16 (1985):28.

[30]Karant-Nunn, "Continuity and Change," p. 38.

[31]Ibid., p. 40.

[32]Williams, *Radical Reformation*, p. 263.

[33]T. J. von Braght, *The Bloody Theatre; or, Martyrs' Mirror*, ed. Edward Underhill (London, 1850), 2:202–17.

speech had been restored after seven years when a pastor gave her a copy of the Lutheran Catechism.[34] The Lutheran clergy were suspicious of such events but did not reject them out of hand.

With the advent of the religious wars, female prophets began to see visions of war and destruction and to make political predictions as well as religious and eschatological ones. Many of these women had been driven from place to place by imperial or Protestant armies and had seen family members die and homes go up in flames, so it is not surprising their visions showed them the end of the world. They were taken seriously, however, and were not regarded as insane or deluded, even though some of them fell into fits and were probably epileptic. During the Thirty Years' War, both Wallenstein and Gustavus Adolphus received female vision-aries bringing them words of warning.[35] In many ways, female prophets were much less threatening than female preachers, for the former had biblical parallels and clear biblical justification. Female preachers, on the other hand, were disobeying the Pauline injunction against women's speaking in church and were moving perilously close to claiming an official, and not just extraordinary, religious role.

The most dramatic public affirmation of faith a woman could make was martyrdom. Most of the female martyrs in Germany were Anabaptists, and the law granted them no special treatment apart from occasionally delaying execution if they were pregnant. Women were more likely to be drowned than beheaded, for it was thought they would faint at the sight of the executioners' sword and would make his job more difficult. Some of them were aware that this reduced the impact of their deaths and wanted a more public form of execution; as a young woman in Friesland put it, "drowning is for dogs and cats."[36] She demanded a public burning or beheading, but the authorities drowned her at night, perhaps because she was crippled and they knew the impact that killing a crippled woman might have. A good indication of the high degree of religious understand-ing among many Anabaptist women comes from their interrogations. They could easily discuss the nature of Christ, the doctrine of the Real Presence, and baptism, quoting extensively from the Bible. As a woman known simply as Claesken put it, "Although I am a simple person before men, I am not unwise in the knowledge of the Lord." Her interrogators were particularly upset because she had converted many people; they

---

[34]Johann Henry Feustking, *Gyneceum Haeritico Fanaticum* . . . (Frankfurt and Leipzig, 1704), p. 178.
[35]Gottfried Arnold, *Unpartheiische Kirchen und Ketzerhistorie* . . . (Frankfurt, 1729), pp. 222–24; 232.
[36]Von Braght, 2:33.

commented, "Your condemnation will be greater than your husband's because you can read and have misled him."[37]

Though most of the women who published religious works during the Reformation were either nuns or noblewomen, there were a few middle-class women who wrote hymns, religious poetry, and some polemics. Ursula Weide published a pamphlet against the Abbot of Pegau, denouncing his support of celibacy in strong martial language.[38] The earliest Protestant hymnals include several works by women, often verse renditions of the Psalms or Gospels. Justitia Sanger, a blind woman from Braunschweig, published a commentary on 96 Psalms in 1593, dedicating it to King Frederick II of Denmark.[39] Female hymn writing became even more common in the seventeenth century when the language of hymns shifted from aggressive and martial to more emotional and pious; it was more acceptable for a woman to write of being washed in the blood of the Lamb than of strapping on the armor of God. Not all female religious poetry from the seventeenth century was meekly pious, however. Anna Oven Hoyer was driven from place to place during the Thirty Years' War and finally found refuge in Sweden. She praised David Joris and Caspar von Schwenkfeld in her writings, which she published without submitting them for clerical approval. Some of them were later burnt as heretical, including her "Spiritual Conversation between a Mother and Child about True Christianity," in which she attacked the Lutheran clergy for laxness, greed, pride, and trust in worldly learning and blamed them largely for the horrors of the Thirty Years' War.[40]

Seventeenth-century women often wrote religious poems, hymns, and prose meditations for private purposes as well as for publication. They wrote to celebrate weddings, baptisms, and birthdays, to console friends, to praise deceased relatives, and to instruct and provide examples for their children. Works published while they were still alive include profuse apologies about the author's unworthiness and presumption. Many were published posthumously by their husbands or fathers and include a note from these men that writing never distracted the author from her domestic tasks but was done only in her spare time.[41] Unfortunately, similar works by sixteenth-century German women have not survived, so that, to exam-

[37]Ibid., 2:202–17.

[38]Robert Stupperich, "Die Frauen in der Publizistik der Reformation," *Archiv für Kulturgeschichte* 37 (1927):227.

[39]C. F. Paullini, *Hoch und wohlgelehrtes Teutsches Frauenzimmer* (Frankfurt and Leipzig, 1712), p. 146.

[40]Arnold, *Kirchen*, pp. 104–107.

[41]Gisela Brinker-Gabler, ed., *Deutsche Dichterinnen vom 16. Jahrhundert bis zur Gegenwart* (Frankfurt, 1978), pp. 28–99.

ine the religious convictions of the majority of women who did not preach, prophesy, publish, or become martyrs, we must consider their actions within the context of their domestic and community life.

I am purposely choosing not to call such actions "private," because no one in the sixteenth century regarded religion or the family as private, as that term is used today. One's inner relationship with God was perhaps a private matter (though even that assertion is arguable), but one's outward religious practices were a matter of great concern for political authorities. Both Protestants and Catholics saw the family as the cornerstone of society, the building block for all other institutions, and every political authority meddled in family and domestic concerns. Thus a woman's choice to serve her family fish or meat on Friday, or to attend the funeral of a friend whose religion was unacceptable, was not to be overlooked or regarded as trivial or personal.

Married women whose religious convictions matched those of their husbands often shared equally in the results of those convictions. If these conflicted with local authorities, and the men were banished for religious reasons, their wives were expected to follow them. As the house and goods were generally confiscated, they had no choice in the matter anyway. Women whose husbands were in hiding, fighting religious wars, or assisting Protestant churches elsewhere, supported the family and covered for their husbands, often sending them supplies as well.

Married women with like-minded husbands demonstrated their religious concerns in different ways. Particularly if they were married to reformers or other prominent individuals, they opened up their homes to students and refugees, providing them with food, shelter, and medical care. Doing so meant buying provisions, brewing beer, hiring servants, growing fruits and vegetables, and gathering herbs for a household that could expand overnight from ten to eighty. Married women also assisted in running city hospitals, orphanages and infirmaries, sometimes at the suggestion of their husbands and sometimes on their own initiative. Katherine Zell, the wife of Matthias Zell and a tireless worker for the Reformation in Strasbourg, inspected the local hospital and was appalled by what she found there. She demanded that the hospital master be replaced as he served the patients putrid, fatty meat, "does not know the name of Christ," and mumbled the table grace "so you can't tell if it's a prayer or a fart."[42] Wealthy women set up endowments for pastors and teachers, and provided scholarships for students at Protestant, and later Jesuit, universities.

[42]Otto Winckelmann, *Das Fürsorgewesen der Stadt Strassburg*, vol. 2 (Leipzig, 1922), p. 76.

Pastors' wives had additional burdens. During the first few years of the Reformation, they were still likened to priests' concubines in the public mind and had to create a respectable role for themselves. They were often living demonstrations of their husbands' convictions and were expected to be models of wifely obedience and Christian charity; the reformers had particularly harsh words for pastors who could not control their wives. Pastors' wives were frequently asked to be godmothers, where they could be "important agents in the diffusion of evangelical domesticity from the household of the clergy to the rest of the population,"[43] but also had to bring the child a gift appropriate to its social standing from the meager pastoral treasury. The demands on pastors' wives were often exacerbated by the lack of concern on the part of their husbands for material matters. Often former priests or monks, they had never worried about an income before and continued to leave such things in God's (or actually their wives') hands.

Less prominent married women also responded to the Protestant call to make the home, in the words of Urbanus Rhegius, "a seminary for the church."[44] They carried out what might best be called domestic missionary activity, praying and reciting the catechism with their children and servants. Those who were literate might read some vernacular religious literature, and as reading was done aloud in the sixteenth century, this was also a group activity. What they could read was limited by the level of their reading ability, the money available to buy books, and the effectiveness of the city censors at keeping out unwanted or questionable material. Women overcame some of the limitations on their reading material by paying for translations, continuing a tradition that had begun before the invention of the printing press.[45] The frequency of widowhood in the sixteenth century meant that women often carried religious ideas, and the pamphlets and books that contained them, to new households when they remarried, and a few men actually admitted that they had been converted by their wives. The role of women as domestic missionaries was recognized more clearly by English Protestants and the Catholics than it was by continental Protestants, who were obsessed with wifely obedience. Richard Hooker, a theorist for the Anglican church, commented that the Puritans made special efforts to convert women because they were "diligent

[43]John Bossy, "Godparenthood: The Fortunes of a Social Institution in Early Modern Christianity," in Greyerz, *Religion and Society*, p. 200.

[44]Quoted in Gordon Rupp, "Protestant Spirituality in the First Age of the Reformation," in *Popular Belief and Practice*, ed. Derek Baker, Studies in Church History, 8 (Cambridge, 1972), p. 169.

[45]Susan Groag Bell, "Medieval Women Book Owners: Arbiters of Lay Piety and Ambassadors of Culture," *Signs*, vol. 7, no. 4 (1982):766.

in drawing away their husbands, children, servants, friends, and allies the same way.''[46] Jesuits encouraged the students at their seminaries to urge their mothers to return to confession and begin Catholic practices in the home; in this way, an indifferent or even Lutheran father might be brought back into the fold.[47]

There are several spectacular examples among noble families of women whose quiet pressure eventually led to their husbands' conversions, and certainly many among common people that are not recorded, but what about a married woman whose efforts failed? What could a woman do whose religious convictions differed from those of her husband? In some areas, the couple simply lived together as adherents of different religions. The records for Bamberg, for example, show that in 1595 about 25 percent of the households were mixed marriages, with one spouse Catholic and the other Lutheran. Among the members of the city council, the proportion was even higher—43 percent had spouses of a different religion, and so this phenomenon was not something that simply went unnoticed by authorities.[48] In cities with strict confessional adherence, two-religion households may have been impossible, but it bears further investigation.

Continued cohabitation was more acceptable if the husband was of a religion considered acceptable in the area. In 1631, for example, the Strasbourg city council considered whether citizens should lose their citizenship if they married Calvinists. It decided that a man would not "because he can probably draw his spouse away from her false religion, and bring her on to the correct path." He would have to pay a fine, though, for "bringing an unacceptable person into the city." A woman who married a Calvinist would lose her citizenship, however, "because she would let herself easily be led into error in religion by her husband, and led astray."[49]

As a final resort, a married woman could leave her husband (and perhaps family) and move to an area where the religion agreed with her own. Such a move was extremely difficult for women who were not wealthy, and most of the recorded cases involve noblewomen with independent incomes and sympathetic fathers. Even if a woman might gather enough resources to support herself, she was not always welcome, despite

[46]Quoted in Collinson, "Role of Women," p. 259.

[47]Hsia, *Society and Religion*, p. 67.

[48]Hans-Christoph Rublack, "Zur Sozialstruktur der protestantischen Minderheit in der geistlichen Residenz Bamberg am Ende des 16. Jahrhunderts," in Wolfgang Mommsen, Peter Alter, and Robert W. Scribner, eds., *The Urban Classes, the Nobility, and the Reformation: Studies on the Social History of the Reformation in England and Germany*, Publications of the German Historical Institute, London, 5 (Stuttgart, 1979), pp. 140–46.

[49]Strasbourg, Archives Municipales, Akten der XXI, 1631, fol. 40.

the strength of her religious convictions, for she had violated that most basic of norms, wifely obedience. Protestant city councils were suspicious of any woman who asked to be admitted to citizenship independently, and questioned her intensely about her marital status. Catholic cities such as Munich were more concerned about whether the woman who wanted to immigrate had always been a good Catholic than about whether she was married or not, particularly if she wished to enter a convent.[50]

Exceptions were always made for wives of Anabaptists. A tailor's wife in Nuremberg was allowed to stay in the city and keep her house as long as she recanted her Anabaptist beliefs and stayed away from all other Anabaptists, including her husband, who had been banished.[51] After the siege of Münster, Anabaptist women and children began to drift back into the city and were allowed to reside there if they abjured Anabaptism and swore an oath of allegiance to the bishop.[52] Both Protestant and Catholic authorities viewed Anabaptism as a heresy and crime so horrible it broke the most essential human bonds.

It was somewhat easier for unmarried women and widows to leave a territory for religious reasons, and in many cases persecution or war forced them out. A widow wrote to the Nuremberg city council after the town had turned Lutheran that she wanted to move there "because of the respect and love she has for the Word of God, which is preached here [Nuremberg] truly and purely"; after a long discussion, she was allowed to move into the city.[53] Women still had greater difficulties than men in being accepted as residents in any city, however. Wealthier widows had to pay the normal citizenship fee and find male sponsors, both of which were more difficult for women, who generally did not command as many financial resources or have as many contacts as men of their class. For this reason and because innkeepers were forbidden to take in any woman traveling alone, no matter what her age or class, the women's cities of refuge were often limited to those in which they had relatives. Women who worked to support themselves generally had to make special supplications to the city council to be allowed to stay and work. Because they had not been trained in a guild in the city, the council often overrode guild objections in permitting them to make or sell small items to support themselves and was more likely to grant a woman's request if they felt she was particularly needy or if her story seemed especially pathetic. A woman whose husband had been killed in the Thirty Years' War asked permission to live in Strasbourg in 1632 and bake pretzels; this permission was

---

[50]Munich, Stadtarchiv, Ratssitzungsprotokolle, 1598, fol. 171; 1601, fol. 24.
[51]Nuremberg, Staatsarchiv, Ratsbücher, Rep. 60b, 1541, fol. 230.
[52]Hsia, *Society and Religion*, p. 12.
[53]Nuremberg, Staatsarchiv, Ratsbücher, Rep. 60b, 1526, fol. 150.

granted to her and to several others despite the objections of the bakers because, in the council's words, "all of the supplicants are poor people, that are particularly hard-pressed in these difficult times."[54] Another woman was allowed to make tonic and elixirs in Strasbourg when a city pastor assured the council "that she is a pious and godly woman who left everything to follow the true word of God."[55]

Noblewomen, both married and unmarried, religious and lay, had the most opportunity to express their religious convictions, and the consequences of their actions were more far-reaching than those of most women. Prominent noblewomen who left convents could create quite a sensation, particularly if, like Ursula of Münsterberg, they wrote about their reasons for leaving and if their actions put them in opposition to their families. Disagreements between husband and wife over matters of religion could lead to exile of the wife, as in the case of Elisabeth of Brandenburg. Mutual toleration might also result, however, as it did for Elisabeth's daughter, also named Elisabeth, who married Eric, the duke of Brunswick-Calenburg. She became a Lutheran while her husband remained a Catholic; his comment was: "My wife does not interfere with and molest us in our faith, and therefore we will leave her undisturbed and unmolested in hers."[56] After his death, she became regent and introduced the Reformation into Brunswick, with the assistance of Matthias Corvinus. Several other female rulers also promoted the Reformation independently in their territories, and still others persuaded their husbands to do so. Later in the century noble wives and widows were also influential in opening up territories to the Jesuits.

Most of these women were following paths of action that had been laid out by male rulers and had little consciousness of themselves as women carrying out a reformation. Their actions were judged by others as well on the basis of their inherited status and power, for despite John Knox's bitter fulminations against "the monstrous regiment of women," female rulers were not regarded as anything unusual in the sixteenth century. Only if a noblewoman ventured beyond summoning and protecting a male reformer or signing church ordinances to commenting publicly on matters of theology was she open to criticism for going beyond what was acceptable.

The best known example of such a noblewoman was Argula von Grumbach, who wrote to the faculty of the University of Ingolstadt in 1523 protesting the university's treatment of a young teacher accused of Lutheran leanings. She explained her reasons: "I am not unacquainted

---

[54]Strasbourg, Archives municipales, Akten der XV, 1634, fol. 34.
[55]Strasbourg, Archives municipales, Akten der XV, 1636, fol. 34.
[56]James Anderson, *Ladies of the Reformation* (London, 1857), p. 123.

with the word of Paul that women should be silent in Church [1 Tim. 1:2] but, when no man will or can speak, I am driven by the word of the Lord when he said, 'He who confesses me on earth, him will I confess, and he who denies me, him will I deny' [Matt. 10, Luke 9] and I take comfort in the words of the prophet Isaiah [3:12 but not exact], I will send you children to be your princes and women to be your rulers.''[57]

She also wrote to the duke of Bavaria, her overlord, about the matter. Neither the university or the duke bothered to reply but instead ordered her husband or male relatives to control her, depriving her husband of an official position and its income to show displeasure. Instead of having the desired effects, these actions led her to write to the city council at Ingolstadt and to both Luther and Frederick the Wise of Saxony to request a hearing at the upcoming Imperial Diet at Nuremberg. Her letters were published without her knowledge, provoking a student at Ingolstadt to write an anonymous satirical poem telling her to stick to spinning and hinting that she was interested in the young teacher because she was sexually frustrated. She answered with a long poem that was both satirical and serious, calling him a coward for writing anonymously and giving numerous biblical examples of women called on to give witness. This poem ended her public career, though she subsequently wrote to Luther and other reformers several times (the letters are no longer extant), received Luther's German works from Georg Spalatin, and visited Luther in 1530. Her story was widely known and was frequently reprinted as part of Lutheran books of witnesses and martyrs, though she died in obscurity.

In the case of Argula von Grumbach, gender clearly made a difference. Political authorities would not have ignored a man of similar status who was in contact with major reformers. Grumbach exhibited a strong sense of herself as a woman in her writings, even before her detractors dwelled on that point alone. Despite the extraordinary nature of her actions, she did not see herself as in any way unusual and commented in her letter to the Ingolstadt city council that, "if I die, a hundred women will write to you, for there are many who are more learned and adept than I am." She recognized that her religious training, which began with the German Bible her father gave her when she was ten, was shared by many other literate women, and expected them to respond in the same way she did, proclaiming "the word of God as a member of the Christian church."[58]

The singularity of Argula von Grumbach is good evidence that gender was an important factor in the way a person responded to the Reformation.

---

[57]"Wie ain Christliche Fraw des Adels . . . , Sendtbrieffe / die Hohenschul zu Ingolstadt" (1523), quoted and translated in Roland H. Bainton, *Women of the Reformation in Germany and Italy* (Boston, 1971), pp. 97–98.

[58]Ibid., p. 100.

Large numbers of literate well-to-do women did not follow her example, and even among Anabaptists, women rarely preached unless they were on the scaffold. The reformers—Catholic and Protestant, magisterial and radical—all agreed on the proper avenues for female response to their ideas. The responses judged acceptable were domestic, personal, and familial: prayer, meditation, teaching the catechism to children, singing or writing hymns, entering or leaving a convent. Public responses, either those presented publicly or those which concerned dogma or the church as a public institution, shocked and outraged authorities, even if they agreed with the ideas being expressed. A woman who backed the "wrong" religion was never as harshly criticized as a man; her error was seen as simply evidence of her irrational or weak nature. On the other hand, one who supported the "right" religion too vigorously and vocally might be censured by her male compatriots for "too much enthusiasm" and for overstepping the bounds of proper female decorum. Thus whatever a woman's status or class, her responses were judged according to both religious and sexual ideology. Because women of all classes heard this message from pamphlet and pulpit, and felt its implications in laws and ordinances, it is not at all surprising that most of them accepted it.

What is most striking about women's response to the Reformation is its individual nature. Women, apart from nuns in convents, were not a distinct social class, economic category, or occupational group and so had no opportunity for group action. They passed religious ideas along the networks of their family, friends, and neighbors, but these networks had no official voice in a society that was divided according to male groups. Even women who reformed territories did so as individual rulers. Men, on the other hand, were preached to as members of groups and responded collectively. They combined with other men in city councils, guilds, consistories, cathedral chapters, university faculties, and many other bodies to effect or halt religious change. Their own individual religious ideas were affirmed by others, whether or not they were ultimately successful in establishing the religious system they desired.

A woman who challenged her husband or other male authorities in matters of religion was thus challenging the most basic assumptions about gender roles and was doing so alone, with no official group to support her. She did not express her religious ideas in collective terms or demand that women as a group be given power in matters of religion because, in both political theory and social reality, women were not a group. An examination of women's responses to the Reformation brings together two lines of research that have previously been separated. The first focuses on individual religious choice, a familiar focus in studies of the reformers themselves but rarely used for ordinary people. The second focuses on common people, but this generally has meant men acting in groups. When we consider women, we are forced to examine the individual responses of average people, and once men have been studied in this way as well, we will have a fuller understanding of the ultimate impact of the Reformation.

*The fortunes and character of marriage were subject to many changes during the Reformation. The most important innovation was the introduction of divorce in the Protestant churches; another landmark in the history of marriage was the Tridentine provision of clerical control over marriages in the Counter-Reformation Catholic church. In his previous work,* Let No Man Put Asunder: The Control of Marriage in the German Southwest: A Comparative Study, 1550–1600 *(1984), Thomas Max Safley, Byron K. Trippet Assistant Professor of History, Wabash College, compares court cases related to marital litigation in selected Protestant and Catholic areas. His present research deals with the history of the family in early modern Germany. The article included here discusses two important forces that affected the fortunes of early modern families: the moral ideas of the community in which families were situated and the economic forces both inside and outside the family that helped to determine the history of familial emotions.*

# [8]

## Civic Morality and
## the Domestic Economy

Thomas M. Safley

### The Individual and the Communal

"So one realizes well," wrote Heinrich Bullinger in his 1548 tract *The Christian State of Marriage,* "what is of concern to those who oppose this ancient, good and meritorious ordinance [parental consent to the marriages of their children]: they are concerned with wealth and want to become rich through marriage: not satisfied that they take children against the wills of their parents, they wish also to win property."[1] The author was writing in opposition to the Catholic principle that the consent of two legally able individuals to wed formed a valid and indissoluble bond. As Zwingli's successor and the leader of Zurich's reformed church, he was concerned about the consequences such marriages could have for civic morality as well as domestic governance and economy. He alleged that secret agreements led to frequent misalliances that squandered family fortunes by placing them in the hands of reckless and undeserving individuals.[2] Parental authority and economic prosperity were closely linked in Bullinger's mind and in the minds of his contemporaries. Deliberate marriage alliances with carefully selected individuals and the orderly devolution of property to legitimate, acceptable heirs formed cornerstones in

---

[1] "Darby man aber wol spurt was denen angelegen ist / die wider dise uralte gute und billiche satzung strytend: jnen ligt rychtumb inn / und wollend mit der Ee rych werdend: und haben nit gnug das sy den eltern jre kind wider jren willen nemmend / sy wollend jnen das gut darzu ouch wider jnen willen angewunnen" (Heinrich Bullinger, *Der christlich Ehestand* [Zurich, 1568], p. 15r).

[2] Ibid., p. 15v.

the edifice of the domestic economy. That Protestant leaders such as Bullinger recognized this fact and used it as a rationale for marital reform suggests that the early modern family was perceived to be an economic unit and that, as such, it was part of the foundation of the common weal, requiring regulation.

These notions are extremely valuable in assessing the Protestant reform of marriage in the sixteenth and seventeenth centuries. Major marital innovations associated with the Reformation included: strengthened parental prerogatives in marriage formulation; a complete divorce with the right of the injured spouse to remarry; and statutory property settlements after a divorce. All had direct effects on domestic authority and property, creating new responsibilities and posing unexpected hazards. As these reforms, but especially those concerning divorce, remarriage, and settlement, were codified in statutes of marital law and were enforced by specialized marital courts, families may have reacted by adopting new strategies to obtain and maintain wealth and status. Indeed, the spirit of Protestantism moved in its reform of marriage, which affected the prosperity of families and sought to foster corporate, communal sensibilities. Max Weber hypothesized that the "ascetic" individual—the person who could view material success as a sign of divine election—was the unique Protestant contribution to capitalist, economic development.[3] Domestic legislation and litigation suggest that this contribution may have occurred differently: through the daily interaction of Protestant marital reforms and familial economic strategies.

The Reformation with its associated marital reforms created a dialectic between individual and communal or familial interests. The expanded role of parents in the marriages of their children, far from vitiating the power of those children to determine their own future, created mutual responsibilities. Children were to submit their marital plans to their parents for approval. Parents were required not to hinder the marriages of their children unduly but rather to help them make responsible decisions. Together, members of the family worked to form marriages that preserved the material and moral interests of kin and community. In the matter of consent, then, the dialectic resolved itself in a higher truth, common interest, and cooperation. The same cannot be said, however, of those reforms pertaining to divorce. The dissolution of a marriage was essentially the act of an individual. It required no authorization and freed the petitioner to remarry. Indeed, through statutes guaranteeing generous property settlements, a

---

[3]"Only the methodical way of life of the ascetic sects could legitimate and put a halo around the economic 'individualist' impulses of the modern capitalist ethos" (From *Max Weber: Essays in Sociology*, ed. H. H. Gerth, C. Wright Mills [New York, 1946], p. 322).

successful plaintiff might anticipate improved material circumstances at the expense of his or her estranged spouse and in-laws. Recognizing the dangers implicit in this situation, Protestant magistrates established procedural and statutory impediments, which made dissolutions usually impractical and occasionally disadvantageous. Likewise, families developed strategies to neutralize this unprecedented threat to domestic economy and authority. Ironically, despite these measures, divorce made possible a great degree of self-determination for wife or husband and gave each a means of coercing the other. It proved a corrosive that acted on the family as an economic unit and, by extension, on the communal interests that Protestants sought to restore. An evaluation of domestic legislation and litigation should serve both to emphasize the conflict of individual and community and to suggest social and economic consequences.

### Marriage in the Community

According to canon law, the free consent of two capable individuals formed a valid matrimonial bond.[4] Canonists considered that free consent to be of vital importance in preserving the sacramental nature of marriage.[5] Nonetheless, they were not immune to suggestions that uncontrolled or secret weddings could lead to great immorality. In 1563, under pressure from reform-minded ecclesiastics, the Council of Trent promulgated the disciplinary canon *Tametsi*, which required the presence of an ordained priest and two or three reliable witnesses for a legal marriage.[6] Nevertheless, though legally culpable, marriages in violation of this canon remained valid and indissoluble.

Although it worked over the years to establish a uniform Catholic wedding, *Tametsi* failed to address what Protestants considered to be the larger disciplinary concerns of parental consent and public oversight. Reformers expressed horror at the immorality and irresponsibility they thought possible under Catholic law. The Strasbourg reformer Martin Bucer fomented against "that supremely godless dogma that the compact of matrimony made verbally by the contracting parties, as they say, binds

[4]George Hayward Joyce, *Christian Marriage: An Historical and Doctrinal Study* (London, 1933), pp. 64–65.

[5]Bartholomew T. Timlin, *Conditional Matrimonial Consent: An Historical Synopsis and Commentary* (Washington, D.C., 1934), p. 4.

[6]"*Decretum de Reformatione Matrimonii.* Cap. I: Matrimonii solemniter contrahendi forma in concilio lateranensi praescripta innovatur: quoad proclamationes dispensare possit episcopus. Qui aliter quam praesentibus parocho et duobus vel tribus testibus contrahit, nihil agit" (*Canones et Decreta Sacrosancti Oecamunici Concilii Tridentini* [Ratisbonae: Georgius Josephus Manz, 1866], pp. 137–39).

at once.''[7] Protestants, for all their dismay over Catholic practice, did not abandon the principle that marriage required the free consent of the betrothed couple. Rather, reformers did what they could to encourage parental participation and to require public control.

The magistrates of the reformed city of Basel, Switzerland, insisted on parental consent and due publicity in addition to the consent of the parties. Males under age twenty and women under age eighteen could not enter a valid marriage without parental consent.[8] Those who had reached legal age could marry without their parents' blessings but were urged not to do so. In fact, the marital code of Basel empowered parents to disinherit those legally capable children who married in defiance of their wishes.[9] Those people who wished to marry were required to announce their intention before their church congregations and to publish an announcement through the city government.[10] In this manner, legal impediments to the proposed union might be discovered. Such statutes had direct consequences on domestic authority and productive functions, by strengthening the ability of kin and community to participate in family formation and by predicating the legal devolution of property upon that participation.

In Lindau, a German city on Lake Constance, provisions for marriage made by the Protestant regime were equally strict. In their Marital Ordinance of 1566, the authorities described matrimony as an "alliance and community between human beings."[11] It required the most open, honest, and earnest expressions of intent.[12] As in Basel, the age of consent was twenty years for men and eighteen years for women.[13] The marriage of minors required the presence of parents as well as two witnesses, without which the union could not be sanctified and was considered void.[14] If minors insisted on marrying in defiance of their parents, they could do so. Their parents, however, were not required to settle property on them.[15] Persons of legal age who wished to marry were required to communicate their intentions to their pastor, who read the banns on the following two Sundays.[16] The wedding had to take place thereafter in church under the

---

[7]*Ehegerichtsordnung,* 7 October 1533, *Gerichtsarchiv* Ue2, St. A. Basel, 13. See also Thomas Max Safley, *Let No Man Put Asunder: The Control of Marriage in the German Southwest: A Comparative Study, 1550–1600* (Kirksville, Mo., 1984), p. 31.

[8]Ibid., 14. See also Safley, *Let No Man Put Asunder,* p. 52.

[9]Ibid.

[10]Ibid., 31.

[11]"Nachdem der Ehstand die höchste und nothwendigste Verbundtnus und Gemeinschaft zwischen den Menshen ist" (*Ehegerichts Ordnung,* 1566, 51.6, St. A. Lindau, p. 298).

[12]"Mit ernstlichen, ausgetrueltem ganzen Herzen, gemuth, willnus Verstandlichen Wortten, ohne alle betrug und Argliss zugehen und beshehen soll" (ibid., p. 299).

[13]Ibid., p. 300.

[14]Ibid., p. 301.

[15]Ibid., p. 303.

[16]Ibid., p. 311.

watchful eyes of community and kin. Aware of the economic and social function of marriage, Protestant reformers clearly sought to emphasize its communal significance through statute and ceremony.

### Divorce and Settlement

Protestant authorities wanted to renew communal and familial oversight in marriage. Yet the creation of divorce with the possibility of remarriage obviously had drastic effects on authority within the family. On a superficial level, it permitted one spouse to abandon the family and form a new alliance elsewhere. More profoundly, divorce compromised the interests in and authority over the family that were held by kin and community. Whereas family formation was tightly controlled, divorce was quintessentially an act both individualistic and anarchic. It required no parental consent, nor did it require advance publicity. The city controlled the legal procedure and organized it in such a way as to frustrate all but the most serious petitions. Nonetheless, any individual whose domestic situation had become insufferable could petition for a divorce.

The individualism implicit in divorce is all the more striking when viewed in light of the generally recognized economic function of the premodern household. Divorce threatened the material interests of all household members and kin. Not only did it remove one person from the array of productive forces, divorce also shattered the material foundations of the family.

Although held necessary in extreme cases of marital distress, separations and divorce troubled Catholic and Protestant authorities alike. These authorities never encouraged them and, as noted, strove to make the legal process difficult, lengthy, and expensive. It is possible to argue that magistrates intended to govern these individualistic impulses by restricting divorce, remarriage, and settlement.

The Catholic separation from bed and board, or "divortium quoad thorum et mensam," relieved spouses of the burden of cohabitation. They remained, however, spiritually bound together. Grounds for this procedure included adultery, abuse, and heresy or apostasy.[17] Once separated, husband and wife entered a limbo of unfreedom. Neither could exercise authority over or demand responsibilities from the other. Either might be declared answerable for the other's well-being, and of course neither could remarry.

Custom rather than statute determined property settlements after a Cath-

[17]Safley, *Let No Man Put Asunder*, p. 75.

olic separation, the status quo ante governing practice. The authorities attempted to separate the private property of each spouse as well as that which each possessed before the marriage. Property acquired during the marriage, on the other hand, was divided evenly between the two. Unless a marital contract existed as a guide to the settlement, the process of dividing property could degenerate into an extended dispute over owner-ship in which the most knowledgeable party—the one who controlled and disposed of it, often the husband—had a distinct advantage.

Protestants treated divorce and settlement in a markedly different man-ner; in many ways these represent their most radical reforms of family life. A divorce among Protestants dissolved the spiritual bonds between husband and wife. Thus freed, the innocent or injured spouse was able to remarry.

All reformers recognized adultery as the only ground for divorce based undeniably on Scripture.[18] Beyond this point, however, unanimity disap-peared in a confusion of individual theory and local practice.

Martin Luther acknowledged three grounds for divorce: adultery, impo-tence, and abandonment.[19] Ulrich Zwingli accepted the Lutheran grounds but added a fourth, contagious disease, as scripturally implicit.[20] Johannes Brenz and Johannes Bugenhagen, among the most influential later apolo-gists for Lutheran marital doctrine, admitted adultery and impotence as causes for divorce. Both, however, found abandonment to be quite prob-lematic.[21] Bullinger listed adultery and abuse as the principal grounds for divorce.[22]

Magistrates were not completely dependent on theologians for their discussion of divorce, remarriage, and settlement. They sought their own means for dissolving failed marriages, for protecting or punishing the parties, and for maintaining civic morality. In the city of Lindau, proven adultery, malicious abandonment, and antecedent impotence were the sole grounds for divorce.[23] The magistrates of Zurich granted divorce in cases of proven adultery or impotence.[24] They exercised judicial discretion to make conviction of a capital crime, malicious abandonment, contagious

---

[18]Hartwig Dieterich, *Das protestantische Eherecht in Deutschland bis zur Mitte des 17. Jahrhunderts* (Munich, 1970), p. 70.

[19]Martin Luther, *Vom ehelichen Leben*, 1522, in *D. Martin Luthers Werke*, vol. 102 (Weimar, 1883–1980), pp. 287–90.

[20]Adrian Staehelin, *Die Einführung der Ehescheidung in Basel zur Zeit der Reformation* (Basel, 1959), p. 50.

[21]Steven Ozment, *When Fathers Ruled* (Cambridge, Mass., 1983), p. 85.

[22]Heinrich Bullinger, *Der christlich Ehestand*, p. 101r.

[23]*Ehegerichts Ordnung*, 1566, 51.6, St. A. Lindau, p. 317.

[24]Walther Köhler, *Zürcher Ehegericht und Genfer Konsistorium* (Leipzig, 1932, 1942), pp. 74–75.

disease, and deadly assault potential grounds for divorce as well.[25] The marital court of Basel showed itself to be one of the most liberal tribunals in practice, granting divorces for reasons of proven adultery, malicious abandonment, deadly abuse, contagious disease, capital crime, and impotence.[26]

By closely controlling grounds and procedures, Protestant magistrates sought to apply communal oversight and control to marital dissolution in much the same manner as to marital formation. On the other hand, the nature of these statutes could not guarantee the interests of family members. Although they frequently participated in it, kin occupied a secondary position in Protestant divorce. Their position recalls the tension between the communal interests favored by reformers and magistrates and the ineluctable individualism of divorce.

The issue of remarriage makes this dilemma clearer. Although there was some disagreement concerning the fate of the guilty spouse, Protestant law generally denied that person any right to remarry. As a result, the families of guilty parties faced the possibility of supporting them as superfluous members of the household or of failing to obtain legitimate heirs through them. Protestant theologians and jurists were unanimous in permitting the innocent spouse to contract a new marriage after a divorce. Yet this party did not escape the stigma attached to such proceedings. To prevent any spouse from deriving undue advantage from a divorce, most marital courts insisted on a waiting period before allowing the innocent person to remarry. In Zurich, that party could form a new union without further ado, an exceptional privilege afforded in few other cities, whereas the guilty spouse had to show evidence of amended behavior in order to remarry.[27] In Lindau, only the innocent spouse could remarry and then only after a period of time to be determined by the court.[28] The guilty spouse was denied remarriage in Basel, too, but the innocent spouse was required to wait a full year before petitioning the court to marry again.[29] Again, the families of innocent parties might suffer disadvantage in the form of the costs of support or lost marital opportunities.

Bullinger referred to divorce allegorically as a remedy for diseased marriages. Although it was created and approved by God, it was a dangerous method, to be reserved for extreme cases.[30] The restrictions placed

[25]Ibid., p. 76.

[26]*Ehegerichtsordnung*, 27 October 1533, *Gerichtsarchiv* Ue2, St. A. Basel, 22. See also Safley, *Let No Man Put Asunder*, p. 131.

[27]Walther Köhler, *Zürcher Ehegericht und Genfer Konsistorium*, p. 113.

[28]*Ehegerichts Ordnung*, 1566, 51.6, St. A. Lindau, p. 320.

[29]*Ehegerichtsordnung*, 27 October 1533, Gerichtsarchiv Ue2, St. A. Basel, 24. See also Safley, *Let No Man Put Asunder*, p. 35.

[30]Heinrich Bullinger, *Der christlich Ehestand*, p. 101r.

on remarriage indicate that Protestant magistrates went a step further, viewing divorce not only in ameliorative terms but also in punitive terms, a means to heal and to punish. These limits further protected familial and communal interests by preventing hasty remarriage.

Nowhere are the conflict inherent in divorce and the jeopardy of familial and communal interests more strikingly demonstrated than in the statutes governing property settlements. The practical consequences of these formulas were to dissolve the family not only as an affective and authoritarian unit but also as an economic unit.

Laws controlling property settlements were part of the marriage codes of Basel, Lindau, Strasbourg, and Zurich. Presumably similar legal arrangements existed elsewhere, too.

In Strasbourg, the magistrates distinguished between the gifts that accompanied the formation of marriage and the property brought to and accumulated during the marriage. Accordingly, all gifts were returned to the donors after a divorce: dowry and *Morgengabe,* a gift presented either to the previously unmarried bride or groom by the previously married spouse or to the virgin bride by her groom, were returned to their original owners. All other property held by the divorced couple was treated as communal property. Strasbourg officials inventoried it and divided it into shares. The innocent spouse received his or her share immediately, but the guilty party lost all direct, independent control. The share of the guilty spouse passed to his or her children or next of kin. The city inventoried this portion and determined the usufruct of one-third, which would serve as a pension for the guilty party. In the event that communal property proved insufficient to provide a pension, the city might support that person as an act of charity.[31]

The marital court of Lindau treated the property of divorced persons in an even more draconian manner. In the event that a couple had no children, all property, including the personal effects of the guilty spouse, all communal property, and all gifts exchanged on marrying, passed to the innocent spouse. In essence, the guilty spouse was declared legally dead, and the survivor inherited the entire estate.[32] The court could act on its own discretion and reserve a portion of the guilty spouse's property, depending on the degree of that person's guilt and capacity for self-support.[33] If legitimate heirs were born to the marriage, then the innocent spouse and those offspring received the entire estate and divided it in

[31]The principles determining shares of communal property were not revealed in the Strasbourg Marital Ordinances. François Wendel, *Le mariage à Strasbourg à l'époque de la reforme, 1520–1692* (Strasbourg, 1928), p. 170.

[32]*Ehegerichts Ordnung,* 1566, 51.6, St. A. Lindau, pp. 321–23.

[33]Ibid., p. 324.

accordance with Lindau inheritance regulations. Again, the legal situation corresponded to the death of the guilty party. Whether that person was minimally supported or was cast completely adrift was left entirely to the discretion of the tribunal.[34]

Property settlements in Basel were also severe, though not as extreme as those of Lindau. The innocent spouse retained control of all his or her private property as well as the dowry. Furthermore, that person received two-thirds of the couple's communal property. The guilty spouse lost all independent control of his or her private property. The city combined it with the final third of the communal property, inventoried it carefully, and administered it in trust. From the proceeds, the guilty spouse received a minimal income sufficient to cover the basic necessities of life. By assuring a minimal income, Basel authorities hoped to prevent further crimes resulting from destitution on the part of the guilty spouse.[35] When the guilty party died, the trust passed to any legitimate heirs or, if there were none, to the municipal treasury.[36]

### Marital Litigation

Protestant magistrates acknowledged openly the intent of their reformed marriage laws to protect the innocent and to punish the guilty. On the one hand, divorce and settlement made possible considerable independence for the petitioning spouse. On the other hand, references to self-support and want in the Lindau and Basel ordinances suggest an awareness that property settlements would rob the guilty parties of all economic independence, making them potential burdens for their families or wards of the state. In punishing marital crime, divorcing for cause, and redistributing family wealth, these authorities seem to have had difficulty reconciling communal and familial interests with the self-determination that dissolutions afforded the individual.

The reformation of marriage therefore created an unresolved tension between the traditional values of family and community responsibility and the supposedly modern impulses of private, individual needs. It is possible to argue that Protestants—theologians and magistrates—firm in the faith that their reforms would strengthen family life, did not foresee this conflict. Parents were urged to take a broader role in the marriages of their children. Divorce was limited in a number of ways. Grounds were re-

---

[34]Ibid., p. 323.
[35]"Und damit das bruchig theil durch mangel leiblicher narung nit in grosser sinden falle" (*Ehegerichtsordnung*, 27 October 1533, *Gerichtsarchiv* Ue2, St. A. Basel, 27).
[36]Ibid.

stricted, objective, and verifiable. Martin Bucer's call for divorce by mutual consent found little acceptance in the Protestant world.[37] Set fees were charged for initiating divorce proceedings, and frequent delays were used to prolong the process, to force reconsideration, and to encourage reconciliation. Even statutory property settlements, in themselves a great hazard to rational planning and orderly devolution of family fortunes, may have acted as a deterrent. Nonetheless, divorce remained an individualistic act, antithetical to the normal interests of kin and community. The scriptural authorization of divorce, the divine purpose of marriage, and the disciplinary responsibilities of magistrates made it impossible consistently to reconcile divorce with the political economy of the family.

Patriarchal authority, family fortune, and communal control—fundamental aspects of the domestic economy—played roles not only in marital regulation but also in marital litigation. An examination of select marital disputes from Catholic and Protestant courts may suggest the effects of religious and legal innovation on early modern marriage and family.

The significance of such cases is not necessarily reflected in statistics. In a few cities, complete series of protocols exist for marriage courts established in the sixteenth century. Recorded over more than four hundred years, these collections preserve thousands of individual cases. At no one time, however, were divorces a commonplace occurrence in early modern Europe. In Basel, a city of some 10,000 inhabitants between 1529 and 1592, the local marital court heard 374 petitions for divorce.[38] In Calvin's Geneva between 1559 and 1569, the Consistory heard nine divorce cases and granted only three.[39] Zurich may prove an exception to the rule of infrequency; its marital court heard 207 divorce cases in a mere seven years, 1525–1531.[40] On the Catholic side, numbers are even more striking. In the diocese of Constance, which stretched from the Bernese Alps north to Stuttgart and from the Rhine River east to Ulm, the *Officialis* heard only 250 *divortia* between 1548 and 1600.[41] In most places, therefore, divorces were exceptional, perhaps even scandalous, events in the life of a family and a community.

---

[37]"And hence is concluded that matrimony requires continuall cohabitation and living together, unless the calling of God be otherwise evident; which union if the parties themselves disjoyn either by mutuall consent, or against the other's will depart, the marriage is then brok'n" (*The Judgement of Martin Bucer Touching Divorce Taken Out of the Second Book Entitl'd of the Kingdom of Christ*, trans. John Milton, in *The Complete Prose Works of John Milton*, II [1643–48; reprint ed., New Haven, 1959], p. 464).

[38]See Adrian Staehelin, *Die Einführung der Ehescheidung*, pp. 181–98; Safley, *Let No Man Put Asunder*, p. 142.

[39]William Monter, "The Consistory of Geneva, 1559–1569," in *Bibliothèque d'Humanisme et Renaissance*, vol. 38 (Geneva, 1976), p. 473.

[40]Walther Köhler, *Zürcher Ehegericht und Genfer Konsistorium*, pp. 109–20.

[41]Safley, *Let No Man Put Asunder*, p. 142.

Disputed marital agreements, whether involving parental consent or not, occurred much more frequently. In Basel, during the period 1550–1600, the marital court revolved 431 contract disputes, roughly one-third of the tribunal's total litigation.[42] At the same time, in the diocese of Constance, the Officialis heard 4,965 disputes of this sort, nearly half of its caseload.[43] Nonetheless, it is impossible to assert confidently that these disputes, unlike divorces, were a commonplace event in the communities of early modern Europe.

Individual cases reflect the circumstances, actions, and values of small groups of people: the married couple; their immediate circle of relatives, neighbors, and friends; and the civil magistrates. As these cases are few in number, what they reveal about the nature of marital law and marital life cannot be extrapolated with certainty to society as a whole. They do, on the other hand, offer a glimpse of the range of ideals and actions that composed marriage.

In 1603, a noblewoman of the Catholic city of Freiburg im Breisgau, Appolonia Meckhen, came forward to testify before the city court that her husband the *Bürgermeister,* Hans Caspar Ingolstetter, beat her savagely.[44] Claiming she feared for life and limb, Meckhen announced her intention to seek a legal separation through the official of the diocese of Constance. The magistrates remonstrated with the couple, urging them to forgive one another and live together peaceably. The Bürgermeister was pleased with the position taken by his official brethren and promised all would be well. For her part, Meckhen was unconvinced and feared, in her words, that they were condemning her to death. Refusing all reconciliation, she was remanded into custody. Two years later, Ingolstetter reappeared before the court, complaining of his wife's refusal to cohabit and demanding a final disposition of their case. Time had not worked its healing miracle. The city appointed a trustee to take control of the couple's property until the dispute was resolved, and Meckhen petitioned the bishop for a separation on grounds of deadly assault. Four months later, her petition was granted.[45]

Although it is safe to assume that some division of property occurred as a result of this separation, no record of this settlement survives. It is not known whether the parties shared the magistrate's acute sense of scandal,

[42]Ibid.
[43]Ibid.
[44]9 July 1603, *Ratsprotokolle* 42, St. A. Freiburg. See also Safley, *Let No Man Put Asunder,* p. 104.
[45]15 September 1605, *Liber sententiarum seu protocollum in reverendissimo officio Officialatus Constantiensis, Handschriften* 145, Eb. A. Freiburg. See also Safley, *Let No Man Put Asunder,* p. 105.

nor does any testimony remain concerning their satisfaction with the resolution of their situation. Meckhen escaped the immediate tyranny of her husband. Yet Ingolstetter retained a degree of economic control. With no statutory guide to such negotiations, the wife's economic security and the continued survival of the household of which she had been a part rested at least in part on her husband's willingness to come to terms.

The situation of Katharina Blanckenfeld highlights the importance of wealth and economic independence, especially for women. Her case can be deduced from an open letter to Martin Luther that she wrote and published in pamphlet form in 1530.[46] A resident of Brandenburg, she obtained a judicial separation from her husband Wolff Hornung. He had allegedly attacked her when she failed to obey him. That she proceeded through an *ordinarius,* in addition to certain tart references to Luther's "nun," suggests that Blanckenfeld was Catholic.[47] Hornung may have been a crypto-Protestant because he appealed to Luther for aid in his case.[48] Blanckenfeld criticized Luther sharply for siding with her husband, claiming that Hornung had abused her during married and had cheated her out of her property after they were separated. They had evidently negotiated a property division, and she itemized the points of contention. She had brought 1,000 gulden to their marriage, but he had returned only 150. He had sold the house in which she lived for 300 gulden but had given her only 100 of it. Finally, in his absence she had paid several of his debts, including 300 gulden to the Elector and 150 gulden to one Klaus Fugen, for which she demanded restitution. At the time of writing, her husband had fled Brandenburg to avoid the justice of the Elector Joachim I and was refusing all efforts to affect a final settlement. Her bitter tone may reflect her helplessness under the circumstances.[49]

The entire case demonstrates the power of the husband during and after

---

[46]Katharina Hornung, *Ein antwort Katharinen Hornung auff D. Marti Luthers notbriefe an Wolff Hornung* (Wittenberg, 1530). That Katharina would dare to challenge Luther in this public manner may seem less improbable if she is identical with the Katharina Hornung who is thought to have been a mistress of the Catholic elector Joachim I of Brandenburg. Indeed, the possibility that she had an illicit relationship with the elector casts an entirely different light on the publication. See *Luther's Works,* 55 vols., ed. Jaroslav Pelikan and Helmut T. Lehman, vol. 49 (St. Louis, Mo., 1958–67), p. 176 n. 36.

[47]That she was Catholic becomes quite likely if, once again, she was the alleged mistress of a Catholic prince.

[48]Wolff can be considered a crypto-Protestant only insofar as he lived in a Catholic territory. He may be the same Hornung often cited in the correspondence of Luther as a carrier. This undertaking, dangerous in some respects, might be seen as proof that Wolff was, in fact, a loyal Lutheran.

[49]That there may have been an illicit relationship with Joachim I raises the possibility that Katharina's financial situation was not desperate. It also suggests a religious motive for the publication.

separation proceedings when tacit control of the family estate remained in his hands. Under Protestant law divorce included a statutory redistribution of property, which presumably would have spared Blanckenfeld much distress. The matter of the property could only increase family and communal interest in the matter.

Catholic *divortia* serve as a reminder that the Reformation created neither the economic family nor the economic individual. A concern for authority and property inspired all alike: Catholic and Protestant, magistrate and citizen. It comes as no surprise, therefore, that individual marital disputes appear similar regardless of confession. The crucial distinction rests on the nature of Protestant reforms. By codifying divorce, remarriage, and settlement, the Reformation made possible a complete disintegration of the family unit along precisely defined lines. A separation from table and bed excused spouses from cohabitation but preserved a network of spiritual and material responsibilities, which could vary considerably from case to case and continued to bind wife to husband and kin to couple. Protestant divorce, established for the public and private good, broke all bonds and set free at least the innocent individual. The resolution of the dispute—the ability for one person to seize the family estate, seek a new marriage partner, and form a new economic unit—rather than the dispute itself distinguishes the Protestant reform of marriage. This resolution also created the tension of divorce in a communal setting.

One fascinating case came to trial in the marital court of Protestant Lindau on 1 April 1602. Catharina Weberin charged a man identified only as Kolb with having promised to marry her and with having made her pregnant on the strength of that promise.[50] She asked that the court enforce his commitment. Kolb denied any promise and accused her of enticing him into sexual relations. The magistrate acted swiftly, fining both parties for fornication and ordering them to wed. One week later, Weberin returned to court in the company of her parents. She claimed to have changed her mind and wished to be excused from marrying Kolb. At this point, the case resembled a divorce. Her parents argued that because of property considerations (''wegen des Guths'') they would rather have the agreement nullified and their daughter's child declared a bastard.[51] A horrified court dismissed this petition and ordered Weberin and Kolb to the altar.

A notebook, kept by one of the marital court judges, Samuel Linns, contains a comment on this case.[52] He claimed that the court had never

---

[50]Notebook, 1 April 1602, 51.10, St. A. Lindau.
[51]Ibid.
[52]Ibid.

witnessed such an extraordinary reversal. He wrote that it had never happened "that a pregnant daughter changed her mind and asked for a divorce [*sic*], as this one did, preferring, rather, to be held a whore than a wife."[53] Clearly, Linns and the court were scandalized by the notion that a person's reputation might be sacrificed in favor of the family's economic status. His comment revealed the unresolved conflict between individual and communal interests. Protestant magistrates advocated the latter in theory but could not always do so in practice. In this case, familial economic concerns could not supersede the moral imperatives of the community.

Family property brought another man by the name of Kolb to court in Lindau.. On 29 July 1606 he appeared to explain a potential instance of multiple simultaneous agreements to marry.[54] He had become engaged to a widow in Ulm on condition that he pay her the sum of fifty gulden and provide her with lifelong use of his house. Kolb's father had refused these conditions, and the son, not much affected by this reversal, found an acceptable alternative. This second marriage candidate, however, refused to marry him until his agreement with the widow from Ulm was officially dissolved. The court obliged. Kolb's situation underscores the dual notions of property and authority in marriage formation.

A final example is the case of *Humerlin* v. *Kuntzlen*. Veronika Humlerin and Ulrich Kuntzlen had been ordered to wed by the marital court on the basis of an agreement followed by sexual relations. On 16 February 1608, Humlerin's father asked the court to dissolve this commitment, charging that Kuntzlen had raped his daughter and that no agreement existed.[55] The daughter confirmed her father's story in all details, sharply reversing earlier testimony. For his part, Kuntzlen denied all charges and requested that Humlerin be questioned in the absence of her family. After several days of testimony, on 8 March, the couple separated by court order without any charges having been filed against either.[56] In an avuncular gesture, the court warned the father that rumors regarding sexual relationship between his daughter and Kuntzlen were circulating in Lindau. Asked if he would not rather have them married, he referred to the young man's poverty and claimed he would never accede to such a union regardless of the family's reputation.

The nature of the evidence in Lindau and in other cities makes it impossible to determine whether parents played a larger role in Protestant

---

[53]"Da die geschwechte tochter also sich widersetzt und die ehescheidung begert hett, wie dise gethon, und lieber fur ein hur denn fur ein eheweib gehalten werden" (ibid.).

[54]Protocol, 29 July 1606, 51.10, St. A. Lindau.

[55]Protocol, 16 February 1608, 51.10, St. A. Lindau.

[56]Protocol, 8 March 1608, 51.10. St. A. Lindau.

litigation than in Catholic. They seem to appear in court more often, but given the lack of detail in most protocols, more cannot be said. These case studies and others reveal clearly, however, that when parents came before the marital court they acted more often in consideration of family property than in consideration of personal reputation.

In cases of divorce, property figured as a frequent cause of the dispute and as the focus of struggle after the case. Several cases demonstrate this point sufficiently. In Lindau on 12 June 1599, a watchmaker named Ulrich Metzlern sued for divorce from his wife, Barbara Lantzingerin.[57] He charged her with abandonment and adultery and so initiated a case that dragged on for more than two years. The procedure was complicated by the absence of the defendant. This raised several thorny procedural issues: how long the abandoned spouse must wait before initiating divorce proceedings; whether a property settlement could occur without proof of the absent spouse's death; and how thoroughly the injured party should seek to establish contact with the miscreant. After all these issues were resolved, witnesses as to the nature of Metzlern's relationship with Lantzingerin—presumably neighbors—were called to testify. On 17 November 1601, the court reached a verdict.[58] Metzlern was required to pay court costs totaling thirty-six gulden. His divorce was granted on the strength of his oath that he did nothing to drive his wife out of the house. A property settlement followed in accordance with municipal statute; all property devolved to Metzlern as the sole heir.

In an interesting coda, the loquacious Samuel Linns, still a member of the court, recorded an extended dissent from this verdict in his notebook.[59] He noted that witness testimony raised the strong suspicion that both Lantzingerin and Metzlern were guilty of immortality and adultery. In addition, the plaintiff was thought to have kept a bawdy house, frequently entertaining persons of dubious character and encouraging them to have sexual relations with his wife. Though these charges were never substantiated, they carried a certain probative value for Linns.

In Basel, on 5 March 1566, Sophia Schnytzeri initiated a divorce from her husband, identified only as Heylmann.[60] She claimed that he had violated their marriage agreement by alienating her property without compensating her. In addition, he had abused her physically, had abandoned her, and, finally, had committed adultery. Heylmann disappeared from Basel, and Schnytzeri received her divorce.

A similar case was brought to the marital court by Catherina Offen-

[57]Protocol, 12 June 1599, 51.10, St. A. Lindau.
[58]Protocol, 17 November 1601, 51.10, St. A. Lindau.
[59]Notebook, 17 November 1601, 51.10, St. A. Lindau.
[60]Protocol, 5 March 1566, *Gerichtsarchiv* U5, 228v–229r, St. A. Basel.

burgin. On 15 January 1566, she charged her husband, Claudi Dorchamps, with alienating her property without compensation and providing her with no means for housekeeping.[61] After the death of their son, Dorchamps left her and committed adultery several times. Dorchamps had since taken up residence outside of Basel and informed the court that it no longer had jurisdiction over him. The divorce was granted.

The element of property is interesting in both of these cases. Although each involved multiple offenses, both complaints began by alleging misappropriation of property. Neither plaintiff denied the rights of their respective husbands to dispose of property. At issue was the matter of compensation. The plaintiffs both assert that their dowries—or at least equivalent values—remained their private possession. Nonetheless, the undisputed power of their husbands to dispose demonstrates that this property had communal characteristics. Conflicts arose through the lack of clear distinctions between these aspects of the wife's portion. Although Basel municipal law made no clear reference to this point, both women insisted that the preservation of their estates within marriage was a legally defensible point.


## Irony of Domestic Reform

In an article, Gerald M. Sider observed that families constitute the social relations of production in preindustrial society.[62] Marriage reproduced these relations, and divorce destroyed them. In the early modern economy, where production and consumption centered largely on the household, the untimely dissolution of a marriage could have disastrous consequences. It exposed dependent children to want. It isolated the guilty party, preventing his or her remarriage. It handicapped the innocent in forming a new marriage. It placed extraordinary restrictions on the estate.

The irony of divorce, this dialectic between individual and communal, is rooted in the perception of the family as an economic unit, functioning within the common weal and necessary for it. Individual action threatened the coherence of the economic unit and, by extension, the common weal. Clearly, therefore, the consequences of divorce concerned all members of early modern communities. Magistrates took steps to ameliorate the most deleterious effects. They increased family participation in marital formation and made marital dissolution costly and difficult. Presumably families took action, too, to prevent catastrophic changes in their fortunes.

[61]Protocol, 15 January 1566, *Gerichtsarchiv* U5, 227v–228v, St. A. Basel.
[62]Gerald M. Sider, "Christmas Mumming and the New Year in Outland Newfoundland," *Past and Present* 71 (1976):102–25.

It is appropriate to ask what the direct and indirect consequences of divorce on the acquisition and transfer of family wealth were. Given the infrequency of these proceedings, the direct results in terms of broken households, though acute for the individuals involved, were not significant for entire communities. The indirect results, which may have taken the form of new strategies controlling family fortune, could have consequences for the accumulation of wealth in and ultimately for the economic development of entire communities.

Families may have sought ways to redistribute property among their members, making it more difficult both for individuals to endanger the patrimony through unwise marriages and for officials to sequester or redistribute it in a post-divorce settlement. One way they might have done so was through changes in marital contracts.

In the city of Strasbourg, François Wendel discovered a curious change in marriage contracts at the time civil divorce legislation passed into law.[63] Families began to write marriage contracts without specifying universal communality of property. Because private property passed to each spouse in the event of a divorce, minimizing communal property reduced the amount that the state could sequester or redistribute. In Strasbourg, strategies for family formation seem to have changed in response to domestic reform. The intention may have been to defend the patrimony from seizure by the authorities. When individual ownership of property by the spouses was emphasized, however, each spouse effectively became a trustee for the property of their respective families. In the event of a divorce, the property could not be appropriated and remained in the family. Here is one clear instance of domestic behavior responding to religiolegal change. Nonetheless, the placement of larger portions of family property at the disposal of either spouse enhanced the options for individual self-determination, thus preserving the essential tension between communal actions and personal opportunities.

In the free, imperial city of Ravensburg, communality of property appears to have declined similarly. A collection of marriage contracts, signed between 1520 and 1620, reveals that great care was taken to distinguish between and preserve the property of each spouse.[64] The city initiated a Protestant reformation relatively late, in 1546, and, though it never established an independent marital court, did permit divorce.[65] Contracts from the post-Reformation period make no mention of communal property. Husbands who received property from their wives guaran-

[63]François Wendel, *Le mariage à Strasbourg*, p. 176.
[64]*Heirat und Erbschaft*, Repertorium IV, pp. 1101–52, St. A. Ravensburg.
[65]Alfons Dreher, *Geschichte der Reichstadt Ravensburg*, 2 vols. (Weissenhorn, 1972), 1:387.

teed its cash value in advance, thus preserving the net worth of the women.

It is possible to compare these two Protestant cities with the German Catholic community of Freiburg im Breisgau. The results, while by no means conclusive, are suggestive. A sampling of the thousands of marital contracts preserved from the period 1500 to 1800 demonstrates that unreserved communality of property between spouses, although by no means universal, remained the rule in this city throughout the early modern period.[66] Of fifty-five contracts sampled, thirty-five established complete communality of property. In the remaining twenty, in which the property of the husband and wife was carefully separated, nearly all involved a person who had children by a previous marriage. Where multiple inheritances occurred, involving complex transfers of property, communality was inconsistent with the inheritance rights of step-siblings as well as of the widowed spouse.

The evidence of marriage contracts is by no means conclusive, merely suggestive. A larger study of a broader range of contracts from a larger number of cities is under way to establish correlations between eased marital dissolutions and altered marital formations. Likewise, the search is on for other familial economic strategies to limit individual action and to safeguard family fortune. Ideally, such a theory would be aided by some direct proof, a firsthand statement linking divorce and settlements to contracts and communality. At present, one can only suggest a possible connection.

Research on the early modern household has firmly established the notion that the family corresponded to an economic unit, in which individual relationships to the figure of authority and individual, productive function determined the fate of family members and of the family as a whole.[67] Protestant theologians and magistrates sought to strengthen the corporate sensibilities that formed and informed the early modern family. Their reforms, especially those pertaining to marriage, created new ties of dependence between husband and wife and between parents and children. The problematic nature of divorce permitting individual action without necessary regard for kin and community, undercutting patriarchal authority, and dissolving relations of production created new challenges to this communal vision. Although the relationships between reformed legislation, economic strategies, and social values remain to be fully explored, it is increasingly clear, despite current interest in the Protestant psyche, that the Reformation affected family and economy through laws that altered the material conditions of life.

[66]*Heirat und Ehe,* C1, St. A. Freiburg.
[67]See Michael Mitterauer and Reinhard Sieder, *The European Family* (Chicago, 1982); Hermann Rebel, *Peasant Classes* (Princeton, 1983).

# PART FOUR

# IMPACT OF THE
# REFORMATION

*What did the Reformation accomplish? Was it a success? How did it shape the lives and minds of the townspeople and rural folk of the Holy Roman Empire? Did the religious reform change the intellectual discourse of the sixteenth century? What effects did confessional divisions have for the political conflict in the Empire? The four essays in this section provide answers to some of these questions.*

*The most fundamental means for the consolidation of the Reformation was education. On the basis of an extensive examination of the visitation records compiled by the territorial Evangelical churches for ascertaining the doctrinal knowledge and religious practices of rural pastors and folk, Gerald Strauss argues that the Reformation should be seen as a failure, measured against the goals and visions of the reformers themselves. Human nature was not changed voluntarily by education, and indoctrination and control very quickly became the instruments for enforcing religious conformity. Above all, Strauss reveals the chasm between popular and official religion, a gap that was widened by the Reformation when a new clerical professional group, the Protestant pastors, asserted their authority over the laity with the backing of the territorial state and city magistrates.*

*Very much in the same spirit, Jane Abray's portrait of the Strassburghers' religion lends support to Strauss's thesis. Even when laypeople saw themselves as good Lutherans, their understanding of piety was quite different from the doctrinal precision of their pastors. Doctrinal eclecticism, toleration, and a concern for practical morality offered a lay counterpoint to the orthodoxy, intolerance, and theological speculation of*

[191]

*the clerical professionals. Thus in the case of Strasbourg, the question of whether the Reformation was a success or a failure was answered by the enduring difference between the religion of the people and that of the Protestant clergy.*

*When Luther, Zwingli, Osiander, and other reformers attacked the "fraudulent miracles" and "popular superstitions" of the late medieval church, they also praised the role of human reason and natural law in the understanding of divine will. The changes in the learned discourses of the later sixteenth century must be interpreted in light of the intellectual revolutions of the Reformation. H. C. Erik Midelfort's reading of Johann Weyer is a good example of the social history of ideas. A student of law and medicine, Weyer (1515–88) was a staunch critic of the belief in witchcraft and the practice of witch hunts: he ridiculed popular superstitions, exposed the tricks of charlatans, and argued for a rational and medical interpretation of what was believed to be witchcraft. Furthermore, he introduced the insanity defense in Roman law into the refutation of witchcraft, thus paving the way for the elimination of witch hunts in the seventeenth and eighteenth centuries.*

*The rise of the territorial state and princely absolutism has traditionally been interpreted as one of the results of the Lutheran Reformation. Recent research has shown that the twin forces of state building and religious control were characteristic of all confessions: conformity in religious belief and behavior was required of all subjects in what amounts to a parallel development of Lutheranism, Calvinism, and Catholicism as state religions. Heinz Schilling argues that confessional allegiance and constitutional form did not match exactly and that Lutheranism served in the city of Lemgo in Northwest Germany as a civic political ideology against the centralizing politics of a Calvinist prince. He thus provides us with an important case study of the social and political tensions of a confessionally divided Germany on the eve of the Thirty Years' War. He cautions us against accepting the traditional wisdom, which saw the seeds of modern democracy in Calvinism and those of authoritarianism in Lutheranism.*

*In a 1978 publication,* Luther's House of Learning: Indoctrination of the Young in the German Reformation, *Gerald Strauss, Distinguished Professor of History at Indiana University, challenges the conventional view of the Reformation. Using ecclesiastical visitation records and pedagogic material, Strauss argues that the Lutheran clerics had failed to impose their vision of a reformed society on the vast majority of the populace, even if they were successful in drilling the rudiments of theology into schoolboys. Strauss's work raises the larger question of the differences between an official religion of the Protestant (and by implication the Catholic) churches and the religion of the people. His thesis has stirred a spirited debate; in the following article, Strauss defends his ideas against critics and calls attention to the centrality of indoctrination and discipline in molding early modern German society. Strauss has published four other books:* Sixteenth-Century Germany: Its Topographers and Topography *(1959);* Historians in an Age of Crisis: The Life and Work of Johannes Aventinus *(1963);* Nuremberg in the Sixteenth Century *(1976); and* Law, Resistance, and the State: The Opposition to Roman Law in Reformation Germany *(1986).*

# [9]

## The Reformation and Its Public
## in an Age of Orthodoxy

GERALD STRAUSS

      How does an ideologically inspired movement pass from its be-
ginnings in a time of struggle to a place of legitimacy and authority? The
study of revolutions, and of other changes equally abrupt and sweeping,
offers few more intriguing questions. How does the movement's leadership control the collective response of its followers? How may this
response be sustained over time? All movements, it seems, tend to follow
a similar course. Ideological emphasis shifts from guiding ideas, and the
transcendent source of these ideas (God, History, or Nature), to institutions and the powerful human agents directing them. Reliance in the
management of people and events passes from exhortation to surveillance.
Long-range goals, originally set to accord with governing ideals, make
way for short-term tasks necessitated by crises. As these begin to determine the making of policy, formerly inflexible norms are bent and ad-
justed. The ineluctable force is now exerted by reality, the real-world
situation with which the movement has to contend. Ideals are relinquished
to an indistinctly perceived future, their urgency attenuated by the press of
immediate problems.
    The very banality of this simple scheme endows it with historical ver-
isimilitude. As an outline of how things change in the process leading
from creative turmoil to settled order, it matches the world of ordinary
affairs as we recognize it, making pattern fit observation in the way to
which social history aspires. It also returns to its earthly base what has
long been dressed up in unworldly spirituality. A sobering experience is in
store for the historical scholar—especially the kind still drawn to the role
played by great men—who charts the passage of a movement from its

heroic to its established phase. My 1978 book, *Luther's House of Learning: Indoctrination of the Young in the German Reformation,* addressed itself to this transition, taking the sixteenth-century Reformation in Germany as a case in point. Although the book was not intended as a demonstration of how ideals succumb to reality, it became just that as my work moved from its original objective, the description of a vigorously pursued pedagogical enterprise, to an interpretation of the results of this undertaking.

*Luther's House of Learning* (the title is taken from Ecclesiasticus, a text much quoted in the pedagogical literature of the Reformation) made the following assertions and tried to offer some evidence for them. (1) An organized effort was made in Lutheran Germany in the first half of the sixteenth century to meet the challenge of the movement's future by imbuing young people with the essentials of Evangelical Christianity and civic morality (in using the term "indoctrination" to describe this effort, I had no pejorative innuendo in mind). (2) This effort represented the joint objectives of theologians and politicians, both groups having grown deeply worried over the unravelling of order in the early events of the Reformation. (3) The undertaking was well supported and systematic (always speaking relatively, of course) and was pursued with great vigor and dedication. (4) It rested upon the best available psychological evidence for the educability of the young and for the prospect of succeeding with the task of training them, provided that techniques of methodical habituation were employed, these techniques being fully explained in the writings of ancient authorities, notably Aristotle. (5) This technique was indeed utilized, most often in the form of catechism instruction, and a small army of pedagogues was kept busy writing catechisms, school texts, primers, readers—all of these incorporating Evangelical ideas. (6) From the very outset of the enterprise, governments monitored the results of their labors through parish visitations—again in a highly systematic fashion—and the unusually revealing written record of these inspections (visitation reports or protocols) told them, and still tells us, that their efforts were not succeeding. (7) On the evidence of these reports, the large mass of the populace exhibited after three-quarters of a century or more of Christian instruction a shocking ignorance of even the rudiments of the Evangelical religion and displayed disheartening apathy toward it. I drew the conclusion that the Reformation must be said to have failed *if* (and I stressed the *if*) it is understood as a serious endeavor to christianize people—all people or at least most—in a meaningful, as opposed to a merely perfunctory, way and if it is agreed that the Lutheran pedagogical enterprise was the heart of this christianizing mission. I suggested several explanations of this failure: the reformers' own ambivalence in pressing their pedagogy on the young—an irresoluteness grounded in large part in their pessimistic anthropology; the debilitating effect on the indoctrination program of the orthodox rigor into which the Lutheran movement settled in its established phase; confusions and doubts brought on by internal controversies about doctrine; and, last and probably most important, the enduring vitality of a popular counterreligion operating at the base of society that rendered the large mass of ordinary people virtually impervious to religious indoctrination from above.

The critical response to this conclusion was vigorous, most likely because the book was seen to be pushing a revisionist thesis in a field that needs no revision according to some of its most committed students but badly needs shaking up in the view of many others. Reviewers seemed to divide along a sharply drawn boundary of scholarly direction and personal engagement.[1] Heiko Oberman has identified this split. "Given the kind of Reformation history that regards the theological factor as a marginal phenomenon of merely circumstantial importance," he wrote in an essay on Luther and the Reformation for which *Luther's House of Learning* served him as a point of departure, "it is not surprising that this thesis has gained support."[2] Reaction to the book does indeed appear to have been governed by a writer's opinions on the place and weight to be given to theology in interpreting the Reformation. As this is also the issue on which the social historian parts company with the older scholarship, it will make a useful focus for this elaboration of my theme.

Most adverse criticism of my book has come from the traditional camp, although—it goes almost without saying—reviewers friendly to my own sense of how religion fits into a period and a culture have also found grounds for disagreement. From my own point of view it is unfortunate that critical comment has concentrated on the last fifty pages of the book, the part entitled "Consequences," in which I raise the question of the success or the failure of the pedagogical experiment and, by extension, of the Reformation itself. This emphasis is unfortunate because it creates the impression that the intent of my book was negative when, to my mind, its

[1]A sampling of reviews: Steven Ozment in *Journal of Modern History*, vol. 51, no. 4 (1979):837–39; Lewis W. Spitz in *American Historical Review*, vol. 85, no. 1 (1980):143; Joachim Whaley in *Times Literary Supplement*, March 21, 1980, p. 336; Jonathan W. Zophy in *Sixteenth Century Journal* 11 (1980):102–103; John M. Headley in *Catholic Historical Review*, January 1981, pp. 112–15; Mark U. Edwards, Jr., in *History of Education Quarterly* 21 (Winter 1981):471–77; Paul Rorem in *Princeton Seminary Bulletin*, vol. 3, no. 1 (1980):99; Kenneth Charlton in *History of Education* 10 (1981):150–52; Lawrence P. Buck in *Historian*, vol. 42, no. 4 (1980):673–74; Scott H. Hendrix in *Sixteenth Century Journal* 16 (1985):3–14.
[2]Heike A. Oberman, "Martin Luther: Vorläufer der Reformation," in E. Jürgel, J. Wallmann, W. Werbeck, eds., *Verifikationen: Festschrift für Gerhard Ebeling zum 70. Geburtstag* (Tübingen, 1982), p. 93.

chief purpose had been to call attention to an important though flawed and ultimately failed undertaking of great historical interest: the German reformers' experiment in mass pedagogy. Failure is no disgrace, although explanation of failure is often read as a judgment on those who tried. No such judgment was intended in my book, however. If we can see clearly now why the German Reformation's pedagogical effort was sure to falter, it is because our perceptions today are so unlike those with which reformers observed their scene. Our awareness of the central role of social reality in shaping every situation allows us to identify the impediments to the reformers' approach to religious and moral education. They, of course, saw things differently, as they were bound to do, given their presuppositions. To indicate that they failed is not, therefore, to dishonor them, nor does it detract from the significance of what they tried to accomplish.

A consideration of this failure should, however, persuade us to think in somewhat altered terms about the immediate and long-range impact of the Reformation on German society, and my argument has come under fire for having exemplified this thought shift. If my way of seeing things is correct, we must accept it as a fact that, for the great majority of men and women in the Lutheran territories of the Holy Roman Empire, the spiritual effects of the Reformation were neither deep nor lasting. Why should this conclusion be considered offensive? From my own perspective as a social historian, one reason suggests itself: because such an assertion undermines an old myth about the Reformation to which so many of us have long subscribed. In this myth, Luther's Evangelical message and its subsequent development in Protestant theology appear as the answer to everyone's prayer for a spiritual renewal. The superiority of the message is assumed, as is the eager acceptance of it by the great mass of the Reformation's loyal partisans. We do not ask: superior for what? Accepted for what reasons? How related to the lives of the men and women to whom it was preached? How understood by them in the context of their own places in the world? One has only to raise such questions to begin to see the conceptual gap dividing the older Reformation scholarship from the new. Practitioners of the latter sort remove their primary attention from the biographical and theological center in the person of Luther and the small circle of his fellow reformers. They direct their interest instead to the circumstances of the Reformation's differential reception in a vast number of distinct urban and rural situations. Inevitably, normative values in interpreting the Reformation make way for descriptive ones. It is this displacement that has aroused the greater number of misgivings.

The most serious objection made to my book is that it proceeds from a false premise. This premise contends that it was the Reformation's "central purpose to make people—all people—think, feel, and act as Christians, to imbue them with a Christian mind-set, motivational drive, and way of life.'' Wrong, it is charged by critics who find the book's credibility seriously weakened by a lack of familiarity with basic Lutheran theology. It is illegitimate, so goes the objection, to claim ''for the Reformation a central purpose no Lutheran reformer ever entertained.'' ''Christianization'' was never the reformers' goal. Luther and his associates, it is argued, could not have expected people to live up to an ideal. Their religious persuasions made it impossible for them to develop such anticipations. Luther never imagined that ''reformation'' could take the form of a transformation of society. Reformation is God's doing, not man's. It comes at the end of time, not before. Luther himself is really a ''pre-reformer,''[3] and categories such as ''success'' and ''failure'' are meaningless in testing the results of his work. They encourage a serious misreading of Lutheran intentions. Moreover, it is wrong to judge the reformers' actions by their high sense of mission. Doing so makes us overlook their many positive achievements, none of which encompassed the moral regeneration of their fellow men and women. It is true that Luther's own fundamental distinction between God's ultimate reformation and a—never attempted—temporal transformation was later dropped by Melanchthon, Zwingli, Bucer, and others of the second and subsequent generations of reformers. Still, they did not, any more than did Luther himself, confuse the however-much-to-be-desired elevation of tone and conduct in life with their real goal as Evangelical reformers, which was to lead people to a saving faith. As theologians, they did not greatly care how the world received the Gospel. None held much hope for the world. True reformation was in God's hands. Men accomplish little. ''One trusts in God to rule the spiritual kingdom while doing the best one can in the affairs of the world.''

Critics who follow this line of reasoning insist that, in judging the reformers' goals, I was misled by an occasional idealistic or ambitious assertion made by them. There is, of course, no shortage of these. Luther himself delivered an extraordinary one in 1528. In a buoyant mood that he found difficult later to recapture, he exulted:

I declare . . . I have made a reformation that will make the popes' ears ring and hearts burst. . . . By the grace of God I have accomplished so much that nowadays a boy or girl of fifteen knows more about Christian doctrine than all the theologians and universities used to know in the old days. For among us the catechism has come back into use: I mean the Lord's Prayer, the Apostles' Creed, the Ten Commandments, penance and baptism, prayer, the cross, living and

[3]Oberman, ''Martin Luther,'' pp. 101, 104, 109. The other quotations in this paragraph are from the reviews cited in note 1, above.

dying . . . also what marriage is, and secular government, what it means to be father and mother, wife and children, parent and son, man servant and maid servant. In short, I have led all estates in society to their right order and have guided them all to a good conscience, so that each knows how he is to live and how he must serve God in his appointed place. And for those who have accepted this, the result has been more than a little benefit, peace, and virtue [*tugent*].[4]

This passage—and others could be quoted to the same effect—suggests what Luther had in mind for the "reformation" that he then believed was being embraced by his fellow men and women. All are to be firmly emplaced in their respective walks of life: "alle stende der wellt . . . zu . . . ordnung bracht," where *ordnung* refers to the external arrangements that establish duties and set boundaries. They are to be led to, and maintained in, this benign equipoise by being brought to good conscience ("zu gutem gewissen . . . bracht"), so that each will know ("das ein iglicher weis") how to conduct himself, both toward God and toward his fellow beings. The appeal, in other words, is by way of the Gospel to the individual's inner self. Its outcome is, personally, a virtuous disposition. Collectively, it is a right-living and right-serving human community.

At the end of the fateful 1520s, Luther was apparently still confident that such a community could be the result of reformation, though he claimed little credit for his own achievements, referring instead to "the good that the gospel has accomplished not only privately, in the individual human mind and conscience, but also publicly, in the conduct of political affairs and in household management" ("tum privatim in hominum animis et consciencius tum publice in politia et oeconomia").[5] If any praise was due to him, it was for having helped to bring the Gospel to young and old, especially to the young. Luther did take pride in the evident success of his two catechisms. "Our tender young people," he wrote in 1530, taking stock of accomplishments, "girls as well as boys, are now so well taught in catechism and Scripture that my heart grows warm as I observe children praying more devoutly and speaking more eloquently of God and Christ than, in the old days, all the learned monks and doctors."[6] This, in Luther's view, was the hoped-for course of the reformation he was making. All men and women—but chiefly the young and the simple at heart—were to be imbued through the catechism with the sum and gist of Scripture, and the result would be a rightly ordered individual conscience, resulting in a human collectivity living in peace and virtue.

---

[4]Luther, preface to Stephan Klingebeil's *Von Priester Ehe* (Wittenberg, 1528), in *D. Martin Luthers Werke, Weimar Ausgabe* (=*WA*), 26:530.

[5]From Luther's lectures on the Song of Solomon, given 1530–1531, published 1539, *WA* 31², p. 613.

[6]Luther writing to Elector Johann, 20 May 1530, *WA* Briefwechsel 5, No. 1572, pp. 325–26.

The point to be made by the historian in judging this scheme is that, whatever its validity or feasibility in terms of Lutheran theology, it was the product of the reformer's increasingly direct involvement in the events activated by the Reformation. The overwhelming public response to his person and, apparently, to his message persuaded Luther of the divine favor shown to the movement whose acknowledged head he had become by the late 1520s. Second, the mass of practical problems created by the rejection of the old Church and brought to him for solution turned his attention increasingly to the worldly consequences of faith. The last of the passages quoted above occurs in a letter from Luther to his sovereign, the elector Johann. It offered the prince encouragement at a difficult moment in the political fortunes of Protestant states. In the mental world of Luther's day, religion and secular concerns interpenetrated seamlessly, for politicians and for ordinary people and for theologians as well. In making this pragmatic linkage of belief and its worldly manifestations, Luther was as little preoccupied as the layman with observing the tidy distinctions between the two kingdoms—God's and the world's—that are held so important in the modern discussion of Lutheranism. Riding the crest of his movement's success in gaining popular approval and political support, Luther was encouraged to look for substantial improvement in public morality as a consequence of the restoration of the gospel. Beset, at the same time, by the religious and social unrest of the Reformation's turbulent first decades, he turned increasingly to political means for actualizing his goal. Hence his close collaboration with Saxon statesmen in the building of a church government, the end product of a process in which the territorywide visitations of 1528 were the first decisive step.[7]

Luther never felt quite at ease with this trend. His many verbal protests against politicians and lawyers reveal his anxiety over the bureaucratic takeover of the church and over the debilitation suffered by civil society as a result of the destruction of its essential nerve, which is Christian love.[8] Still, although objections to the politicization of civic life—a process of

---

[7]The precise nature of Luther's involvement with the electoral Saxon state in the formation of the Saxon *Kirchenregiment* has been the subject of a vigorous controversy. For a discussion of this debate, see Hans-Walter Krummwiede, *Zur Entstehung des landesherrlichen Kirchenregimentes in Kursachsen und Braunschweig-Wolfenbüttel* (Göttingen, 1967), pp. 13–47; also Irmgard Höss, "The Lutheran Church of the Reformation: Problems of Its Formation and Organization," in Lawrence P. Buck and Jonathan W. Zophy, eds., *The Social History of the Reformation* (Columbus, Ohio, 1972), pp. 317–39.

[8]For a few examples of these protests, see *Eine Predigt, dass man Kinder zur Schule halten solle* (1530), WA 30², p. 566; Tischreden (=TR) I, No. 349 (1532); III No. 3622 (1537); preface to *Das fünffte, sechste, und siebend Capitel S. Matthei gepredigt und ausgelegt* (1532), WA 32, pp. 299–300; sermon of 6 January 1544, WA 49, p. 298. For an extended treatment of this issue, see my *Law, Resistance, and the State: The Opposition to Roman Law in Reformation Germany* (Princeton, 1986), chap. 7.

which Luther was keenly aware—fell easily from the reformer's lips, his actions did far more to support the trend than to oppose it. In any case, Luther's ambivalence on matters of politics and legislation soon gave way to a much more positive posture toward worldly laws, a posture associated, in Luther's own day, with Philip Melanchthon and, in later decades, with the controversialist theologians and ecclesiastical administrators who came to dominate the Lutheran establishment in the second half of the sixteenth century. A mere twenty years after Luther's death, the editor of his Table Talk, Johann Aurifaber, a loyal partisan of what he took to be authentic Lutheranism, noted sadly that "politicians, lawyers, and courtiers run the church now, directing religion like worldly affairs."[9] With this change in the direction—in both senses of the word—of the Lutheran movement in Germany, the question of whether a "moral transformation" of society could be reconciled with basic Lutheran theology became moot. The social turmoil of the 1520s had left a profound impression on ecclesiastical and political ruling circles. Above all other lessons, it had taught them that religious ideas could have revolutionary consequences. After 1525 it was no longer possible as a matter of practical politics to segregate faith from worldly affairs. If the latter were to be held stable, the former, too, must be placed under governance. Bracing authority became the paramount task of church and state, and anxiety over holding public belief in a condition of orthodoxy replaced the earlier zeal for spreading the word as a liberating message.

From about the middle of the sixteenth century, therefore, governments insisted on conformity in religion and practiced stringent supervision in order to obtain it. As the execution of religious policy became the business of the state, responsibility for putting it into effect passed from ecclesiastical to political personnel. This development received its most sweeping expression in the publication of *Kirchenordnungen*, comprehensive church constitutions through which the religious institutions of territories and cities were closely meshed in their operations with the politics of the territorial and urban state. An example will indicate the intent and range of these documents. A directive addressed by Duke Christian I to provincial administrative courts in Saxony, in 1587, declared that,

whereas a great contempt for God's word has been observed in many places, and people are lax and lazy in their attendance of church and their attention to God's word, and whereas governments are obliged to act against such contempt for God's word, it is ordered that one official person be appointed in every congregation . . . to make a weekly inspection in church, to see which chairs and pews are

---

[9]From the preface to Aurifaber's edition of Luther's *Tischreden* (1566), printed in Johann Georg Walch, ed., *Dr. Martin Luthers sämmtliche Schriften*, vol. 22 (Halle, 1743), col. 49.

unoccupied two or three Sundays in a row, and persons who have been absent and have not obtained permission for unavoidable cause shall pay a fine of six Groschen into the common chest, or, if they refuse, shall be put in prison for two nights and two days. And if a court shall be shown to be lax or recalcitrant in enforcing this order, it shall be accountable to the electoral district office for its failure.[10]

The same directive required that individuals found to be deficient in their knowledge of the Lutheran catechism be barred from "taverns, baptisms, church fairs and other such entertainments, nor is their presence to be tolerated at a carousing" until they could bring a clean bill in writing from their pastor.[11] Local officers were instructed to roam the village environs on Sundays to spot anyone standing or walking about during divine service. Such offenders, if they ignored the first warning, were imprisoned. If obstinate, they were put in the pillory. Blaspheming, "insulting remarks" about God, mutterings to the effect "that the Lord is not omnipotent or not just" were to be punished by death or mutilation. Careless cursing led the offender straight to the stocks. "And anyone in the village who hears such things, and does not report them, shall be punished more severely than the criminals [*verbrecher*] themselves."[12]

The pattern contained in this example of church legislation from Luther's own Saxony—vigilant political surveillance followed in cases of infraction by heavy-handed punishment—came to be adopted everywhere, and not only by the major states. Towns imposed such rules on their citizens, and even villagers found their religious behavior regulated by those who held jurisdiction over them. A Village Ordinance (*Dorfordnung*) issued by the counts of Castell for their village of Obereisenheim in Franconia in 1579, set a fine of fifteen pfennig for anyone missing adult catechism class and a much more substantial penalty of one pound for absence from Sunday service.[13] Nor was the surveillance/punishment sequence a monopoly of Protestants. Trying to cope with identical difficulties in advancing their own reformation, Catholic rulers adopted it in step with their Lutheran rivals. In Tyrol, for instance, beginning in the late 1570s, the government of Archduke Ferdinand II compelled parishioners

[10]*Ehegerichts Ordnung des Ambtes Stolbergk* (1587). Staatsarchiv Dresden Loc. 8832: "Ambt Stolbergks Acta," 63 recto and verso. *Ehegerichte* in Saxony were local courts situated in the electorate's administrative districts (*Ämter*) and in domains of landowners with administrative and legal jurisdictions.

[11]Ibid., 63 verso–64 recto.

[12]Ibid., 67 recto and verso.

[13]Printed in Emil Sehling, ed., *Die evangelischen Kirchenordnungen des 16. Jahrhunderts* (Leipzig, 1901–13), continued by the Institut für evangelisches Kirchenrecht der evangelischen Kirche in Deutschland (Tübingen, 1955–), XI[1], pp. 687–88. This collection will hereinafter be cited as Sehling.

to obtain "confession receipts" (*Beichtzettel*) from their priests. The names of recipients were transmitted to the local district chief, the *Pfleger*, who kept a list (*Beichtregister*) of them and sent a copy of it to the central administration in Innsbruck, where officials stood ready to go after slackers and resisters.[14] By such means did the archduke hope to raise the religious and moral temper of his duchy. Bavaria offers an even clearer example of a state girded to act on the proposition that reformation meant religious and moral rectification, and that this beneficial change could be achieved only by the joint forces of state and church. Unwilling to leave the supervision of religious life to the Bavarian church (even though this church was effectively linked to the state apparatus through "political" lay members sitting on its controlling organ, the Council for Spiritual Affairs), the duchy's zealously Catholic rulers empowered their provincial chiefs, the *Rentmeister,* to gather information (*auskundschaften*) about the populace's adherence to official religious mandates during their annual circuit ride (*Umritt*) round their districts. As shown by the elaborate instructions issued to them (many such instructions survive in the Bavarian State Archive in Munich[15]), no aspect of the enforcement of "true religion" escaped the vigilance of these exalted bureaucrats. Make certain, they were told, that town and village notables go regularly to church. Inspect booksellers' and bookbinders' shops for heretical volumes, and follow up all allegations and rumors by "visiting" (that is, by seeking out and interrogating) suspected householders. Trace to their sources all talk about people crossing "sectarian borders" (that is, from Catholic Bavaria to Protestant regions such as Regensburg and the Palatinate). Report all religious discussions said to have taken place among citizens (these had been banned). Question priests on their parishioners' loyalty, reliability, state of religious knowledge, and performance of religious duties. Compare this body of information with the delinquency reports that priests were required to make to the secular authorities. Inspect all monasteries, and "visit" the superiors and brothers, pressing each to divulge what he knows about his fellow members' offenses, such as breaking fasts and keeping concubines. Although the supervision of religious behavior was only one of the Rentmeister's many obligations, it was, in the age of Reformation and Counter-Reformation, given top priority. Catholics and Protestants were in rare agreement on this point.

But what aspect of religion mattered most to the authorities? What

---

[14]Joseph Hirn, *Erzherzog Ferdinand II von Tirol: Geschichte seiner Regierung und seiner Länder* (Innsbruck, 1885–88), 1:177–79.

[15]Bayerisches Hauptstaatsarchiv, Munich, G.R. 1262, No. 4, from the year 1584 on.

mattered to them above all other things was a condition of general orthodoxy, uniformity, and collective loyalty. Outward behavior was bound to count more heavily in the practice of these virtues than belief and inner conviction. For this reason, the Lutheran insistence on salvation by faith alone began to cause some concern among observers of the many social problems arising from the theological devaluation of works. Christoph Scheurl, for example, a prominent jurist in Nuremberg, no Lutheran himself, but nonetheless a trusted legal adviser to his Protestant city, warned his magistrates that, although the *sola* in *sola fide* was still being disputed by the experts, people seemed to be all too eager to act on it. "How devoid of works we have become now," he noted, "is, alas, plain for all to see."[16] To counteract this perceived decline in public commitment to moral action, church and state leaders put their trust in social discipline, the instruments of which were catechism training and systematic visitations. No theological scruples kept authorities from trying to impose "Christian discipline" (*Zucht*) on young and old, although their definition of "discipline" now included articles of belief as well as norms of conduct. Examples from the Old Testament served as precedents for this endeavor. King Josiah abolished idolatry and brought the religious practice of his state into harmony with its laws. Nehemiah cleansed religion of all foreign contamination. King Jehoshophat enforced the law upon the people of Judah. Citing these, and others, as examples for emulation, the *Kirchenordnung* of the County of Hohenlohe (for example) takes "visitation" to mean the institution of godly doctrine ("die lehr gotlichs worts") and the imposition of *Christliche Zucht* on all subjects. "In these last and perilous times," the document declares (it was published in 1558), with Satan gaining strength every day, only a government-promoted effort could keep civic life and religion from disintegration.[17] A law-and-order mentality thus combined with eschatological expectations to explain the transfer of religious initiative from individuals to institutions and to justify the passage of religious voluntarism into social control. Churchmen and statesmen joined hands in promoting this shift.

Although they were not fully articulated until after Luther's death, the developments described on the preceding pages certainly owe something to the reformer's own frequently voiced sense of frustration. The euphoria

---

[16]Scheurl in a 1530 memorandum on the projected Nuremberg-Brandenburg church constitution, Germanisches Nationalmuseum Nuremberg, Merkel-Handschrift 129, 5 verso.

[17]For the text see Sehling XV[1], pp. 120–32, especially pp. 129–30: "Von der oberkeit als beschützerin der kirchen." See also Gunther Franz, *Die Kirchenleitung in Hohenlohe in den Jahrzehnten nach der Reformation: Visitation, Konsistorium, Kirchenzucht und die Festigung des landesherrlichen Kirchenregiments, 1556–1586* (Stuttgart, 1971), pp. 40–41.

of Luther's early years as a reformer did not long outlast the troublesome 1520s. By 1530 it was gone, as dejection became the dominant mood in which Luther contemplated the worldly scene. For years now, he wrote in 1541, we Germans have been allowed to hear the precious word preached without falsification. "But how gratefully and honestly we have received and kept it is a dreadful thing to see." Only a few (*gar wenig*) want to accept it gratefully (*danckbarlich annemen*). The greater part shows itself to be impudent, licentious, faithless, lazy, thieving, given to consorting with evil sects and wicked heretics and "all this under the name and appearance of the gospel" while their real gods are Mammon and greed. "Thus Germany is ripe and rotten with all manner of sins against God," he concluded, which is why the Turk has been sent to punish us.[18] Luther took much of this dismal picture of Germany's moral condition from data newly brought to light by government visitations, in the planning for which in his own state of Saxony he had played a prominent part. The widespread apathy and ignorance discovered by the visitors convinced authorities, Luther and Melanchthon foremost among them, that "discipline" was now required above all other needs. As the chief theoretician of the Wittenberg movement, Melanchthon developed a doctrine of positive law that encouraged Protestant governments to overcome the earlier Lutheran ambivalence on the use of law, and to undertake, through legislation, the indoctrination of men and women in morality and *pietas*.[19] Such legislation was doing God's own work.[20] Hence the many mandates and directives concerning religion, the proliferation of which is the characteristic expression of politics in the second half of the sixteenth century.

Decrees and directives, however, tell us little about their impact on society. They may persuade us that "moral transformation" by way of a system of discipline was, indeed, the objective of both ecclesiastic and secular administrators, but they are silent on the results of this undertaking (although the ceaseless reissue of them in subsequent decades suggests that their results were less than perfect). For this reason visitation reports are an especially vital source for judging the social consequences of reformation in Germany. Visitations were designed to test the effectiveness of religious policy. They are, of course, official documents too, but they contain direct information obtained at first hand on the site, revealing the responses of ordinary people to government policy. Visitations were held frequently—at least annually, in most places—and carried out me-

[18]*Vermahnung zum Gebet wider den Türken* (1541), WA 51, pp. 585–89.

[19]Melanchthon, *Loci communes theologici* (1521), trans. L. J. Satre, in Wilhelm Pauck, ed., *Melanchthon and Bucer*, Library of Christian Classics, 19 (London, 1969), pp. 50, 53.

[20]Melanchthon, *Oratio de legibus*, printed in Guido Kisch, *Melanchthons Rechts- und Soziallehre* (Berlin, 1967), p. 196.

thodically. They were called "church visitations" (*Kirchenvisitationen*) not because churchmen alone conducted them (they did not) but because the unit of inspection was the church parish. Teams of ecclesiastical and lay officials passed from village to village and town to town (although they did not go to the larger cities, where magistrates were too jealous of their autonomy, and too powerful, to subject themselves to surveillance). There they put questions, taken from printed questionnaires, to local officials (pastors, schoolmasters, mayors, bailiffs, and council members) and to a selection of ordinary folk (women and men, old and young, rich and poor). Answers were written down by scribes at the site; later they were transcribed verbatim or in detailed paraphrase to fair copies. These were then gathered in volumes for use by appropriate government agencies. Most of these copies have survived, many in excellent condition. They may be read in state, municipal, and church archives throughout Germany. A few have been published.[21] They hold invaluable—and so far largely unexploited—evidence for discovering both the facts and the quality of life at the grass roots of society.

This claim, first made in my 1978 book, has been disputed. Many critics have asked whether, by their very purpose, the visitation reports do not overemphasize abuses and shortcomings. Were visitors not instructed to find faults? Were they not "intended to ferret out problems, not successes"? Clerical informants, in particular, must have had a "tendency to see sin everywhere." Taking the visitation reports at face value, it has been suggested, is like writing the history of our time from the police blotter. Still, I do not think that these are fatal objections, though they are valid cautions. Visitation reports, like all other historical documents, are "texts" in that they incorporate unspecified attitudes and are shaped by a net of largely unacknowledged circumstances. There is—to pick out one difficulty among many—the problem of "self-labeling," as emphasized now by the interactionist approach to the study of deviant behavior. ("Deviance" is, of course, what the visitation protocols were meant to pick out.) The recent literature on this subject shows how easily a "description" of phenomena becomes "ascription" when supposedly factual accounts of behavior are laced with value judgments brought to their observations by investigators harboring a preformed attitude toward what they see.[22] One must, of course. recognize this tendency on the part of six-

---

[21]See the partial list of printed and archival visitation materials in Ernst Walter Zeeden and Hansgeorg Molitor, eds., *Die Visitation im Dienst der kirchlichen Reform*, 2d ed. (Münster, 1977). For additional references, see my *Luther's House of Learning* (Baltimore, 1978), especially the notes to chaps. 12 and 13.

[22]See, for example, *Theories of Deviance*, ed. S. H. Traub and C. B. Little, 2d ed. (Itasca, Ill., 1980), pp. 241–42; Kai T. Erikson, "Notes on the Sociology of Deviance," in E. Rubington and M. S. Weinberg, eds., *Deviance* (New York, 1973), p. 27.

teenth-century visitors. Still, such circumspection belongs to the historian's basic equipment, and I see no reason why, when used along with other relevant materials, visitation records should not be trusted.

I have been finding additional materials that support my original interpretation. They include the copious records of local and patrimonial courts in Saxony, the so-called *Ehegerichte*, administrative and judicial tribunals on which clergymen had no place.[23] Concerned with problems of law and order in daily life, these bodies produced masses of records in which the picture conveyed of the country's religious condition matches that of the visitations exactly. Another source to be set beside visitation documents is the deliberations of territorial Estates (*Stände*), notably the unceasing stream of "grievances" (*gravamina, Beschwerden*) addressed by them to their sovereigns.[24] Grievances were very differently generated from visitation protocols. The latter were the products of centralized planning and execution; in the case of the former, masses of local complaints coalesced into regional and corporate protests. In indicating the state of religion and morality in society, however, the two sets of records are in full agreement. From Catholic Bavaria comes still another source to compare with visitation data: the already mentioned reports made to the Munich government by provincial Rentmeister. They contain the very same disappointing descriptions of religious conditions as the records of the duchy's parish visitations.[25]

The evidence from visitation reports seemingly cannot therefore be set aside as inherently untrustworthy. It may be assumed, of course, that exaggerations of failures slipped into the reports. In all likelihood, however, such hyperbole is balanced by some judicious doctoring of evidence in the opposite direction—in order to improve somewhat on the dismal facts of what was observed. Psychologically, the latter distortion makes as much sense as the former. No document is a clear window to reality. Only a much more systematic study of visitations than anything undertaken so far will reveal their real strengths or weaknesses as primary evidence for the consequences of reformation.

There are signs that such studies are now under way.[26] Additional

---

[23]Staatsarchiv Dresden, Locs. 8832 and 9905.

[24]For a lengthy discussion of this grievance literature, see my *Law, Resistance, and the State*, chap. 8.

[25]For a discussion of these reports in one district of Bavaria, see Hans Hornung, *Beiträge zur inneren Geschichte Bayerns vom 16.–18. Jahrhundert aus den Umrittsprotokollen der Rentmeister des Rentamtes Burghausen* (Munich, 1915).

[26]E. W. Zeeden of Tübingen has been overseeing work on visitations for some time. It is one of the projects of the Sonderforschungsbereich Spätmittelalter und Reformation at that university. See the bibliography by Zeeden and Molitor cited in n. 21. In France, the Centre National de la Recherche Scientifique has prepared a useful scheme for content analysis of visitation records.

visitation material is being unearthed from state, municipal, and church archives where it has been hiding from all but local historians.[27] It is also becoming clear that much more can be accomplished with these documents than has been attempted in the past, perhaps even the kind of serial history of religion envisioned by Pierre Chaunu.[28] But even before the fruits of these fresh labors have been brought in, we may agree with the judgment of Gabriel LeBras that, though visitation records, being human documents, are sure to contain errors, "the critical use of them will give us more truth about the prosperity or the poverty of the faith than is found in our literary fantasies." This, it seems to me, is the salient point: we need to move beyond the stereotypical view of the Reformation so long dominant in our work with the sources. The impulse to this forward step may well come from the lessons to be drawn from the visitations, namely that reform, conceived as religious and moral transformation, was not gaining much ground.[29]

One always returns to the question: why was this so? Why the failure to get through? Why the resistance? I think much more can be said in accounting for this lack of success than was suggested in my 1978 book, though I still think that the explanation offered there is sound. New factors keep emerging. Not until I began to work with the records of regional assemblies, for instance, did I sufficiently appreciate the extent to which the religious policies of state and church governments were impeded by the territorial nobility. As they attempted to implement their religious decrees, governments found themselves stymied by noble landlords anxious to protect their *ius patronatus*. The grievances of most members of the nobility were about the meddling of church consistories and superintendents in their *Gerichtbarkeit* or *Hofmarkrecht* or ius patronatus or Ehegericht—the cherished jurisdictions that defined their aristocratic liberties. Constant reiteration of complaints shows that these liberties were being violated. It also demonstrates, however, that the assault was being

See *Répertoire des visites pastorales de la France: Première série: Anciens diocèses (jusqu'en 1790)* I: *Agde-Bourges* (Paris, 1977), *Annexe*. Useful references to archival materials relating to visitations appear in the articles gathered in Georges Livet, ed., *Sensibilité religieuse et discipline ecclésiastique: Les visites pastorales en territoires protestants . . .* , *XVIe–XVIIIe siècles* (Strasbourg, 1975). See also the notes to pp. 156–59 of Paul Münch, *Zucht und Ordnung: Reformierte Kirchenverfassungen im 16. und 17. Jahrhundert* (Stuttgart, 1978).

[27]For example, Staatsarchiv Weimar, Reg N, *Ergänzungsband*, especially nos. 364–587.

[28]As described by Chaunu in Pierre Chaunu, "Une histoire religieuse sérielle," *Revue d'histoire moderne et contemporaine* 12 (1965), pp. 7–34.

[29]For a strongly dissenting view forcefully argued and well documented, see James M. Kittelson, "Successes and Failures in the German Reformation: The Report from Strasbourg," *Archive for Reformation History* 73 (1982):153–75, and "Visitations and Popular Religious Culture: Further Reports from Strasbourg," in Philip N. Bebb and Kyle C. Sessions, eds., *Pietas et Societas: New Trends in Reformation Social History* (Kirksville, Mo., 1985), pp. 89–101.

resisted. Cities often associated themselves with the nobility in these complaints. Given the utter dependence of princely rulers on their territorial estates for revenues raised from taxes, such parliamentary protests were by no means empty gestures. As for the nobility, its success in resisting intrusions was the measure of its survival as an autonomous estate. This tug-of-war must have been a heavy drag on the efforts of ecclesiastical and political bureaucrats to impose their regulations on the populace. As such it was surely a cause of their inability to make reformation effective.

Their efforts were further enfeebled by the notorious doctrinal dissension that split Lutheranism in the second half of the sixteenth century. Abundant evidence exists for the destructiveness of these divisions, which—touching almost every pastor in the church apparatus—reached down to every parish and congregation. The resulting embitterment of religious tempers may be difficult for us to appreciate. Contemporaries, however, were very much aware of it. Frequent *Änderungen*—doctrinal and administrative alterations—"are making citizens more distrustful, more defiant [*trutzig*], and more insolent every day."[30] Incessant disputes on the fine points of theology were causing "lay people and common folk to doubt the very articles of the faith and to hold the preachers, indeed the entire religion, in contempt."[31] In Saxony, in the 1560s, 1570s, and 1580s, the state frequently intervened to remove ministers from their pulpits following theological readjustments by the territory's chief ideologues. Those allowed to remain had to make open *Damnation und Revocation,* public recantations of their former beliefs and repudiations of those theologians from whom they had been derived—of the "Philippist" Victorinus Strigel, for example, a professor at the University of Jena, a leading advocate of the "synergist" position on divine grace and the human will, and a suspected follower of "Crypto-Calvinism" on the question of the Eucharist.[32] One can imagine the effect on a pastor's flock of such public humiliation. Partisans for one side or the other of this issue must have badly confused their auditors as they held forth from their pulpits with pro-Victorinus and anti-Victorinus fulminations.[33] The vast

[30]Christoph Scheurl in a memorandum to the Nuremberg Council, 1530. Germanisches Nationalmuseum Nuremberg, Merkel-Handschrift 129, 20 recto.

[31]From a memorandum by the Saxon jurist Melchior von Osse to Duke August of Saxony, written in 1555. Printed in O. A. Hecker, ed., *Schriften Dr. Melchiors von Osse* (Leipzig and Berlin, 1922), p. 294.

[32]For the effect of the "Crypto-Calvinist" controversy on one small-town Lutheran pastor, see my article "The Mental World of a Saxon Pastor," in Peter N. Brooks, ed., *Reformation Principle and Practice . . .* (London, 1980), pp. 165–67.

[33]Staatsarchiv Weimar Reg N, Nos. 376–88, contains a large number of documents illustrating the situation created on the parish level by this controversy in the 1560s and as late as the early 1570s.

body of writing produced by such a controversy (others concerned "anti-nomianism," "Osiandrism," "adiaphora," "Majorism," and so on) was evidently of absorbing interest to professional theologians.[34] The attitudes that these quarrels created in the minds of the theologically uninvolved are another matter.

The estrangement likely to have been the consequence must have been substantially deepened for the majority of ordinary people by the increasingly class-specific edge given later in the century to the Protestant message. R. W. Scribner has recently shown how the aim of Evangelical propaganda moved from popular to burgher targets and how this shift was made visually explicit in Lucas Cranach's graphic work on behalf of the Lutheran Reformation.[35] Other studies, too, have suggested that the conservative bent of established Lutheranism, particularly its emphasis on patriarchal authority and household property, made its strongest appeal to privileged proprietor groups,[36] a segment of society estimated to amount to no more than 20 percent of the whole.[37] The polarization resulting from this change in the Evangelical message's social direction must have affected the public response. Gabriel LeBras has noted that the practice of religion has never been the same for different classes of Christians.[38] The Reformation did not alter this state of affairs. Whatever Protestantism's original allure as spiritual enlightenment and religious liberation, once it had solidified itself as a politically defined church, it played the part of a provider of theologically and socially safe religious norms. The catechism was the ideal tool for indoctrinating the public in this kind of religion. Once this point had been recognized in the years following the events of 1525, Lutheran pedagogy moved its emphasis decisively from Scripture reading to catechetical instruction.[39] Lamenting the "blasphemous and shameless way in which the children of poor people grow up nowadays," a legal adviser to the government of Nuremberg recommended in 1530 that two German-language schools be set up in that city, "in which simple people's children will be taught some writing and the catechism . . . so

[34]A good impression of the sheer bulk of this kind of writing is given by repertory books in the Staatsarchiv Weimar, Reg. N, "Religionswesen," especially the *Ergänzungsband*, nos. 364–587 and 687–721.

[35]R. W. Scribner, *For the Sake of Simple Folk: Popular Propaganda for the German Reformation* (Cambridge, 1981), p. 247 and illus. 165 and 167.

[36]Berndt Balzer, *Bürgerliche Reformationspropaganda: Die Flugschriften des Hans Sachs in den Jahren 1523–1525* (Stuttgart, 1973). For England, see the suggestive remarks on this subject by J. J. Scarisbrick on pp. 173–74 of the book cited in n. 46 below.

[37]Peter Blickle, *Deutsche Untertanen: Ein Widerspruch* (Munich, 1981), p. 57.

[38]Gabriel LeBras, *Etudes de sociologie religieuse, vol. 1: Sociologie de la pratique religieuse dans les campagnes françaises* (Paris, 1955), p. 363.

[39]For an elaboration of this argument, see Richard Gawthrop and Gerald Strauss, "Protestantism and Literacy in Early Modern Germany," *Past and Present* 104 (1984):31–55.

that these children, who between the ages of five and ten are of no use either as servants or as laborers, will be kept from running wild in the streets.''[40] In this proposal we hear the authentic voice of established Lutheranism. Catechization in the rudiments of religion, with heavy stress on the duties arising from the fourth commandment: such was the approach to be taken now toward the majority of people. A historian looking at a later period has remarked that, ''when the members of a community are divided into classes . . . meeting only in relations of authority and subordination, it is futile to expect that they will meet in the same church.''[41] Lutheran churchmen, however, did harbor such expectations. When their hopes turned to disappointment, they were dismayed and puzzled.

They should not have been. Their own visitation reports showed them that another reason existed for the apathy displayed by so many toward the officially sanctioned faith. Sixteenth-century folk practiced their own brand of religion, which was a rich compound of ancient rituals, time-bound customs, a sort of unreconstructable folk Catholicism, and a large portion of magic to help them in their daily struggle for survival. This underground religion was not necessarily incompatible with the Lutheran creed. Still, when clergymen, intolerant of its primitivism, tried to stamp it out, hostilities developed at every point of contact. We have a somewhat distorted view of this conflict, for our idea of folk magic has been formed largely by the spectacular witch scares of the seventeenth century. The actual practices of folk belief were ordinary, unspectacular, and usually harmless. They had to do mainly with keeping oneself safe and coping with daily life. The facts about them lie buried in local records such as the visitation documents, from which a great deal can be learned about them.

Lutheran clerics abhorred this rival religion, supposing it, quite correctly, to be a popular alternative to the church, its ministers, and its teachings. Until recently, the opinions of modern scholars have reflected this disdain. Their views illustrate the preoccupation with the normative that has traditionally guided Reformation historiography. They also reveal the largely unquestioned assumption that the religious concerns preached so passionately from the pulpit met an equally heartfelt response from the mass of auditors. In such attitudes, Reformation scholarship shows itself to be backward compared with work done in the religious history of other periods. Our knowledge of the Reformation's reception by ordinary people is still largely undifferentiated, and this deficiency explains, I think,

[40]Memorandum by Johannes Müller, 1530, Germanisches Nationalmuseum Nuremberg, Merkel-Handschrift 129, 92 recto–93 recto.

[41]Hugh McLeod, *Class and Religion in Late Victorian London* (Hamden, Conn., 1974), p. 281.

the rather stern rejection by a number of reviewers of my conclusions concerning the "failure" of the Reformation. But the withdrawal, or defection, of groups of people from established churches and official religions is a common phenomenon. Fintan Michael Phayer has described it for nineteenth-century Bavaria, Joseph Moody for the French working class in the Second Empire, and K. S. Inglis, Owen Chadwick, Kitson Clark, Standish Meacham, Hugh McLeod, and James Obelkevich for Victorian England.[42] Obelkevich observes in his excellent study of *Religion and Rural Society* that

what parishioners understood as Christianity was never preached from a pulpit or taught in Sunday school, and what they took from the clergy they took on their own terms. . . . The Church . . . had become too closely associated with the elite and with elite culture to be attractive to most villagers, [and it] was almost entirely lacking in religious institutions of the middle range—monks, nuns, saints, shrines, processions, pilgrimages, rosaries, candles—which might have reduced the gap between transcendent deity and ordinary villagers. . . . The Church offered no "moral equivalent" to the magic and superstition that proliferated in the villages. Since the clergy were incapable of shaping a more popular version of the faith, villagers were left to do so themselves.[43]

These sentences relate to England in the middle of the nineteenth century, but they could have been written to describe the sixteenth-century German Reformation. "What is popular religion?" asks Obelkevich. He answers:

First of all, it is religion. To treat it as ignorance, superstition, debasement, or as compensation or mystification is to misconceive it. No less than the religion of the elite, it is a realm of the sacred, with its own pattern of symbol, ritual, and morality. At the same time, popular religion is popular: it grows out of the experience of the many, expressing their wider outlook and values and often their ambivalence toward a hegemonic faith.[44]

[42]Fintan Michael Phayer, *Religion und das gewöhnliche Volk in Bayern in der Zeit von 1750–1850 (Miscellanea Bavarica Monacensia* 21 [Munich, 1970]); Joseph N. Moody, ed., *Church and Society: Catholic Social and Political Thought and Movements, 1789–1950* (New York, 1953), 138; K. S. Inglis, *Churches and the Working Classes in Victorian England* (London, 1963); Owen Chadwick, *The Victorian Church,* 2 vols. (New York, 1966) 1:325–36, 2:235–36; G. S. R. Kitson Clark, *Churchmen and the Condition of England, 1832–1885* (London, 1973), chaps. 9–10; Standish Meacham, *A Life Apart: The English Working Class, 1890–1914* (London, 1977), pp. 15–16, 200; Hugh McLeod as in n. 41, especially chap. 2: "Who Went to Church?"; James Obelkevich, *Religion and Rural Society: South Lindsey, 1825–1875* (Oxford, 1976).

[43]James Obelkevich, *Religion and Rural Society,* p. 279.

[44]James Obelkevich, ed., *Religion and the People, 800–1700* (Chapel Hill, 1979), p. 7.

If this can be said by a historian of Victorian Britain, why not by a Reformation scholar?[45]

The answer may be that too few of us who work on the German Reformation have grasped the importance of what Keith Thomas has demonstrated for seventeenth-century England and what John Bossy has tried to show for late sixteenth-century France and Italy: that a change occurred in the normative meaning of religion as a result of the Reformation, a shift away from piety and toward doctrine or creed. The result of this shift, which placed unprecedented emphasis on the central necessity of a coherent doctrine, was—Thomas writes—"an across-the-board downgrading of alternative views of religion and knowledge." In this derogation, the word "magic" came to be applied indiscriminately to all forms of popular religion. German visitation records bear out the aptness of this formulation, as they do Thomas's further assertion that, while before the Reformation, the Church was "a limitless source of supernatural aid, applicable to most of the problems likely to arise in daily life," Protestant theologians tried to abolish "this whole apparatus of supernatural assistance," although—plainly—"the problems for which the magical remedies of the past had provided some sort of solution were still there."[46] Because the problems would not go away, and the new religion offered no simple corrective for them, people sought their own remedies.

It seems to me that the reluctance of Reformation historians to accept this view of how ordinary people construct their religion has less to do with a shortage of sources than with the uncritical acceptance by so many of us of what, earlier in this chapter, I called a myth about the Reformation. The proponents of this myth know only the normative faith, the one developed by theologians and delivered from university lecterns and church pulpits. They do not ask how this faith was received by those for

[45]The reluctance of Reformation historians to draw the sum even of their own investigations is illustrated by Bernard Vogler, "Die Entstehung der protestantischen Volksfrömmigkeit in der rheinischen Pfalz zwischen 1555 und 1619," *Archiv für Reformationsgeschichte* 72 (1981):158–95. Vogler concludes (p. 195) that Protestantism as a product of a "rational and urban culture" initiated a "secularization of thought" by demanding a piety detached from sacred objects and by banning old fears and anxieties about hell and demons. Vogler's own evidence suggests, however, that things remained the same for most people, thus contradicting his conclusion. Most of the evidence is set out in the three volumes of Vogler's *Vie religieuse en pays rhenan dans la seconde moitié du 16e siècle, 1556–1619* (Service de reproduction des thèses, Université de Lille III, 1974).

[46]Keith Thomas, *Religion and the Decline of Magic* (London, 1971), pp. 76–77; John Bossy, "The Counter-Reformation and the People of Catholic Europe," *Past and Present* 47 (1970):51–70 and *Christianity in the West 1400–1700* (Oxford, 1985). For a vivid picture of the stark contrast between the old faith and the new, see J. J. Scarisbrick, *The Reformation and the English People* (Oxford, 1984), chap. 8: "Rival Evangelisms."

whom it was intended or how it fitted into their world. The reformers themselves were more curious than this about the public reaction to their labors. Holding themselves responsible for people's lives, as well as for their souls, they asked hard questions about the reception of the faith they tried so vigorously to bring to their flocks. Through these questions they discovered that they were failing in their best efforts.

I do not think that we should interpret this failure as a judgment on the worth of their objectives, but it does seem to be a sign of the instinct people have for protecting themselves from uplifting ideas forced upon them from above. Whether we read this sign as a sad comment on human behavior or as an encouraging one depends on how we feel about the idea.

One of the highlights of recent Reformation research is the work on Strasbourg, perhaps the most vibrant intellectual center in sixteenth-century Germany. One of the many excellent studies of this Alsatian city is a recent work of synthesis that examines the religious history of Strasbourg during the entire century of the Reformation. Lorna Jane Abray, associate professor of history at the University of Toronto at Scarborough, published a book, The People's Reformation: Magistrates, Clergy, and Commons in Strasbourg, 1500–1598 (1985), in which she analyzes the interplay of forces between the three constituent elements of civic society in defining the socioreligious body of believers. There emerges from her research a fascinating picture both of the contests between the reformed clergy and the laity in defining orthodoxy of belief and correct behavior and of the enduring differences between clerical and lay understandings of piety.

# [10]

## The Laity's Religion: Lutheranism in Sixteenth-Century Strasbourg

LORNA JANE ABRAY

What did the Reformation mean to laypeople in the sixteenth century? This is one of the most tantalizing questions we can raise about the early modern period and one that evidence from the free imperial city of Strasbourg can help to answer.[1] In Strasbourg the early Reformation was characterized by intense competition for popular support on the part of proponents of several visions of a purified Christianity: Catholic, humanist, Evangelical, radical, and spiritualist. By the mid-1530s the city was officially Protestant, and Lutheranism was emerging as the dominant force in the Strasburghers' religious lives. Yet questions about doctrine and morality, and about the proper division of power between the clergy and the secular rulers, would not be fully resolved until 1598, when Strasbourg at last ratified the Formula of Concord, a detailed definition of Lutheran orthodoxy. The city's long reformation, nearly a century in the making, was the product of an interplay of clerical, magisterial, and popular designs for the Christian church.

The clergy's program to reform the faith is the clearest of these three designs, for the preachers themselves codified it in confessions of faith and catechisms. The magistrates produced no such documents, but they did legislate church ordinances that, together with the surviving records of their debates (particularly the minutes of the Senate and XXI, the city's

[1]This essay is an adaptation of chapter 7 of Lorna Jane Abray, *The People's Reformation: Magistrates, Clergy, and Commons in Strasbourg, 1500–1598* (Ithaca and Oxford, 1985). Manuscripts cited in the notes are to be found in the Archives Municipales de Strasbourg, or AMS (which also houses the Archives du Chapitre St. Thomas, or AST), and in the Bibliothèque Nationale et Universitaire de Strasbourg, or BNUS.

main governing body) and the masses of other government papers, make it possible to recreate the lay political elite's understanding of what a proper reformation should involve. When we turn to the lay population at large the meaning of the Reformation becomes truly difficult to grasp. The majority of the magistrates' lay subjects—let us, for convenience, call them "the people"—considered themselves to be "good Protestants," and sources of information about what they meant by this phrase are not scarce, although they are fragmentary. No general statements issued by the people are comparable to the clerical and magisterial documents. We must try to piece together popular religion from a mass of hints and anecdotes that yield no more than themes and tendencies. These broad patterns in popular religion, when combined with the magistrates' opinions and illuminated by clerical statements, give us a fascinating glimpse of the laity's religion during the decades in which Lutheranism took shape.

The Protestant reformation in Strasbourg began with Evangelical preaching by clergymen stimulated by Martin Luther's ideas. From the beginning, lay responses to the clerical reformation varied. Some Strasburghers let events roll on without them, ignoring the new preachers as once they had ignored their priests. There were parents here who preferred to send their children to unlicensed teachers to learn the three Rs, because the legal parish schools spent too much time on religious instruction.[2] Other people took an active part in the Reformation, arguing in the taverns and marketplaces or even fomenting riots.[3] Some of these men and women later grew cool toward the new established church, for the enthusiasms of the 1520s often gave way to indifference once the Protestant faith had been institutionalized. Although the majority accepted the progressive Lutheranizing of their new church, important minorities followed sectarian leaders, or preferred Swiss to Lutheran definitions of reform, whereas still other Strasburghers rejected Protestantism entirely and remained loyal to the old church. All these people, even the comparatively apathetic, were united by their insistence on their right to define their own beliefs. We do the Strasburghers an injustice if we assume that they cared so little for the greatest abstract issues of their day—salvation and morality—that they would accept blindly what the more learned told them, whether the more learned were Catholic priests, Lutheran pastors, Calvinist divines, or sectarian preachers.

Strasburghers in the sixteenth century heard a welter of conflicting

---

[2]AST 372, third foliation, fol. 20r–v (1546).
[3]Miriam Usher Chrisman, *Strasbourg and the Reform* (New Haven, 1967), pp. 104–105, 138–40, and 144; Thomas A. Brady, Jr., *Ruling Class, Regime, and Reformation at Strasbourg, 1520–1555* (Leiden, 1978), pp. 203–204.

opinions and often reached their own conclusions. The case of a member of the aristocratic Zorn von Plobsheim family shows this process at work. He wanted to read the Bible, and in 1530, Luther's translation was not complete, so he took what he could from Luther and added other parts in translations done by Anabaptists and by a follower of Huldrych Zwingli. Then, with a fine disregard for the theological differences of his translators, he had the separate parts bound together and sat down to read it all for himself.[4] A generation later the president of the Church Assembly, Johann Marbach, complained about local printers who published hymnals that mingled Schwenckfeldian and Anabaptist hymns with Lutheran chorales.[5] Throughout the century the city's residents could continue to pick, to mix, and to choose. Daniel Sudermann, an immigrant to the city, described his religious evolution: "First I was a Catholic [in Liège]. But soon, in 1558, I went to the Calvinist school. I attended Lutheran services as well. Heard the Anabaptists. In 1594 I came to understand the truth."[6] Sudermann was forty-four when he found his truth in the teachings of a spiritualist, Caspar Schwenckfeld.

Few Strasburghers set down their experiences even as summarily as did Sudermann. All of them, if they chose, could expose themselves to as many ideas as he did, and all without leaving their own territory, as Strasbourg always had heretical congregations within its walls. For all that, most people preferred the established Lutheran church to its rivals and developed their ideas in response to its direction. These Lutherans, although they were the majority, are the people about whose religious lives we know least. The easiest way to approach them is to begin with the external framework the clergy created for them. From there we can review some of the evidence about widespread beliefs not necessarily spelled out in confessions and church ordinances—like superstitions and bigotry—before turning to the men who ruled Strasbourg and left in their records our most comprehensive picture of lay values.

The orthodox had no difficulty in meeting whatever need they felt for public worship.[7] Every morning at five o'clock in summer and six o'clock in winter the assistant pastors of the seven parishes held a short early service with prayers and a half-hour exhortation to piety. At eight or nine the cathedral preacher gave a sermon on a biblical text, working his way

---

[4]The Bible is now in the BNUS, R 10087.

[5]Minutes of the Senate and XXI (RP) for 1576, fols. 632r–637v.

[6]Hans Horning, *Daniel Sudermann als Handschriftensammler: Ein Beitrag zur strassburger Bibliothekgeschichte* (Tübingen inaugural diss., 1956), p. 23. Sudermann had immigrated to Strasbourg in 1585.

[7]For the evolution of services, see René Bornert, *La réforme protestante du culte à Strasbourg au XVIe siècle (1523–1598): Approche sociologique et interprétation théologique* (Leiden, 1981).

through the Testaments according to an annual schedule, and there was another daily service in the cathedral in the late afternoon. On Sunday morning there was an early service in each parish, intended for servants in particular; they could hear the word of God and then return to mind the house while their employers attended the longer second service, which began with an organ recital and hymn singing by the congregation.[8] Standing before the altar, the pastor then led his parishioners in a general confession of sins, reminding them of God's mercy and forgiveness and reciting other prayers with them. There followed more singing before the pastor moved to his pulpit to join the congregation in a silent recitation of the Lord's Prayer. He then announced his text and preached for about an hour. Later came prayers for the well-being of the congregation as a whole and also for particular members, for example, the sick. Another round of singing and a blessing completed the service, which ended with a final organ recital. Four times during the year this service was given over to a review of parts of the catechism. At noon on Sunday those avid for instruction could take part in a second service at the cathedral and could even return there for a third in the early evening. Meanwhile, in the afternoon, catechism classes had been held in each parish for the youngsters. Special services of prayer and penance were held every Tuesday, once a month there was a half holiday for these exercises, and four times a year a full day was given over to them.

The sacraments naturally had a place of their own. Parishioners could take communion every Sunday in the cathedral, fortnightly or monthly in the other parishes, and in all the churches on Easter Sunday, Whitsunday, Christmas, and New Year's Day. They were urged to attend a preparatory service the preceding Saturday evening, at which their pastors reminded them of the importance of the sacrament and went through the long list of those who should exclude themselves or should be excluded as unworthy. Those wishing to do so—and the practice was encouraged—could remain for further instruction and for a voluntary private confession of sin. The other sacrament was baptism, and like the Lord's Supper, it was intended to be communal. A child's father was to arrange it with his pastor in advance, which gave the pastor an opportunity to veto unsuitable godparents. The clergy admonished parents not to pick sponsors on "worldly" grounds (for example, to establish a connection with a powerful family) but to choose pious members of the church who would help to ensure that the child received a Christian education. In an emergency a

---

[8]Miriam Usher Chrisman, *Lay Culture, Learned Culture: Books and Social Change in Strasbourg, 1480–1599* (New Haven, 1982), pp. 154–55, 166, notes that hymnals were among the books most likely to be owned by the laity. She argues that the laity absorbed much of their biblical knowledge through the Psalms.

child could be baptized at home and even in the absence of a clergyman. When this happened, the child was to be brought before the congregation later, not for rebaptism, but for the public prayers that acknowledged its membership in the visible church.

Marriage was no sacrament, but it remained a religious act as well as a secular one and again a public one. When people whom the pastor did not know presented themselves, he had the right to examine them on their beliefs. Reading out the banns to the rest of the congregation reinforced the social nature of the contract.

Encouraged by their doctors to turn to the clergy for help, the sick and the dying readily did so. Pastors came into their homes to offer them the Lord's Supper and to pray with them, and also commended their cases to their congregations for public prayer. When Johann Marbach was summoned to Jacob Sturm's deathbed in 1553, he found Sturm unable to talk but fully conscious. Marbach stayed with him until the end, reading to him from the Gospel according to St. John.[9] Funeral services were kept brief and were devoted to strengthening the living.

For young Strasburghers the clergy offered a special Sunday service at which girls and boys were drilled on the fundamentals of their faith. The 1534 Church Ordinance specified that they were to learn the articles of faith, the Lord's Prayer, and the Ten Commandments. Parents or guardians, masters, and teachers were obliged by law to get their charges to these lessons; the older children and young adults were particularly recalcitrant. Many of the pastors instituted special prizes for diligent students. In 1551 Christoff Kolöffel, who was then eleven, recited his whole catechism before the congregation, along with twenty-eight other youngsters. Each of them got a new Strasbourg penny; children in other parishes might get a little book instead.[10] The city schools emphasized religious training, including instruction in hymn singing. Pious parents could supplement all this with home instruction, and books were available to help them. One local manual recommended that family Bible readings be held four times daily.[11] By the time children were ready to take communion for the first time, the pastors could reasonably expect them to understand the elements of their faith.[12] It is likely that most of the children brought up in the city did, although there was no guarantee that all this indoctrination would remain alive in a child's mind.

---

[9]Marbach's diary, AST 198, fols. 100r–101r.
[10]Kolöffel's recollections, BNUS ms. 847, fol. 18r; Nicolas Florus, *Kurtze und einseltige Auslegung des 91 Psalmen* (Strasbourg, 1576), p. 5; AST 198, fol. 123v.
[11]*Tischgebete für die Kinder* (Strasbourg, 1557), sig. A iii recto.
[12]Isaac Kessler, *Kurtz Examen und Underricht vom Sacrament des heyligen Abentmals . . . Für die Christliche Jugendt* (Strasbourg, 1556), gives a good example of what was expected.

Through sermons, books, private instruction, and catechizing, the clergy devoted endless energy to educating their flocks. Decades passed before these efforts bore fruit, and many adult Strasburghers, from the magistrates on down the social scale, long remained vague about the tenets of their faith. In 1534 a member of the Council of XV, Peter Sturm, told his fellow magistrates that he was too preoccupied with official business to know what he believed, and he declined to express any opinion about the Tetrapolitan Confession presented to the emperor in the city's name in 1530; many of his fellow magistrates were equally unsure of themselves.[13] Admittedly a formal confession of faith would be daunting to nontheologians, and Sturm's successors in the next generation regularly expressed their distaste for theology.[14] Other Strasburghers showed an equal incomprehension of simpler material, and comments in the parish registers of the 1560s identify people unable to answer even the most basic questions about their faith. Parishioners turned up who could not recite the Lord's Prayer or the Ten Commandments, and men and women who remembered parts of their catechism into adulthood were evasive when asked about the Lord's Supper.[15] By the 1570s this phenomenon was on the wane. The laity had come to know what they were supposed to believe.

One old lesson that continued to be pounded home was that of God's power. Both natural and man-made disasters—fires, floods, bad harvests, plagues, wars, and defeats—were set down to the operation of God's wrath. Pastor Nicolas Florus, for instance, commenting on the Hundred and Thirty-seventh Psalm ("By the Waters of Babylon"), explained that the Jews had been subjected to the anguish of exile for neglecting their religious duties and that this sort of calamity could be visited on the Germans just as easily. The magistrates sounded similar themes in the preambles to their statutes.[16] Both sets of authorities argued that God operated on a theory of collective responsibility, so that the sins of the few could result in divine punishment for the whole city.[17] When disaster threatened, the first reflex was supposed to be toward prayer and repentance; the greater the danger, the greater was the need for collective atonement and improvement. This was not always forthcoming, as shown by the stream of complaints about frivolous, worldly behavior during the

[13]Manfred Krebs and Hans Georg Rott, eds., *Elsass,* pt. 1: *Stadt Strassburg, 1522–1532,* and *Elsass,* pt. 2: *Stadt Strassburg, 1533–1535* (Gütersloh, 1959–60), pt. 2, no. 523.
[14]AST 55/3, fol. 26r (1563); RP 1563, fols. 396v—397r.
[15]AMS N26, pp. 309, 393, 469.
[16]*Der CXXXVII Psalm* (Strasbourg, 1587), sigs. B ii verso and B iv verso; BNUS ms. 39.894, "Christliche Erinnerung eines erbarn Rhats," 1585.
[17]RP 1540, fol. 273v; AST 80/39 (1541); RP 1546, fol. 618v; RP 1547, fols. 178v–183v; RP 1564, fols. 418v–419r; RP 1566, fol. 270v.

mid-century crisis that began with the Schmalkaldic War.[18] To balance the fear of God's power, the clergy also emphasized his love for his people, which was demonstrated by good harvests, healthy babies, and, most of all, by the promise of salvation. Release from danger was to be celebrated by prayers of thanksgiving.[19] Whether individual Strasburghers were more impressed by God's love or by his wrath cannot be known, but they clearly believed he intervened directly in their collective and personal lives.

They also believed in the Devil, and some of them were willing to risk their souls by consulting his agents. Strasbourg had its "warsager," or soothsayers, who could find lost or stolen objects and who claimed to know what was going on miles away or in the future. One of these was Batt Ott, reputed to have been a priest in the city before the Reformation, and in and out of it thereafter, attracting a large clientele, particularly among the country folk who had moved into town. Pastors and magistrates agreed that he was involved in the Devil's business. The clergy preached against divination and banned its practitioners and their clients; the magistrates expelled Ott and absolutely forbade their subjects to consult anyone like him.[20] Such measures did not put an end to the thirst for illicit knowledge, particularly about the course of the future, and throughout the century Strasburghers sought out any books of prophecies and prognostications that escaped the censors.[21] The warsager Ott was stopped, but others replaced him, some of whom claimed to be healers. Their activities shaded into black magic and witchcraft in the authorities' judgments.[22]

Accusations of witchcraft and sorcery begin to occur in the city records in the early 1560s. Peter Aller's wife was thought to be a witch because of her quarrelsome disposition. A woman was burned in 1564—the first execution in a long time, according to the chronicler who recorded it. In

[18]For example, RP 1546, fols. 299v, 334v, 393v–394v, 460r, 561r–v; RP 1547, fols. 35r–v, 78v, 248v, 250v, 293r.

[19]RP 1571, fol. 1010v, on the news of the Christian victory over the Turks at Lepanto; Jean-Pierre Kintz, *La société strasbourgeoise du milieu du XVIe siècle à la fin de la guerre de Trente Ans, 1560–1650: Essai d'histoire démographique, économique, et sociale* (Paris, 1984), pp. 219–21, on childbirth.

[20]Daniel Specklin, "Les collectanées de Daniel Specklin," ed. Rodolphe Reuss, *Bulletin de la Société pour la conservation des monuments historiques d'Alsace (BSCMHA)*, n.s. 14 (1889), no. 2364; AMS R3, fol. 255v (1537); RP 1544, fols. 334v–335r, 408r, 411r; Kessler, *Kurtz Examen*, sigs. B vii recto–B viii verso.

[21]For example, Otto Brunfels, *Almanach . . . von dem xxvj Jar an, bitz zuo Endt der Welt* (Strasbourg, 1526); Johann Carion, *Practica und Prognostication* (Strasbourg, 1545).

[22]RP 1556, fols. 187v, 189r; RP 1566, fol. 528r; AST 67/II, fols. 14v–17v (1566); AST 67/III, fols. 46v–48r (1567); RP 1568, fol. 91r.

1579 a woman in the Krutenau district (one of the city's poorest quarters) was supposed to have laid a spell on her husband, filling his body with chopped straw; she too was burned. Two years later, as a result of neighbors' complaints, the magistrates burned another woman from the same district. There were more executions in 1581, 1587, and 1588, about the time that Johann Fischart translated and published Jean Bodin's *Demonomania*. In 1593 several people were in prison awaiting judgment on charges of witchcraft.[23] The magistrates did not always believe the evidence submitted to them.[24] They also made some effort to keep stories about the Devil, witches, and magic out of their subjects' hands. In 1533 they refused to allow a printer to bring out a tale about an appearance by the Devil in nearby Schiltigheim. Thirty years later they ordered Diebolt Berger not to print a song about a witch burned in the county of Helffenstein. In 1587 they rejected a book about Faust on the grounds that the young people were already too much interested in the black arts and such a book would only lead more of them astray.[25]

Official prohibitions did little good when both the magistrates' executions and the clergy's sermons confirmed the reality of the Devil and his works. The sense of malign powers brooding over vulnerable humans is brilliantly evoked in Hans Baldung Grien's spare and haunting print, "The Stable-Hand Bewitched." There he lies, toppled on his back, his feet toward us, his face partially concealed, struck down. Behind him the horse in his care turns its head to eye him uneasily. We look to find the cause of his destruction and there, at the side, peering through the small stable window, is the dreadful face of the crone who ruined him, Satan's agent.[26]

Like the warsager and the witches, strange visionaries and prophets found a following in the city despite official condemnation. Melchior Hofmann, Clemens Ziegler, and Lienhard and Ursula Jost all had connections with the Anabaptists, but there were also independent figures, such as Martin Steinbach. Steinbach was an illiterate cooper from Sélestat who claimed to be the Holy Ghost, the prophet Elias, and a light of truth. His disclosures were more than a little obscure, even to his followers, yet he

---

[23]For Aller's wife, RP 1562, fol. 255r–v. Sébald Büheler, "La chronique strasbourgeoise de Sébald Büheler," ed. Léon Dacheux, *BSCMHA*, n.s. 13 (1888), nos. 415 (1564) and 539 (1579); Léon Dacheux, ed., "Fragments de diverses vieilles chroniques," *BSCMHA*, n.s. 18 (1898), no. 4078; BNUS ms. 998, pp. 130–31 (1593).

[24]For example, RP 1569, fol. 777r–v, and RP 1585, fol. 336v.

[25]See the chronicle begun by Sebastian Brant, "Annales de Sébastien Brant," ed. Léon Dacheux, *BSCMHA*, n.s. 15 (1892), no. 3579. RP 1563, fol. 382v; RP 1587, fol. 615v.

[26]Reproduced in Marianne Bernhard, *Hans Baldung Grien: Handzeichnungen, Druckgraphik* (Munich, 1978), p. 76.

did attract both men and women, and according to a chronicler his sect's articles got into print. Pastor Matthis Negelin considered the Steinbachians enough of a problem to write a book against them.[27]

Some Strasburghers thus showed a taste for special revelations, and there was a widespread fascination with the biblical prophets and the Apocalypse. The magistrates discouraged sermons on these matters, but the preachers went ahead, whether from their own interest or to preempt or refute false exegetes. In 1568 Melchior Speccer published a commentary on Matthew 14 and more particularly on the second coming of Christ. It drew a great deal of its color from the Revelation and from the early modern fascination with monstrous and deformed infants.[28] A few years later Johann Marbach took a rather different tack in *On Miracles and Miraculous Signs.*[29] In it Marbach attacked Jesuit propaganda about miracles and exorcisms; the book was addressed to the people of Bavaria and Augsburg but could also have been used against doubts that Catholic migrants to Strasbourg might plant in Lutheran minds. What particularly bothered Marbach was the effect of the Jesuit claim that, although Catholics still experienced miracles, the Lutherans had not produced a single one in fifty years. Marbach first hinted broadly and then announced flatly that Father Peter Canisius's success as an exorcist should be attributed to the Devil's collusion. Against this sort of wickedness Marbach flourished the Lutheran miracles: the exposure of Antichrist and the destruction of the papacy; the "wonderful" reception of Luther's teaching; the translation of the Bible. Marbach might have described this as fighting superstition with true religion, but it was perhaps not very effective against the Strasburghers' craving for horrors, supernatural tales, and visible manifestations of God and the Devil. Superstition and orthodoxy are notoriously hard to separate, and the Strasburghers' religion certainly contained a good dollop of the former.

Historians have made much of the Strasburghers' toleration of those whose views were unorthodox in the confessional sense—the relatively lenient treatment of sectarians, the willingness to allow Catholics to live in the city, and the charity shown to Calvinist refugees.[30] This toleration was real but limited, because official policy and public opinion tolerated individuals rather than faiths. The non-Lutheran denominations were all con-

---

[27]For Hofmann, Ziegler, and the Josts, see Krebs and Rott, *Elsass.* Information on Steinbach is scattered; the most convenient source is Reinhard Lutz, *Verzaichnus . . . der kaetzerischen, und verdampten Leer Martin Steinbachs . . .* (Strasbourg, 1566). Negelin's book is not extant.

[28]AST 75/52, fol. 761r; Melchior Speccer, *Auslegung des Evangelii Matthei am XIV Capitel* (Strasbourg, 1568), a work for lay readers.

[29]*Von Mirackeln und Wunderzeichen* (Strasbourg, 1571).

[30]*The People's Reformation*, chap. 3, n. 44, and chap. 5.

demned, and the Strasburghers' religion was heavily tinged by this condemnation. For many people the confessional debates reduced themselves
to automatic attacks on abstract labels such as "popery," fed by the
century's gift for scurrilous invective on the order of calling Jesuits "Jesu-
wider," or opponents of Christ.[31] For the illiterate, pictures told the tale.
In the early days of the reformation, there were woodcuts depicting the
pope as Antichrist, as a mercenary, or riding on the seven-headed beast of
Revelation in the company of the Great Whore. In 1577 Tobias Stimmer
did a woodcut, which also carried verses by Johann Fischart, showing
"The Weird and Grotesque Mill" that ground up priests to expose their
kernels: monsters and demons.[32] Lutheran congregations sang battle
hymns against the Catholics:

> From false lips does their talk proceed,
> From disunited hearts,
> Their doctrine's empty, baseless creed,
> Which gives the conscience smarts;
> With purgatory, absolution, mass
> And ban, the world misled it has.[33]

Peter Canisius, who was in Strasbourg around the middle of the century,
described a play performed in the Latin school, which dealt with a man
made ill by swallowing Catholic ideas and cured by vomiting up Catholic
objects of worship.[34] Catholics were not the only victims of these attacks;
the Lutheran clergy habitually referred to Caspar Schwenckfeld as
"Stinkfield."[35] As one prominent laywoman noted, what was lacking in
all of this was any sense of Christian charity.[36] The Lutheran clergy
undoubtedly felt themselves under siege in Strasbourg in the second generation of the Reformation, thanks in particular to pressure from Catholics
and Calvinists outside the city, and tried to develop a fortress mentality in
their congregations.[37] To some extent this tactic worked. Lambert
Daneau, a professor of theology in Geneva en route to Leiden with his

---

[31]For example, Johannes Fischart, *Nacht Rab oder Nebelkraeh* (Strasbourg, 1570).

[32]R. W. Scribner, *For the Sake of Simple Folk: Popular Propaganda in the German Reformation* (Cambridge, 1981), pp. 94, 71, and 161 and illus. 78 and 131.

[33]Johannes Janssen, *History of the German People at the Close of the Middle Ages*, trans. M.
A. Mitchell and A. M. Cowie, 16 vols. (London, 1896–1925), 11:290, quoting hymnbooks of
1562 and 1566. There were secular songs against the Catholics as well as hymns; see Büheler,
"La chronique," pp. 363–69.

[34]Janssen, *History of the German People*, 13:182–83.

[35]AST 180/53, fols. 575r–634r, Marbach's six sermons against "Stenckfeld" (1556).

[36]Katherine Zell, *Ein Brieff an die gantze Burgerschafft* (Strasbourg, 1557).

[37]AST 100, unnumbered piece (1579), a sermon by Johann Liptitz on holding to the true
faith.

family in midwinter 1582, described his arrival in the city at sundown, in a driving rainstorm. Inn after inn turned him away, and the city's chief magistrate refused to help him.[38] The anti-Catholic and anti-Calvinist popular demonstrations of 1559 and 1581 reveal a current in the Strasburghers' religion that was far removed from toleration but was likewise part of their sense of being Lutheran.[39]

To move deeper into the meaning of Lutheranism for sixteenth-century Strasburghers we need to find a sample of laypeople who left a regular record of their reactions to the reformation. The only group that did so were the members of the Senate and XXI. Using them as a sample of the lay majority raises difficulties because the magistrates were not typical townspeople. They were older, better educated, more sophisticated and wealthier than their subjects, and all were men. Yet the magistrates' opinions, taken in their eighty-year sweep, can serve as a guide to the lay understanding of the Reformation. In the 1520s the magistrates were outpaced by early converts to the new faith; in the late 1540s and toward the end of the century they stepped ahead of their subjects by negotiating with Catholics and Calvinists. In each case, however, they worked themselves back closer to popular opinion in about a decade.

Like their subjects, the rulers of Strasbourg were not all Lutheran.[40] Some, like Ludwig Wolff von Renchen, Adolff Braun, and Wolf Sigismund Wurmser, remained Catholic. Others adopted a Protestant position but set their own interpretation on it. Jacob Sturm seems to have leaned toward Schwenckfeld's views, and Michael Theurer made no secret of his admiration for the spiritualist. Jacob Wetzel von Marsilien was fascinated by the Anabaptists, but he may well have been Catholic like other members of his family. A very few of the magistrates accused of Calvinism had some inclination to the Genevan faith; Josias Rihel always refused to condemn it. Adolff Braun was never reelected to the Senate after the discovery that he had circulated a Jesuit attack on Johann Marbach in the city, and Wetzel was dismissed from the Council of XV as a result of difficulties more constitutional than religious. The others had normal, even illustrious, careers. All of them managed to work effectively with their Lutheran colleagues, just as their heterodox subjects had managed to coexist with the Lutheran majority.

Again, like their subjects, the magistrates were not all, or were not always, consistent. Nicolas Fuchs was a determined advocate of pro-Calvinist foreign policies, whereas Jacob von Molsheim and Michael

[38]AST 100, unnumbered piece, "Lambertus Danaeus in Apologia adversus Doct. Jacobum Andreae."
[39]For these disturbances, see *The People's Reformation*, pp. 59–60, 116–17, and 149.
[40]For the examples that follow, and other cases, see ibid., appendix A.

Lichtensteiger were equally adamant in their support for the Formula of Concord and its condemnation of Calvinism. On the other hand, many of their colleagues slid into contradictions. Johann Carl Lorcher voted against the Calvinists one month and against the Lutherans another. The passage of time changed the opinions of other men, banking the enthusiasm of one and kindling that of another. Claus Kniebis had led the militant Evangelical faction in the 1520s, but by 1547 he rejected the idea of prolonging the Schmalkaldic War. His contemporary, Martin Betschold, had been slow to accept the Protestant preachers, but in 1546 he urged the passage of two of their most cherished projects, a uniform liturgy and a means to examine parishioners on their beliefs.

Individually and as a corporation, the magistrates of Strasbourg proclaimed themselves to be Christian. Very early, perhaps by 1524 and certainly by 1526, the majority of them had become Evangelicals. After 1529, when they abolished the Mass, they consistently defended the Protestant cause, committing themselves and their city again and again to the Augsburg Confession. Twice, in 1546 and in 1592, they went to war for it. Between these wars they pursued an aggressive foreign policy that challenged the Habsburg plans for Europe. Defeat in the Schmalkaldic War did not blunt their resolve to fight the Catholic powers where and how they might. Their links with the French Huguenots brought them the suspicion of Lutherans east of the Rhine and the constant menace of French siege and conquest. Still they persisted. For the Protestant cause they would risk both their autonomy and their prosperity.

What was this Protestantism that meant so much to them? It was the accomplishment of God's will, for the magistrates were no less convinced than were their clergy that their own way was God's way. In their public statements they stressed their desire to advance the honor of God, a theme that recurs as the justification for their policies in their 1527 mandate against the sects, in a 1559 address to the guilds, a 1568 blasphemy statute, and eventually in their 1597 condemnation of Calvinism.[41] The explanation was no empty rhetorical flourish but the accurate expression of one of their deepest convictions.

A sincere piety informed the magistrates' discharge of their responsibilities. In 1564 Johann Schenckbecher set down this prayer in his diary: "On the sixteenth of September the Council of XV elected me to replace the late Diebolt Gerfalck on that council. May our beneficent and merciful God grant that I may fill this office for the praise and honor of his holy name, for the succor of many people, and the salvation of my soul."[42]

---

[41]Krebs and Rott, *Elsass,* pt. 1, no. 92; AMS IV/48/31; BNUS R22, pt. 12; AST 84/113.
[42]AST 1655, fol. 31r.

The following year Hans Hammerer said much the same thing to his colleagues on being elected to one of the regime's highest offices: "Since it has pleased God almighty to put me in this office this year, I want to pray to him that he will lend me his divine grace and wisdom, so that I may better fulfill my task."[43] As they were in the privacy of their chambers, so they were in public. At the close of the annual ceremony of reciprocal oaths between magistrates and citizens, the oligarchs joined the burghers in a prayer for divine guidance. Every year on the day following this ceremony the magistrates invited their subjects to a special church service where all those present solemnly repeated this appeal.[44] At regular intervals throughout the year they authorized special prayer days to implore God to grant protection to the city. Likewise they called for special public prayers during their most difficult enterprises; Jacob Sturm personally requested such a service before the Catholic-Protestant colloquy at Worms.[45]

The magistrates' religion was not the increasingly convoluted doctrinal edifice that the Lutheran clergy in and out of Strasbourg constructed in the sixteenth century. Eventually they approved that edifice, for sooner or later they always bowed to the clergy's technical competence and accepted their theological judgments. Still, they accepted precise statements of doctrine more because these statements were politically expedient and might help to settle quarrels than because they thought precision necessary to salvation. Their attitude was rather like that of someone who admires a beautifully detailed topographic map, indicating every feature on the road from one place to another, but who travels that road guided only by a bare sketch on a scrap of paper. Although it took the framers of the Book of Concord hundreds of pages to lay down the essence of their version of the Christian faith, the magistrates regularly did so in a paragraph.

In 1529, fully nine months after they had abolished the Mass, the members of the Senate and XXI summed up the "principle parts of our true Christian faith, necessary to the soul's salvation, as: That Almighty God, out of his love for mankind, sent his beloved only-begotten son, our Lord Jesus Christ, into this world. While truly divine, he took on a human nature. He died for us and rose again for our justification."[46] The magistrates wanted a faith that they themselves could understand. Carl Mieg said it about the Tetrapolitan Confession in 1534: "I hope that as a

[43]RP 1565, fol. 1v.

[44]AST 80/35 (1539); AST 80/40 (1544).

[45]RP 1540, fols. 378v/380v.

[46]Hans Virck et al., eds., *Politische Correspondenz der Stadt Strassburg im Zeitalter der Reformation,* 5 vols. in 6, Urkunden und Akten der Stadt Strassburg, pt. 2 (Strasbourg, 1882–89, and Heidelberg, 1928–33), vol. 1, no. 682; compare no. 718.

layman, I won't be trapped into something I don't understand and then forced to confess and believe it."[47] Barthel Keller said it about the Formula of Concord a generation later: "This is over my head and I am reluctant to bind my conscience to it."[48] The Formula was finally accepted by the next generation of magistrates, but only after it had been presented to them as something not for the laity to master. For themselves, the magistrates preferred creeds to confessions.

Very few members of the Senate and XXI discussed their personal beliefs before their colleagues, but statements by a Catholic, Adolff Braun, by the probably Lutheran Wolfgang Schütterlin, and by a possible Calvinist, Josias Rihel, have survived.[49] Braun said: I subscribe to the Old and New Testaments and to the Apostles', Nicean, and Athanasian Creeds. I was saved by the unique sacrifice of Jesus Christ, the son of God and Man. Of the sacraments I believe that Scripture tells us. Braun was bending over backward to be accommodating. The Protestant Schütterlin, under no such pressure, was scarcely more forthcoming: I learned my catechism here in the St. Lawrence chapel, he began, and I stand by it. I am not Zwinglian, Calvinist, or Lutheran, for I follow Christ who saved me. I believe in the teachings of the Christian faith, simple and unbeclouded. I believe that God created me, that Christ saved me, and that the Holy Ghost leads us to the truth. I was baptized in the name of the Trinity. Of the sacraments I believe what every Christian can and should believe from God's Word. Rihel echoed Schütterlin's story: I was born into a Christian, Evangelical family and was brought up to oppose error. I learned my worthlessness from the Ten Commandments, my salvation and sanctification from the articles of faith, take my comfort and resolution from hearing God's word and receiving the sacraments. Let people pin what party label on me they will, I recognize no name but Christian.

What is striking is that these statements are so simple that they are interchangeable. Except for the biographical details, Rihel could have used Schütterlin's words, or Schütterlin Braun's. In the last third of the sixteenth century a Catholic, a probable Lutheran, and a possible Calvinist all chose to express their faith in the broadest possible terms. They might just as well have stood up and recited the Apostles' Creed. They had faithfully reproduced the content of the Senate and XXI's 1529 statement on the essentials of Christianity, and their fellow magistrates found their explanations quite adequate. There was no close questioning, no attempt to pin a colleague down and force precision on him. They all agreed on the

---

[47]Krebs and Rott, *Elsass*, pt. 2, no. 523.

[48]RP 1577, fols. 725v–732v.

[49]AST 100, unnumbered piece (1570), RP 1577, fol. 357r–v, and AST 326/22 (1595), respectively.

essentials, and it was better to stop there than to push on to the areas where they disagreed.

Jacob Sturm was perhaps the only magistrate of the first generation to appreciate the subtleties of the doctrines in dispute, and he was well aware that his colleagues did not share his interest. As he said in 1534, they could not be expected to sit through a reading of the Tetrapolitan Confession nor to remember what was at the beginning if they did reach the end. Sturm wanted his colleagues to vote on the Confession and wanted them to vote intelligently, so he proposed that each man take home a copy to study for a week. The result demonstrated that his colleagues were not prepared to turn themselves into theologians. Jacob Meyer, Hans von Blumenau, and Philips von Kageneck all said they would accept any decision reached by the majority. Carl Mieg hoped things would be kept simple, whereas Peter Sturm, Jacob's brother, dodged the question and said only that the preachers' sermons were too violent.[50] This same sort of attitude would crop up again in the next generation, for example in Johann Carl Lorcher's refusal to read the whole Formula of Concord because it was too long and too complicated.[51]

Such distaste for theology should not be construed as an indifference to religion or willful ignorance of the ideas in the Bible, because the magistrates could quote Scripture to their purposes. Nicolas Götz retold the parable of the good Samaritan to justify the admission of a French refugee.[52] In 1574 the Senate and XXI defended the lay supremacy with an ingenious gloss on the story of Moses, Aaron, and the golden calf.[53] The magistrates' lay subjects were scarcely indifferent to religion. Postmortem inventories of their possessions made in the early seventeenth century show that half the pictures they chose to decorate their homes portrayed religious scenes.[54]

What the magistrates wanted from Lutheranism was not confessional precision but peace and salvation. They avoided doctrinal debate in their own chambers because it fostered division, and they sought to prevent such debate among their people for the same reason. The Creeds provided an adequate statement of the Christian faith. A church that taught the fundamentals and no more could be a true church and yet a broad church that all Strasburghers might accept. It would not deny any belief necessary

---

[50]Krebs and Rott, *Elsass*, pt. 2, no. 523 (1534); see Brady, *Ruling Class*, pp. 192–93.
[51]RP 1577, fols. 727v–728v.
[52]RP 1572, fols. 910r–911r.
[53]RP 1573, fols. 878r–881v.
[54]Jean-Pierre Kintz, "La société strasbourgeoise du milieu du XVIe siècle à la fin de la guerre de Trente Ans, 1560–1650: Essai d'histoire démographique, économique, et sociale" (doctorat d'état, Strasbourg, 1980), p. 874.

to salvation in the next life, but it would not destroy harmony in the present world. This was the church that the magistrates wanted for Strasbourg.

The Senate and XXI urged its clergy to preach the barest minimum of doctrine. At a synod held in 1539, it cautioned the preachers to choose their sermon texts from the Gospels and not to take up "the Prophets or other difficult books." The clergy's explanations of the Bible should not be about "subtle or high-flown materials, but about those which come within the understanding of the common people and are likely to contribute to their improvement." What they wanted the clergy to do was to enjoin their parishioners "to behave like pious Christians . . . to go to the sermons, to send their children to catechism classes, and not to neglect anything befitting pious Christians."[55] The lay rulers stressed ethics, not dogma; as far as they were concerned, on matters of subtle doctrine it was better by far that their people remain in tranquil ignorance than that they take up a pugnacious certainty.

A real divergence between clerical and lay thinking can be found in the arguments about the use of compulsion to enforce orthodoxy. The clergy tended to intolerance and the laity toward greater charity. This was a divergence of tendencies rather than an absolute distinction. As we have seen, a streak of bigotry against other confessions ran through the Lutheranism of Strasburghers in both estates, and the city's legendary toleration must be balanced against this current in both lay and clerical thinking. Just as we can collect evidence of lay bigotry, we can produce evidence of clerical charity. These cases, however, were dramatic reversals of the norms.

Early in the reformation Martin Bucer and Wolfgang Capito had both argued that Christian magistrates must use their sword against heretics. As Bucer put it, it was a new and dangerous error to hold that lay rulers ought not to concern themselves with their subjects' beliefs as long as the public peace was not endangered.[56] The clergy continued to feel that this error was all too widespread in Strasbourg.[57] Marbach complained in 1572, "These days we have unfortunately fallen into the habit of leaving everyone free to take up not just the old religion, but also those which are expressly forbidden by the Religious Peace of Augsburg. so that people join all the other sects, like the Anabaptists, the Schwenckfelders, and the Calvinists, and all this publicly and without any prejudice to them."[58]

[55]AST 75/52, fol. 761r; RP 1574, fol. 316r–v.
[56]Philippe Dollinger, "La tolérance à Strasbourg au XVIe siècle," *Hommage à Lucien Febvre*, 2 vols. (Paris, 1953), 2:242–43.
[57]RP 1545, fols. 35v–37v; RP 1548, fol. 294r.
[58]AST 87/60, fol. 13r.

Things were scarcely so easygoing, and Catholics, sectarians, and Calvinists all had reason to argue that they suffered for their faiths because official policy restricted or denied their right to public worship. Even so, there was some ground for Marbach's complaint, and Strasbourg did earn a reputation for toleration or, in modern terms, for moderation.[59] Sebastian Franck's judgment has been repeated by nearly every commentator: "What is elsewhere punished by execution, in Strasbourg brings no more than a whipping." Refugees entering the city regularly told the magistrates that they had been attracted by the city's renowned mercy and charity toward the victims of religious persecution.[60]

Not only did the Senate and XXI take in the oppressed from other lands, it defended the principle of freedom of conscience. As one of its members remarked in 1580, quoting the late Emperor Maxmilian, "There is no greater tyranny than to dictate to consciences."[61] The magistrates would forbid certain forms of behavior—blasphemy, disruption of the Sabbath, participation in the services of rival faiths—but they did not normally try to force Lutheran observances on their people; church attendance was not mandatory for adults. The magistrates usually granted their subjects the same privilege they granted each other, freedom from being forced to account for one's beliefs. Throughout the century the laity remained true, truer than did their clergy, to the early Protestant notion that no mortal could or should usurp God's privilege to see into the human heart. Freedom of conscience in Strasbourg was just that, and it did not extend to the freedom to act. Yet any liberty here was the work of the laity, not the clergy.

The laity's insistence on freedom of conscience undoubtedly grew out of aversion to mastering the complexities of an evolving Lutheran orthodoxy. For most men and women in Strasbourg in the sixteenth century, religion was fundamental to the understanding of the meaning of human life. The clergy provided the Strasburghers with their basic religious instruction and organized the forms of their public worship, but although the laity accepted the general guidance of their pastors, they were not willing to limit themselves to ideas and practices approved by Lutheran theologians. A simple Bible-based religion everyone could understand, good morals that everyone could appreciate and practice, a church in which the clergy served the laity and did not dictate to them—to secular Lutherans in Strasbourg this was the essence of the Reformation.

---

[59]The distinction is Dollinger's ("La tolérance," p. 249).
[60]RP 1571, fol. 1015r–v, and RP 1572, fol. 905v.
[61]RP 1580, fols. 259v–260r.

*The most perplexing problem in interpreting sixteenth-century texts is the need to place and read them in their larger social contexts, the features of which are not always clear to readers of a later age. In addressing himself to the problem of the social history of ideas, H. C. Erik Midelfort, associate professor of history at the University of Virginia, has concentrated on the history of witchcraft. In line with his previous work,* Witchhunting in Southwestern Germany, 1562–1684: The Social and Intellectual Foundations *(1972), Midelfort is now examining the history of madness in early modern Germany. A crucial figure in the debates on witchcraft and insanity was the sixteenth-century physician Johann Weyer. Through a careful reading and a contextual analysis of Weyer's writings, Midelfort shows how the insanity defense, as formulated in Roman (civil) and canon law, was gradually incorporated into the debate on witchcraft. The following essay, which is drawn from his forthcoming book on the subject, discusses medical, legal, and religious discourses as they competed to define social reality.*

# [11]

# Johann Weyer and the Transformation
# of the Insanity Defense

## H. C. Erik Midelfort

From the earliest times of which we have records, men have recognized that criminal sanctions cannot be applied unhesitatingly to the mentally retarded and mentally disordered. In the West, a large body of ancient Roman jurisprudence elaborated an explicit insanity defense, and these principles were taken over in medieval canon law. From ancient times onward, Western jurists conceded that, if a defendant was mad (*furiosus*), if he did not know what he was doing, and if he was clearly not pretending to be mad, then he should not be punished, for as the legal phrase had it, "his madness is punishment enough."[1] It is worth emphasizing that the language used in describing and elaborating the ancient and medieval insanity defense was the legal language of *furor, insania, mentis alienatio,* and *dilucida intervalla.* The judgments were legal, and lawyers were in charge. In Germany, too, as Roman law made its way into common practice from the fifteenth century onward, the insanity defense was a strictly legal matter, with no observable influence from medicine or theology.[2]

[1]See generally Theodor Mommsen, *Römisches Strafrecht* (Leipzig, 1899), pp. 75–77; Karl Binding, *Die Schuld im deutschen Strafrecht: Vorsatz, Irrtum, Fahrlässigkeit: Kurzes Lehrbuch* (Leipzig, 1919), p. 11; Georg Dahm, *Das Strafrecht Italiens im ausgehenden Mittelalter* (Berlin, 1931); Woldemar Engelmann, *Irrtum und Schuld nach der italienischen Lehre und Praxis des Mittelalters* (Berlin, 1922); Stephan Kuttner, *Kanonistische Schuldlehre von Gratian bis auf die Dekretalen Gregors IX* (Vatican City, 1935), pp. 85–116.

[2]Rudolf His, *Das Strafrecht des deutschen Mittelalters, erster Teil: Die Verbrechen und ihre Folgen im allgemeinen* (Leipzig, 1920), pp. 66–68; Eberhard Schmidt, *Einführung in die Geschichte der deutschen Strafrechtspflege,* 2d ed. (Göttingen, 1951), pp. 67–68.

[234]

In the course of the sixteenth century, German law came increasingly to include explicit references to Roman law and Roman procedures and in this process to include large chunks of canon law as well.[3] Nowhere is this more evident than in the history of the crime of witchcraft. As understood by most secular jurisdictions in 1500, witchcraft was the crime of *maleficium*, of harmful magic understood as the production of physical harm through illicit, demonic means. The *Malleus maleficarum*, by Heinrich Institoris and Jacob Sprenger, however, had tried to shift the focus away from the actual harm done to the spiritual state of infidelity and heresy that made *maleficium* possible. In the view of the two Dominican authors, the pact with the devil was the heart of the crime of witchcraft. From a canon-legal point of view, with an emphasis on states of mind and sinful intentions, this shift of understanding was reasonable, but we may well ask why the secular law found it plausible. Some years ago I suggested that the secular courts of Germany came to accommodate the clerical views of Institoris and Sprenger because the secular reasoning of codes such as the 1532 Imperial *Carolina* was muddled.[4] The advance of scholarship has now added another piece to the puzzle.

Michael Kunze has recently drawn attention to the fact that the single most important *German* book on law in the sixteenth century, Ulrich Tengler's *Layenspiegel*, was not originally the powerful apology for the *Malleus* that historians have usually assumed. When Tengler published his work in 1509, he treated witchcraft only very briefly and as an afterthought to his section on Jewish corruption and usury. In one paragraph he added that witches and magicians were also heretics who harmed the Christian faith and "especially cooperate with the evil spirit (with God's permission) to cause the elements to clash, making storms and producing many kinds of harm to men and beasts."[5] Tengler concluded that they should, "as heretics," be stripped of "all their honors and offices and be excluded from the Christian community" and that "appropriate inquisitions" should determine what punishments or other actions should be added. In passing it is worth noting that this clause seems to assume that witches often had honors and offices to give up, that they were in other words probably men of wealth and influence rather than marginal women.

---

[3]See, for example, Ulrich Zasius's discussion of the three kinds of furiosi, *Opera Omnia* (Lyon, 1550; reprint ed., Aalen, 1965), vol. 3, cols. 336–37, paragraphs 3–5.

[4]Midelfort, *Witch Hunting in Southwestern Germany, 1562–1684: The Social and Intellectual Foundations* (Stanford, 1972), pp. 22–23.

[5]Ulrich Tengler, *Layen Spiegel: Von rechtmässigen Ordnungen in burgerlichen und peinlichen Regimenten* (Augsburg, 1509), at the end of pt. 1. In the Strasbourg 1510 edition, this passage is at fol. 36r. Michael Kunze, *Der Prozess Pappenheimer* (Ebelsbach, 1981), pp. 175–76.

In column references Tengler referred learnedly to Roman and canon law but also unspecifically to the *Malleus maleficarum*.[6] As it happened, the reference was far too unspecific for Ulrich's son Christoph, who was a priest and a "doctor of arts and canon law." When Christoph the theologian undertook to edit a second edition of his lawyer father's work, published in 1512, he made a variety of additions including the Golden Bull of Charles IV and a large chunk of the *Malleus maleficarum*.[7] He explained that witchcraft involved such incredible events that some jurists even doubted whether witches existed. As a result, witchcraft was not everywhere prosecuted, and it had lately got "completely out of hand." The *Malleus* had the solution to this overwhelming problem, and in some detail Christoph Tengler summarized its provisions, the use of accusation, inquisition, and torture in ferreting out the evil of witchcraft, a crime now described as mainly committed by women. Instead of one paragraph on witchcraft, the theologically infected *Layenspiegel* now had ten pages on the crime. In this form the *Layenspiegel* was popular throughout the first half of the sixteenth century.[8]

This infusion of canon law did not, however, immediately affect the insanity defense in the Holy Roman Empire, but in the second half of the sixteenth century a different sort of assault, combining medicine and theology, broke down the isolation of German jurisprudence. In 1563 Johann Weyer published the first edition of his extraordinary *De praestigiis daemonum* (On the Tricks of the Demons) and succeeded in fundamentally altering the terms of legal discourse from then on. This large claim runs counter to conventional wisdom on the subject. The profound scholar Friedrich Schaffstein concluded, for example, that between 1550 and 1750 there was no development at all in the area of legal responsibility.[9] Jurists from the end of the period were still repeating the wisdom of 1550, he thought, but we will see that the witchcraft controversy had an unexpected impact. Even though medicine did not produce any decisive or new psychiatric insight in the sixteenth century, the insanity defense was pushed in a new direction by the controversy surrounding Johann Weyer.

Among scholars Weyer has been famous for constructing a lengthy and learned argument that the women accused of witchcraft were not guilty of harming anyone and that they therefore should not be burned to death.

---

[6]The column note says simply: "vi mall. male cum ibi no."

[7]*Der neu Layenspiegel* (Augsburg, 1512), fols. 159r–163v.

[8]The original edition of 1509 was reissued in Strasbourg by M. Hupfuff in 1510 and 1511. Christoph Tengler's edition with his extensive additions appeared not only in 1512 but also in 1514, 1518, 1527, 1530, 1532, 1538, and 1544.

[9]Schaffstein, *Die allgemeinen Lehren vom Verbrechen in ihrer Entwicklung durch die Wissenschaft des gemeinen Strafrechts* (Berlin, 1930), p. 98.

Instead these women (and he thought that witches [*lamiae* or *sagae*] were overwhelmingly women) merely hallucinated or dreamed that they had entered a pact with the devil, that they flew off to the sabbath with him, that they had sex with him, and so on. Weyer reached this extraordinary conclusion not by claiming, as a modern skeptic might, that the devil was nonexistent but paradoxically by affirming that he was far more powerful than was usually thought. A host of modern scholars have charged that Weyer was trying to draw a conclusion that his premises unfortunately would not permit.[10] They have held that, if the devil was as powerful as Weyer said he was, then witchcraft was not only possible but likely, and Leland Estes has even advanced the remarkable claim that Weyer's approach actually fomented witch hunting rather than dampening it as he had intended.[11]

To clarify this controversy will require us to back up a bit in order to obtain a better view of Weyer's enterprise and argument as a whole. It will not do to confine our attention strictly to Weyer's legal views, important as they were. Crucial to the development of Weyer's views was a complex exposure to the best Renaissance thinking on the nature of magic, religion, and heresy. As a trained physician he could of course marshal the opinions of Hippocrates and Galen whenever he wanted, but more striking is his willingness to draw radical religious conclusions from medical evidence. As we will see, moreover, Weyer was thoroughly familiar with the Roman tradition of civil and canon law.

Among Weyer's most important early experiences were the year or two he spent as a servant and assistant to the famous scholar Heinrich Cornelius Agrippa of Nettesheim. As a youth of sixteen or seventeen, Weyer lived with Agrippa in Bonn and came to regard him fondly as "my revered teacher,"[12] using his secretarial position to gain access to occult works that were circulating then only in manuscript.[13] From Agrippa Weyer evidently imbibed a permanent dislike for Aristotle and for the peripatetic tradition, but he developed a strong distaste as well for that element in the Platonic tradition that emphasized the power of magical

---

[10]H. R. Trevor-Roper, *The Crisis of the Seventeenth Century: Religion, the Reformation, and Social Change* (New York, 1968), pp. 149, 172. Sydney Anglo, "Melancholia and Witchcraft: The Debate between Wier, Bodin, and Scot," in *Folie et Déraison à la Renaissance* (Brussels, 1976), pp. 209–222; Christopher Baxter, "Johann Weyer's *De Praestigiis Daemonum:* Unsystematic Psychopathology," in Sydney Anglo, ed., *The Damned Art: Essays in the Literature of Witchcraft* (London, 1977), pp. 53–75; E. William Monter, "Law, Medicine, and the Acceptance of Witchcraft, 1560–1580," in his *European Witchcraft* (New York, 1969), pp. 55–71.

[11]"The Medical Origins of the European Witch Craze: A Hypothesis," *Journal of Social History* 17 (1983):271–84.

[12]*De Praestigiis Daemonum* (Basel, 1583), Bk. II, chap. 5, col. 162.

[13]In this way Weyer came to read Trithemius's *Steganographia*, for example: *De Praestigiis Daemonum*, Bk. II, chap. 6, col. 169.

words. In this distaste Weyer found himself rejecting Agrippa's *De occulta philosophia* and sympathizing rather with Agrippa's later *De vanitate scientiarum*. Late in life when he was accused of uncritical dependence on Agrippa, Weyer observed that even Agrippa himself came to reject many of his early occult ideas.[14] Probably more important to Weyer than any specific doctrines of Agrippa was his mentor's example as a broadly learned, tolerant man with a distinct (perhaps even heretical) religious position of spiritualism. Weyer must also have known that in 1519 Agrippa had successfully defended a woman accused of witchcraft in Metz; Agrippa's argument had claimed that a woman could not be held for witchcraft solely because her mother had been a witch, for such a conclusion would deny the power of baptism to free Christians from the grip of the devil.[15] Weyer also used this argument, but it is more important here to observe that Weyer may have learned in this way to employ essentially religious arguments in legal cases. As we will see, much of his later opposition to witchcraft doctrine was religious in nature. From Agrippa Weyer may have imbibed a broad religious tolerance as well, for Agrippa had been hounded from city to city all his life on account of religious views that were surely unorthodox and may have been a form of Nicodemite spiritualism.[16] It is of interest that, despite the openly magical operations of *De occulta philosophia*, Weyer never identified Agrippa as a magician of any sort, preferring to demonstrate (accurately but misleadingly) that Agrippa was not the author of the notorious fourth book of *De occulta philosophia* and to remark that Agrippa had heartily repudiated genuinely dangerous magicians.[17]

Despite his year or two with one of Europe's leading neo-Platonist magicians, therefore, Weyer came away from Agrippa unimpressed by Plato and appalled at learned magic. What he took away from Agrippa was perhaps a Nicodemite ability to keep his religious views to himself, a suspicion that accusations of witchcraft were irreligious, and a tendency to mix religion, medicine, and law into an amalgam that was for his day unusual if not unorthodox.

Second only to the importance of Agrippa for Weyer was his obvious if always unstated debt to Martin Luther and the Protestant Reformation. In his published works Weyer never explicitly admitted to being a Protestant

[14]Liber apologeticus, in Weyer, *Opera Omnia* (Amsterdam, 1660), pp. 625–26, replying to Leo Suavius [Jacques Gohory].
[15]Agrippa, *Opera Omnia*, vol. 2 (Lyon, 1660?), pp. 687–91 at p. 688.
[16]Paola Zambelli, "Magic and Radical Reformation in Agrippa of Nettesheim," *Journal of the Warburg and Courtauld Institutes* 39 (1976):69–103.
[17]*De Praestigiis*, (1583), Bk. II, chap. 5, cols. 161–64; Liber Apologeticus, *Opera Omnia*, pp. 626–27; cf. Agrippa, *De Occulta Philosophia* I, c. 39, *Opera Omnia*, 1:69, where Agrippa sharply condemns the gnostic magi.

of any sort, and a hundred years ago Catholic partisans were still trying to claim him for the Catholic camp. It is all too evident from his constant attacks on fraudulent priests, false Catholic miracles, possessed convents, superstitious peasants, and phony exorcisms, however, that Weyer could scarcely have been a pious Catholic, not even an "Erasmian" Catholic. His references to Protestants, and especially to Philipp Melanchthon, were warm and admiring, and he dedicated various editions of his works to the Lutheran magistrates of Frankfurt and Bremen. Most important, Weyer represented at its fullest Lutheran pitch the conclusion that the devil was overwhelmingly powerful and deceptive: for those who thought that they could act with assurance, Weyer noted that the devil could exploit and manipulate even sincere actions and intentions. Lutherans were not of course alone in holding that the devil was the ruler of this world, but Catholics had retained a measure of confidence in the prescribed rituals of the Church, whereas Calvinists often argued that the age of miracles was over and that the devil had a mainly spiritual influence over the world.[18] Lutherans, by way of contrast, were often left with the disconcerting view that the devil was loose in the land and that he could indeed work wonders but that ritual materials and ritual actions such as blessed salt, holy water, and exorcism were powerless. Prayer and fasting were all that could be recommended, and they provided no real assurance or guarantee. This world was a dangerous and deceptive place.

The third crucial influence on Weyer's legal views was Erasmus, not the cardboard stereotype of a mild-mannered, liberal, right-thinking man recently ridiculed by Christopher Baxter[19] but the serious religious thinker for whom the views of the early church retained an authority undiminished by a thousand years of Constantinian Christianity. When Erasmus asked by what right the Church punished heresy with death, he was probing what he saw as the unwarranted merger of ecclesiastical and secular concerns. Jesus' parable of the tares (Matthew 13) made it clear enough (to Erasmus at least) that heretics should not be uprooted from the Christian community for fear of eradicating true Christians as well. This was one of the most common arguments for religious toleration in the sixteenth century and one that we should not confuse with modern liberal arguments that depend on relativist or pluralist foundations. The point was that, even on Christian grounds, Erasmus and others like him could not find religious warrant for eliminating those with whom the Church disagreed. Johann Weyer cited Erasmus with some frequency but nowhere more fervently

---

[18]D. P. Walker, *Unclean Spirits, Possession, and Exorcism in France and England in the Late Sixteenth and Seventeenth Centuries* (Philadelphia, 1981); H. A. Kelly, *The Devil at Baptism: Ritual, Theology, and Drama* (Ithaca, 1985).

[19]Baxter, "Johann Weyer's *De Praestigiis Daemonum*," pp. 53–54, 69–72.

than on just this point, one that assimilated witchcraft and heresy (just as the late medieval church and Christoph Tengler had taught) but then asked by what right such witch-heretics were to be executed. As we shall see, this Erasmian argument served a crucial function in Weyer's general theory.

The fourth and final area of general influence on Weyer was the Renaissance idea of melancholy, an idea that was very much on the rise among physicians and literary men even as it waned in power for artists and philosophical students of genius. Already in 1515 the famous jurist Andrea Alciati had written that many supposed witches had more need of purification by hellebore (the usual purge for excess melancholy) than by fire: "Non paucae helleboro potius quam igne purgandae."20 At about the same time Agrippa was speculating that the force of the melancholy imagination might be great enough actually to cause a person to ascend while asleep to places that the waking could hardly attain.21 By the 1550s Girolamo Cardano could combine these bits and pieces and could argue forcefully that witches suffered from melancholy, which drove them to imagine that they did many wondrous and horrible things.22 When Giovanni Battista della Porta wrote his famous book on natural magic, it was becoming widely accepted that various herbs and poisons could cause fearful dreams and hallucinations and that some witches used a special salve that induced a deep trance accompanied by visions of flight and of the witches' sabbath.23 The theories of melancholy and of hallucinatory drugs therefore gave sixteenth-century Europeans a plausible and entirely natural way of explaining the apparently voluntary confessions made by those convicted of witchcraft. They were theories with which Weyer made himself thoroughly familiar, but until the witchcraft debate unleashed by Weyer's *De praestigiis,* these ideas had little or no legal impact. What was it that Weyer added to the thought of Agrippa, Luther, Erasmus, Cardano, and Porta?

There are, of course, many remarkable features of Weyer's book; in many respects it was a uniquely powerful, if sometimes confused, treatise. For one thing Weyer recounted his tales and anecdotes with such a tongue-in-cheek seriousness that one must suspect that he had read

[20]Joseph Hansen, *Quellen und Untersuchungen zur Geschichte des Hexenwahns und der Hexenverfolgungen im Mittelalter* (Bonn, 1901), pp. 263–64 citing Alciati's *Parergon* of 1515.

[21]*De Occulta Philosophia* III, c. 43; *Opera,* p. 440.

[22]G. Cardano, *De rerum varietate* (Basel, 1557), chap. 8; cf. Peter Burke, "Witchcraft and Magic in Renaissance Italy: Gianfrancesco Pico and His *Strix,*" in Anglo, *The Damned Art,* pp. 32–52, at pp. 41, 48.

[23]Porta, *Magiae naturalis* (Naples, 1558); cf. Lynn Thorndike, *A History of Magic and Experimental Science,* vol. 6 (New York, 1941), pp. 418–22. Hans Peter Dürr, *Dreamtime: Concerning the Boundary between Wilderness and Civilization* (Oxford, 1985), pp. 8–9.

Rabelais.[24] Amid a flood of stories concerning gullible peasants, lascivious women, and lusty priests, Weyer retold the history of Faust and the story of the Pied Piper of Hamelin, along with stories of monstrous births and mixed fables from the worlds of Herodotus and Pliny and Merlin. He called some of his tales true and other fabulous and occasionally asserted that a story told straight-facedly had just as much credibility as a previous story he had explicitly called fiction.[25] The effect of such fabulous word heaps was to call into question any story for which there was no firsthand evidence. It was an artful literary technique that deployed the grotesque as a weapon against the monstrous.

By calling the legends, fables, and traditions of more than two thousand years into question, Weyer made it clear that credibility depended on more than just the authority of the storyteller or the plausibility of the story. He illustrated his skepticism by personally investigating the local scandals and monstrous events of his region and by emphasizing throughout his book that his accounts depended upon the testimony of his own eyes or those of other careful observers.

In any event, Weyer was not content to say that melancholy hallucinations *could* explain the fantastic confessions of witches, or that physical processes *could* explain the odd tumors, lungstones, frosts, and strange mishaps often attributed to the devil, or even that fraud *could* be an explanation for apparently successful exorcisms. Any contemporary of Weyer might have coped easily with his arguments if they had rested on no more than could-have-beens. What made Weyer notably exasperating for his opponents was his claim that he had personally investigated countless weird events and "unnatural" circumstances, and he had rarely returned in a state of perplexity. Rather, Weyer was one of the early masters of intrepid debunkery. He could say with more than mere plausibility that teenage girls and young women needed a sex life rather than the austerities of a convent. He could prove that locally celebrated miracles of extended fasting were actually fraudulent. He could bring even the unwilling reader to admit that he had a point when he examined a presumed case of sexual difficulty that rested on natural organic obstacles rather than on maleficium—and who was not amused (even if bitterly offended as well) by Weyer's account of the wax phallus used by Katherine Loe to ward off demonic assaults?[26] It must have seemed that time and again Weyer knew in a new way, and it is no accident that Weyer's opponents were quick to learn his method of close observation. Jean Bodin, for example, for all his

---

[24]Christopher Baxter calls the flavor "Rabelaisian." This topic would repay much closer literary study. See Baxter, "Johann Weyer's *De Praestigiis Daemonum*," p. 73.

[25]*De Praestigiis* (1583) I, c. 16; col. 82.

[26]*De Praestigiis* (1583) V, c. 36; cols. 635–36.

theological, medical, and legal differences with Weyer, also adduced a new body of closely observed material from which to argue for the reality of witchcraft.[27] That, after all, was the problem with the empirical investigation of wonders and demonic possessions, of monsters and miracles. As often as one showed that a specific case was natural in origin or fraudulent in construction, another observer could rise up to say, truly enough, that that did not make miracles, demon possession, or witchcraft impossible. It was easy to introduce doubts about witchcraft but hard to prove a case *per impossibile*.

Instead of claiming that the Bible no longer provided an accurate picture of the world, Weyer took up the opposite position: that the Bible, properly understood, gave no support to the witch hunters of the sixteenth century. Employing a razor-sharp philology, Weyer scrutinized the actual words for witchcraft in Hebrew and Greek as used in the Old and New Testaments and concluded, shrewdly enough, that the Bible knew nothing of pacts with the devil and that the "witch" of the Old Testament had been essentially a poisoner rather than a heretic. We know that one of the most important transformations in the history of European witchcraft was the late medieval canon legal and theological redefinition of witchcraft as heresy and apostasy, emphasizing the denial of faith rather than harm by hidden, magical means, as earlier laws had understood the crime. Weyer was pleased to grasp this transformation with both hands, for it meant that the crime of witchcraft had lost its solid basis in the Word of God. It meant, moreover, that witchcraft should be punished exactly as heresy should be, but here Weyer introduced one of his most explosive arguments. Echoing but sharpening Agrippa's argument on behalf of the woman accused of witchcraft in 1519, Weyer exclaimed that if the essence of the crime was the witch's renunciation of her baptism and of Christ, then surely that was a crime that all Christians, including even St. Peter, committed repeatedly throughout their lives.[28]

Weyer's point did not here depend on proving that a given witch was insane. Rather it depended on establishing a bond between every fallible Christian and the suspected witch-apostate, for in so doing he would get the suspected witch off the hook. As a profound Erasmian Weyer felt the force of Erasmus's plea that Christians should not do all of God's work for Him, that vengeance was after all His, not ours. Heresy, in particular, did not merit the death penalty. In Book VI, chapter 18, Weyer saw fit to reprint in six columns a long section of Erasmus's *Apology* of 1520 in

---

[27]Bodin, *De la démonomanie des sorciers* (Paris, 1580), preface, fols. a3v–i3r, 180v–186v.
[28]Agrippa, *Opera*, 2:688–89 on baptism and faith; Weyer, *De Praestigiis* (1583), cols. 243–44.

which Erasmus interpreted the parable of the tares to mean that heresy should not be severely punished in this world. Heretics and witches, Weyer argued, needed better religious instruction, to be sure, but their deviations from the Catholic faith should not be capital crimes. In extending Erasmus's argument this way, Weyer brilliantly wielded the double-edged sword of the heresy indictment. Accepting the late medieval reformulation of witchcraft as heresy, Weyer claimed that the only plausible crime committed by old women accused of witchcraft was the mental crime of heresy, for which no one should ever be killed. Even the learned magicians of Renaissance Europe (Weyer's *magi infames*) were only sinfully, deliberately, and intentionally committing the offense of heresy and blasphemy. From this Erasmian or spiritualizing position, the only criminals worth punishing in this life were the physically dangerous, the *venefici*, the *Giftmischer,* the poisoners.

If this analysis is correct, as I think it is, then recent critics are off base when they charge that Weyer simply shifted the capital charge of witchcraft from old women to the learned (male) magicians.[29] Despite the outrage Weyer felt toward the blasphemies of the magicians, he did not generally urge their execution. Instead, Weyer insisted on religious grounds that, if witchcraft was a spiritual crime, as heresy and blasphemy and apostasy were, then the proper remedy was spiritual as well. Weyer's religious arguments directly showed not that witchcraft was an impossible crime but that capital punishment was inappropriate for witches whose crimes were religious.

It was an argument of some force in Weyer's day, for the Erasmian tradition in Europe, although in retreat after 1560 or 1570, was never completely routed. Compelling as these arguments were in sixteenth-century terms, Weyer had not yet succeeded in showing that the crime of witchcraft was literally impossible; only when he turned to the argument from law did Weyer find an argument *per impossibile*. On a legal basis Weyer went well beyond a reformulation of the insanity defense to an amazing claim that witchcraft was an impossible crime.

Weyer's references to Roman and canon law were extensive, and expert, ranging freely among the massive texts of Justinian, Gratian, and Pope Gregory IX. In Book VI of the *De praestigiis,* Weyer considered the legal question of how magicians, witches, and poisoners should be punished. Magicians, we have seen, were fraudulent, blasphemous, irreligious, and deliberately deceptive; even so they did no physical harm with their purely verbal charms and empty rituals. They deserved to be admon-

---

[29]Anglo, "Melancholia and Witchcraft," p. 213. Baxter seems especially confused by this problem; see "Johann Weyer's *De Praestigiis Daemonum,*" pp. 53–54, 66–71.

ished and warned not to disturb the religious peace of their communities; they might be fined and even exiled, but because they did no real (physical) harm, they should not be executed.[30] On the other hand poisoners did do real damage and deserved the fullest rigor of the law. We will not pause here to concern ourselves with Weyer's interesting distinction between *magi infames* and *venefici,* for our interest in the history of the insanity defense draws us on to the witches, the *lamiae.* Witches, Weyer claimed, could not be guilty of the crime of witchcraft for several reasons, some having to do with their mental condition, some with the nature of the alleged acts, and some dealing with the law itself. As we have seen, Weyer held that witches were feeble, hallucinating, insane old women, and he cited numerous places in Justinian's *Digest* and in later commentaries where special leniency was shown to the aged, to the feeble, to the mentally deranged, and to women.[31] The cases he cited were well chosen, but the odd thing about this argument is that the most zealous witch hunters also recognized and even stressed the idea that witches were usually aged, feeble, credulous, helpless women. Precisely their qualities as marginal women made witchcraft seductively attractive to them. Vigorous men, it was commonly held, had the strength and common sense to resist the temptations of the devil, whereas old women easily fell prey to demonic entrapment precisely because they had no other social or physical resources. So most of Weyer's legal references to the leniency deserved by women could cut in the opposite direction as well. The same was not true of madness. No witch hunter, however eager to denigrate women, could afford to concede that witches were out of their minds or driven by forces beyond their control.[32] Jean Bodin, for example, constructed a memorably ridiculous argument that women did not usually fall into melancholy disorders at all, as Weyer had claimed; so bent was Bodin on asserting the sanity of the witches.[33] Although this position made no medical sense even in the sixteenth century, it does suggest that Weyer's

[30]Cols. 655–61.

[31]Weyer repeatedly cited the following passages on madness: *Digest* 1.18.13–14, 48.9.9, 47.10.3, 9.1.1, 9.2.5, 48.8.12, 26.7.61, 29.7.2.3, 50.17.5, 26.5.12.2; *Code* 4.38.2; on the aged and on women, *Digest* 3.2.13, 48.8.4.2, 48.19.16, 29.5.3.7–11, 50.6.5, 48.18.8, 1.5.9; *Code* 5.67, 9.9.29, 1.18.3, 6.9.6, 9.8.5.

[32]See the perceptive remarks of Hans-Peter Dürr, *Dreamtime,* pp. 1–11.

[33]Bodin, *De la démonomanie,* fol. 226r–231v. Monter, "Inflation and Witchcraft: The Case of Jean Bodin," in T. K. Rabb and J. Seigel, *Action and Conviction in Early Modern Europe: Essays in Honor of E. H. Harbison* (Princeton, 1969), pp. 371–89; Noel L. Brann recognized, as others have more recently, that Bodin's argument was desperate and ill founded by sixteenth-century standards: "The Renaissance Passion of Melancholy: The Paradox of Its Cultivation and Resistance," (Ph.D. diss., Stanford University, 1965), pp. 361–67; see also C. Baxter, "Jean Bodin's *De la Démonomanie des Sorciers:* The Logic of Persecution," in Anglo, *The Damned Art,* pp. 76–105; Ursula Lange, *Untersuchungen zu Bodins Démonomanie* (Frankfurt, 1970).

argument had touched an extremely sensitive nerve in the legal thinking of even the best minds of Europe.

When Weyer turned to the nature of the alleged acts of the witches, he hit upon an essential element of the crime as most jurists conceived it. The crucial nexus between the terrifying power of the devil and the corrupt will of the witch was the supposed pact with the devil, a notion that scholastic theory had elaborated on the model of the feudal oath of homage. Weyer was on firm biblical ground when he pointed out that the Scriptures say nothing of such a contract or pact, but legally speaking, Weyer had an even more potent argument in his analysis of the Roman law of contract. If he could show that there was no binding agreement between human and demonic agents, then it would follow that witches could not really order the devil to do anything, nor could the devil require any action of his witches. In essence their relations would be comparable to those that obtained between the devil and ordinary mortals: that is, the relation of predator and victim. Let us pursue Weyer's legal argument and his legal references more carefully.

It would have been easy but unproductive to argue that Roman law knew nothing of contracts between men and spirits, and so Weyer looked carefully at the nature of contracts of all sorts. He pointed out, for example, that contracts were invalid wherever one party was ignorant of crucial facts. In general, valid contracts depended on *bona fides*.[34] Therefore any contract with the devil was null on grounds that the devil fraudulently withheld information from his intended clients.[35] Moreover the Roman law of partnership disallowed "leonine" contracts in which one party could only gain and the other could only lose:[36] this description exactly fitted the position of witches, who often expected monetary or sexual gain only to be disappointed by the failure of the devil to live up to his promises. Ultimately, the witch stood only to lose and the devil only to gain. Weyer also held that contracts did not bind if they were entered with *dolus malus* (intentional deceit),[37] which certainly described the action of the devil, who used cunning, tricks, and deception to defraud and seduce the whole world.[38] In addition, Weyer insisted that pacts with the devil

---

[34]*Digest* 12.1.41. For a summary of Roman provisions on "pacta" (informal bargains), see W. W. Buckland, *A Text-Book of Roman Law from Augustus to Justinian* (Cambridge, 1921), pp. 524–29; see generally Sven Erik Wunner, *Contractus: Sein Wortgebrauch und Willensgehalt im klassischen römischen Recht* (Cologne, 1964).

[35]*De Praestigiis* (1583), col. 780.

[36]*Digest* 17.2.29.

[37]*De Praestigiis* (1583), cols. 780–81; *Digest* 4.3.7.

[38]On deceit in Roman contracts, see Buckland, *Text-Book*, pp. 589–90, 714–17; Weyer, *De Praestigiis* (1583), col. 781; *Digest* 4.2.6.

were void because they rested upon force and fear.[39] With a long string of references to Justinian's *Digest,* Weyer made out a case for the sheer *legal* impossibility of witchcraft. Witches could not will that the devil willed; their intentions were necessarily incongruent, resting on the witches' error, ignorance, and lack of a well-formed will.[40] These legal references make clear Weyer's essential argument: the devil was so potent, so overwhelming in strength and malice, that any contract with him would have no more force than would a contract between a grown man and an infant. No one would blame a small child for the damage done by an adult even if the adult claimed that he was merely acting upon the orders of the child: the disparity of wills make the liaison void.[41]

Weyer's assault on the witches' contract was followed by an assault on the alleged damage willed by the witches. It did not matter that witches might desire to harm their neighbors or even that they might try to incite the devil to harm their communities. The devil really needed no encouragement and could act (with divine permission) without any supposed aid from the witch. Roman law did not punish anyone for merely contemplating a crime, even if the Roman jurists regularly scrutinized intentions to determine the severity of any crime. A naked intention devoid of any action was beyond punishment,[42] for thoughts were free.[43] Moreover, certain crimes simply could not be committed; certain actions by definition were beyond human ability. No one can even seem to will what he actually cannot do.[44] And despite the fact that one could steal houses and crops and even trees, soil, or rocks, the Roman law declared that no one could steal real estate: it was an impossible crime (although of course one could be defrauded of one's title to a property).[45] So even if one "attempted" to steal landed property, it would be clear at once that this was merely fanciful and absurd.[46] Indeed, anyone who tried to intend or attempt the impossible might be thought mad. Here we have one of the major reasons why Weyer claimed that witches were mentally disordered. The claim was not merely empirical, as his opponents sometimes thought; it was embedded in Weyer's far more radical claim that witchcraft was an

[39]*De Praestigiis* (1583), cols. 782–83; *Digest* 19.2.15, 19.1.31, 19.2.41, 4.2.1, 4.2.6; *Code* 2.4.13; *Digest* 4.2.9. On fear in Roman contracts, see Buckland, *Text-Book,* pp. 588–89.

[40]Cols., 780–83; *Digest* 14.2.8, 2.1.15, 50.17.174, 12.1.12, 39.3.2.6.

[41]*De Praestigiis* (1583), cols. 772, 780, 781; *Digest* 4.4.13, 35.1.5, 50.17.4. On agency in Roman contracts, see Buckland, *Text-Book,* pp. 529–35.

[42]*Digest* 26.5.12.2; 33.10.7; Code 6.25.5.

[43]"Nihil sit liberius," *De Praestigiis* (1583), col. 777; Ulpian as quoted at *Digest* 48.19.18: "cogitationem poenam nemo patitur."

[44]*Digest* 50.17.174; "Nolle adire hereditatem non videtur, qui non potest adire"; *Digest* 29.2.4; 50.1.21.

[45]*Digest* 47.2.25.

[46]*De Praestigiis* (1583), col. 778.

idiotic or lunatic attempt to do the impossible. Weyer was so sure that the belief that one had a pact with the devil (and that one had, for example, flown off to the sabbath and had intercourse with the devil) was evidence of mental illness that he suggested a new way of interpreting malicious thoughts and desires as well. When an accused witch thought of harming others through witchcraft, Weyer claimed that she was really only harming herself, for the murderous or malicious intent could only rebound upon the subject. With such intentions, it was as if the mind jammed and the malice exploded internally. Citing the Roman law limiting the praetor's competence to compel himself to do anything, Weyer asserted that such harmful thoughts were harmful only to the one who thought them. Because the witches' destructive ideas were all internal, they actually suffered from them rather than inflicting them.[47] The legal argument was fanciful here, another real stretch beyond what Justinian's jurists had had in mind, but the result was a remarkable use of a legal principle to achieve a "modern" insight into the psychology of hatred.

These audacious claims depended, as we have seen, on a massive erudition in Roman and canon law. Weyer ingeniously extracted principles of contract law, of agency and voluntary action, and of crimes that cannot exist, from the whole range of ancient and ecclesiastical law, often stretching the implications well beyond any ancient intention. His procedures were occasionally fanciful and often willful, dragging current relevance out of rulings that had never before been applied to witchcraft or to any crime at all. His legal case did rest, however, on a profound reverence for the wisdom of the ancient Romans. Indeed, Weyer's zeal to show that witchcraft was an absurd crime overlooked one major objection that Weyer's opponents might have made forcefully. This was the objection that the crucial "pactum cum daemone" was not a contract to be understood in Roman terms at all. In papal formulations from the fourteenth and fifteenth centuries, for example, the witches' pact was often described as an act of "homage" to the devil, a feudal gesture of servitude rather than the compact between well-informed equals that Weyer so impressively debunked.[48] If the pact was an act of homage, perhaps it could be understood only in feudal terms rather than in ancient Roman language; perhaps Weyer's argument would have had trouble in this context. The way things turned out, we need not answer this question, for most jurists between 1550 and 1600 thought about witchcraft in the same

[47]*Digest* 36.1.13–14, 26.5.4, 46.1.71.
[48]Siegfried Leutenbauer, *Hexerei- und Zaubereidelikt in der Literatur von 1450 bis 1550* (Berlin, 1972); Hansen, *Quellen*, pp. 2, 4, 17, 49. For the changes in the Roman law of contract in the feudal period after Justinian, see György Diosdi, *Contract in Roman Law from the Twelve Tables to the Glossators* (Budapest, 1981), pp. 148–228.

Roman terms that Weyer chose. A feudal understanding of the witches' pact is indeed visible in some sixteenth-century drawings of the witches' sabbath, but lawyers across the Holy Roman Empire had been thoroughly Romanized by 1550.

So it seems that on legal grounds Weyer tried to prove that the central crime of witchcraft was impossible and that on religious grounds the laws governing heresy should ordain only minor disciplinary actions rather than execution. Scholars have not generally thought that Weyer's case was as clear as this analysis suggests partly because they (and especially the English scholars) have held up Reginald Scot as the model of radical skepticism against which Weyer should be measured. It is plain by now that Weyer's skepticism did not at all rest upon doubting the physical powers of demons, which he did not deny in principle, even if many of the alleged actions of the devils were actually the fraudulent inventions of Catholic priests. Yet modern readers have gone astray in understanding Weyer not just because they have read Reginald Scot or Jean Bodin. Weyer himself contributed to the confusion in two major ways.

Throughout *De praestigiis daemonum* Weyer took such pains to un-mask the fraudulent actions of priests, exorcists, diviners, and magicians that he sometimes seemed to be claiming that the devil could not actually do wondrous acts, that he could not really imitate God's miracles. If the reader tentatively drew this conclusion from Weyer's book, he was bound to be appalled and disturbed at the obvious inconsistencies in Weyer's argument when Weyer conceded, as he often did, that the devil could actually do much more than merely tempt and delude his human vic-tims.[49] Thus Weyer was really confusing when he tried to sum up his conclusions regarding the power of demons: he claimed that many things were impossible for the devil when he had already conceded that demonic wonders did occasionally occur.[50] Some of Weyer's objections to the pact with the devil are of just this prudential variety, as if his claim were that a pact could occur but usually did not. If this was all of Weyer's argument, we would have to agree that it was critically flawed.

Weyer sowed confusion in a second area when he considered the appro-priate punishments for witchcraft. Early in *De praestigiis* he heaped up scorn and outrage over the actions of the learned magicians (the *magi infames*) who befouled Scripture with their claims to know the future, to enchant their enemies, raise the dead, summon demons, cast out demons, and generally surpass the powers of nature. Most of what they did was pure illusion and self-delusion, Weyer claimed, and yet his indignation

---

[49]*De Praestigiis* (1583), I, c. 10, col. 48; I, c. 12, cols. 55–60.
[50]Ibid., I, c. 25, cols. 132–35; III, c. 3–4, cols. 242–52.

over their blasphemies was so intense that he occasionally implied that the death penalty was appropriate for them. Some readers have concluded that Weyer's denunciation of the magi was so zealous that he illogically transferred to them the rage reserved for witches by most of his contemporaries.[51] Certainly Weyer took such pains to distinguish the old, decrepit, ignorant, foolish women accused of witchcraft from the learned, vigorous, and cunning men who practiced various magic arts that one could be forgiven for hastily concluding that Weyer approved of the death penalty for magicians and that, if he did so, his argument was hopelessly unsound. Had he not shown that their claims were just as illusory as those of the witches?

With respect to the crimes of the magi, it is plain that Weyer was indeed appalled at their blasphemies, but he nowhere argued that magicians should actually be executed. He made it clear enough in Book VI that execution should be reserved for those who physically harmed others with their poisons or in any other way. I do not believe that anyone in Weyer's day took seriously the flights of rhetorical excess in which Weyer claimed heatedly that magicians were nefarious criminals to whom the criminal code should apply in all its rigor. It was only that, compared with old and feeble women, the magicians at least entered knowingly upon their course of heresy and blasphemy. With respect to the powers of the devil, however, Weyer did contradict himself. In his own experience he regularly found natural causes for all of the supposed demonic wonders of his day, but on biblical authority he could not conclude that the devil had no physical powers any more. Considering the diabolically infested world of the New Testament, we can see Weyer's problem. Weyer never fully resolved this confusion, this conflict between experience and doctrine, but his basic argument did not hinge on it in any event. He could easily concede vast powers to the devil because the essence of witchcraft was the pact, the agreement of man and devil, and the pact did not depend in any serious way upon the actual physical powers of the devil. The confusion on this score was real but inconsequential. On essential points, therefore, Weyer's argument was coherent and original.

This is not to say that Weyer won his argument. Instead, many jurists (perhaps most) reacted in shock at the audacity of Weyer's claim. Here was a physician who made bold to inform his legal colleagues that a crime

[51]Ibid., VI, c. 1, cols. 653–57; Baxter, "Johann Weyer's *De Praestigiis Daemonum*," pp. 66–71. Citing the *Twelve Tables*, Weyer claimed that the death penalty was intended for "the magician and poisoner," not the "deluded old woman who is ignorant of all arts; "magus et veneficus hic intellegitur, non illusa vetula, cunctarum expers artium;" col. 654. Speaking of the local reverence for traveling exorcists, Weyer protested that, if anyone tried to prohibit their activities, a cry went up that one was "touching the apple of God's eye." Still, this is great wickedness deserving of death, "Hoc grande nefas, et morte piandum," col. 656.

they had prosecuted for centuries (in one form or another) was not in fact a crime at all but an impossible absurdity.

Weyer was, therefore, immediately charged with exceeding his competence, with interfering in matters beyond his professional ken, with "medical imperialism" as some would call it in our times. Weyer was actually far from regarding medicine as a replacement for Stoic and Christian counsels, but he did insist that physicians had valuable advice on matters usually left to others.[52] Moderate though he was on anger, he did represent an early form of medical omnicompetence, which we have also seen in his view that modern marvels all had physical explanations and his notion that only the physically dangerous should be punished. What were jurists to make of Weyer's arguments?

By and large lawyers ignored or misunderstood Weyer's claim that witchcraft was impossible because the pact with the devil was impossible. This claim depended, as we have seen, on Weyer's extraordinary and unorthodox readings of Roman law. Lawyers could not, however, ignore Weyer's empirical claim that those accused of witchcraft were usually mad. From now on jurists seem to have felt that they had to take medical testimony seriously. In this sense Weyer had an amazing impact even on those who disagreed with him. Moralists and theologians, jurists and political theorists, from Jean Bodin to King James VI of Scotland, undertook to refute Weyer's offensively reductionist arguments not by hitting them directly but by adding new empirical (often medical) data.

In the case of Jean Bodin I have already mentioned his peculiar claim that the women accused of witchcraft could not have been melancholy because only men were subject to that malady. Although such an argument made a bit of philosophical sense if one connected melancholy only with the Aristotelian topos of human genius, it made no medical sense in Bodin's day and no one that I know of followed Bodin in this argument. Bodin's sensitivity on this issue does indicate, however, just how crucial the question of melancholy had become.

Another response to Weyer was that of the Swabian jurist (later of Rostock) Johann Georg Godelmann, who published a *Tractatus de magis venificis et lamiis* in 1591 that adopted Weyer's categories verbatim. Those accused of witchcraft might be *magi* (magicians), *venefici* (poisoners), or *lamiae* (witches), and Godelmann was quick to agree with Weyer that *lamiae* were (mainly) women who imagined that they had a pact with the devil and that they did all sorts of evil on its basis; as he said in the German version of this treatise, the devil attacked women because they were more often "unsteady or flighty, credulous, malicious, ill-humored, melancholy or depressed, but especially old, worn-out women

[52]*De ira morbo* (Basel, 1577), p. 152.

who were foolish and awkward, badly grounded in the Christian faith, and unsound old hags."[53] Their pacts with the devil were only illusory, but necromancers and learned magicians did have a real pact with the devil that Godelmann believed worthy of severe punishment and even death. While attempting to defend witches from unjust accusations, in other words, Godelmann left open the argument that at least some persons did have a contract with the devil. Godelmann argued strenuously against abuses of torture and in favor of cautious procedures, but in strictly theoretical terms he was not the radical opponent of witchcraft trials that Weyer was. Yet despite the illogical features of his argument, Godelmann was crucial in the process of restructuring the insanity defense. Precisely because he thought that the witches' pact was a real possibility, Godelmann did not think that one could just assume that supposed witches were mentally ill. On this empirical question medical advice had to be sought.[54]

Even those who disagreed vehemently had to accept the logic of analysis here. Peter Binsfeld, for example, was openly upset at the number of skeptics at large, men who held that witches should not be punished because their confessions were all fantasy and illusion. He conceded that the devil could pervert the imagination and "make something appear other than it is."[55] And he had to concede that those who dream while asleep or fall into madness are not capable of sin (as long as they are asleep or mad), for sin was "by nature a matter of free will."[56] Even so he argued strenuously that witches did fly through the air to the sabbath and that, when the devil deluded their senses and their fantasy, they had already consented to this invasion. Binsfeld recognized that the crux of Weyer's argument was the impossibility of having a pact with the devil. If the pact was impossible, then witchcraft was impossible; consequently Binsfeld aimed the Latin version of his treatise on witchcraft at Weyer.[57]

---

[53]Johann Georg Godelmann, *Von Zäuberern Hexen und Unholden: Warhafftiger und Wolgegründeter Bericht* (Frankfurt, 1592), p. 162. According to Sönke Lorenz, Godelmann anticipated most of this argument in a 1584 Rostock disputation: *Disputatio de magis, veneficis, maleficis et lamiis: Praeside Ioanne Georgio Godelmanno* (Frankfurt, 1584); see his "Johann Georg Godelmann—Ein Gegner des Hexenwahns?" in Roderich Schmidt, ed., *Beiträge zur Pommerschen und Mecklenburgischen Geschichte* (Marburg, 1981), pp. 61–105.

[54]Godelmann repeatedly raised the question of melancholy, claiming in Bk. II, cap. 2, "Lamiae errant et melancholicis vexantur morbis," and repeating the tag "ubi autem est caput melancholicum, ibi Diabolus habet praeparatum balneum" (*Tractatus de Magis, Veneficis et Lamiis* [Frankfurt, 1591] p. II, 10).

[55]*Tractat von Bekanntnuss der Zauberer und Hexen: Ob und wie viel denselben zu glauben* (Munich, 1591) fol. a2v, 25r.

[56]Ibid., 31r.

[57]*Tractatus de confessionibus maleficorum et sagarum recognitus et auctus: An et quanta fides iis adhibenda sit* (Trier, 1591); this Latin version bears a title similar to the German treatise cited in the previous note, but the Latin *Tractatus* has 633 pages compared with the 75 leaves (and large type) of the German (*Tractat*).

Unlike many modern readers of Weyer, Binsfeld seized upon the truly novel and dangerous element in Weyer's book: "he refers almost all the evil devices of witches and sorcerers to fantasy, melancholy, and illusion, and judges their league and pact to be imaginary and impossible."[58] Binsfeld spent much of this Latin work trying to prove on biblical and philological grounds that the demonic pact was possible, and he presented a fully up-to-date legal discussion of witchcraft confessions, accusations, and trial procedure. Repeatedly he attacked Weyer's understanding of Scripture and of Roman law.[59] Even if Weyer was wrong on these points, however, Binsfeld seems to have felt the force of Weyer's psychiatric claims, for he insisted that, despite their possible delusion, witches' confessions were believable. When a confessed witch accused someone else of witchcraft, of course, the charge was less credible than it would have been from an honorable source, but two or three such accusations would suffice as an *indicium* for torture of the new suspect.[60] Refusing to see things in black and white, Binsfeld was elaborating the shades of gray.

The key point in all of this for the workings of the insanity defense is that Binsfeld exercised an exquisite care in judging the extent of guilt in persons suspected of crime. Although he rejected Weyer's claim that witches were necessarily mad, he did not fall into the extreme opposite position, as did Bodin, who held that witches could hardly be melancholy at all. Binsfeld illustrated his flexibility in a sympathetic account of a woman who had fallen into desperation, desolation, and weakness of spirit; in this low condition she had allowed herself to be tempted into witchcraft. Instead of being executed, she was sent into exile, but after a year she came back home, explaining that she had been miserable in exile. Turning herself in to the magistrate voluntarily, she begged to be executed rather than sent away again. Binsfeld took pity on her and insisted that she should not be executed.[61] Binsfeld's repeated arguments with Weyer seem to have jostled him into a more sensitive position on the insanity defense.

This sensitivity to the gray, intermediate areas seems to have impressed Peter Heig, a professor at the University of Wittenberg, who in 1596 was asked to advise on a difficult situation in which a woman had taken the lives of her children. Heig thought that she was clearly depressed but not fully mad. She was melancholy. Instead of repeating what had become tired legal commonplaces about *furor* and *malitia*, Heig seized upon the witchcraft controversy swirling around Johann Weyer and cited specifical-

[58]Ibid., p. 23.
[59]Ibid., pp. 24–27, 395–400, 462, 478, 530–32, 555.
[60]Ibid., pp. 248, 260, 280.
[61]Ibid., pp. 568–74.

ly the works of Bodin, Godelmann, and Binsfeld to justify a moderate position in which the melancholy mother was punished mildly and sent into exile.[62] In adapting the insanity defense to the witchcraft controversy, Heig made medical testimony or medical thinking a crucial part of the analysis of degrees of guilt. One might be melancholy and desperate and therefore not fully culpable but also not entirely innocent either.

Heig was not the only one to remake the insanity defense along medical lines. Already in 1594 Dieterich Graminaeus, a legal counselor to the duchy of Berg, wrote to his duke, Johann Wilhelm, that, with the world coming to an end, Satan was raging as never before. As a result the evaluation of confessions and accusations was harder than ever. The recent confusion over witchcraft, for example, had led to contradictory assertions that witchcraft was all fantasy or that witches all needed to be executed on account of their horrid offense to God's majesty. On such questions Graminaeus favored the opinions of Binsfeld and Godelmann, just as Heig had; like Binsfeld he held that one of the actual causes of witchcraft was "the abandonment of spirit as happens frequently with women, or too much sadness and a contrary timidity."[63] In other words, Graminaeus held that precisely those psychic conditions that Weyer might hold up in order to get suspected witches off the hook constituted the very cause of their crime. Reflecting the changed attitudes in the duchy of Jülich-Cleves, he rejected Weyer's arguments as extreme and even Godelmann's as fatally flawed,[64] but melancholy was for him a plausible defense. Weyer's discourse, if not his conclusions, was beginning to affect legal argument.

When Christoph Besold (1577–1638) of Tübingen took up the task of compiling an encyclopedic thesaurus of the terms in general use throughout the German Empire, his first edition of 1629 made no reference to melancholy.[65] As with his earlier works on Roman law, Besold was content to stay within the conceptual framework of Justinian. He dealt with the mad as *furiosi*.[66] When Besold's *Thesaurus* was reprinted with additions in 1659, however, it contained a lengthy discussion of melancholy, with the familiar recommendation that melancholy fantasies could

[62]Petrus Heigius, *Quaestiones iuris tam civilis quam Saxonici . . . edita nun primum cura Ludovici Person*, 2 vols. (Wittenberg, 1609–19), vol. 2, Q. 38, pp. 332–35.

[63]Graminaeus, *Inductio sive Directorium, Das ist: Anleitung oder underweisung wie ein Richter in Criminal und peinlichen sachen die Zauberer und Hexen belangendt sich zu verhalten* (Cologne, 1594), fol. (i)ii verso and pp. 92–93.

[64]Ibid., fol. (i)v verso, pp. 140–57.

[65]*Thesaurus Practicus, Continens explicationem terminorum atque clausularum, in Aulis et Dicasteriis Romano-Germanici Imperii usitatarum* (Tübingen, 1629).

[66]*Ad Tit. I, III, IV, V, et VI Lib. I: Pandectarum Commentarii Succincti* (Tübingen, 1616), pp. 55, 176–77.

be treated by playing along with them.[67] One reason for the addition was that in 1654 the papal physician Paolo Zacchia's writings on forensic psychiatry were published with the first full medical discussion of the insanity defense.[68] With an amazing grasp of the whole legal, theological, and medical literature, Zacchia spoke of melancholy as producing an insanity that was not quite the same as furor: "Melancholia arises from the natural melancholy humor, furor from the unnatural."[69] Some jurists held that melancholiacs suffered only in their imagination, whereas furiosi suffered in their reason, but Zacchia rejected this conclusion, claiming that the melancholy often suffered in their reason as well.[70] Even so the melancholy were often mad in only one respect or on only one subject, and so they could often testify or be tried for their misdeeds. With explicit reference to Johann Weyer, Zacchia admitted that many supposedly possessed by the devil were actually mad or melancholy: "Among the common people 'demoniac' is the name given to many demented persons."[71] He did not deny that there were true possessions, of course, but claimed that "they are properly called demoniacs who are driven into insanity from a melancholy weakness which the demons use as if it were an instrument to possess them."[72] The most commonly afflicted were "ignorant persons [idiotas] and wenches [mulierculas], and among the latter especially virgins who are not yet purged by being of mature age and are accounted as demoniacs when they are not."[73] Citing Martin Delrio (who knew Weyer well) Zacchia pushed this discussion in the direction of a cautious forensic medicine, in which the medical condition of witnesses, testators, and suspects was of immediate and obvious importance.

The invasion of medical thinking into the insanity defense was even more evident in the separate question Zacchia devoted to hysteria, the female disorder related to a wandering or "suffocated" uterus. Women were, he said, subject not just to female disorders, however, but to all kinds of insanity; despite the claims of Hippocrates to the contrary, "women rarely avoid melancholy," and it was evident that "for every single demon-possessed man (whom we enumerate in the class of melan-

---

[67]*Thesaurus Practicus . . . Additionibus Dn. Joh. Jacobi Speidelii . . . cum novis additionibus . . . Christophori Ludovici Dietherns* (Nuremberg, 1659), no. 40: Melancholi.

[68]Written between 1621 and 1650, the *Questiones medico-legales* were first printed in 1654. I have used the 1701 Lyon edition. On Zacchia, see Margarete Helms, *Die psychopathologischen Anschauungen bei Paulus Zacchias in Hinsicht auf den Beginn einer forensischen Psychiatrie* (M.D. diss., Munich, 1957).

[69]*Quaestiones*, vol. 1, Bk. II, title 1, Q 9; p. 132.

[70]Ibid., p. 132; Helms, *Die psychopathologischen Anschauungen*, p. 37; Jean Fernel had also opposed such a distinction. Zacchias cited his *Pathologia*, Bk. V, chap. 6.

[71]*Quaestiones*, vol. 1, Bk. II, title 1, Q 18, "De Daemoniacis, Fanaticis, etc.," p. 150.

[72]Ibid., p. 151.

[73]Ibid.

cholics), six hundred women are possessed by the demon, as Codronchi says (*De morb. venef.*, Book II, chapter 8). Moreover, this is certain, that when women go mad with melancholy disease, they are far worse off then men: their madness is both more intense and more incurable."[74] It followed that medical testimony would often be necessary to clarify the mental state and degree of legal responsibility of melancholy women.

Zacchia's work had a truly European impact, but in Germany the insanity defense had already undergone a kind of medical transformation in the thought of Benedict Carpzov, who was probably the most important German commentator on criminal law in the seventeenth century. Carpzov (1595–1666) was for forty years a member (and for a time the head) of the famous Leipzig "Schöffenstuhl," the panel of judges who heard appeals from all over Germany but especially from the eastern regions of the Empire, settled in the Middle Ages by Saxons, whose descendants were obliged to confer with Saxon judges on countless matters; Carpzov was also a member of various Saxon superior courts, a professor of law in Leipzig, and for eight years a privy councillor at the Dresden court. In 1635 he published the main work on which his fame rested: *Practica nova imperialis Saxonica rerum criminalium*.[75] In this work Carpzov tried to create a German criminal law for the Empire, one that was based more on Charles V's famous criminal code of 1532 (the *Carolina*) than on Italian commentators. In the process Carpzov rethought all the basic elements of criminal law, including, of course, the insanity defense. Essentially Carpzov was still working within the Roman legal tradition, however, so that criminal intent (*dolus*) was still mainly an intellectual affair of knowing what one was doing and what the consequences of one's acts might be. Ignoring the medieval canon lawyers, who emphasized both the will and the intellect as components of any crime, Carpzov followed mainly the Roman jurists and was relatively unconcerned by the possibility that one's will might be so bound or driven that one could not be deemed responsible for one's acts.[76]

Confronting Johann Weyer's conclusion that all of the old Roman laws concerning furor should apply to melancholia, Carpzov took refuge in Peter Heig and insisted that melancholy was not the full excuse that raging madness was. One had to make distinctions.[77] There were in his view two

[74]Ibid., vol. I, Bk. II, title I, Q 22, "De suffocatis ex utero," p. 158.
[75]I have used the three-volume eighth edition published in Wittenberg in 1684.
[76]For a sharp critique of the shortcomings of Carpzov's understanding of liability and responsibility, see the useful work of Franz Lubbers, *Die Geschichte der Zurechnungsfähigkeit von Carpzow bis zur Gegenwart unter besonderer Berücksichtigung der Doktrin des gemeinen Rechts* (Dr. Jur. diss., Jena, 1936; published Breslau-Neukirch, 1938), pp. 3–7.
[77]For citations of Heig, see Lubbers, *Geschichte der Zurechnungsfähigkeit*, p. 22; Carpzov, *Practica nova*, 3:367, 371–72.

sets of rules in fact, one for the furiosus and another for the melan-
cholicus. Agreeing amiably with the long tradition that I have already
outlined, Carpzov held that the furiosus should not be punished at all, for
his furor was punishment enough.[78] Despite his usual stress on the intellect, Carpzov said that this made perfect sense because will was essential
to crime, and a *furiosus* acted involuntarily. The Schöffen in Leipzig also
deployed this rule, for example, in March of 1623 when they decided that
an insane murderer was not to be punished. Following the letter of the
Roman law, they decreed further "that he should be taken by his friends
and relatives [von seiner Freundschafft] to a special place in secure custody, there to be held with chains and bands so that he will not be able
further to harm himself or others."[79] This rule was also binding for those
who became insane after committing a crime. Punishment of any sort,
whether corporal, capital, or pecuniary, had to wait for the criminal to
enjoy a lucid interval.[80] This was true, Carpzov held, not only because
madness was "punishment enough," but because the madman had to be
treated as if he were absent or dead, and if the analogy was strict, then one
obviously could not punish him as long as he was mad. These rules
regarding furor had to be applied with great caution, he admitted, for the
proof of furor was difficult. To assist in deliberations, Carpzov recommended that physicians be consulted, but the trouble, as we can see, was
that physicians were not trained to recognize furor. They could diagnose
mania, phrenitis, melancholy, and other diseases but not the legal category. A similar situation often exists today, of course, when lawyers ask
psychiatrists to translate their thinking into the legal categories of responsibility and freedom. Even if the madman was declared not guilty because
of his furor, however, Carpzov was eager to remind his readers that the
suspect "is not to be let go or set free at once, but should be held in
custody by his own people and even in chains and shackles if necessary,
not as a punishment for any crime but lest he do himself or others some
damage,"[81] and he cited the appropriate references to the familiar Roman
texts. All of this thinking about furor was subject to the major limitation
that, if it could be shown that "the madman was responsible for provoking [*sua culpa*] his own madness," he should be punished, yet not so
severely as would be right if he were fully sane and fully guilty.[82] So
much for the furiosi.

The melancholy were another story. "If a criminal commits a crime on

[78]Ibid., p. 368.
[79]Ibid.
[80]Ibid., p. 369.
[81]Ibid., p. 370.
[82]Ibid., p. 371.

account of melancholy, he should be no means go unpunished, and yet the ordinary penalty should be remitted on that account, and another milder one can safely be imposed.''[83] Such a ruling left the insanity defense in confusion, but Carpzov maintained that there was an obvious difference between the furious and the melancholy: ''The furious are those who lack mind and common sense [''qui mente et sensu communi caret''], whereas the melancholy are persons of desperate and agitated mind, imagining to themselves and saying absurd and sad things [''homines desparatae et emotae mentis, absurda et tristia sibi fingentes atque dicentes''].''[84] Carpzov was not speaking of those who were merely melancholy by temperament, those whose humoral temper made them usually fearful, lustful, greedy, or angry. No, he was speaking of the melancholy-mad, but they were not completely insane. Even those suffering strange delusions and laboring under the temptation to kill themselves had a sadness that had not usually brought them to a ''total mental alienation, nor has it flatly deprived them of understanding; and so there is no doubt that they do their misdeed willingly and with malice.''[85] Thus a plea of melancholy did not necessarily take one off the hook. As an example, Carpzov recounted the judgment given in 1608 to a woman who confessed that she had murdered her own child. By her account she had been driven to this deed by a black man who had come to her in a dream; she seemed likely to have acted out of ''sadness, melancholy, and depression,'' and so the ''ordinary'' death penalty was remitted. Instead she was to be tied into a sack with a dog, a rooster, a snake, and a cat and thrown into the water to be drowned. If the place had no suitable water, she was to be executed with the wheel.[86]

Carpzov clearly felt he had to deal with the melancholy, but he gave them no quarter. Some of his animus against them may have arisen from his sharp and prolonged effort to refute the arguments of Johann Weyer.[87] We can see plainly in Carpzov's case the way in which medical language and medical consultation entered the law of insanity; jurists did not accept the argument as Weyer had posed it, but they did adopt Weyer's terms of discourse, as further interpreted especially by Peter Heig.[88]

With this turn to medical language and medical consultation, the insanity defense entered a strangely modern phase. If lawyers and judges were no longer the best judges of whether a suspect was capable of

[83]Ibid., p. 372.
[84]Ibid., p. 371.
[85]Ibid., p. 372.
[86]Ibid.
[87]Ibid., 1:308–16.
[88]Lubbers, p. 22, holds that Heig was the first to see melancholy as a legal problem, but such a view obviously leaves out of account the very sources Heig cited: Binsfeld, Godelmann, and Bodin, all of whom were reacting to Weyer.

committing a particular crime or fit to be punished, they began to worry, as they rarely had before, that madness might be feigned. Here too, of course, there was a Roman legal precedent, as a glance at *Digest* I, 18, 14 would show.[89] Commentators, however, had ignored the possibility of pretense until that point when jurists were compelled by their own language, the language of melancholy, to seek expert medical testimony.

In 1654, for example, Justus Oldecop of Halberstadt wrote a treatise on criminal procedure that was highly critical of the loose use of torture to extract confessions.[90] One of the major difficulties in current legal practice, he thought, was the ease with which suspects feigned illness in order to avoid jail or torture or punishment. Some simulated demon possession, whereas others pretended to be suffering from "enthusiasm" or to be caught up in ecstasy.[91] Women were prone to feign suffocation of the womb or pregnancy. In order to detect and unmask such deceits, one needed expert physicians. Following Zacchia, Oldecop listed five ways of uncovering fraud and emphasized especially the role of medical knowledge in distinguishing true madness from false.[92] Gone was Carpzov's tortured distinction between furor and mere melancholy madness, a distinction that we can perhaps see as a last desperate effort to retain a legal category separate from the medical. For Oldecop, however, the real problem was that "there is almost no disease more easily and frequently imitated than insanity."[93] Two kinds of insanity were common, he thought: melancholy plain and simple and melancholy mixed with furor. "There is this certain difference between the two, that the former are quiet, timid, sad, and dejected in spirit, whereas the later are worked up and in perpetual motion, restless, rash, and wrathful."[94] Both kinds resulted in sleeplessness, and a careful physician would know both well and would be able to tell them from the false. Often sleeplessness was a good enough litmus test by itself, "for Celsus rightly says that for the mad sleep is as difficult as it is necessary."[95] Such extreme disorders did not develop overnight but built up with the excess humors over a long period. Without prodromal symptoms one should remain gravely suspicious of malingering. Moreover, the mad usually exhibited queer opinions, such as

[89]"If . . . no suspicion is left that he was not simulating insanity when he killed his mother . . ."

[90]*Observationes Criminales Practicae congestae et in quinque titulos . . . tributae,* signed by Oldecop in Halberstadt, 12 January 1654. I have used the edition published in Frankfurt an der Oder, 1685. This edition contains a remarkable appendix, pp. 349–72, listing forty-two cases in which innocent persons were unjustly tortured and condemned.

[91]Ibid., pp. 150–51: "Enthusiasmum pati . . . aut in Ecstasin rapi."

[92]Ibid., pp. 153–54.

[93]Ibid., p. 158.

[94]Ibid., p. 159.

[95]Ibid., p. 160.

thinking oneself dead and therefore avoiding food and drink (taking one of the classic tales of melancholy); deceitful simulators of madness never imitated these opinions, Oldecop thought, but how long would this statement remain true if Oldecop's descriptions of true madness made their way out of Latin and into the popular imagination?[96] Recognizing this dilemma, he passed on the advice of a "most learned physician" that mad suspects should be whipped "with this purpose and intention, that if he be truly mad these blows might divert the humors to the beaten parts; but if he really dissimulate, by the strength of those same blows he may recover, even if he doesn't want to."[97] On and on he went with medical tests for true madness. Among his favorite authorities for all of this were Carpzov and Peter Heig, but it should be obvious that Oldecop was living with a new fear. Now that the insanity defense was medical, how could one be sure that only the mad were protected by it?

He was not the only one to feel this new threat. Just one year later, in 1655, Johann Andreas Frommann published a treatise on the legal treatment of the insane that agreed that melancholy madness was an adequate excuse. Citing a case out of Carpzov from 1623, Frommann analyzed the mental condition of a murderer whom the physicians examined and found to be suffering a "melancholy delirium" so that his head was all "confused and mixed up."[98] Such persons were not to be punished. We notice that, although Carpzov raged against the melancholy for not fully qualifying as furiosi, Frommann and Oldecop did not share this harsh attitude. Frommann, however, was concerned about deceit and composed a chapter entitled "De ficto et simulato furore."[99] Again medical opinion was essential in the testing for true madness.

By midcentury these anxieties had become commonplace. In 1672, for example, law professor Samuel Stryk tried to establish that madness could actually be divided not into species (as Carpzov and Heig had tried to do) but into grades, running from full dementia to melancholy. Medical advice was necessary to distinguish the grades and to weed out the fraudulent, a task made even more complex by the proverb: "Sometimes it is wise to simulate madness."[100] Citing Carpzov, Stryk insisted that learned and experienced physicians could make all the difference,[101] and his

---

[96]Ibid., pp. 161–62.

[97]Ibid., p. 162.

[98]*Hypotyposis Juris Furiosorum singularis quam deo ter opt. max. miserabilium eiusmodi personarum defensore justissimo dirigente*, a doctoral disputation (Strasbourg, 1655), p. 63.

[99]Ibid., pp. 70–83.

[100]Samuel Stryk, "Disputatio octava inauguralis de dementia et melancholia (March 8, 1672)," in his *Opera Omnia*, 14 vols. (Frankfurt and Leipzig, 1743–53), 2:202–12, at cap. I, no. 15, p. 204.

[101]Ibid., cap. II, no. 16, p. 206.

discussion of melancholy in particular became a treatment of the medical literature.[102] Although he usually accepted the opinion of Zacchia, Heig, and especially Carpzov, Stryk disagreed on the subject of melancholy; in its mildest forms, to be sure, melancholy did not constitute a defense, but in its highest, worst forms (*summa melancholia*), it did obliterate the "rational faculty" and constitute a full insanity defense. Even after their delusions, in quiet moments, these melancholiacs were punished by the awareness that they might go mad at any time: "satis est, ad reliqua quacunque tempore hos insanire paratos esse."[103] This made a neat parallel to the Roman dictum that the furiosus was punished enough by his own furor, but it made medical judgment absolutely central because there was no longer a fully autonomous, legal judgment of reason, intent, and malice.[104]

This is surely not the place to pursue the German insanity defense into the eighteenth century, but we may at least note in passing that jurists remained anxiously dependent upon a medical understanding of madness. By the mid-eighteenth century the insanity defense was involved in widespread abuse, if we may believe the testimony of Jacob Ernest Friedrich Crell, a jurist who charged that many, when accused of a crime, sought out pliant physicians willing to attest to their madness. Injustice and confusion were the result.[105] It was the dawn of the medicolegal world in which we live today, but the point of this chapter is that the origins of the European (and especially German) insanity defense lie back in the remarkable work of Johann Weyer, who seized upon the exclusively legal language of furor and infused it with the medical discourse of melancholy. In the process jurists gained the ability to see more than the abstract qualities of reason and will. By confronting the medical interpretation of troubled suspects, legal minds may have been encouraged to cope with an empirical reality that could easily be lost in the maze of scholastic legal categories. It is true, however, that medicine in the sixteenth and seventeenth centuries had its own scholastic labyrinth. By inviting medical comment, by insisting on medical advice, lawyers and jurists also forfeited some of their sovereign independence of judgment. It may have been a good thing, on the whole, but it opened a new loophole for the clever defendant: the pretense of madness. This had always been a pos-

---

[102]Ibid., cap. IV, pp. 208–209.

[103]Ibid., cap. V, no. 8, p. 211.

[104]For a brief discussion of Stryk, see Lubbers, *Geschichte der Zurechnungsfähigkeit*, pp. 41–44, which criticizes Stryk for failing to follow the pioneering work of Pufendorf on natural law, in which freedom of the will was the central issue.

[105]"Observationes de probatione sanae mentis . . . defend. Iac. Ernest. Frider. Crellius . . . 5 Dec. 1737," in Christoph Ludwig Crell, *Dissertationum atque Programmatum Crellianorum Fasciculi XII* (Halle, 1775–84), fasc. V, pp. 731–46, at pp. 732–33.

sibility, to be sure, but with the growth of forensic medicine the option appears to have become somewhat easier to employ. In any event it is a tortuous path from Weyer's witches to Peter Heig's melancholy but culpably murderous mother, to the fraudulent madmen that worried Carpzov, Oldecop, Frommann, and Stryk. The path I have traced suggests an unsuspected power in the melancholy metaphor, a power that transformed the insanity defense into something closer to what it is today.

*Two central themes have informed the writings of Heinz Schilling, professor of history at the University of Giessen, the Federal Republic of Germany: the Calvinist movement and the relationship between religion and politics in early modern Germany and the Netherlands. In 1981 he published a detailed analysis of confessional politics in the County of Lippe in Northwest Germany, in which he documents how a Calvinist prince, supported by his officials and an ideology of an absolutist state, tried to impose confessional and political uniformity on the Lutheran town of Lemgo. The ensuing conflict between prince and city is an illuminating case study of one of the results of the 1555 Religious Peace of Augsburg, one clause of which gave the rulers the power to determine the confessional allegiance of their subjects; the book is a microscopic study of state building and princely absolutism in action and of the constitutional constraints placed upon dynastic ambitions. Professor Schilling is also the author of a study on Dutch exiles in the sixteenth century (1972), the coauthor of a general history of Germany (1984), and the author of many articles on religion, society, and politics in early modern Germany and the Netherlands.*

[262]

# [12]

# Between the Territorial State and Urban Liberty: Lutheranism and Calvinism in the County of Lippe

HEINZ SCHILLING

Translated by Thomas A. Brady, Jr.

I

The study of the Reformation as "an urban event," which was originally stimulated by the appearance in 1962 of Bernd Moeller's *Reichsstadt und Reformation* (English: *Imperial Cities and the Reformation* [1975]), has greatly expanded and deepened our insights into both the societies and the mentalities of early modern Europe. The paradigm of "City and Reformation," which has dominated German and international research for nearly a generation, now needs to have its (understandable) onesidedness corrected through new research emphases, without in any way surrendering its unusually fruitful research agenda. In particular, the field's horizon needs to be broadened in content, chronology, and interpretation.[1]

---

[1]Because I have been asked to present my research on the Reformation and confessionalism to a broader, chiefly non-German-speaking public, I present here the case study and the conclusions from my book *Konfessionskonflikt und Staatsbildung: Eine Fallstudie über das Verhältnis von religiösem und sozialem Wandel in der Frühneuzeit am Beispiel der Grafschaft Lippe*, Quellen und Forschungen zur Reformationsgeschichte, 48 (Gütersloh, 1981). I have also integrated some more recently published studies: "Wandlungs- und Differenzierungsprozesse innerhalb der bürgerlichen Oberschichten West- und Nordwestdeutschlands im 16. und 17. Jahrhundert," in M. Biskup and K. Zernack, eds., *Schichtung und Entwicklung der Gesellschaft in Polen und Deutschland im 16. und 17. Jahrhundert* (Wiesbaden, 1983), pp. 122–74; "Reformierte Kirchenzucht als Sozialdisziplinierung?" in W. Ehbrecht and H. Schilling, eds., *Niederlande und Nordwestdeutschland* (Cologne and Vienna, 1983), pp. 261–327; "The Reformation and the Hanseatic Cities," *Sixteenth Century Journal* 14 (1983):443–56; "European Crisis of the 1590s—The Situation in the German Towns," in P. Clark, ed., *The Crisis of the 1590s* (London, 1985), pp. 135–56; " 'History of Crime' or 'History of Sin'?" in Tom Scott and E. Kouri, eds.,

In the area of content, we chiefly need a much stronger integration of the territorial principality into Reformation research, which could be approached through the obvious tie between city and land. The new social-historical approaches, which have been tested on the urban Reformation, ought to be applied to this topic as well, so that we may move beyond the older literature on the territories and their churches, which was dominated by political, constitutional, and church-historical concerns. Together with the territories, the supraterritorial planes of the region and the Holy Roman Empire itself ought to figure more prominently in scholarly field of vision. Because of the peculiar constitutional structures of early modern Germany, the social-historical dimension of the Reformation, along with the ensuing developments in church life and religion, can be adequately studied only by embracing all levels of public life—from the *Haus* (household) to the neighborhood, from the village and town to the territory, the region, and the imperial circle, right up to the various organs of the Empire itself, principally the imperial court and the courts of law.

The chief chronological revision must do away with the traditional division at 1555, which the "City and Reformation" paradigm has in certain respects fixed even more rigidly than before.[2] The fact that most studies of the Reformation end at 1555 at the latest has led to the separation of overarching lines of development that historically belong together. This is true of the history of the bourgeoisie, as well as of the formation of the early modern State, the formation of the Holy Roman Empire's government in the same era, and even the history of church and church polity, where the main consequences of the Reformation were by no means fully worked out by 1555. It seems more reasonable to deal with the social history of the Holy Roman Empire in terms of the chronological span from 1450 to 1650.

Corresponding to these revisions, the framework of interpretation must be expanded from the issue of the connection between religious and secular forces in the Reformation to broader, more inclusive problems of

*Politics and Society in Reformation Europe: Essays for Sir Geoffrey Elton on his Sixty-Fifth Birthday* (London, 1987), pp. 289–310. As these publications contain extensive references to sources and literature, my notes below include only the briefest annotation.

[2]The era after 1555 has not been entirely excluded. See, for example, the contributions on Würzburg, Bamberg, and Emden in B. Moeller, ed., *Stadt und Kirche im 16. Jahrhundert* (Gütersloh, 1978). There are also the studies on the "late Reformation," such as H.-C. Rublack, *Gescheiterte Reformation* (Stuttgart, 1978); K. von Greyerz, *The Late City Reformation in Germany* (Wiesbaden, 1980); H. Schilling, "Bürgerkämpfe in Aachen zu Beginn des 17. Jahrhunderts," *Zeitschrift für historische Forschung* I (1974):175–231; Schilling, "Dortmund im 16. und 17. Jahrhundert—Reichsstädtische Gesellschaft, Reformation, und Konfessionsierung," in G. Luntowski, ed., *Dortmund—1100 Jahr Stadtgeschichte* (Dortmund, 1982), pp. 151–202. Because these are by definition studies of individual cities, they could not serve as bases for revision of the scheme of periodization based on the year 1555.

the specific mediations of religion and social formations in early modern (or "Old European") societies in general. This brings the phenomenon of confessionalization directly into focus as, on the one hand, a direct consequence of the Reformation and, on the other, a movement possessing its own dynamic, which profoundly transformed early modern Europe in general and the multiconfessional, politically fragmented Holy Roman Empire in particular. The movement so intensified the interpenetration of religion and society, confession, and politics, that there arose irreconcilable, total confrontations that endangered peaceful social life as such.[3] This dialectical process of confessionalization drove forward the modern secularization of political life, in which the decisive turning point came during the long years of the great religious wars of the earlier seventeenth century, when Europe was plunged into chaos.

In German historiography, "confessionalization" has become an independent paradigm of social history.[4] Squarely in the center stands the connection between ecclesiastical and religious forces and the rise of the early modern state with its modern social discipline. Confessionalization appears here as a driving element of the long process that transformed the old, status-ordered world of Europe into the modern, industrial society of the nineteenth and twentieth centuries. Confessionalization was a transitional phenomenon, but it also had an epochal quality of its own. The decisive point is that, during the century between 1550 and 1650, the premodern European conception of politics worked most powerfully both as structure and as event. In contrast to the secularized political conception of the present day, this older European concept of politics included both the church and religion in accordance with the maxim "religio vinculum societatis," which means that religion was not—as at present— a social sector or factor but a pillar of State and society, indispensable to human social life.

---

[3]See above all R. Koselleck, *Kritik und Krise: Eine Studie zur Pathogenese der bürgerlichen Welt,* 3d ed., Suhrkamp Taschenbuch Wissenschaft, 36 (Frankfurt am Main, 1973).

[4]Developed by Wolfgang Reinhard and Heinz Schilling, working on Tridentine Catholicism and Protestantism, respectively. In addition to the introduction to my *Konfessionskonflikt und Staatsbildung,* see H. Schilling, "Konfessionalisierung als gesellschaftlicher Umbruch," in S. Quandt, ed., *Luther, die Reformation, und die Deutschen* (Paderborn, 1982), pp. 35–51; Quandt, "The Reformation and the Rise of the Early Modern State," in James D. Tracy, ed., *Luther and the Development of the Modern State* (Minneapolis, 1986); W. Reinhard, "Konfession und Konfessionalisierung in Europa," in W. Reinhard, ed., *Bekenntnis und Geschichte* (Munich, 1981), pp. 165–89; Reinhard, "Zwang zur Konfessionalisierung?" *Zeitschrift für historische Forschung* 10 (1983):257–77. More recently, confession has appeared as a "social and ideological element" in the historical literature in the German Democratic Republic though with the limitation that it is not considered an adequate basis for periodization from the viewpoint of dialectical materialism. H. Langer, "Religion, Konfession, und Kirche in der Epoche des Übergangs vom Feudalismus zum Kapitalismus," *Zeitschrift für Geschichtswissenschaft* 32 (1984):110–24, here at p. 121.

The events of church history, therefore, including radical changes such as the Reformation, had direct political and social effects. During the second half of the sixteenth century, ecclesiastical, political, and social developments combined to form politically significant confessions. This is the process of confessionalization. In order to describe the Reformation and confessionalization as part of a single process, which we must do, we can borrow a concept from the natural sciences and speak of a social-historical "syndrome": all the different aspects of history—politics, society, constitution, law, and individuals, along with religion and collective mentalities, stood in a relationship of constant mutual interaction, producing effects on the territorial, national, and even global levels.

The Holy Roman Empire's middling and small territories, in which the religious transformation of the sixteenth century coincided with the breakthrough of the princely absolutist state, lend themselves especially to the study of the conjuncture of sociopolitical with ecclesiastical and religious processes that forms the essence of confessionalization. To the territorial princes, often equipped with but modest means of power, deliberate confessionalization became a welcome instrument for the intensification of authority and for building up the state. Not only did confessionalization present an opportunity to domesticate the church and eliminate it as a rival for power, but the confessional churches also incorporated all subjects into a system of pastoral and moral influence and control. The churches thus promoted the formation of a uniform body of princely subjects. Confessionalization was a preparation, according to Gerhard Oestreich, for the social discipline of absolutism.

Against these religious and sociopolitical innovations often arose a stiff resistance that mobilized religious and confessional counterforces. The most instructive cases are those in which the territorial princes struggled against self-conscious territorial cities. Such cities formed financial, economic, and administrative centers that were often quite independent of the territory itself. In the wake of the urban reformation they developed further their religious and ecclesiastical autonomy and heightened thereby their own sense of independence. This was the typical course of events in northwestern Germany, where the rise of the early modern state came about fifty years later than in South Germany. The middling and larger territorial cities, mostly members of the league known as the Hansa, had traditionally been thoroughly independent in this region. These cities and their burghers were especially hard hit by the political and social changes wrought by the rise of the early modern state. They also formed the spiritual crystallization points and the social and political centers of both the religious movements and the ensuing confessional conflicts, whether between Protestantism and Counterreformation Catholicism or between the different Protestant orthodoxies.

The history of the territories in northwestern Germany provides several good case studies for this complex of problems. One is confrontation of Protestant citizens' movements with absolutist princely Counter-Reformation in the Westphalian bishoprics of Münster[5] and Paderborn. In these two cathedral cities, the issue was posed between the maintenance or even expansion of Hanseatic traditions of liberty and self-administration and integration into the territorial state as episcopal residences and centers of administration. Another instructive case would be East Frisia, where during the sixteenth century there formed a political, social, and religious front intimately connected with the struggle over the confessional allegiance of the church. The territorial princes—initially Count Edzard II (1558–1598)—chose orthodox Lutheranism and tried with Lutheran help to establish a territorial state under princely control. The peasants of the western marshes, who were economically strong and had strong traditions of political freedom, joined with the rising burghers of Emden under the banner of Calvinism to fight the count's plans. This front, which is highly interesting in terms of both the history and the sociology of confessionalism, burst into open conflict about 1600 and ended with the victory of Emden and Calvinism.[6]

Even more interesting, from the standpoint of the sociology of religion, is the case of the county of Lippe in eastern Westphalia. Whereas East Frisia presents the alignment taught by historical science and classical sociology of religion—Calvinism and bourgeois freedom, Lutheranism and princely authority—in Lippe the connections were reversed. Here Calvinism allied with the early modern authoritarian state and Lutheranism with civic autonomy and freedom, both corporate and individual. As a result we may add a fourth task to the three outlined above, namely, to test the conventional judgments of the history and sociology of confessionalism about the antithetical political and social affinities of Calvinism and Lutheranism.

## II

The events in Lippe can briefly be sketched. The rise of the territorial state and a corresponding social order in this Westphalian county occupied the whole sixteenth century and much of the seventeenth. Between the princes and the Hanseatic city of Lemgo, by far the county's most impor-

[5]See the richly insightful study by R. Po-chia Hsia, *Society and Religion in Münster, 1535–1618* (New Haven, 1984).

[6]See H. Schmidt, *Politische Geschichte Ostfrieslands* (Leer, 1975); M. Smid, *Ostfriesische Kirchengeschichte* (Leer, 1974); H. Schilling, "Reformation und Bürgerfreiheit: Emdens Weg zur calvinistischen Stadtrepublik," in Moeller, *Stadt und Kirche*, pp. 128–61.

tant city, arose violent struggles, which sometimes coincided with quarrels within the city. The most acute phases were the first third of the sixteenth and the first fifteen years of the seventeenth century, just the times when the religious and institutional reform of the church were at issue: first the Lutheran Reformation, then the second, Calvinist, one. During the 1530s the conflict involved only Lemgo and its relationship to the territorial prince, but with the coming of Reformed (that is, Calvinist) confessionalism, it broadened by century's end to include the entire territory, though Lemgo remained its center.

At Lemgo, as elsewhere in the area of the Hansa in northwestern Germany, the Reformation came to the point of breakthrough in the 1530s in the form, typical for the region's cities, of an oppositional movement to the civic magistrates and the territorial prince. Court Simon V (1511–1536), a decided supporter of the old faith, had even secured a decision by the territorial diet against Lutheranism, which was approved, out of both conviction and policy, by a majority of Lemgo's city council. At Lemgo, unlike other such places, no local priest turned Lutheran, so that, lacking a local clerical leader, the Lutheran reformation here acquired the character, even more pronounced than elsewhere, of a communal movement of the citizenry. This had several causes, among them economic ones: the beginnings of overpopulation and several bad harvests and food shortages had presented the lower and middling citizens with new threats to their existence. They demanded the restoration of communal rights to pastures, woods, and fisheries, which the political elite had either appropriated or restricted to their own advantage. The principal elements in the rebellion syndrome, however, were the reform of the church and the expansion of the state. In accordance with the character of premodern European society, the constitutional and religious lines of conflict also had far-reaching social consequences.

Like a stone thrown into a pond, the popular movement for the Reformation, moved out from the center in ever-widening social and political ripples, until it brought the water's entire surface in motion. At Lemgo, as in other Hanseatic cities, Lutheran sentiments among the citizens first surfaced when German hymns were entoned without warning during a church service. The spontaneous singing of Evangelical songs by the congregation during the Mass, which in the later Middle Ages had the priest as its only actor and the faithful as its largely uninvolved objects, expressed a desire for religious self-determination. Once they penetrated the citizenry, Evangelical ideas set in motion a process that gave birth to the first true church congregation, which could now appear before God as a collective subject through its common song. Building on this action, it could begin the Reformation through political action.

Ecclesiastical and religious events thus directly altered the balance of political and social power in the city and in the territory, for the communal movement in the church evoked a corporate movement of the citizens, which forced the city council to favor the Reformation. This change strengthened for a whole generation the political weight of the citizenry, or its representatives, such as guilds, assemblies, or neighborhood organizations. The urban political structure of Hanseatic cities possessed two centers, the city council and the commune, and the emphasis now shifted from the governmental to the popular pole. As late as the Interim crisis at midcentury, the citizens could still make their own will effective in the city council. Several of the older magistrates had refused to convert to Lutheranism, which changed the elite not in a revolutionary way but merely by effecting the movement into the council of some younger sons of old senatorial families and some social climbers of merchant and artisan backgrounds.

The burghers' movement for the Reformation also had broader effects on Lemgo's position in the territory, especially its relationship to the territorial prince. Because the Reformation came to victory as a citizens' movement, it posed a political opposition to the simultaneous beginning of absolutist state building in the territory. The count's long-range goal was to make himself more independent from the nobles and towns as intermediary powers, which would surrender their autonomy in line with the modern principle of the state by renouncing their long-standing rights of dominion in favor of the prince's *superioritas territorialis* (territorial sovereignty). In the Reformation struggles there emerged for the first time in Lippe's history the hitherto latent conflict between two contrary constitutional and social models—the corporate-communal model of the cities and the princely-authoritarian model of the early modern state. The first phase ended with a strengthened city and citizenry, after the count failed to bind his subjects to his own Catholicism, whereupon his successor, Count Bernhard VIII (1536–1563) converted the entire land to Lutheranism. In Lippe the Lutheran Reformation was thus not just a "prince's reformation" in the interest of the count and his territorial state. It was what I have called a "Hanseatic reformation." It revitalized Lemgo's endangered autonomy. For a long time thereafter attempts to integrate the city fully into the territory and its bureaucracy had no hope of success.

Three-quarters of a century passed before Count Simon VI (1563–1613), a grandson of Simon V, tried once more to create in Lippe the type of princely state that was already well advanced in other German territories. The chief target had to be the city of Lemgo, because its recently strengthened political, ecclesiastical, and economic autonomy blocked the path toward a unified territory under princely sovereignty. Chances of success were now incomparably better than in the early sixteenth century, for the Religious Peace of Augsburg in 1555 had significantly improved the constitutional and ecclesiastical positions of the Protestant princes in their own territories, especially vis-à-vis the Hanseatic towns.[7] Conflict flared anew between city and prince and between citizens and civic oligarchy, taking a course similar to that of the 1530s. Just as in the previous century, ecclesiastical and religious questions provided the spark for a quarrel that brought together the political, legal, and social lines of conflict. The conflicts had in the meantime grown even sharper and more fundamental, for during the last quarter of the sixteenth century, the process of confessionalization had produced three integral world views— Tridentine Catholicism, orthodox Lutheranism, and Calvinism—that embraced all aspects of both public and private life. In the decades toward the turn of the seventeenth century, therefore, every confessional conflict became a total political and social confrontation that cut at the heart of the ability to live together.

In Lippe the struggle began when Count Simon VI announced his conversion to Calvinism through a public celebration of the Lord's Supper according to the Reformed usage. This change of religion rested on the count's personal religious decision, which in turn flowed from his humanist, Philippist education and his social involvement with the Calvinist dynasties of western Germany, such as Hesse-Cassel, the Wetterau counts, and the Palatinate. The conversion also had far-reaching political and social consequences, for the count, drawing on the episcopal powers that the Peace of Augsburg's principle of "cuius regio, eius religio" had authorized for the Protestant princes, spurred his political and theological advisers to introduce Reformed religion into the Lutheran county. It was therefore necessary to make a formal change in doctrine on the basis of the Heidelberg Catechism and to purify churches and worship from the relics of "papist" superstition that the Lutherans had retained, such as votive pictures and altars, the exorcism in the baptismal formula, the use of church bells to warn against storms and to call the people to worship, the blessing of the fields, and especially the Lutheran eucharistic service, which was replaced by memorial service, in which bread, not the blessed elements, was received seated at the communion table. Just as in Lutheran Württemberg and Catholic Bavaria, confessionalization meant princely state building in Reformed Lippe, where the count introduced reforms of the administration, tax structure, and justice at the end of the sixteenth

[7]For details see H. Schilling, "Konfessionskonflikt und hansestädtische Freiheiten," *Hansische Geschichtsblätter* 97 (1979):36–59.

century. The new church reform was supposed to bring administrative unity and centralized bureaucratic control to the territorial church, within which the civic church of Lemgo possessed, for the time being, extensive autonomy over personnel, institutions, and worship.

The changes were propagated as a Second Reformation. Following Luther's reformation of doctrine, religious practice and life in general would now be reformed in a Protestant sense, in that the individual, the family, and the urban or rural neighborhood would now be subjected to a system of ecclesiastical discipline that aimed at a transformation of religious, spiritual, and moral life. From these changes a new Christian way of life was to arise, the content of which was to be defined by the Reformed theologians and political elite around the prince's court. Civil and ecclesiastical bureaucracies were to be permeated by the same spirit of religious and moral discipline. Furthermore, all officials—from the pastor and bailiff in the villages and hamlets to the superintendents and district officials in the towns up to the chancellery personnel and privy councillors in the central administration at court—were to be bound together in a strict hierarchy. Regular inspections, reports, and visitations were to guarantee the flow of information from below and from above. Special attention was given to the schools, from the village schools to the urban elementary and Latin schools up to the Calvinist institutions of higher education. For attendance at the latter—Bremen, Burg Steinfurt, and Herborn, all of which lay outside the county of Lippe—the prince established special scholarships. These provisions were meant to assure that the next generation of subjects and especially of civil and ecclesiastical officials should be educated in the new confession's ways and simultaneously in the spirit of the new social and political models. As the prince's episcopal authority was made evident to the subjects, above all through the prayers for the princes and his family every Sunday, the prince assumed a sacral character and the evident proximity to God so characteristic of the age of the baroque and absolutism.

It was not to be expected, of course, that the Lutheran nobles and towns would accept this program without resistance, and they reacted with radical opposition to the massive challenge from the prince. The conflict-ridden nature of the confessional transformation nonetheless gave the prince a chance to break the autonomy of estates and towns, which the Lutheran Reformation had strengthened, and thus to force, through the instrument of Calvinism, the formation of a unitary territorial state with a uniform body of subjects.

The new ecclesiastical policy found supporters only among the teachers and theologians, some of whom were Calvinist refugees from orthodox Lutheranism elsewhere, among the jurists of the central administration, among a few noble families, and among a sector of the urban political elite. These men opted from political or religious conviction for the prince and his ecclesiastical, political, and social model, keeping an eye on the chances for their own advancement. The leaders of the opposition to Calvinism, however, which also opposed the early modern territorial state, were men who were oriented politically to the traditional model of corporate-communal, local autonomy and religiously to Lutheranism. The combination did not arise solely from the political constellation that made Lutheranism a natural collection point for opposition to the Calvinist prince, for behind it stood an affinity between religious and sociopolitical conceptions, between Lutheran spirituality and the corporate-communal mentality in town and land.

The least engaged group were the nobles, from whose ranks only the Kerssenbrock family committed itself against the Second Reformation by instituting private Lutheran worship at their Castle Barntrup. The ecclesiastical and political reforms were passively tolerated by most nobles and were supported by others, such as the Donop family, which had become acquainted with Calvinism while on military service in the Netherlands.

The peasants behaved quite differently, and resistance developed in many villages, especially against pastors who were prepared to accept the reforms or even actively promoted them. The peasants refused to perform services for such pastors, slaughtered their hogs, and treated them with the contempt that in premodern agrarian Europe was reserved for aliens. These rebellions were hardly dangerous, though they reveal that the peasants regarded the church reforms and the corresponding advance of princely power as an alien invasion of the world of the village. To them, such acts threatened the time-honored social structure and religious usages that protected them from the dangers of everyday life. They had to stand by and see their own pastors introduce these dangerous innovations.

The resistance proved especially stout in the village of Sonneborn, where several leading peasants (*Meier*) were tenants of the above-mentioned Lutheran noble family of Kerssenbrock. Shortly before, since the village had become Lutheran, the church had been adorned by a splendid set of paintings based on the *biblia pauperum,* which was now to fall victim to Calvinist puritanism. The paintings, which displayed the passion and death of Christ, had apparently impressed the Sonneborn peasants with the sacral nature of the Lutheran eucharistic service, which now was to give way to the sober, rational atmosphere of the Calvinist communion service.

The village congregation, summoned by the church bells, met in a parish assembly under the presidency of their dean and decided on countermeasures. Their envoys confronted the pastor and the churchwarden and shouted their rage. Through the removal of the high altar and other sacral objects, the polemic against exorcism, the ringing of church bells against thunderstorms and other ritual acts, and above all the new, purified Lord's Supper—which had the congregation sit at table as for an ordinary meal—the pastor had "deprived our Lord God of power." Worse, when he broke the bread, he put himself in the Lord's place. The peasants could hardly have expressed more clearly how the purification of worship—determined by a group of intellectuals at a distant court— ignored their own religious needs. The incident also revealed the conflict with the Lutheran Reformation, which both urban and rural folk had adopted as their own cause.

In this second phase of the struggle over the ecclesiastical, political, and social formation of the early modern territorial state, as in the first phase, the chief bastions of Lutheranism lay in the towns. This time there were disturbances in the territory's smaller towns, such as Blomberg, Horn, Salzufflen, and Detmold—the comital residence. The bitterest resistance, however, and most dangerous to the count occurred once again in Lemgo, for the financial, economic, and political resources of this middling Hanseatic city were equal to those of the count himself, making the struggle one between two equal opponents. The resistance also became radicalized, because the struggle came to concern political and ideological fundamentals. Under the banner of Lutheranism, the forces for the autonomy of the premodern, corporate world fought against those of the early modern princely state, which attacked under the banner of Calvinism. The conflict of Lippe versus Lemgo, as the acts of the imperial courts later named the quarrel, lasted more than a decade, and the smoldering Lemgo case, which now and again rekindled, also threatened the count's successful subjugations—by tactics or force—of the nobles, the peasants, and the smaller towns.

During the struggle's initial phase, the city council assumed the leadership of the resistance, but when several senators began to yield to the count's political and ecclesiastical might, a split developed within Lemgo's political elite and decisively weakened it. At Pentecost 1609 the magistrates of Lemgo signed a treaty that meant the city's de facto subjection to the prince and the territorial state. With demonstrative pomp and show of might, Count Simon VI and his civil and ecclesiastical officals rode into the city. He replaced the Lutheran pastors with Reformed ministers and introduced broad, general reforms that began the political and social integration of the long independent "Punktherrschaft"[8] of Lemgo into the territorial state.

Contrary to the common cliché of a passively obedient Lutheranism, in

---

[8]I take this concept from H. Stoob, "Westfälische Beiträge zum Verhältnis von Landesherrschaft und Städtewesen," *Westfälische Forschungen* 21 (1968):69–97.

this situation the resistance developed from below, rising from the citizenry and the corporately minded circles of the guilds and communal representatives. The deposed Lutheran clergy, pastors, and teachers, who were still living in the city, laid the spiritual and propagandistic basis for this act of religious and political self-defense, to which they also provided theological legitimacy.

A powerful popular movement arose, fed by a dangerous alliance of Lutheranism with typically premodern European demands for liberty and self-determination. The citizens' collective will aimed not at change but at maintaining the religious situation. The civic church's administrative autonomy and the Lutheran confessions gained great symbolic value, for they represented the historic accomplishment of the citizenry back in the Reformation era. In accordance with the burghers' corporate understanding of right and traditional legal symbolism, the citizenry gathered in the market, renewed their citizen's oath, and formed an association for defense of the city with might and main, without reservation. They also formed a citizens' committee, which de facto took power from the city council and assumed direct rule over the city. The movement had found its social basis among the artisans and shopkeepers, supported by the Lutheran civic clergy and that part of the political elite that rejected the early modern territorial state and staked its economic, political, and cultural survival—in short, its entire spiritual and material existence—on the burghers' traditional world.

Just as in the villages, though with far more dangerous consequences, at Lemgo the resident Reformed ministers and princely officials saw themselves and their families threatened with persecution and extortion by the burghers. The Reformed theologian Heinrich Dreckmeier, whom the prince had just recently named superintendent of the civic church of Lemgo, saved his own life only through a very risky fight.

The military and political struggles to which this confrontation led lasted almost a decade and brought the city and the territory close to financial and economic ruin. Each side sought to injure the other wherever possible. The Lemgoers, for example, fired cannon from their own walls at the count's nearby Castle Brake, while the count had his men drive away the burghers' livestock, which they let graze outside the city's gates, and on several occasions imposed a total blockade against the city.

In the tense times on the eve of the Thirty Years' War, when the confessional fronts confronted one another with irreconcilable ideological, political, and military enmity, every confessional conflict was liable to act like a spark in a powder keg. The northwestern part of the Empire was especially endangered because of the Netherlandish-Spanish war. Following the conclusion of the Twelve Years' Truce, each side tried to prevent the other from building new strongholds in neighboring German lands. In Lippe, to be sure, though there was no trace of a Catholic-Protestant conflict, a victory for the politically more aggressive and better-connected Calvinists would have weakened the Catholic bloc's position in the region. Furthermore, the case of Lemgo versus Lippe was of concern on a region and even an imperial level, because both parties entered suit at the imperial courts—the High Court (*Reichskammergericht*) controlled by the estates and the emperor's court (*Reichshofrat*)—and also sought to mobilize other imperial organs, such as the Lower Rhenish-Westphalian Circle and the neighboring Lower Saxon Circle, plus the electors and the emperor himself. Each tried to involve its own coreligionists. Lemgo approached the Lutheran Hanseatic cities of Minden, Herford, Hameln, Osnabrück, and Lübeck—the Hansa's capital—plus the Lutheran princes of Hesse-Darmstadt and Schaumburg and the cathedral chapters of Minden and Osnabrück. The count of Lippe tried to involve the Elector Palatine, Hesse-Cassel, the United Provinces of the Netherlands, and the government of the city of Bremen, which on account of the quarrel fell into a conflict between confessional loyalty and urban solidarity. The neighboring Catholic regimes of electoral Cologne and Paderborn, plus the Hanseatic city of Münster, also intervened.

Although the Lippe-Lemgo confessional conflict had repercussions throughout the region, hostilities did not spread beyond the county. On the contrary, everything worked to isolate the quarrel, for precisely because the danger was so great that confessional conflicts out of control could plunge the region, the Empire, and even all Europe into chaos, there developed a zealous, and in the end successful, effort to restore peace.

The successful peacekeeping effort in the case of Lemgo versus Lippe is all the more remarkable because the mediation aided not the prince and the rising princely state but the city. That it did so is already evident in the form of the peace concluded in 1617 through the mediation of the neighboring bishop of Paderborn. In this agreement, called the Röhrentrup Decree, city and prince appear as formally equal parties to the treaty, which was hardly compatible with the principle of princely sovereignty or with the uniform territorial authority of the modern state. In this peace the count guaranteed his own city its Lutheran doctrinal confession and the organizational and legal independence of its parish church. He also guaranteed the constitutional autonomy that the city had won during the Middle Ages and that he had tried to suppress along with its Lutheranism. He also had to concede important economic liberties.

Lemgo had survived, and for the most part won, the conflict with the territorial government of Lippe, even though in general the early modern territorial state was advancing and, compared with the Reformation era, the protection of imperial law for northwestern Germany's territorial cities was weaker than it had been earlier. Right down to the end of the old Empire, Lemgo was never fully integrated into the territorial state of Lippe, within which the city maintained itself as an ecclesiastically, politically, and socially autonomous system. The upholding of his independence, just at the beginning of the seventeenth century, when the princes were making their most dangerous assault on traditional urban autonomy in northwestern Germany, was unthinkable without the mobilization through Lutheranism of the burghers' will to liberty and autonomy and its corporate-communal resources. This coalition between Lutheranism and burghers' liberty in the traditional, corporate sense also protected Lemgo from the autocratic and absolutist princely state during the remainder of the early modern era.

## III

From a detailed religious, legal, constitutional, social, and ideological analysis of the events thus sketched, we may draw conclusions that apply beyond the case itself to the structure and dynamic of early modern society in the Holy Roman Empire and in the rest of Europe. They may be summarized in six points.[9]

(1) *The functions of church and confession in the process of state building.* Neither the Reformation nor the Second Reformation was an exclusively religious event. Despite their autonomous, primary quality, the religious and ecclesiastical developments were embedded in an overarching social process, which may be described as the transformation of the old territorial lordship into the early modern type of state, or as the development of the institutionalized territorial state with its uniform body of subjects. The struggle for the spiritual and religious basis of the territorial society and for the confessional basis and organization of the church was no less important for the foundation of this early modern type of state than were the taxation and the army favored by the constitutional historians. If we follow Norbert Elias in seeing in military power and taxation the "key monopolies" of state building conceived as a process of monopolization, we must recognize that the state's monopolization of the church in the Protestant states came earlier and created important preconditions for the achievement of the other two key monopolies. This statement was especially true of the many small and middle-sized territories,

[9]For details and nuances, see my *Konfessionskonflikt und Staatsbildung*, pp. 365–91, with much comparative material.

which were the dominant form in the Empire and in which the army played a minor role or none.

The Protestant princes assumed roles as emergency heads of the Evangelical churches at the point when those institutions stood in their organizational and administrative infancy. The princes were thus able to monopolize the administration and government of the new territorial churches, bringing an important sector of public life under modern (that is, permanent and centralized) state power without any participation by intermediate powers. The organized and confessionally uniform territorial church bound all inhabitants, down to the most remote hamlet far into the body of the territory—an important step toward the formation of a uniform territorial social order, to which the individual felt he or she belonged. The older local loyalties, such as typically medieval ones to religious ecclesiastical units outside the territory, faded accordingly into the background.

These generalized connections between the renewal of the church and the rise of the early modern state were hampered in practice by many forms of opposition and countertendencies. An instructive example of the latter is the county of Lippe, where the Lutheran Reformation did not, as Karlheinz Blaschke demonstrates for Saxony, "weaken" or even "neutralize the potential foes of the territorial state"[10] but, on the contrary, decisively strengthened them. In such cases, which were not so rare, during the second half of the sixteenth century the process of confessionalization offered the territorial prince a welcome opportunity to make up for ground lost earlier during the Reformation era.

(2) *The social character of confessional conflict and the limits of political action in the confessional age.* The history of churches and confessions provides an especially good perspective from which to study more precisely the critical conflict-ridden aspects of state building in the early modern era and the attendant social changes. This statement is especially true of the participation of the popular classes, who appear at most indirectly in military and tax affairs, because they were excluded from the territorial diet. Certain things may be said about the origins, course, and possibilities for solution of such confessional conflicts that embraced entire societies. Within the "conflict syndrome," which embraced nearly all aspects of public life, the question of religion and confession formed a crystallization point around which other important social problems settled. Religious issues already played a comparable role during the later Middle Ages. Through the establishment of a competing system of churches and doctrine—that is, through *confessionalization*—the social weight of re-

---

[10]K. Blaschke, "Wechselwirkungen zwischen Reformation und dem Aufbau des Territorialstaates," *Der Staat* 9 (1970):347–64, here at p. 352.

ligious differences had nonetheless gained greatly in significance, to the point at which they could form the core of competing political programs. In the case of Lippe, Calvinism became the guarantor of the early modern, sovereign, princely state, whereas Lutheranism became the paradigm of traditional privileges and civic liberties, that is, of the burghers' self-administration and the city's removal from the region of direct princely rule. Tridentine Catholicism, which does not figure directly in this case study, could assume the same function. In fact, none of the three confessions was bound to one of these political programs.[11]

Their confessional ties enabled local forces in town and land to legitimize more generally and effectively the political resistance, which often drew strength from the defense of local rights. The religious contrasts by their very visibility, as in the Lord's Supper, enabled groups that had otherwise been excluded from the increasingly academic juristic and political discussion of the day to formulate their criticism of the sovereign's invasions.

The confessional issues also made social conflict in principle incapable of solution. The confessionally shaped mentality of conflict thus differed qualitatively from that of a pluralistic society, which must constantly keep open the possibility of compromise. The inability to compromise shows how the confessionalization of politics barred the way to certain forms of sociopolitical action. It plunged European societies into a state of aporia in both domestic and external affairs that could be altered only through a change of paradigm. There are, to be sure, some historical connections and some parallels between the confessional parties of the early modern era and modern political parties, but the qualitative differences are decisive, especially the confessional parties' claim to exclusivity and their acceptance of total confrontation, even when socially destructive. There could be no line of continuity, therefore, between the confessional and the modern form of political action, the path to which necessarily meant the throttling of religious conflicts, the political and social demotion of the confessions, and the transformation of systems with claims to totality into private associations with merely particular religious claims. In German church law, this change was completed during the second half of the seventeenth century.

Socially, too, the confessional conflicts belong entirely to the premodern type of political movements, for most confessional parties and fronts were vertically and not horizontally structured. Confessions were little suited to the articulation of class antagonisms or to becoming vehicles of class conflict. Running as they did straight through the elites and

[11]See point 5 below.

sometimes even through urban families, religious conflicts contributed above all to the differentiation of elites that early modern society constantly produced.

(3) *Burghers, city, and territorial state.* In the history of German cities and the German bourgeoisie, the struggle over Lutheranism during the first third of the sixteenth century and the resistance to confessionalization at the beginning of the seventeenth century developed as a religiously expressed defense of the burghers against the authoritarian tendencies of the magistrates within and the challenge of the territorial state without. The structural peculiarities of civil society (*societas civilis*) in premodern Europe meant that this struggle over the civic constitution always involved ecclesiastical, social, and economic positions.

Such struggles took place in nearly all the middling and larger cities—and in all the Hanseatic ones—of northern and northwestern Germany. With a few exceptions, the cities were not trying to rid themselves of territorial authority and then become imperial cities. Rather, they wanted to maintain the position of a medieval city inside the territory. Between the territory and the Empire, their liberties were often greater than those of an imperial city. The burghers expected the "higher authority" of the territorial prince to remain at the level of medieval lordship, bound by liberties and customs, which were conceived as an order superior to both territorial prince and population. This claim to autonomy, which was shared with other subordinate units that participated in medieval forms of lordship—such as the nobles and the church—was incompatible with the idea of the early modern princely states, for it disrupted uniform territorial sovereignty and emasculated the principles of a sovereign supreme state.

The internally and externally directed claim of the Hanseatic burghers to freedom and self-determination, which was in a certain sense republican, grew stronger during the Reformation era.[12] The territorial princes had also considerably improved their political and legal position, chiefly through the Religious Peace of Augsburg. When the decisive struggle came at the turn of the seventeenth century, two strong opponents confronted one another, which made the struggle all the more bitter. In the long run, however, in northwestern Germany the princely state had greater stamina, so that most Hanseatic cities were subjected to and integrated into the territorial state. The last case was mighty Brunswick, which succumbed in 1671. The case of Lemgo shows, however—and Emden is comparable—that it was possible for a city to win.

---

[12]For details see H. Schilling, "Gab es einen Hansestadt—Republikanismus?" in H. Koenigsberger, ed., *Republiken und Republikanismus in der frühen Neuzeit in Europa*, Schriften des Historischen Kollegs (Munich, 1986).

Viewed in the light of social history, these events are part of the long-term process that transformed the civic burghers into the territorial bourgeoisie of the early modern era. In Lippe, as generally in Germany, the old civic burghers maintained a strong position both spiritually and socially, right down to the end of the Old Empire.[13] The pressure to choose between these two modes of bourgeois existence was felt, at least in norhwestern Germany, only by the upper stratum of the burghers, whereas since the Thirty Years' War the guildsmen normally had no alternative to the urban economy and way of life.

(4) *The minor territories, the Empire, and religion: limits and consequences of the peace.* The handling of the case of Lippe versus Lemgo on the levels of the region and the Empire reveals basic characteristics of early modern history. First, the German minor territory did not attain full sovereignty during the early modern era, for it was not able to handle this kind of conflict as a purely internal problem. It did not succeed in blocking its subjects' hostile political activities beyond the territory's bounds. In this case, several conditions were responsible for the state's failure: the need to conform to the Empire's system of law and order, confessional loyalties that crossed territorial boundaries, and the city's traditional supraregional ties. The restraints on the count of Lippe's freedom of action, which became ever more apparent in the course of the quarrels, ultimately imposed limitations on princely sovereignty within the minor state. There was obviously a threshold with respect to the size of the territory and its ruler's rank (count or prince), and only above that threshold was it possible to achieve true internal sovereignty. The minor state, of which there were many strewn across the Empire, ought to be regarded as a special type in German history, which loses its typical social and political preconditions and limits when it is regarded as merely the detritus of the large territories or as an irritation to them. This statement is especially true of the position of the cities and the burghers within the territory, for their subjection to the centralized state in the Prussian-Brandenburg manner was the exception rather than the rule.

The second basic characteristic is that, even at the peak of confessional polarization in the Empire, there existed at the supraterritorial levels mechanisms of political order that could tame the disruptive forces of confessionalism. The imperial system of law and order, which was established by the Religious Peace of Augsburg to dampen religious and political conflicts through the imperial circles and the imperial courts, proved

---

[13]See M. Walker, *German Home Towns: Community, State, and General Estates, 1648–1871* (Ithaca, 1971).

its ability in the case of Lippe versus Lemgo at a time when elsewhere the confessional situation was already one of total confrontation. In Bohemia only a few years later, the peacekeeping system did not work. This comparison points us toward an insufficiently clarified problem: what conditions in the early modern Empire, or in any historical order, determine whether or not a peacekeeping system will properly function? In the Lippe case we can observe two prerequisites. First, the neighboring powers and the confessional parties in the Empire, including the aggressively Calvinist Palatine Elector, recognized a pacification of the Westphalian regions as corresponding to their own interests. Second, Lippe was a weak, inconsequential territory. Neither condition applied to Bohemia in 1618, for the kingdom belonged to the inalienable core of the Habsburg house lands, and the Elector Palatine, as leader of the anti-Habsburg and Calvinist opposition in the Empire, sought in Bohemia a decisive increase in political and confessional power. The conflict, therefore, could not be controlled. The chaos of the ensuing Thirty Years' War heightened the sense of a need to eliminate the confessional principle as a political category. Society's sense of self-preservation finally won out, and from then on the secularized state guaranteed the peaceful coexistence of the churches and sects. The storms of the Reformation, which had stirred up both church and society, were over.

(5) *Lutheranism and Calvinism.* In the county of Lippe during the early modern era, Calvinism established a "prince's reformation," that is to say, it intensified authority and stabilized princely rule. Lutheranism, on the contrary, appeared as a "resistance ideology" of a burgher association, in which role it made the subjects capable of solidarity and political action against early absolutist tendencies in their territory. This constellation proves that the identification of *Lutheranism* with the inculcation of passivity, withdrawal from politics, and the strengthening of the authoritarian state, and conversely of *Calvinism* with democratic constitutional principles and commitment to freedom and human rights, cannot be maintained, at least not in so general a form. The events at Lemgo prove that *Lutheranism* did not, contrary to the widespread view, ossify after 1555 and respond supinely to the wishes of the ruler or the state. Well into the seventeenth century, it is wrong to speak, as Helmut Plessner does, of a principle of "Lutheran indifference to everything connected with politics." At the critical moment, when the Lutheran confession of the civic parish was at stake, orthodox Lutheranism revealed itself to be a political power possessed of undiminished dynamism. It struck an alliance with the burghers' demands for freedom and autonomy, and it legitimated the political resistance of the antiabsolutist opposition. The goal of this coali-

tion was to limit authority in theory and practice, or better, to prevent the development of a new kind of public authority, which no longer recognized the traditional limits on lordship.

In the county of Lippe, on the other hand, the political and social forces allied with Calvinism differed entirely from the analogous elements in lands where Calvinism opposed the ruler and his established church, as in France, the Netherlands, and England, or, within the Empire, on the Lower Rhine or in the county of East Frisia. In Lippe and in other Reformed territories of the Empire, Calvinism allied with the doctrine of sovereignty, not with the natural law doctrine of resistance, as in western Europe. In Lippe the Second Reformation thus formed an important step toward integration of the particularist units into the territorial state. It is suggestive that the Reformed church in Lippe took its constitution not from Geneva—it was thus not "Calvinist" in the strict sense—but from the state churches of the type represented in Basel and Zurich and discussed in the Netherlands and for a time at Heidelberg. Even later, when Calvinist-Presbyterian elements entered the church polity of Lippe, the appointment of ministers in the Reformed church of the territory remained strictly in princely hands. In Lutheran Lemgo, in contrast, the parish still took part in the calling of pastors in the seventeenth and eighteenth centuries. In this confessionally transposed situation, at the end of the eighteenth century the Lutheran city of Lemgo charged that the Reformed church denied its parishioners a voice in the management of ecclesiastical affairs.

These findings should not be idealized. In Lemgo, too, the burghers' spirit faded and gave way to the usual oligarchy, which thus had nothing to do with democracy in the modern sense. Still, neither did Calvinism wherever it opposed the early modern state—not in the Calvinist urban republic of Emden, or in the United Provinces of the Netherlands, and not in Puritan England or America. It is nonetheless argued time and again, and correctny, that these Calvinist-related movements of revolt belong to the tradition that ate gave birth to modern freedom and human rights. The same should be granted the analogous movements that marched under the banner of Lutheranism.

(6) *The Reformation and the Second Reformation*.[14] In the history of Lippe, the Reformation and the Second Reformation appear as two religious waves, different in development, realization, and sponsors. One

[14]The problem of the Second Reformation was discussed and debated in October 1985 at a scholarly symposium sponsored by the Verein für Reformationsgeschichte. The papers and discussions are published in H. Schilling, ed., *Die reformierte Konfessionalisierung in Deutschland: Das Problem der "Zweiten Reformation,"* Schriften des Vereins für Reformationsgeschichte, 195 (Gütersloh, 1986).

was the religious "burghers' movement," carried by the thirst for salvation among all social strata of the city and pushing up "from below" against the rulers' will; the other was the "made" Reformation, the theological and religious goals of which spoke only to an elite around the ruler and were introduced into the individual congregations by fiat, against the religious needs and expectations of the faithful. Were these differences of such a qualitative kind that the autonomous character of religious experience might have shifted from the era of the Lutheran to that of the Calvinist reformation? Does the Calvinistic renewal movement at the end of the sixteenth century represent, in contrast to the Reformation, another and different type of religiosity?

The political and social consequences of these differences are clear. On the one hand, there was indeed a qualitative, and not merely a functional, affinity between Calvinism and the territorial bureaucracy, which was convinced on both private and sociopolitical grounds of the need for changes. On the other hand, there was a clear association between Lutheranism's traditionalist theology of history and the burghers' desire to secure the status quo. In this respect it is important that, on the basis of the practical enforcement of the Second Reformation, Calvinism could also attract persons who had little interest in theology or religion. For this reason crypto-Calvinism and Philippism in Germany became gathering points for physicians, literati, and jurists—that is, for humanists from faculties other than theology. Under pressure from Lutheran orthodoxy, they converted to Calvinism in order to hide their liberal ideas about religion and life under the mantle of Philippism.[15] The cultural, literary, and scholarly consequences of this movement remain to be investigated.

---

[15]The idea of a reform of life appears also in Lutheranism during the second half of the sixteenth century though without producing comparable results. The history of the concept of the Second Reformation needs to be expanded accordingly. See the concluding discussion in ibid.

# Bibliographical Essay

This essay is meant not to cover the entire field of the Reformation but rather to offer a selective guide to the most important works in the social history of religion in the German Reformation. The emphasis is understandably on works in English, but the most important contributions in French and German have also been included. The following abbreviations are used for journal and monograph series citations:

ARG       *Archiv für Reformationsgeschichte*

QFRG     Quellen und Forschungen zur Reformationsgeschichte

*P&P*      *Past and Present*

*SCJ*      *Sixteenth Century Journal*

SVRG     Schriften des Vereins für Reformationsgeschichte

VIEGM    Veröffentlichungen des Instituts für Europäische Geschichte Mainz. Abteilung für Abendländische Religionsgeschichte

## General Survey of Literature and Sources

For more comprehensive bibliographical and historiographical guides to the Reformation, see the annual bibliographical supplement to the *ARG: Literaturbericht;* Lewis W. Spitz, *The Protestant Reformation, 1517–1559* (New York: Harper & Row, 1985), pp. 385–429; the bibliographical handbooks published by the Center for Reformation Research, St. Louis, including: Steven E. Ozment, ed., *Reformation Europe: A Guide to Research* (St. Louis: Center for Reformation Research, 1982); and the series *Sixteenth Century Bibliography;* for a comprehensive survey from the early sixteenth century to contemporary approaches, see A. G. Dickens and J. Tonkin, *A Historiography of the Reformation* (Cambridge: Harvard University Press, 1985).

For bibliographical reviews and surveys of current literature in the social history of religion, see R. W. Scribner, "Is There a Social History of the Reformation?" *Social History* 2 (1977):483–505; his "Religion, Society, and Culture: Reorientating the Reformation," *History Workshop* 14 (1982):2–22; "Interpreting Religion in Early Modern Europe," *European Studies Review* 13 (1983):89–105; and *The German Reformation* (Atlantic Heights, N.J.: Humanities, 1985). See also Kaspar von Greyerz, "Religion und Gesellschaft in der frühen Neuzeit: Einführung in Methoden und Ergebnisse der sozialgeschichtlichen Religionsforschung," in Société suisse d'histoire économique et sociale/Schweizerische Gesellschaft für Wirtschafts- und Sozialgeschichte, ed., *Religiosität—Frömmigkeit: Religion Populaire* (Lausanne, 1984), pp. 13–36. Specifically on the urban Reformation, see Hans-Christoph Rublack, "Forschungsbericht Stadt und Reformation," in Bernd Moeller, ed., *Stadt und Kirche im 16. Jahrhundert* (=SVRG 190) (Gütersloh: G. Mohn, 1978), pp. 9–26; and the updated survey by Kaspar von Greyerz, "Stadt und Reformation: Stand und Aufgaben der Forschung," *ARG* 76 (1985):6–63.

### Collected Essays and Conference Volumes

The published papers of several important conferences may serve as milestones in gauging the directions of research in the social history of religion. See Miriam Usher Chrisman and Otto Grundler, eds., *Social Groups and Religious Ideas in the Sixteenth Century* (Kalamazoo, Mich.: Medieval Institute, 1978); Wolfgang J. Mommsen, Peter Alter, and Robert W. Scribner, eds., *Stadtbürgertum und Adel in der Reformation* (Stuttgart: Klett-Cotta, 1979), with essays in English and German; Hans-Joachim Köhler, ed., *Flugschriften als Massenmedium der Reformationszeit* (Stuttgart: Klett-Cotta, 1981), with essays in English and German; Kaspar von Greyerz, ed., *Religion and Society in Early Modern Europe, 1500–1800* (London: George Allen & Unwin, 1984), which covers all the countries of Western Europe; and Heinz Schilling, ed., *Die reformierte Konfessionalisierung in Deutschland: Das Problem der "Zweiten Reformation"* (=SVRG 195) (Gütersloh: G. Mohn, 1986), which collects essays at the October 1985 conference at Reinhausen on the Calvinist Reformation in Germany. Four collections of essays in English are particularly helpful for the beginning students; see Lawrence P. Buck and Jonathan W. Zophy, eds., *The Social History of the Reformation* (Columbus: Ohio State University Press, 1972); Peter N. Brooks, ed.,

*Reformation Principle and Practice: Essays in Honour of A. G. Dickens* (London: Scolar, 1980); Philip N. Bebb and Kyle C. Sessions, eds., *Pietas et Societas: New Trends in Reformation Social History* (Kirksville, Mo.: Sixteenth Century Publishers, 1985); Sherrin Marshall and Philip N. Bebb, eds., *The Process of Change in Early Modern Europe: Festschrift for Miriam Usher Chrisman* (Athens, Ohio: Ohio University Press, 1988).


Transmitting the Reformation


The ideas of the Reformation were transmitted by a multiplicity of media. A great deal of work has been done on printing; see especially Miriam Usher Chrisman's exhaustive study of printing in Strasbourg: *Lay Culture, Learned Culture: Books and Social Change in Strasbourg, 1480–1599* (New Haven: Yale University Press, 1982), and *Bibliography of Strasbourg Imprints, 1480–1599* (New Haven: Yale University Press, 1982). Two shorter articles by Richard G. Cole are also of use; see his "The Reformation Pamphlet and Communication Processes," in Ingrid Batori, ed., *Städtische Gesellschaft und Reformation* (Stuttgart: Klett-Cotta, 1980), and "Reformation Printers: Unsung Heroes," *SCJ* 15 (1984):327–39; see also Bernd Moeller, "Stadt und Buch: Bemerkungen zur Struktur der reformatorischen Bewegung in Deutschland," in W. J. Mommsen et al., eds., *Stadtbürgertum und Adel in der Reformation*, pp. 25–39. See also the new study by Paul A. Russell, *Lay Theology in the Reformation: Popular Pamphleteers in Southwest Germany, 1521–1525* (Cambridge: Cambridge University Press, 1986). More recently, historians have extended their study of the communications process to include oral, ritualistic, carnivalesque, musical, and pictorial transmission of the reform message. Of fundamental importance is Robert W. Scribner's original study of the antipapal and pro-Lutheran woodcuts of the early Evangelical movement: *For the Sake of Simple Folk: Popular Propaganda for the German Reformation* (Cambridge: Cambridge University Press, 1981). See also Jane O. Newman, "The World Made Print: Luther's 1522 New Testament in an Age of Mechanical Reproduction," in *Representations* 11 (1985):95–133. On the important subject of preaching, see R. W. Scribner, "Practice and Principle in the German Towns: Preachers and People," in Peter N. Brooks, ed., *Reformation Principle and Practice*, pp. 95–118; his "Oral Culture and the Diffusion of Reformation Ideas," in *History of European Ideas* 5 (1984); and "Reformation, Carnival, and the World Turned Upside-down," *Social History* 3 (1977):303–29; see also Bernd Moeller, "Was wurde in der Frühzeit der Reformation in den deutschen Städten gepredigt?" *ARG* 75 (1984):176–93; and his "Einige

Bemerkungen zum Thema: Predigten in reformatorischen Flugschriften,''
in Köhler, ed., *Flugschriften als Massenmedium der Reformationszeit,*
pp. 261–68.


## Cities and the Reformation

The classic study is Bernd Moeller's 1962 essay: *Reichsstadt und Reformation* (=SVRG 180) (Gütersloh: G. Mohn, 1962); English translation
by Mark Edwards and H. C. Erik Midelfort: *Imperial Cities and the
Reformation* (Philadelphia: Fortress, 1972). The urban Reformation is
inexplicable without a prior understanding of the history of late medieval
German cities; for a brilliant interpretive survey, see Erich Maschke,
''Deutsche Städte am Ausgang des Mittelalters,'' in Wilhelm Rausch,
ed., *Die Stadt am Ausgang des Mittelalters* (Linz, 1974), pp. 1–44. One
of the earliest works in English on the urban Reformation is Miriam Usher
Chrisman's study of Strasbourg: *Strasbourg and the Reform* (New Haven:
Yale University Press, 1967). The Alsatian imperial city has received a
great deal of attention; see Thomas A. Brady, *Ruling Class, Regime, and
Reformation at Strasbourg, 1520–1555* (Leiden: Brill, 1978); Lorna Jane
Abray, *The People's Reformation: Magistrates, Clergy, and Commons in
Strasbourg, 1500–1598* (Ithaca: Cornell University Press, 1985). For
Augsburg, see Philip Broadhead, ''Popular Pressure for Reform in
Augsburg, 1524–1534,'' in W. J. Mommsen et al., eds., *Stadtbürgertum
und Adel,* pp. 80–87; and his ''Politics and Expediency in the Augsburg
Reformation,'' in P. Brooks, ed., *Reformation Principle and Practice,*
pp. 53–70. See also Robert W. Scribner, ''Civic Unity and the Reforma-
tion in Erfurt,'' *P&P* 66 (1975):29–60, and his ''Why Was There no
Reformation in Cologne?'' *Bulletin of the Institute of Historical Research*
49 (1976):217–41. For reformation in the Hanseatic cities, see Heinz
Schilling, ''The Reformation and the Hanseatic Cities,'' *SCJ* 14
(1983):443–56; and his ''Konfessionskonflikt und hansestädtische
Freiheiten,'' *Hansische Geschichtsblätter* 97 (1979):36–59. On Zwickau,
see Susan Karant-Nunn, *Zwickau in Transition, 1500–1547* (Athens:
Ohio University Press, 1987). On Nuremberg, see Günther Vogler,
*Nürnberg, 1524–25: Studien zur Geschichte der reformatorischen und
sozialen Bewegung in der Reichsstadt* (Berlin: VEB Deutscher Verlag der
Wissenschaften, 1982). Recent studies have explored urban religious
movements in the second half of the sixteenth century as well. See Kaspar
von Greyerz, *The Late City Reformation in Germany: the Case of Colmar,
1522–1638* (=VIEGM 98) (Wiesbaden: Franz Steiner, 1980); and Hans-
Christoph Rublack, *Die Gescheiterte Reformation: Frühreformatorische
und protestantische Bewegungen in süd- und westdeutschen geistlichen*

*Residenzen* (Stuttgart: Klett-Cotta, 1978). For general reflections on the urban reformation, see Steven E. Ozment, *The Reformation in the Cities* (New Haven: Yale University Press, 1975); and Hans-Christoph Rublack, "Political and Social Norms in Urban Communities in the Holy Roman Empire," in K. von Greyerz, ed., *Religion, Politics, and Social Protest.*

## The Clergy

We often forget that the Reformation was spearheaded by clerics of the Catholic church who paradoxically presided over a vehement anticlerical movement. In addition, the problem of the social character of the clergy in the second half of the sixteenth century, especially the Catholic clergy, has yet to be elucidated by further studies. The most important works to date are: Henry J. Cohn, "Anticlericalism in the German Peasants' War," *P&P* 83 (1979):3–31; Hans-Joachim Goertz, "Aufstand gegen den Priester: Anticlericalismus und reformatorische Bewegung," in Peter Blickle, ed., *Bauer, Reich, und Reformation* (Stuttgart, 1982), pp. 182–209; Robert W. Scribner, "Memorandum on the Appointment of a Preacher in Speyer, 1538," *Bulletin of the Institute of Historical Research* 48 (1975):248–55. The most important work on the formation of the Protestant clergy is Bernard Vogler's *Le clergé protestant rhenan au siècle de la réforme, 1555–1619* (Paris, 1976), and his three-volume thèse de doctorat, which contains more details. For the Protestant clergy in Saxony, see Susan Karant-Nunn, *Luther's Pastors: The Reformation in the Ernestine Countryside.* (=Transactions of the American Philosophical Society 69) (Philadelphia: American Philosophical Society, 1979); and Gerald Strauss, "The Mental World of a Saxon Pastor," in Brooks, ed., *Reformation Principle and Practice,* pp. 157–70. Very little work has been done on the Counter-Reformation Catholic clergy in Germany; for a recent study on the German College in Rome, see Peter Schmidt, *Das Collegium Germanicum in Rom und die Germaniker* (Tübingen: M. Niemeyer, 1984).

## Confessions and Society

No other European society was as divided along confessional lines as early modern Germany. Recent scholarship has studied the confessionalization of society not from the viewpoint of the development of church doctrines but as a political and cultural phenomenon that helped to shape the character of German society down to the present. Ernst Walter Zeeden was the first to note the importance of this phenomenon; see his

*Die Entstehung der Konfessionen: Grundlagen und Formen der Konfessionsbildung im Zeitalter der Glaubenskämpfe* (Munich: Oldenbourg, 1965) and his *Konfessionsbildung: Studien zur Reformation, Gegenreformation, und Katholischen Reformation* (Stuttgart: Klett-Cotta, 1985). For the struggle between a Calvinist prince and a Lutheran city in the German Northwest, see Heinz Schilling, *Konfessionskonflikt und Staatsbildung: Eine Fallstudie über das Verhältnis von religiösem und sozialem Wandel in der Frühneuzeit am Beispiel der Grafschaft Lippe* (=QFRG 48) (Gütersloh: G. Mohn, 1981). For Strasbourg's strong Lutheran identity, see Erdmann Weyrauch, *Konfessionelle Krise und soziale Stabilität: Das Interim in Strassburg (1548–1552)* (Stuttgart: Klett-Cotta, 1978). The development of a Catholic Counter-Reformation culture has been the subject of R. Po-chia Hsia, *Society and Religion in Münster, 1535–1618* (New Haven: Yale University Press, 1984); see also Wolfgang Reinhard, ed., *Bekenntnis und Geschichte: Die Confessio Augustana im historischen Zusammenhang* (Augsburg: Vögel, 1981); his "Gegenreformation als Modernisierung? Prolegomena zu einer Theorie des konfessionellen Zeitalters," *ARG* 68 (1977):226–51; and "Zwang zur Konfessionalisierung?" *Zeitschrift für Historische Forschung* 10 (1983):257–77. On toleration and interconfessional relations, see Joachim Whaley, *Society and Religious Toleration in Hamburg, c. 1580–1785* (Cambridge: Cambridge University Press, 1985); Paul Warmbrunn, *Zwei Konfessionen in einer Stadt: Das Zusammenleben von Katholiken und Protestanten in den paritätischen Reichsstädten Augsburg, Biberach, Ravensburg, und Dinkelsbühl von 1548 bis 1648* (=VIEGM 111) (Wiesbaden: F. Steiner, 1983); and Peter Zschunke, *Konfession und Alltag im Oppenheim: Beiträge zur Geschichte von Bevölkerung und Gesellschaft einer gemischtkonfessionellen Kleinstadt in der frühen Neuzeit* (=VIEGM 115) (Wiesbaden: F. Steiner, 1984). An important study of the mutually reinforcing relationship between confessionalization and state building is Volker Press's study of the Palatinate; see his *Calvinismus und Territorialstaat: Regierung und Zentralbehörde der Kurpfalz* (Stuttgart, 1970). For a shorter sample of Press's voluminous writings, see his "Soziale Folgen der Reformation," in Marian Biskup and Klaus Zernach, eds., *Schichtung und Entwicklung der Gesellschaft in Polen und Deutschland im 16. und 17. Jahrhundert* (=*Vierteljahrsschrift für Sozial- und Wirtschaftsgeschichte*, Beiheft 74) (Wiesbaden, 1983), pp. 196–243.

## Women and the Family

A number of interesting works in these hitherto neglected topics have opened up new ways of seeing the Reformation. Historians who specialize in women's history or family history have shown that the reforms in the sacrament and institution of marriage must be understood in the larger context of redefinitions of gender roles for women. In traditional Reformation historiography, the study of women has been limited to a few prominent individuals. A pioneering work that expands the perspective so that it includes women in different social classes is Miriam U. Chrisman, "Women and the Reformation in Strasbourg, 1490–1530," *ARG* 63 (1972):143–67. For more recent studies, see Susan Karant-Nunn, "Continuity and Change: Some Effects of the Reformation on the Women of Zwickau," *SCJ* 13 (1982):17–42; Lyndal Roper, "Going to Church and Street: Weddings in Reformation Augsburg," *P&P* 106 (1985):62–101; and her " 'Discipline and Respectability': Protestantism and the Reformation in Augsburg," *History Workshop* 19 (1985):3–28; Merry Wiesner, "Luther and Women: The Death of Two Marys," in Raphael Samuel, James Obelkevich, and Lyndal Roper, eds., *Religion and Society* (London: Routledge and Kegan Paul, 1986); and her *Working Women in Renaissance Germany* (New Brunswick, N.J.: Rutgers University Press, 1986). The ideals of sixteenth-century family life are presented in Steven E. Ozment, *When Fathers Ruled: Family Life in Reformation Europe* (Cambridge: Harvard University Press, 1983), and his *Magdalena and Balthasar: An Intimate Portrait of Life in Sixteenth-Century Europe Revealed in the Letters of a Nuremberg Husband and Wife* (New York: Simon & Schuster, 1986). For the tighter control of marriage by civic magistrates and parents as a result of the Reformation, see Thomas Max Safley, *Let No Man Put Asunder: The Control of Marriage in the German Southwest: A Comparative Study, 1550–1600* (Kirksville, Mo.: Sixteenth Century Journal Publishers, 1984).

## Religion and Rural Society

The focus of recent research on this theme is the Peasants' War of 1525, for which there is an abundance of literature. See Peter Blickle, *Die Revolution von 1525,* 2d rev. ed. (Munich: Oldenbourg, 1981); English translation by Thomas A. Brady, Jr., and H. C. Erik Midelfort, *The Revolution of 1525* (Baltimore: Johns Hopkins University Press, 1981). For collections of essays, see B. Scribner and G. Benecke, eds., *The German Peasant War, 1525: New Viewpoints* (London: George Allen & Unwin, 1979). Also see Janos Bak, ed., *Journal of Peasant Studies,* vol. 3, no. 1 (1975), special issue on the Peasants' War; Hans-Ulrich Wehler, ed., *Der deutsche Bauernkrieg, 1524–26* (=*Geschichte und Gesellschaft, Sonderheft 1*); Peter Blickle, ed., *Revolte und Revolution in Europa* (=*Historische Zeitschrift,* Beiheft 4, NF) (Munich: Historische

Zeitschrift, 1975); Rainer Wohlfeil, ed., *Der Bauernkrieg, 1524–26: Bauernkrieg und Reformation* (Munich: Nymphenburger, 1975); Bernd Moeller, ed., *Bauernkrieg-Studien* (=SVRG 189) (Gütersloh: G. Mohn, 1975); for peasant protests in early modern Germany, see Peter Blickle, *Deutsche Untertanen: Ein Widerspruch* (Munich: C. H. Beck, 1981); Blickle, ed., *Aufruhr und Empörung? Studien zum bäuerlichen Widerstand im Alten Reich* (Munich: C. H. Beck, 1980) and *Bauer, Reich, und Reformation: Festschrift für Günther Franz* (Stuttgart: E. Ulmer, 1982); Winfried Schulze, *Bäuerlicher Widerstand und feudale Herrschaft in der frühen Neuzeit* (Stuttgart: Fromann-Holzboog, 1980); Schulze, ed., *Aufstände, Revolten, und Prozesse: Beiträge zu bäuerlichen Widerstandsbewegungen im frühneuzeitlichen Europa* (Stuttgart: Fromann-Holzboog, 1983). For a succinct English introduction to Schulze's findings, see his "Peasant Resistance in Sixteenth- and Seventeenth-Century Germany in a European Context," in *Religion, Politics, and Social Protest: Three Studies on Early Modern Germany,* by Peter Blickle, Hans-Christoph Rublack, and Winfried Schulze, ed. Kaspar von Greyerz (London: George Allen & Unwin, 1984), pp. 61–98. See also Tom Scott, "Reformation and Peasants' War in Waldshut and Environs: A Structural Analysis," in *ARG* 69 (1978):82–102, 70 (1979):140–68. On the impact of the Reformation in rural areas, much work needs to be done. See Thomas Barnett-Robisheaux, "Peasants and Pastors: Rural Youth Control and the Reformation in Hohenlohe, 1540–1680," *Social History* 6 (1981):281–300. An attempt to emphasize the religious rather than the political character of the Reformation impact is made in a recent monograph on the rural Reformation in Alsace: Franziska Conrad, *Reformation in der Bäuerlichen Gesellschaft: Zur Rezeption reformatorischer Theologie im Elsass* (=VIEGM 116) (Wiesbaden: F. Steiner, 1984). A number of fascinating cases in Lutheran Württemberg reveal the conflict between rural popular religion and official church and doctrine well into the early eighteenth century; see David W. Sabean, *Power in the Blood: Popular Culture and Village Discourse in Early Modern Germany* (Cambridge: Cambridge University Press, 1985).

## Education and Indoctrination

Gerald Strauss has recently concluded that the Reformation failed in general to indoctrinate the populace and that a chasm continued to exist between the religion of the people and that of the establishment; see his *Luther's House of Learning: Indoctrination of the Young in the German Reformation* (Baltimore: Johns Hopkins University Press, 1978). For a critique of Strauss, see James M. Kittelson, "Successes and Failures in the German Reformation: The Report from Strasbourg," *ARG* 73 (1982):153–75. L. Jane Abray has reformulated the question so that it concerns the conflict between the religion of the clergy and the religion of the people; see *The People's Reformation* (see under "Cities and the Reformation"). One of the lasting contributions of the Reformation, however, was the spread of literacy in Protestant Germany; see Richard Gawthrop and Gerald Strauss, "Protestantism and Literacy in Early Modern Germany," *P&P* 104 (1984):31–55.


Creating the "Other"

The establishment of confessional "centers," by definition, also created marginal groups that were excluded from religious and political discourse. Historians have increasingly recognized the sharp distinctions between religion, as it was learned by the clergy, enforced by the governments, and understood by the people. Thus in addition to the interconfessional conflicts between the Catholics, the Lutherans, and the Calvinists, social historians have turned to the study of marginal groups in early modern German society: witches, the insane, Jews, magicians, and Anabaptists. For witch hunting in Germany, see H.-C. Erik Midelfort, *Witch-hunting in Southwestern Germany, 1562–1684: The Social and Intellectual Foundations* (Stanford: Stanford University Press, 1972); and Gerhard Schormann, *Hexenprozesse in Nordwestdeutschland* (Hildesheim: Lax, 1977). For the study of madness, see H.-C. Erik Midelfort, "Madness and Civilization in Early Modern Europe: A Reappraisal of Michel Foucault," in B. Malament, ed., *After the Reformation: Essays in Honor of J. H. Hexter* (Philadelphia: University of Pennsylvania Press, 1980), pp. 247–65; his "Madness and the Problems of Psychological History in the Sixteenth Century," *SCJ* 12 (1981):5–12; and "Sin, Melancholy, Obsession: Insanity and Culture in Sixteenth Century Germany," in Steven L. Kaplan, ed., *Understanding Popular Culture: Europe from the Middle Ages to the Nineteenth Century* (New York: Mouton, 1985), pp. 113–46. On Jews, see R. Po-chia Hsia, "Printing, Censorship, and Antisemitism in Reformation Germany," in S. Marshall and P. Bebb, eds., *The Process of Change in Early Modern Europe: Festschrift for Miriam Usher Chrisman*. There is a vast literature on Anabaptism. For works that examine the social character of the Anabaptist movement, see Claus-Peter Clasen, *Anabaptism: A Social History, 1525–1618* (Ithaca: Cornell University Press, 1972); James M. Stayer and Werner O. Packull, eds., *The Anabaptists and Thomas Müntzer* (Dubuque, Iowa: Kendall/Hunt, 1980). Klaus Deppermann, *Melchior Hoffman: Soziale Unruhen und apokalyptische Visionen im Zeitalter der Reformation* (Göttingen: Vandenhoek & Ruprecht, 1979); Hans-Jürgen Goertz, ed., *Umstrittenes Täufertum, 1525–1975* (Göttingen: Vandenhoek & Ruprecht, 1975). The question of magic and popular religion has not received the same attention that Keith Thomas has given the subject for early modern England, but for a stimulating introduction, see Robert W. Scribner, "Ritual and Popular Religion in Catholic Germany at the Time of the Reformation," *Journal of Ecclesiastical History* 35 (1984):47–77; and his "Cosmic Order and Daily Life: Sacred and Secular in Pre-Industrial German Society," in Greyerz, ed., *Religion and Society*, pp. 17–32.

# Index

agriculture, 81, 88–89, 97
Agrippa, Heinrich Cornelius, 237–38, 240
alchemy, 96–97
Alciati, Andrea, 240
Alva, duke of, 98
Anabaptists, 12, 32, 88, 157; and communal eating, 69; and family, 52, 63–64; in Münster, 12, 50–69; Münster, immigration to, 54, 63; Münster, number in, 57; and polygamy, 55–56, 59–60, 153; and property, 55; and prophecy, 55–56; solidarity of, 56; and women, 52, 55, 57–60, 162–63, 167, 170
Anahans, Contz, 105, 108, 111–12, 114
Andernach, Gunther von, 96
Andlau, Peter von, 15
Anhausen, Abbey of (Saxony), 135
anthropology, social, 3–5
anticlericalism, 19–20, 22, 30, 52, 139, 225; guilds and, 65; in Münster, 52, 65; in Nördlingen, 106, 113–14; in Nuremberg, 36, 38, 42; peasant, 38–39; in print, 84–86; ritual of, 137. *See also* clergy
apothecaries, 76, 89, 96
apprentices, 18, 115. *See also* artisans
Aristotle, 99, 150, 195, 237, 250
artisans, 22–23, 26–27, 30, 64–65, 81, 96, 123, 143, 153, 167, 223; in Münster, 54, 62–63; in Nördlingen, 103, 106–7, 112–13, 115; in Nuremberg, 36, 38–40. *See also* apprentices; journeymen
artists, 36–38, 41, 44–46; and lay culture, 76, 85, 210; and woodcut production, 78, 90, 210

Artz, Ulrich, 19
Augsburg: magistrates of, 24, 26–27, 106; and the popular reformation, 30; and ritual, 124, 128, 131, 135–36, 138, 143; and women, 153, 159–60
Augsburg, Peace of, 231, 262, 270, 279–80
Augsburg Confession, 227
Aurifaber, Johann, 201

Bächtold-Stäubli, Hanns, 3
Baldung Grien, Hans, 78, 90, 223
ballads, 72, 74–75, 101, 123, 139, 223; text of "The Song of Contz Anahans," 108–10
Bamberg, 166; bishop of, 37
baptism, 45, 127, 156–57, 219–20, 242, 270
Basel, 15, 25, 96, 132, 134, 139, 176, 178–79, 180–83, 187–88
bastardy, 66, 185
Battista della Porta, Giovanni, 240
Bautzen, 139–41
Baxter, Christopher, 239
Beck, Balthasar, 88
Beck, Reinhardt, 88
beguinage, 60, 160. *See also* nuns
Beham, Barthel, 44
Beham, Sebald, 36, 44, 46, 133
Bensing, Manfred, 6
Berg, Duchy of, 253
Berger, Diebolt, 223
Bernhard VIII, Count of Lippe, 269
Besold, Christoph, 253
Betschold, Martin, 227

Matthys, Jan, 55
Maximilian I, 18, 232
Meacham, Standish, 212
medicine, 75, 80–81, 88–89, 220; forensic,
    261; and the insanity defense of witches,
    249–50, 257–58; and Paracelsus, 96; and
    witchcraft, 192, 233–34, 236–37, 240,
    253–54, 260
melancholy, 240–41, 250, 252–54, 260; and
    the insanity defense, 255–59; and women,
    261. *See also* insanity defense
Melanchthon, Philip, 198, 201, 205, 239
Memmingen, 24, 136, 156, 161
Mentzen, Anna, 130
*menu peuple*, 115
merchants, 11, 25, 61–62, 64, 81, 93–94,
    139
Metz, 238
Meyer, Jacob, 230
midwives, 80, 156–57
Mieg, Carl, 228–30
Mieg, Daniel, 26
millenarianism, 12, 19; and Anabaptism, 52,
    55–56, 60–61, 63–64, 68–69; and wom-
    en, 60–61, 69. *See also* prophecy
Minden, 275
mining, 6, 75, 91
mirales, 192, 239; Lutheran, 224
Mittenzwei, Ingrid, 6
Mock, Hans, 112
Moeller, Bernd, 11, 16, 29n, 263
Mollenhecke, Heinrich, 56
Molsheim, Jacob von, 226
monks, 36, 53, 85–86, 106, 113, 137, 154,
    203
Moody, Joseph, 212
*Morgengabe*, 180
motherhood, 151
Mühlhausen, 43–44, 135
Munich, 167, 203, 207
Münster, 12, 30, 32, 124, 135, 137, 140,
    153, 160, 167, 267, 275; and the anabap-
    tist revolt, 50–69
Müntzer, Thomas, 43–46, 161
Murner, Thomas, 81–82, 92
mysticism, 161–62
myth, 14–15, 241; chivalric tales and
    Greco-Roman legends, 79–80, 91–92;
    hagiography, 79–80, 82–83

*Nachbarschaften*, 64
*Narrenschiff, Das*, 78, 81
nature: and lay culture, 75, 84, 88–91;
    powers of (in Scripture), 248
Nebra, 136
Negelin, Matthis, 224

Netherlands, the, 275, 282
Nettesheim, 237
Neuendorf, 131
New Jerusalem, 51, 55
Nicodemism, 152–3, 238
Nördlingen, 72, 101, 105, 112; city council
    of, 113, 117–18; and communalism, 103–
    4; and the Holy Roman Empire, 102, 106;
    *menu peuple* of, 115; and printing, 107
novels, 75, 93–94
nuns, 58, 135, 145, 151–54, 158–60, 241
Nuremberg, 4, 25–26, 32–49, 106, 131,
    204; and city council, 35–36, 38, 160;
    Imperial Diets in, 35–36; preaching in,
    34–35, 37; and the St. Clara convent,
    158; and women, 167
Nützel, Kaspar, 26

Obelkevich, James, 212
Obereisenheim, 202
Oberman, Heiko, 17, 29n, 196
occultism, 96–97, 237–38. *See also* magic;
    witchcraft
Ochino, Bernardo, 152
Oestreich, Gerhard, 266
Oldecop, Justus, 258–59, 261
Osiander, Andreas, 34, 44, 192
Osnabrück, 52, 275

Paderborn, 267, 275
Palatinate, the, 270, 275, 281
Pappus, Johann, 95
Paracelsus, 96
parental authority, 146, 173, 175, 177, 181,
    186–87, 220
patricians, 22–24, 30–31; in Augsburg,
    128–29; and Catholicism, 25–26; and lay
    culture, 76, 86; in Münster, 53, 61; in
    Nuremberg, 35–36, 48, 158; in
    Strasbourg, 25–26, 86, 218
Paul, Vincent de, 160
Paul III, Pope, 159
peasants, 12, 23, 32, 107–8, 111, 114–15,
    118, 241, 272–73; Assemblies of, 38–41;
    attack on ritual, 122–23
Peasants' War, 6, 9, 29–30, 32, 52, 54, 72,
    84, 136, 156; in ballads, 101–2, 108–12
Pencz, Georg, 44
Peringer, Diepold, 41–43
Peutinger, Conrad, 106
Pfarrer, Mathis, 26
Pfeiffer, Heinrich, 43, 45–46
Phayer, Fintan Michael, 212
Pirckheimer, Charitas, 158
Pirna, 123, 130–31
plague, 80

Library of Congress Cataloging-in-Publication Data

The Germany people and the Reformation.
  Bibliography: p.
  Includes index.
  1. Reformation—Germany. 2. Germany—Church history—16th century. I.
Hsia, R. Po-chia
BR309.G37  1988      274.3'06      87-47863
ISBN 0-8014-2064-4 (alk. paper)
ISBN 0-8014-9485-0 (pbk. : alk. paper)